Japanese Grammar

by

HIDEICHI ONO

Assist. Professor of Tokyo University
of Foreign Studies
Lecturer at Takachiho College
of Commerce
Lecturer at the Association for
Overseas Technical Scholarship

1973
THE HOKUSEIDO PRESS
TOKYO

© Copyright, 1973, by Hideichi Ono

First Printing March, 1973
Fifth Printing November, 1976
ISBN 0–89346–004–4

Published by The Hokuseido Press
3-12, Kanda-Nishikicho, Chiyoda-ku, Tokyo

PREFACE

It is a fact that numerous books have been written on the Japanese language, yet there have been no suitable, comprehensive texts for its study—very few serve any grammatical and logical purpose. This has led to the preparation of the present work "**Japanese Grammar**" which is intended for both beginners and those who wish to pursue the study of Japanese at a more advanced level. The author of this grammar spent several years in research and inquiry into current Japanese grammar, grammatical function, syntactical details, and the grammar's scope of study. The result is the present volume—some of the exclusive and important features of this volume may be summarized as follows:

Following the Preface there is a special section, "An Outline of the Japanese Language", which provides useful and general information about Japanese pronunciation, sentence patterns, and verbal and adjectival conjugations. First, the author is to take his readers on a study tour of this section, the world of the Japanese language, before departure. This volume is made up of fifty-four lessons and each lesson follows a strictly grammatical order. The majority of the lessons in the book, except Lessons 52, 53, and 54, consistently follow the same system—**rule**, **drill**, and **exercise**. The author's idea is, as it were, to enable the readers to go hand in hand with the study of each of these sections—the reason is that the study of the *rule* itself cannot be independently brought to a successful end. Thus, the readers are requested not to disregard this interrelated order—progress by degrees based upon rule, drill, and exercise which are worth serious study. In particular, the *rule*, with grammatical explanations based on a scientific description of the language, is written in both Japanese and in Roman letters with their English translations, so that students of the Japanese language, especially beginners, may learn the language and its grammar with far greater ease and precision. The *drill* and *exercise* sections, blended with all words and terms and reading matter conforming to modern usage, have been given by the language symbolic characters (hiragana, katakana, and Kanji) only—each of these sentences is also accompanied by its English translation; these latter two sections, in conjunction with the former rule section, will, undoubtedly, be welcomed by foreign students, research students, and trainees whose intention is to probe more definitely and deeply into

the intricacies of that most difficult and complex of all languages—
Japanese. The sections *drill* and *exercise* are intended to help the
student concentrate on the study of reading, writing, and speaking
after his getting maximum benefit from grammar and structural
comprehension in the *rule* section.

The selection and arrangement of contents provides the student with
a well-rounded command of the Japanese language by fostering ability
to read a wide variety of materials. The series contains selections
from the pens of some writers. In view of the nature of this work
for non-native speakers studying Japanese, major or minor changes
in vocabulary, style, Kanji, etc. were inevitable. Drastic modifications
have been thoroughly necessary—therefore, the original authors' names
have been purposely withheld to spare them annoyance. The author
wishes to record here his profound gratitude to these writers.

The author also expresses his sincere thanks to his American
friend Mr. Paul Craven who kindly gave valuable suggestions and
helpful criticism and looked over the manuscript of this book.

The author hopes that the readers will acquire, by using this
Grammar Book, a sound sense of Japanese grammar in current Japanese. Besides, it is the hope of the author that this book, as well as
facilitating the study of the Japanese language, will also contribute to
friendly understanding between the peoples of Japan and all other
countries.

Embracing the opportunity of this publication, the author has to
express his thanks to Mr. Junpei Nakatsuchi, the publisher of the
Hokuseido Press, for his kind help.

March 1973

Hideichi Ono

CONTENTS

An Outline of the Japanese Language

The nature of the combination of Japanese sounds is illuminated through comparison with that of the English language. The former ends entirely with vowels, with the exception of the syllabic nasal sound ン [n], such as **kaigan**, a seashore and **mikan**, an orange. This nasal sound ン [n] nearly corresponds to the English articulation [n]; but this articulation is, in fact, conducted in two ways in Japanese. When the Japanese syllabic nasal ン can be articulated just as the phonetic sign [n] in English, the tip of the tongue is pressed against the upper gum. On the other hand, in Japanese, when words end mainly with ン or some vowels follow it, the articulation of [n] used in English is not adaptable. In this case, the tongue back is raised up to the velum to close off the mouth. This is exemplified as follows:

(A) The same articulation as the English [n]:

        señsui, diving   **meñkai**, an interview

        hañtai, opposition   **shiñdai**, a bed

(B) The Japanese ン unlike the English [n]:

        kōgen, a plateau   **mon**, the gate

        san-en, three yen   **tan-i**, a unit

Other than this nasal sound, all of the Japanese fifty sounds end with vowels. That combination of sounds which ends with a vowel evidenced in the Japanese language is regarded as an **open syllable**; this syllable is formed of a consonant + a vowel. In English the combination of sounds ends with either vowel or consonant — here is a marked difference. The proportion of consonants to vowels in this combination in English is high; in other words, the consonant cluster, a series of consonants, figures heavily in the construction. That combination of sounds ending with a consonant evinced in the English language is called a **closed syllable**.

Note: The English phonetic symbols employed herein are according to the International Phonetic Association.

In addition, as the main feature of the closed syllable, the combination of sounds always ends on a consonant, with the exception of such short vowels as [ə] and [i]. That is, in English there are found no terms ending with the sounds [æ], [ʌ], [e], [ɔ], or [u]. This case is simply demonstrated as follows:

kokuban, blackboard [blǽkbɔ:d]

daijin, minister [mínistə]

chōmen, notebook [nóutbuk]

kakujitsu, surety [ʃúəti]

shikai, dentist [déntist]

enpitsu, pencil [pénsl]

jitensha, bicycle [báisikl]

As to the difference of accent between Japanese and English, the former is recognized as the **pitch accent** and the latter as the **stress accent.**

When observing the Gothic words in the following sentences, the form of a lower or higher pitch can be detected. In **Hi ni atarimashō,** Let's warm ourselves at the fire, and **Hi ni atarimashō,** Let's bask in the sun, the term **hi ni,** at the fire, is marked with the pitch accent "‾hi＿ni" and the term **hi ni,** in the sun, "＿hi‾ni." Likewise, such words as **hashi,** an edge, **hashi,** chopsticks, and **hashi,** a bridge, must be pronounced respectively as "hashi", an edge, "‾ha＿shi", chopsticks, and "＿ha‾shi", a bridge. Antithetic to this nature, in English those words composed of more than two syllables are all to be accentuated someplace; that is, the stress accent goes on, never permitting even a word to be pronounced flat as in Japanese.

Such consonants as [f], [v], [θ], and [ð] in English cannot be found in Japanese and are simulated by those consonants included in the lines ハ (ha), バ (ba), サ (sa), and ザ (za) of the Japanese 50 Sounds Table. The consonant in the line ハ (h) corresponds to the English [f] and [h], the consonant in the line バ (b) to [v] and [b], and the consonant in the lines サ (s) and ザ (z) to [θ] and [s] and to [ð] and [z]. The consonant [s] found in the Japanese letters サ (sa), ス (su), セ (se), and ソ (so) is pronounced in such a way that the tip of the tongue is let down, permitting to slightly touch the back of the lower teeth; so, the sound of friction occurs between the front part of the palate and the front of the tongue. But for the English consonant [s] the upper and lower teeth are drawn close, nearly in touch with each other. Then the left and right rim of the tongue must be pressed against the upper gum; in this way the fricative sound [s] is brought out from between the tip of the tongue and the teeth ridge. When pronouncing ザ (za), ズ (zu), ゼ (ze), and ゾ (zo), the tip of the tongue is once pressed against the gum and released as vocalization is initiated. Therefore, these sounds have assumed the quality of [dz], and not of the sound [z]. In the case of [z] in English, the tip of the tongue is not in contact with the upper teeth ridge. Some Japanese terms with the sound [dz] are **zaibatsu,** plutocracy, **zuga,** drawing, **zeikan,** the customs, and **zōtei**, presentation.

The Japanese consonants シ (sh), シャ, シュ, and ショ nearly correspond to the voiceless sound [ʃ] in English. Also, the Japanese consonants ジ (j), ジャ, ジュ, and ジョ are similar to the voiced sound [ʒ] in English. The sounds シ (sh) and ジ (j) in Japanese are not made from a hollow in the middle of the tongue by lifting up its left and right rim as in pronouncing the English [ʃ] and [ʒ]; in Japanese it's also unnecessary to protrude the lips forward in a pucker. Particularly the sound ジ (j), in words like ジテンシャ (jitensha), a bicycle, can be pronounced with the tongue touching the upper jaw.

The Japanese consonants チャ (ch), チュ, and チョ are quite the same as the English affricate [tʃ]; but they are less pronounced than [tʃ] which strengthens the expiration by protruding the lips forward.

The Japanese consonants ハ (h), ヘ, and ホ are less pronounced than the English glottal [h] which has an intense vibration of the vocal chords and an inward shift of its point of articulation.

The Japanese consonant in the line ラ (l) can be pronounced with the tip of the tongue touching the upper gum as if rebounding, especially when it is inserted between vowels. But the English fricative [r] must be pronounced so that the tip of the tongue would absolutely not touch the upper gum.

The Japanese consonant in the line カ (k) and ガ (g) is slightly different from the English plosive [k] and [g]; the latter is pronounced in a stronger expiration, with the tongue much more emphatic, pressing against the upper jaw and also leaving the point of articulation behind. The voiced form of カ (k) is ガ (g). To ascertain the difference, some of these words are given here:

kabin, a vase   kettle [kétl], **yakan**
kome, rice   couple [kʌ́pl], **fūfu**
gendai, the present day   gauge [geidʒ], **keiki**
gunka, a war song   good-bye [gúdbái], **sayōnara**

The English nasal [ŋ] is used in Japanese as well. As for the plosive [g], respiration comes into the mouth whereas, in the nasal [ŋ], it enters the nose. Some of these words are given as follows:

gaikoku, a foreign country   kage [kaŋe], shade
gichō, the chairman   kagaku [kaŋaku], science
goji, a wrong word   kagi [kaŋi], a key

The Japanese consonant in the line タ (t) and ダ (d) approximates the English plosive [t] and [d]. The sounds in Japanese generally belong to those called the post dental and are pronounced in such a way that the front of the tongue touches the back of the upper teeth, whereas in English the tip of the tongue is pressed against the gum. The voiced form of タ (t) is ダ (d).

As to the nasal ム (m), words ending with ム are commonly pronounced [mu] in Japanese; but in English this nasal must be pronounced with the tips more forcibly closed.

The distinct assimilated sound found in Japanese is not noticeable in English, causing Englishmen and Americans in particular who are not familiar with Japanese difficulty in pronouncing the assimilated sounds like -kka- in the place name **Hokkaidō** and -ppo- in **Sapporo**. Faced with such a sound as this, they are sure to ignore the represented sound and pronounce it by putting an accent on the preceding syllable, as [hókaido] and [sǽpərou].

The Japanese semi-vowel [ワ] corresponds to the English [w]; but the Japanese [ワ] is not pronounced by rounding the lips and protruding them forward; therefore, the opening of the mouth is more or less wider, its shape being longer horizontally.

The Japanese semi-vowels ヤ (y), ユ and ヨ are quite similar to the English [j]; but in Japanese the tongue is much lower, friction thus being reduced.

All of those consonants used in Japanese and English are classified in the table on the next page: Gothic letters indicate Japanese consonants and close letters English ones.

There are five vowels ア [a], イ [i], ウ [u], エ [e], and オ [o] in Japanese; but those vowels which can be used in English amount to eleven; that is, [ɑ], [æ], [i], [u], [e], [ɛ], [o], [ɔ], [ə], [ʌ], and [a]. If the English vowels are further subdivided, they run as follows: the seven short vowels [i], [e], [æ], [u], [ʌ], [ɔ], and [ə]; the five long vowels [i:], [u:], [ɔ:], [ɑ:], and [ə:]; the nine diphthongs [iə], [ei], [ɛə], [ai], [au], [uə], [ou], [ɔi], and [ɔə]; and the two triphthongs [aiə] and [auə].

In English there are nine diphthongs, while Japanese words ending with イ [i], such as **koi**, love, **kui**, regret, and **kai**, a meeting, are merely regarded as such. Other words like **warau**, to laugh, **you**, to get drunk, **niou**, to smell, **kau**, to buy and **narau**, to learn, are not diphthongs, each being only the continuance of different syllables. That is, each of them goes under the following syllablication—**wara**[w]**u**, to laugh, **yo**[w]**u**, to get drunk, **nio**[w]**u**, to smell, **ka**[w]**u**, to buy, and **nara**[w]**u**, to learn. Such words as **akai**, red, **aoi**, blue and **usui**, light, end with [i] and the phonetic signs [ai], [oi], and [ui], used within these words might possibly be regarded as diphthongs. But

Method of articulation \ Limit of articulation	Lips (labial)		Teeth and tongue point (dental)	Teeth ridge and tongue point (alveolar)	Hard palate and tongue back (palatal)	Soft palate and tongue back (velar)	Throat (glottal)
	Both lips	Lips and teeth (labio-dental)					
Plosive (mute)	p, b p, b			t, d t, d		k, g k, g	
Nasal	m m			n n	ñ	ŋ ŋ	
Fricative		f, v	θ, ð	s, z s, z ʃ, ʒ; r	ʃ, ʒ		h h
Affricate				ts, dz tʃ, dʒ	tʃ, dʒ		
Lateral				l (flowing sound) l (liquid consonant)			
Semi-vowel	w				j		

in any case, that diphthong or triphthong manifested in English is, in fact, non-existent in Japanese.

There are some long vowels even in Japanese, and they were once pronounced as the dissyllables [aa], [ii], [uu], [ee], and [oo] in certain time-honored words, excluding borrowed words. Therefore, even at present, such an indication as おとうさん (otōsan), Father, きゅうきゅうしゃ (kyūkyūsha), an ambulance, おおどおり (ōdōri), a main street, and ええ (ee), Oh yes!, is prevalent. But these underlined terms regarded as long vowels are actually only the continuance of two vowel phonemes, a nature which is really different from the pure stretching of long vowels seen in English. Because of this Japanese peculiarity, the sign ― has been devised to indicate those long vowels found in such denizens as フォーク (fork), ボート (boat), and プール (pool).

Japanese vowels [ア], [イ], [ウ], [エ], and [オ] nearly correspond to the English vowels [a], [i], [u], [e], and [o]. Now, the exact intra-oral point of articulation, diagrammed as follows, is singularly taken up.

Vowels like [イ], [エ], and [ア] are articulated around the front of

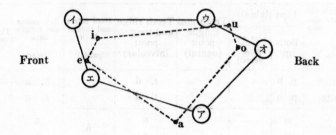

the tongue—such a vowel is called a **front vowel**. Vowels like [ウ] and [オ] are articulated around the back of the tongue—such a vowel is called a **back vowel**. As can be imagined from the picture above, the tongue drops down more for [エ] than [イ] and it is much lower for [ア]. In other words, the opening of the mouth naturally becomes larger in the shift from [イ] to [エ] to [ア]. In the case of [オ], the tongue is lower than [ウ] and also the mouth is slightly wider. The Japanese vowel [ア] is pronounced in such a way that the mouth is a bit wider than the English vowel [a], with the tongue protruding less. The Japanese vowel [イ] is nearly the same as [i] in English; but the English vowel [i] has its point of articulation slightly behind the midpoint of the Japanese [イ] and the English [e]. As for the Japanese vowel [エ], the tongue is a bit lower and the mouth a little wider than for the English [e]. As for the Japanese vowel [ウ], the opening of the lips is merely narrowed, with no need of rounding them. The English vowel [u], however, is regarded as one of the rounded, back, and close vowels; in line with this feature, it is quite indispensable to purse the lips. Also, as compared with the Japanese [ウ], the English [u] is articulated at a lower point. The height of the tongue for the Japanese [オ] and the English [o] is nearly the same; the small difference is that the point of articulation of [o] is slightly forward. This sound in Japanese, different from that in English, is to be pronounced freed from tensing the mouth and sqeezing it into a circle; that is, the Japanese vowel [オ] has not the deep and slow quantity of being kept within the mouth.

Japanese 50 Sounds Table

(With Hiragana and Katakana)

あ ア	い イ	う ウ	え エ	お オ					
a	i	u	e	o					
か カ	き キ	く ク	け ケ	こ コ	が ガ	ぎ ギ	ぐ グ	げ ゲ	ご ゴ
ka	ki	ku	ke	ko	ga	gi	gu	ge	go
さ サ	し シ	す ス	せ セ	そ ソ	ざ ザ	じ ジ	ず ズ	ぜ ゼ	ぞ ゾ
sa	shi	su	se	so	za	ji	zu	ze	zo
た タ	ち チ	つ ツ	て テ	と ト	だ ダ	ぢ ヂ	づ ヅ	で デ	ど ド
ta	chi	tsu	te	to	da	ji	zu	de	do
な ナ	に ニ	ぬ ヌ	ね ネ	の ノ					
na	ni	nu	ne	no					
は ハ	ひ ヒ	ふ フ	へ ヘ	ほ ホ	ば バ	び ビ	ぶ ブ	べ ベ	ぼ ボ
ha	hi	hu	he	ho	ba	bi	bu	be	bo
					ぱ パ	ぴ ピ	ぷ プ	ぺ ペ	ぽ ポ
					pa	pi	pu	pe	po
ま マ	み ミ	む ム	め メ	も モ					
ma	mi	mu	me	mo					
や ヤ	い イ	ゆ ユ	え エ	よ ヨ					
ya	i	yu	e	yo					
ら ラ	り リ	る ル	れ レ	ろ ロ					
ra	ri	ru	re	ro					
わ ワ	い イ	う ウ	え エ	を ヲ					
wa	i	u	e	o					
ん ン									
n									

Japanese sentence patterns are classified into the nine patterns, against the five in English.

Pattern 1

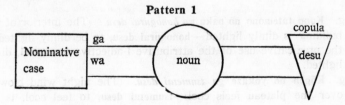

e.g. **Kare *wa* kaikatsu de, kōdōteki de, kibikibi to hagire no yoi *seinen desu.*** (He is a cheerful, active, smart and sharp young man) —the nominative case **wa** in this sentence indicates an essential and inevitable relationship and suggests such shading as the adverb **always** or **generally**. That is, **wa** is used when the speaker is going to give an explanation regarding the subject, after presenting it first; that is, the particle **wa** is the theme or topic of the sentence. And the predicate of this sentence will be an explanation giving new information about the particular noun or pronoun presented as the theme or topic.

e.g. **Kare *ga* sekiri de *nyūinchū desu.*** (He is in hospital with dysentery)—**ga** indicates a temporary or irregular (accidental) relationship and suggests such shading as the adverb **now** or **at this moment**. That is, ga is used only with subjects that identify clearly the performer or agent of the predicate. This sentence is concerned with who is in hospital. That is, what the speaker wants clarified is "who is concerned with the matter described in the predicate," and the subject should be the solution of the predicate.

e.g. **Chichi *wa majime* de *chūjitsu* de *ohitoyoshi desu.*** (My father is honest, faithful, and good-natured)—the words **majime**, honesty, **chūjitsu**, faithfulness, and **ohitoyoshi**, a good-natured person, are noun forms derived from the na-adjectives **majime na**, honest, **chūjitsu na**, faithful, and **ohitoyoshi na**, good-natured. De in **majime de** and in **chūjitsu de** is the connective used in a compound sentence employing the copula desu and may be considered to be an abbreviation of that verb.

Pattern 2

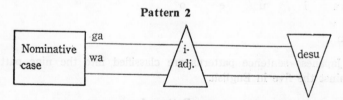

e.g. **Kono tatemono no naka *wa honogurai desu.*** (The interior of this building is dimly lighted)—**honogurai desu**, to be dimly lighted, is the predicative use of the attributive i-adjective **honogurai**, dimly lighted.

e.g. **Kōgen no yokaze *ga tsumetai desu.*** (The night wind blowing over the plateau feels cool)—**tsumetai desu**, to feel cool, is the predicative use of the attributive i-adjective **tsumetai**, cool.

Pattern 3

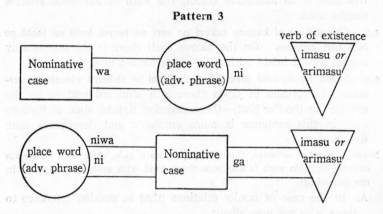

The restriction of a topic led **by wa** is loose because of its function of presenting the theme; and thus, **wa** accordingly reaches far. The feeling of approach taken by **wa** extends over and as far as the **imasu** or **arimasu** at the end of the sentence, while that by **ga** is quite closely connected to these verbs of existence. And thus, the formation of **Pattern 3** should be approached from the intended use of the nominative cases **wa** and **ga**.

e.g. **Yōtsui o yararete shimo hanshin fuzui no kanja wa, watashi no tonari no beddo ni imasu.** (A patient, semi-paralysed from a wound in his back bone, lies on the bed next to me)—when the nominative case is an animate object, the verb of existence **imasu** can be used.

e.g. **Nerima no jieitai no eimon o haitta tokoro no koya ni shichi hachi nin no hei ga imasu.** (In a hut just inside the camp gate of the Self Defense Force in Nerima there are seven or eight soldiers)

e.g. **Kono kyōshitsu no mado giwa no tsukue niwa, mijikai hige o hayashi, kami o kirei ni waketa se no takai ryūgakusei ga imasu.** (At the desk by the window in this classroom there is a foreign student of tall physique, wearing a short moustache, and with his hair parted neatly)—the expression **tsukue niwa**, at the desk . . . in this sentence is more emphatic and descriptive than **tsukue ni**.

e.g. **Kiiroi kabe no yōfū nikai date ni natta seifu no ryōyōjo wa Meguro no oka no ue no miharashi no yoi tokoro ni arimasu.** (The two-storied foreign-style government sanatorium with yellow walls is on a hill in Meguro commanding a fine view)—when the nominative case is an inanimate object, the verb of existence **arimasu** can be used.

e.g. **Chigai dana *ni* kogane zukuri no sori no tsuyoi kofū na tachi *ga* hito furi *arimasu*.** (On the alcove shelf there is the one sharply curved sword inlaid with gold, old-fashioned in style)

e.g. **Nihon no Kyūshū *niwa* Tōyō dai ichi to shōsuru zōsenjo *ga arimasu*.** (In Kyushu in Japan there is a shipyard said to be the greatest in the Far East)—the expression **Kyūshū niwa**, in Kyushu . . . in this sentence is more emphatic and descriptive than **Kyūshū ni.**

Note: The verb **arimasu**, there is..., is, as a rule, used with inanimate objects; but this verb is also sometimes used with animate objects as in the following:

A. In the case of family relations (that is, making reference to those who are now alive):

Watashi wa san nin no musuko ga *arimasu*. (I have three sons)

B. In the case of a universal fact:

Watashi wa hōtō o shinai ga, hōtō o suru hito mo *arimasu*. (I myself would not lead an intemperate life, but there are some who waste their energies in dissipation)

C. In the case of an old story (that is, a historical fact):

Muromachi jidai ni Ashikaga Yoshimasa to iu hito ga *arimashita*. Kono hito wa Kyōto no Higashiyama ni ginkakuji o tatemashita. (There was a man named Ashikaga Yoshimasa in the Muromachi era. This man built the temple Ginkakuji at Higashiyama in Kyoto)

Note: **Igaku kankei no shomotsu de zatsuzen to shita kare no heya no naka ni, aoi kasa no sutando ga *tsukete arimasu*.** (In his room in the midst of the disorder of books concerning medical science, there is a lighted desk lamp with a blue shade)—**tsukete arimasu**, to be on, is a transitive verb. The phrase **aoi kasa no sutando ga tsukete arimasu** is induced from the following construction—*Dare ka ga* **aoi kasa no sutando** *o tsukemashita*, Someone switched on a desk lamp with a blue shade. This form denoting consequence nearly corresponds in meaning to the form denoting continuance used with an intransitive verb; the difference is that the former is effected by the third person pronoun but the latter has no such nuance. **Aoi kasa no sutando ga *tsukete arimasu*.** (A desk lamp with a blue shade is on)—**tsukete arimasu** is a transitive verb. **Aoi kasa no sutando ga *tsuite imasu*.** (A desk lamp with a blue shade is on)—**tsuite imasu** is an intransitive verb.

Pattern 4

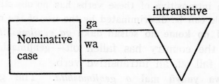

Those verbs which do not take the objective particle o are called intransitive verbs. In Japanese the relationship between the intransitive and transitive states is found to be obscure, quite different from that in English.

e.g. **Kono sagyōjō dewa, jokō *ga* goretsu ni naran de mishin to shūjitsu mukai atte *hatarakimasu*.** (In this workshop, the factory girls, ranged in five lines, work at the sewing machines all day long)—hatarakimasu, to work, is an intransitive verb; this verb indicates a person's activity.

e.g. **Komatta koto ni natta to, shachō *wa* tsukue ni hiji o tsuite *kangae komimashita*.** (The director, worried about being in an awkward position, rested on his elbows on the desk, lost in thought)—kangae komimashita, was lost in thought, is an intransitive verb; this verb indicates a man's mental activity.

e.g. **Seinen no ikoji na kanjō kara, ranbō na rikutsu o iu musuko to, unmei ni shitagai jijō no kōten o matsu to iu chichi to dewa sore zore no kangae *ga* hijō ni *chigaimasu*.** (The son, bandying unreasonable words in the perversity of youth, and the father, in his mind, following destiny and waiting for a more propitious time—their minds differ greatly)—chigaimasu, to differ, is an intransitive verb; this verb indicates a relationship.

e.g. **Kono rōjin *wa* tesuri ni tsukamaru yō ni shite, yasumi yasumi yonkai made *agarimashita*.** (This aged man rested again and again leaning against the banister as he climbed up to the fourth floor) —agarimashita, climbed up, is an intransitive verb; this verb indicates a change of position.

e.g. **Me o saegiru mono mo naku yuruyaka na kifuku o tsuraneta kōya ni osoroshii hodo no shonetsu to shikki to *ga tachikomemasu*.** (Over a gently undulating stretch of the wide plain with nothing to block the eye, a terrible heat and moisture prevails)—tachikomemasu, to prevail; to envelop, is an intransitive verb; this verb indicates a natural phenomena.

Note: Such verbs as genjiru, to fall off, to decrease, and warau, to laugh, take the same form in both the intransitive and transitive states. In the sentence the intransitive of these verbs has no objective particle o; the transitive role can be discriminated by the use of the objective particle.

e.g. **Kokunai no kome no seisan daka** *ga genjimashita.* (The output of rice in the country has fallen off)—**genjimashita** comes from **genji-ru**, to fall off, an intransitive verb.

e.g. **Seifu wa yunyū mai** *o genjimashita.* (The government has decreased its rice imports)—**genjimashita** comes from **genji-ru**, to decrease, a transitive verb.

e.g. **Kodomo** *ga waraimasu.* (A child laughs)—**waraimasu** comes from **wara[w]-u**, to laugh, an intransitive verb.

e.g. **Kodomo** *o waraimasu.* (We laugh at the child)—**waraimasu** comes from **wara[w]-u**, to laugh, a transitive verb.

Note: Such verbs as **tobu**, to fly, **aruku**, to walk, **sanpo suru**, to take a walk, **hashiru**, to run, and **tōru**, to pass, are intransitive verbs but the particle o here should be introduced into the sentence as if the nouns preceding these verbs were in the objective case.

e.g. **Hato no mure ga wa o egaite, Kasumigaseki no kanchōgai no takai tatemono to tatemono to no aida** *o tonde imasu.* (A flock of pigeons, circling, are flying between the high buildings of the governmental office streets of Kasumigaseki)—**tonde imasu**, to be flying, comes from **tob-u**, to fly, an intransitive verb; the particle o preceding this verb denotes a place of passage.

Pattern 5

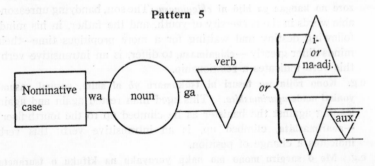

Some sentences in Japanese appear to have two subjects; one would serve as the subject of the entire sentence; that is, **wa** in this pattern takes the function of presenting the theme. The other would serve as complement or object; that is, **ga** in this pattern takes the role of the secondary theme under **wa** presenting the major topic. The restriction of a topic by **wa** is loose because of its function of presenting the overall theme; and thus, wa accordingly reaches far. On the contrary, the method of limitation in both time and distance of the particle ga is one that strives for more clarity; therefore, the sphere of limitation taken by ga is narrower than that of wa.

e.g. **Kono kōjōchō *wa* ano kōin *ga ki ni irimasen*.** (This factory manager dislikes that factory hand)—wa in kono kōjōchō, this factory manager, extends as far as . . . ki ni irimasen, to dislike, at the end of the sentence and within its extention ki ni irimasen goes to ano kōin, that factory hand. The subject in this sentence is kōjōchō and not ano kōin; that is, kōjōchō should be thought to be the subject for the phrase ano kōin ga ki ni irimasen. And also, the object for which this factory manager has a dislike is that factory hand; from this idea ano kōin in ano kōin ga is treated as an objective case. This pattern comes from the following basic phrase: kono kōjōchō no ki ni iranai ano kōin, that factory hand this factory manager dislikes.

e.g. **Nihon *wa* gyogyō *ga sakan desu*.** (In Japan the marine industry is well developed)—the subject in this sentence is Nihon, Japan, and not gyogyō, fishery; that is, Nihon should be thought to be the subject for the phrase gyogyō ga sakan desu. And also, the complement as treated here for sakan desu from the na-adjective sakan na, prosperous, is gyogyō. The basic phrase is Nihon no sakan na gyogyō, Japan's prosperous marine industry.

e.g. **Nihon *wa* kōbutsu shigen *ga toboshii desu*.** (Japan is lacking in mineral resources)—the subject in this sentence is Nihon, Japan, and not kōbutsu shigen, mineral resources; that is, Nihon should be thought to be the subject for the phrase kōbutsu shigen ga toboshii desu, to be lacking in mineral resources. And also, the complement as treated here for toboshii desu from the i-adjective toboshii, lacking, is kōbutsu shigen, mineral resources. The basic phrase is Nihon no toboshii kōbutsu shigen, Japan's short mineral resources.

e.g. **Watashi *wa* omuretsu *ga tabetai desu*.** (I would like to eat an omelet)—omuretsu ga, an omelet, is treated as an objective case for tabetai desu, would like to eat, the auxiliary of hope. The basic phrase is Watashi no tabetai omuretsu, an omelet which I would like to eat.

e.g. **Kare *wa* yonka kokugo *ga hanasemasu*.** (He can speak four different languages)—yonka kokugo ga, four different languages, is treated as an objective case for hanasemasu, can speak, a potential auxiliary. The basic phrase is **Kare no hanaseru yonka kokugo,** the four different languages he can speak, or **Kare wa yonka kokugo o hanasu koto ga dekimasu,** He can handle four different languages.

Pattern 6

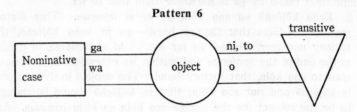

e.g. **Nihongo no sensei *wa* min-na kono ryūgakusei *o* homemasu.** (All of the Japanese teachers praise this foreign student)—o in this phrase **kono ryūgakusei o,** this foreign student, a noun (a person), shows the direct object and **homemasu** from **home-ru,** to praise, is a transitive verb. Sentences in this pattern can be converted into the direct passive voice (the objective case with the particle o in this active voice in this syntax being changed into the nominative case for the passive voice). The direct passive voice of this active voice sentence is **Kono ryūgakusei *wa* Nihongo no sensei min-na *ni* (or *kara*) homeraremasu.** (This foreign student is praised by all of the Japanese teachers)—ni or kara in **Nihongo no sensei min-na ni** or **Nihongo no sensei min-na kara** indicates the agent of passive action.

e.g. **Tan-nin no Nihongo no sensei *wa* kono joshi ryūgakusei no yūshū na seiseki *o* homemasu.** (The Japanese teacher in charge praises this female foreign student's excellent record)—o in the phrase **yūshū na seiseki o,** excellent record, a noun (a thing), shows the direct object. The passive voice would be: **Kono joshi ryūgakusei no yūshū na seiseki *wa* tan-nin no Nihongo no sensei *ni* (or *kara*) homeraremasu.** (This female foreign student's excellent record is praised by the Japanese teacher in charge). But such an inanimate subject as **yūshū na seiseki,** excellent record, cannot actually be used in the passive form.

Note: **Kare wa me no sameru yō na kono kosui no utsukushi sa *ni* kokoro o utarete imasu.** (He is deeply touched by the dazzling beauty of this lake)—utsukushi sa, beauty, a noun form derived from the i-adjective **utsukushii,** beautiful, is an inanimate object and the perpetrator of the action in the passive voice. In the case of an inanimate object as the perpetrator of an action in the passive voice, kara is never used; the particle **ni** always replaces the particle **kara**.

e.g. **Chotto mae, watashi *wa* shōbō jidōsha no sairen *o* kikimashita.**
(Just a little while ago, I heard the fire engine siren)—o in the
phrase **shōbō jidōsha no sairen o**, the fire engine siren, is an inanimate object and **kikimashita** from **kik-u**, to hear, is a transitive
verb.   The spontaneous voice sentence is **Chotto mae, shōbō jidōsha
no sairen *ga* kikoemashita** (or *kikoete kimashita*), Just a little while
ago, the fire engine siren was audible (or became audible)—the expression **kikoete kimashita** from **kikoete kuru**, to become audible, is
made up of two verbs, **kikoete** (to be audible)+**kuru**, to come; that
is, a compound verb.   The form denoting approach can be applied
in the sentence as **te** or **de**+ the subsidiary verb **kimasu**, to come
—this carries the meaning of the beginning and the progress of
an action coming toward the speaker or subject.   When an animate
object is in subjectivity and inanimate object in objectivity and
then a transitive verb is used, the person worthy of subjectivity
is, as it were, left behind; and instead a thing itself will be underlined in its own spontaneous action, phenomenon, and quality—
such a tendency as this is quite Japanese.   In particular, the subject
denoting an inanimate object is often applied with verbs of perception such as **mi-ru**, to see and **kik-u**, to hear.   And thus, such a
passive voice as this only is quite possible.

e.g. **Watashi *wa* me no mae ni umi *o* mimasu.**   (I see the sea right
before my eyes)—the passive voice of this sentence is **Me no mae
ni umi *ga* miraremasu,** The sea can be seen (or: is visible) before
my eyes—**miraremasu**, can be seen; to be visible, is in the passive
voice.   Otherwise, this sentence can also be expressed as **Me no
mae ni umi *ga* miemasu,** The sea can be seen before my eyes—
miemasu, to be seen; to be visible, is in the spontaneous voice.
The use of the nominative case **umi**, the sea, an inanimate object,
is quite possible because this subject in the passive is applied with
such a verb of perception as **mi-ru**, to see.   And the expressions
miraremasu and **miemasu** evident in these two sentences have respectively such shading as: **raremasu** in **mi-raremasu** is the auxiliary
of possibility and this expression is used in the sense that something is in sight if one has a desire to observe it; on the other
hand, the expression **mi-emasu**, to be visible, is used in the sense
that something exists there, irrelevant to the will of an observer.
The use of the expression **miemasu** (an intransitive verb) is more
common than the expression **miraremasu**.

e.g. **Kono Indo-jin *wa* uchi no pātii de sashimi *wa tabemasen deshita*.** (This Indian did not eat slices of raw fish at the party of my house)—**wa** in the phrase **sashimi wa**, slices of raw fish, is an objective term which shows the receiver of the action. The expression **sashimi wa** is more emphatic and descriptive than the expression **sashimi o.**

e.g. **Kore o keiki to shite, kanojo *wa* jibun no ketten *ni ki ga tsukimashita*.** (Taking this opportunity, she became aware of her own defects)—**ni** in the phrase **jibun no ketten ni**, one's own defects, shows the other party or the object.

e.g. **Kare *wa* shinyū *to zekko shimashita*.** (He broke off with his close friend)—**to** in the phrase **shinyū to**, with one's close friend, shows the other party of an action which needs a companion.

Pattern 7

e.g. **Shachō *wa* hidari no ude *ni* sutekki *o kakemashita*.** (The director put a walking stick over his left arm)—**hidari no ude ni**, over one's left arm, is an adverb phrase as the indirect object and the particle **ni** in this phrase shows a spatial point of arrival or direction. The phrase **sutekki o**, a walking stick, is here treated as the direct object. And the verb **kakemashita** from **kake-ru**, to put, is a transitive verb. Generally the common order in this pattern places the indirect object (a noun or an adverb phrase) first and then the direct object appears. On the other hand, we may say, **sutekki *o* hidari no ude *ni*.**

e.g. **Kono ochūgen *o* tan-nin no sensei *e todokete kudasai*.** (Please send this Bon present to the teacher in charge)—the particle **e** in the phrase **tan-nin no sensei e**, to the teacher in charge, shows the other party.

e.g. **Ohima nara, kon-ban watashi *wa* anata *o* Asakusa no Kokusai gekijō no 'Haru no odori' *ni*** (or: *e*) **osasoi shimasu.** (If you are free, tonight I'll invite you to enjoy "A Dance of Spring" at the Kokusai Theatre in Asakusa)—the particle **ni** or **e** in the phrase **'Haru no** odori' **ni** (or: **e**), A Dance of Spring, can be used rather freely without any strict direction. The difference of function between **ni** or **e** indicating a place is as follows: **ni** is used as a shifter in the sense of "a fixed position with the implications of the process of shift"; and **e** is used as a shifter in the sense of "a direction of movement".

e.g. **Kono Amerika-jin no kōkan kyōju** *wa* **Nihon no daigakusei** *ni* **kōkogaku** *o* *oshiemasu.* (This American exchange professor teaches Japanese university students archaeology)—**Nihon no daigakusei ni**, Japanese university students, denotes the indirect object (an animate object) and **kōkogaku o**, archaeology, the direct object (an inanimate object). From this pattern the indirect passive voice (the objective case preceding either of the particles **ni** or **to** in the active voice in this pattern being expressed as the subject in the passive voice) can be induced. The indirect passive voice of this active voice pattern is **Nihon no daigakusei** *wa* **kono Amerika-jin no kōkan kyōju** *ni* (or: *kara*) **kōkogaku** *o* *oshieraremasu,* Japanese university students are taught archaeology by this American exchange professor. Otherwise, we may say and write this sentence **Kono Amerika-jin no kōkan kyōju** *wa* **Nihon no daigakusei** *ni* **kōkogaku** *o* *oshiete yarimasu.* (This American exchange professor teaches Japanese university students archaeology)—**oshiete yarimasu** consists of the two verbs **oshiete** from **oshieta**, taught and **yarimasu** from **yar-u**, to give, a subsidiary verb which is used when doing a favor for a subordinate or an equal. The passive voice is **Nihon no daigakusei** *wa* **kono Amerika-jin no kōkan kyōju** *ni* (or: *kara*) **kōkogaku** *o* *oshiete moraimasu,* Japanese university students are taught archaeology by this American exchange professor—**oshiete moraimasu** consists of the two verbs **oshiete** from **oshieta**, taught and **moraimasu** from **mora[w]-u**, to receive, a subsidiary verb which is used when the subject of the sentence is given some help by somebody else.

Note: The form of the passive voice of vowel stem verbs and that of the potential of these verbs are exactly the same; that is, such forms as the passive voice and the potential can be similarly induced from any vowel stem verb in the present / future form.

e.g. **Kono kenkyū ryūgakusei** *wa* **kono daigaku no Nihongoka no shunin kyōju** *ni* (or: *kara*) **Nihon kindai bungaku** *o* *oshieraremasu.* (This foreign research student is taught Japanese modern literature by the chief professor in the Japanese Department at this university)

—oshie-raremasu from oshie-ru, to teach, a vowel stem verb, is the passive voice; and o in the phrase Nihon kindai bungaku o, Japanese modern literature, is used as an objective particle in the passive form.

e.g. Kono daigaku no Nihongoka no shunin kyōju *wa* kono kenkyū ryūgakusei *ni* Nihon kindai bungaku *ga oshieraremasu*. (The chief professor in the Japanese Department at this university can teach this foreign research student Japanese modern literature)—oshie-raremasu from oshie-ru, to teach, is the potential; and ga in the phrase Nihon kindai bungaku ga, Japanese modern literature, is treated as an objective particle in the potential form.

e.g. Kinō watashi no yūjin no Yamada-san *wa* Yamanote sen no shanai de suri *ni* ni man en zaichū no saifu *o suraremashita*. (Yesterday my friend Mr. Yamada had his purse with 20,000 yen in it stolen by a pickpocket in a Yamanote Line train)—ni in the phrase suri ni, by a pickpocket, shows the other party as the indirect object and o in the phrase saifu o, a purse, denotes the direct object. This pattern is in the third person passive voice and can be induced from the following active voice sentence: Yamanote sen no shanai de suri *ga* ni man en zaichū no saifu *o surimashita*, A pickpocket relieved someone of his purse with 20,000 yen in it in a Yamanote Line train—surimashita comes from sur-u, to steal. The owner of the objective term saifu, a purse, is not explicitly evidenced in this sentence; that is, the omission of any owner whose interests are affected by some action is standard in the third person active voice. This owner, however, can be expressed first in the passive voice, enabling it to take the role of the nominative case.

Note: Kyō kaisha e iku tochū, watashi *wa* ame *ni furaremashita*. (Today on my way to the company, I was caught in the rain)—the phrase ame ni furaremashita, was caught in the rain, is in the third person passive voice. The active voice phrase of this sentence is Ame *ga furimashita*, It rained—in Japanese not only transitive verbs but such an intransitive verb as fur-u, to rain, can also be expressed in the passive form.

e.g. Watashi *ga* imōto *ni* shinkyoku no rekōdo *o katte yarimasu*. (I will buy a record of a new composition for my younger sister)— ni in the phrase imōto ni, for my younger sister, shows the other party as the indirect object and o in the phrase shinkyoku no rekōdo o, a record of a new composition, the direct object. This sentence is transformed into Imōto *ga* watashi *ni* (or: *kara*) shinkyoku no rekōdo *o katte moraimasu,* My younger sister will have me buy a record of a new composition. In the case of the subsidiary verb (. . . **te moraimasu**), a rearrangement of the subject and object occurs, as seen in **Imōto *ga* watashi *ni*** from the original **Watashi *ga* imōto *ni.***

e.g. **Obasan *ga* watashi *ni* shinkyoku no rekōdo *o* kaimasu.** (My aunt will buy a record of a new composition for me)—this sentence is transformed into **Obasan *ga* watashi *ni* shinkyoku no rekōdo *o* katte kuremasu,** My aunt will buy a record of a new composition for me. In the case of the subsidiary verb (. . . **te kuremasu**), there occurs no change of position between the nominative and objective cases, as seen in the **Obasan *ga* watashi *ni* shinkyoku no rekōdo *o*** of both sentences.

e.g. **Keikan *wa* shūjin *ni* amigasa *o* kaburasemashita.** (A policeman had the criminal wear a face-concealing straw hat)—**ni** in the phrase **shūjin ni**, the criminal, indicates the other party as the indirect object and **o** in the phrase **amigasa o**, a face-concealing straw hat, an inanimate object as the direct object, and **kaburasemashita** comes from the verb **kabur-aseru**, to have someone wear something, in the causative form. The basic sentence is **Shūjin *wa* amigasa *o* kaburimashita,** The criminal wore a face-concealing straw hat—with the causative form, the nominative case of the basic sentence can be expressed by only the particle **ni** as the agent of causative action in transitive verbs; that is, **kaburimashita** from **kabur-u**, to wear, is a transitive verb, so the agent of causative action will be indicated by the particle **ni** as **shūjin ni**, the criminal.

e.g. **Chichi *wa* musuko *ni*** (or: *o*) **ginkō *e* ikasemasu.** (The father will get his son to go to the bank)—**ni** in the phrase **musuko ni**, one's son, indicates the other party as the direct object and **e** in the phrase **ginkō e**, to the bank, a spatial point of arrival or direction as an adverb phrase for the indirect object. And **ikasemasu** comes from the verb **ik-aseru**, to get someone to go to . . . , the causative form. The basic sentence is **Musuko *ga* ginkō *e* ikimasu.** (The son will go to the bank)—with the causative form, the nominative case of the basic sentence can be expressed by either the particle **ni** or **o** as the agent of causative action in intransitive verbs; that is, **ikimasu** from **ik-u**, to go, is an intransitive verb, so the agent of causative action will be indicated by the particle **ni** or **o** as **musuko ni** or **musuko o**, one's son.

Pattern 8

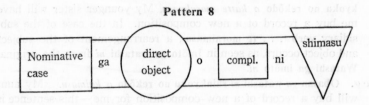

In this pattern **ga** and not **wa** is generally used—in this syntax the use of the particle **ga** is more reasonable because **ga** has a function somewhat similar to that of identification, and is always used with the subject which is to be identified with the facts or occurrences described in the predicate.   In other words, the particle **ga** is used in situational expressions in which one intends to identify a matter or event he is informed of with a particular subject.

 e.g. **Naganen tsukaete kita shujin ga nakunari, kono hōkōnin wa mō saitai no nozomi mo noren o wakete morau nozomi mo sutete shimatta koto *ga*, kare *o* hōtōmono *ni shite shimaimashita*.** (His master, to whom he had long been devoted, breathed his last; and this apprentice had no longer any intention of making a home and starting in his own business elsewhere with that same shop curtain —that made him a prodigal)—**o** in the phrase **kare o**, him, shows the direct object and **ni** in the phrase **hōtōmono ni**, a prodigal, serves as a complement in this syntax; that is, **ni** is used as a modifier in the sense of a complement for the direct object **kare o**, him.   The particle **ni** in the phrase **hōtōmono ni**, a prodigal, is used in the sense of fixing a position through a shift.   And the verb **shite shimaimashita** comes from **shite shima[w]-u**, to make— this is a true compound verb.   The form denoting conclusion can be expressed with the **te** or **de**-form+the subsidiary verb **shima[w]-u**, had+the past participle.   This carries the meaning that an action is to be performed up to the last moment.

 e.g. **Tsuma no muchi to buyōjin *ga* otto *o* keibakyō *ni shimashita*.** (The wife's ignorance and carelessness accelerated the driving of her husband into a turf fan)—**o** in the phrase **otto o**, one's husband, shows the direct object and **ni** in the phrase **keibakyō ni**, a turf fan, is used as a modifier in the sense of a complement for the direct object **otto o**, one's husband.

Pattern 9

```
                                            to, ku
  ┌──────────────┐          ╭───────╮                    ╲narimasu╱
  │ Nominative   │   wa     │  noun │     ni               ╲      ╱
  │ case         │──────────│       │─────                  ╲    ╱
  └──────────────┘          ╰───────╯                        ╲  ╱
                                                              ╲╱
```

In this pattern **wa** and not **ga** is used as the nominative case (the theme)—in this syntax the use of **wa** is more reasonable because **wa** places emphasis on self-speciality; that is, this **wa** implies that consciousness which emphasizes the difference between self and others. And the predicate of this sentence will be an explanation giving new information about the particular noun or pronoun presented as the theme or topic.

e.g. **Kare *wa* shakaishugisha *ni*** (or: *to*) ***narimashita***. (He became a socialist)—the difference between . . . **ni narimashita** and . . . **to narimashita** (became) found in this expression is as follows: **ni** is used in the sense of fixing a position through a shift, while **to** of a result brought about by something or some action. **Pattern 9** is a variation on **Pattern 8**; that is, **Jidai *ga* kare *o* shakaishugisha *ni* shimashita**, The age shaped him into a socialist. In other words, the construction . . . **o**, direct object, . . . **ni**, complement, in **Pattern 8** can be converted into **Pattern 9** . . . **wa** . . . **ni narimasu**. Also, the expression . . . **wa** . . . **ni** (or: **to**) **narimasu** in **Pattern 9** can be revised into the syntax using a copula (is; am; are), that is, **Pattern 1** as seen in **Kare *wa* shakaishugisha *desu***, He is a socialist.

Note: **Kanojo *wa* aka*ku* narimashita**. (She became red in the face)—**akaku** in this sentence is an adverb from the **i**-adjective **akai**, red. Such an adverb as this is not indicated by either the particle **ni** or **to** in this syntax.

Japanese verbs can be classified into three categories: vowel and consonant stem verbs and irregular verbs. Any verb root ending with either of the vowels *e*-**ru** and *i*-**ru** is called a vowel stem verb. Any verb root ending with **u**, a consonant+**u**, is called a consonant stem verb. The verbs **suru**, to do and **kuru**, to come, are among the irregular verbs which do not belong to either vowel or consonant stem verbs. Also **suru**, to do, in the irregular verb group, is put after those nouns in which a sense of action is inherent. For example, **sentaku suru**, to wash one's clothes—the noun **sentaku**, washing+**suru**, to do— assumes the grammatical changes of the irregular verb group.

Such verbs as **mi-ru**, to see, and **tabe-ru**, to eat, are called vowel stem verbs. First of all, the vowel stem verb **mi-ru**, to see, is taken up as a model and conjugated as follows:

Vowel Stem Verb see	Affirmative Present		Negative Present	
	Plain Form	Polite Form	Plain Form	Polite Form
Indicative mood	mi-ru	mi-masu	mi-nai	mi-masen
	mi-ta (past)	mi-mashita	mi-nakatta	mi-masen deshita
Volitional & Presumptive	mi-yō	mi-mashō	mi-mai	(mi-masumai)
	mi-ru darō	mi-ru deshō	mi-nai darō	mi-nai deshō
	mi-ta darō (past)	mi-ta deshō	mi-nakatta darō	mi-nakatta deshō
	mi-tai (desiderative)	mi-tai desu	mi-taku nai	mi-taku arimasen
	mi-saseru (causative)	mi-sasemasu	mi-sase nai	mi-sasemasen
	mi-saserareru (causative passive)	mi-saseraremasu	mi-saserare nai	mi-saseraremasen
	mi-rareru (potential and passive)	mi-raremasu	mi-rare nai	mi-raremasen
Connective or Participial (*te*-form)	mi-te			
	mi-nagara			
Conditional	mi-reba			
	mi-tara (past)			
Imperative	mi-ro	mi-nasai	mi-runa	(mi-masuna)

In the normal polite style, the ending of a sentence employs the polite form whereas all other verbs, adjectives, and copulas within the sentence are in the plain form. The use of the polite style in this manner is, as a rule, quite fashionable and the common spoken Japanese. But, these plain forms within the sentence will occasionally be transformed into the polite style; it must be acknowledged that this is mainly due to the speaker's subjective feelings. Besides, if the phrase or clause preceding the principal clause suggests a habitual or customary shading, or a universal truth, the tense in this phrase or clause can be indicated by the plain present/future form, never influenced by the tense of the principal clause in the sentence.

e.g. **Kono kaishain wa itsumo densha nai ni burasagatta yokomoji no kōkoku o *mimasu*.** (This company employee always looks at an advertisement in foreign letters posted inside the tramcar)—**mi-**

masu, polite form, from **mi-ru**, plain form, to see—this is a complete form imposing a need for no other additional words; in other words, this is a root form of the verb. The polite form of vowel stem verbs can be obtained by dropping the last syllable **ru** and adding **masu** to the stem.

The plain present form **mi-ru**, to see, is a form attached to such nouns as "a person", "a noun form" which imply the meaning of "the thing that . . ." or "what" (a fact), and "time" ("when" in English) and used to modify these nouns.

e.g.   **Anata ga soko ni *miru hito* wa shōi gunjin desu.** (That person whom you see there is a disabled serviceman).

e.g.   **Raishū eiga o *miru koto* o watashi wa kanojo ni yakusoku shi-mashita.** (I promised to go and see a movie with her next week) —**miru koto**, to see; seeing, is a noun phrase substituted for a regular noun like the expression **kanshō**, appreciation; therefore, **eiga o miru koto**, to see a movie or seeing a movie, is transformed from the expression **eiga no kanshō**, the appreciation of a movie.

e.g.   **Watashi wa meiga o *miru toki* ga ichiban tanoshii desu.** (The most pleasant time for me is when I look at some notable paintings).

e.g.   **Sengetsu watashi wa Shinjuku no Mitsukoshi depāto no nana kai no garō ni naraberareta suisaiga no tenrankai o *mimashita*.** (Last month I saw the exhibition of water color paintings hanging in rows in the seventh floor gallery of the Mitsukoshi department store in Shinjuku)—**mi-mashita**, saw, is in the polite past form.

The expression **yō** in **mi-yō** or **mashō** in **mi-mashō** refers to the will of the speaker or the speaker's sounding out the other party. Moreover, the use of the volitional form is pursued through the grouping of three forms—the simple volitional form (vowel stem verbs+**yō** or **mashō**) is commonly translated "will", "shall", or "let's"; the imminent volitional form (such verbs+**yō to shimasu** or **yō to omoimasu**) is well expressed by "be going to", "be about to", "be ready to", or "to try to"; and the interrogative volitional form (such verbs+**yō ka to omoimasu**) is commonly translated as "(I) think (I) might".

e.g.   **Nan to ka jikan o mitsukete konban rebyū o *mi-mashō*.** (I will manage to find some time to see a revue tonight).

e.g.   **Engawa ni atsumatte, otsukisama o *mi-mashō*.** (Let's gather on the veranda and look at the moon).

e.g.   **Kodomo tachi wa utsukushii hoshi zora o *mi-yō to shimasu*.** (The children are trying to look up at the beautiful starry sky).

e.g. **Watashi wa yukata gake de, Bon odori o** *mi-yō to omoimasu.* (I,
in a 'yukata' [a bath-dress], am going to see the "Bon Festival
Dance").

e.g. **Watashi wa ima kara terebi o** *mi-yō ka to omoimasu.* (I think
I might watch television from now).

e.g. **Watashi wa yoru jū ji igo terebi o** *mi-mai.* (I'll not watch
television after ten o'clock in the evening)—the negation of the
volitional form is expressed by **mai**, plain form, or **masu mai**, polite
form; but the expression **masu mai** is not commonly used.

The conjectural form is used when the speaker relates in conjecture
the state or condition of an object which is obscure. The expression
darō, plain form, or **deshō**, polite form, is used to indicate the conjectural form. This **deshō** is related to verbs, nouns, and adjectives
quite freely. In the case of verbs, **deshō** is put after the plain present
form of any verb.

e.g. **Otōto wa kondo no Doitsu no kijutsu o** *mi-ru deslo.* (My younger
brother will go and see jugglery from Germany this time).

e.g. **Hawai no Amerika-jin kankōkyaku wa 'Kabuki' ga** *mi-tai desu.*
(American tourists from Hawaii would like to see a 'Kabuki' play)
—**tai desu** in **mi-tai desu**, would like to see, is the auxiliary of hope.

e.g. **Watashi wa otōto ni Ueno dōbutsuen o** *mi-sasemasu.* (I'll get
my younger brother to go and see the Ueno Zoo)—**mi-sasemasu**, to
get one to see, is in the causative form.

e.g. **Watashi wa chichi ni shokubutsuen o** *mi-saseraremasu.* (I'm made
to go and see a botanical garden by father)—**mi-saseraremasu**, to be
made to see, is in the causative passive form.

Note: As far as vowel stem verbs are concerned, there is no difference in
form between the potential and the passive voice.

e.g. **Nikai no mado kara Fuji-san ga** *mi-raremasu.* (I can see Mt. Fuji
from the window upstairs)—**raremasu** in **mi-raremasu**, can see, is
the potential auxiliary.

e.g. **Yūjin ga watashi no hō e kuru no ga** *mi-raremasu.* (My friend
is seen coming toward me)—**raremasu** in **mi-raremasu**, to be seen,
is the passive voice.

e.g. **Konyakusha no kao o** *mi-te,* **kanojo wa hanikamimashita.** (Looking at her betrothed's face, she felt shy)—**mi-te**, looking at . . . ,
is in the continuative or participial construction. This form is
obtained by replacing the final vowel **a** of the plain past form by
e. In the case of vowel stem verbs, these plain past forms can
be obtained by dropping the last syllable **ru** and adding **ta** to the

stem, as **mi-ta** from **mi-ru**, to see.

An action in progress or a state of being is obtained by the **te**-form of vowel stem verbs+**imasu**. This form is obtained by replacing the final vowel **a** of the plain past form by **e**.

  e.g. **Kanojo wa shōuindō no hōseki o *mi-te imasu*.** (She is looking at some jewels in the show window)—**mi-te imasu**, to be looking at . . . , is in the polite present progressive form.

  e.g. **Kono shōnen wa terebi o *mi-nagara*, ringo no kawa o muite imasu.** (This boy is peeling an apple while watching television). "While (or: although) . . ." is expressed by **nagara**. **Nagara** is a connective particle expressing an action or condition parallel to another, and it also expresses paradox. In the case of vowel stem verbs, "while or although . . ." can be obtained by dropping the last syllable **ru** and adding **nagara** to the stem.

  e.g. **Nihon-jin wa dare demo ryō heika o *mi-reba*, kangeki shimasu.** (Any Japanese who looks at the Emperor and the Empress is deeply impressed)—**mi-reba**, if one looks at . . . , indicates a hypothetical subjunctive condition concerned with the present and future, as well as a counterhypothesis to the present facts. In the case of vowel stem verbs, the hypothetical subjunctive condition can be obtained by dropping the last syllable **ru** and adding **reba** to the stem. The relationship between **mi-ru**, to look at . . . and **kangeki suru**, to be deeply impressed with . . . in this sentence, is an inevitable theory common to the public at large. The proposition with **reba** denotes a theory.

Besides the expression **reba**, such expressions as **to**, and **nara** or **nara ba** indicating hypothetical subjunctive conditions can be used with vowel stem verbs.

  e.g. **Ikoku de nisshōki o *mi-ru to*, kangeki shimasu.** (If I happen to see the rising-sun flag in a foreign country, I'm deeply touched by it)—the relationship between **mi-ru**, to see and **kangeki suru**, to be deeply touched by . . . in this sentence, is a matter of fact which acts upon the single person "I", a Japanese resident or a tourist in a foreign country; that is, the phrase with **to** preceding the principal clause suggests a shading like "in such a case as when . . ." or "whenever . . .".

  e.g. **Chashitsu o *mi-ru nara*, mite kudasai.** (If you would look at my tearoom, please take a look)—**nara** or **nara ba** indicates a mere subjunctive clause which exerts no restricting influence over the principal clause.

e.g. **Ta-nin no me kara** *mi-tara*, **junboku de, sunao de, ohitoyoshi de,
mōshibun no nai musume deshita.** (As she would have appeared to
others she was simple-hearted, obedient, and good-natured—she
was a daughter beyond criticism)—**mi-tara**, if one had seen . . . ,
indicates a counterhypothesis to the past facts. Such hypothesis
as evident in Japanese is quite different from that in English; in
other words, in Japanese there is found no distinct difference
between the indicative mood and the subjunctive mood. However,
a hypothesis in opposition to past facts is indicated, in its if-clause,
by the conditional suffixes **tara, ta nara** or **ta nara ba** in the case
of vowel stem verbs. And, in this main clause there are no exact
verbal expressions and rules of concord which relate to the conditional mood—style and wording in the main clause can be preferably varied, closely associated with the speaker's subjective
feelings and the sense of conversation through the medium of
him. In the case of vowel stem verbs, this hypothetical subjunctive condition can be obtained by dropping the last syllable **ru**
and adding **tara, ta nara** or **ta nara ba** to the stem. The **ta** found
in these suffixes is derived from the plain past form of any vowel
stem verb. Therefore, another clue for the formation of this
subjunctive condition is found in the plain past form of vowel
stem verbs, that is, this plain past form+**ra, nara** and **nara ba.**

e.g. **Yama no ue no bon no yō na man marui utsukushii tsuki o** *mi-
nasai.* (Please look at the beautiful moon, perfectly round like a
tray, above the mountains)—**mi-nasai**, Please look at . . . , is a
complete form with an imperative meaning.

Secondly, any verb root ending with a consonant is called a consonant stem verb. The polite form of verbs in this category can be
obtained by dropping the last syllable **u** and adding **imasu** to the stem.
On the other hand, the polite form of vowel stem verbs can be obtained
by dropping the last syllable **ru** and adding **masu** to the stem. In the
case of vowel stem verbs, the plain past forms can be obtained by
dropping the last syllable **ru** and adding **ta** to the stem, while consonant
stem verbs in the plain past form involve a sound change before adding
ta or **da**; that is, there are four euphonic changes—an **i**-euphonic
change, a euphonic change to the syllabic nasal sound, a euphonic
change of assimilation, and a euphonic change of friction. Rules for
these sound changes are illustrated as follows:

Such a verb as ha*k*-u, to put on shoes, undergoes an **i**-euphonic
change—the plain past form is ha*i*-ta. But here the verb i*k*-u, to

go, is an exception; the plain past form is i*t*-ta.

Such verbs as ka*m*-u, to bite, and to*b*-u, to fly, undergo a euphonic change to the syllabic nasal sound—the plain past forms are ka*n*-da and to*n*-da. But here the verb shi*n*-u, to die, is an exception; the plain past form is shi*n*-da. Note: Oyog-u→oyo*i*-da (swam).

Such verbs as ka*ts*-u, to win, so*r*-u, to shave, and wara[*w*]-u, to laugh, undergo a euphonic change of assimilation—the plain past forms are ka*t*-ta, so*t*-ta, and wara*t*-ta.

Such a verb as ka*s*-u, to lend, undergoes a euphonic change of friction—the plain past form is ka*shi*-ta.

The consonant stem verb kak-u, to write, which undergoes an i-euphonic change, is taken up as a model and its conjugation shown in the following table.

Consonant Stem Verb **write**	Affirmative Present		Negative Present	
	Plain Form	Polite Form	Plain Form	Polite Form
Indicative mood	kak-u	kak-imasu	kak-anai	kak-imasen
	kai-ta (past)	kak-imashita	kak-anakatta	kak-imasen deshita
Volitional & Presumptive	kak-ō	kak-imashō	kak-umai	(kak-imasumai)
	kak-u darō	kak-u deshō	kak-anai darō	kak-anai deshō
	kai-ta darō (past)	kai-ta deshō	kak-anakatta darō	kak-anakatta deshō
	kaki-tai (desiderative)	kaki-tai desu	kaki-taku nai	kaki-taku arimasen
	kak-aseru (causative)	kak-asemasu	kak-ase nai	kak-asemasen
	kak-aserareru (causative passive)	kak-aserare masu	kak-aserare nai	kak-aserare masen
	kak-eru (potential)	kak-emasu	kak-e nai	kak-emasen
	kak-areru (passive)	kak-aremasu	kak-are nai	kak-aremasen
Connective or Participial (*te* or *de*-form)	kai-te			
	kak-i			
	kak-i nagara			
Conditional	kak-eba			
	kai-tara (past)			
Imperative	kak-e	kak-inasai	kak-una	(kak-imasuna)

The plain present form **kak-u**, to write, and the polite present form **kak-imasu**, to write, are complete forms requiring no additional words.

Besides, the plain present form **kak-u** is a form attached to such nouns as "a person", "a noun form" which imply the meaning of "the thing that . . ." or "what" (a fact), and "time" ("when" in English) and used to modify these nouns. This case is simply demonstrated as follows: **kak-u hito**, a person who writes . . . , **kak-u koto**, to write; writing, and **kak-u toki**, when one writes . . . **Kak-imashita**, wrote, is in the polite past form.

In the case of consonant stem verbs ending with **u**, the volitional form can be obtained by changing the last syllable **u** to **i** and adding **mashō** to the stem. The verb **kak-u**, to write, in this form is as follows: **kak-imashō**, (I)'ll write and Let's write. Also, the imminent volitional form is **kak-ō to shimasu**, (I) am ready to write or **kak-ō to omoimasu**, (I) am going to write, and the interrogative volitional form is **kak-ō ka to omoimasu**, (I) think (I) might write.

The expression **darō**, plain form, or **deshō**, polite form, is used to indicate the conjectural form. In the case of verbs, **darō** or **deshō** is put after the present form of any verb. And thus, the verb **kak-u**, to write, in the conjectural form is **kak-u deshō**, will write. The negation of the volitional form is **kak-u mai**, plain form, or **kak-imasu mai**, will not write, polite form, although this latter expression **kak-imasu mai** is not commonly used.

The desiderative (would like to) is expressed by the auxiliary of hope **tai**, plain form, or **tai desu**, polite form, attached to the second base of any verb (the verb form used with the polite -masu endings), as **kaki-tai desu**, would like to write, from **kaki-masu**, to write.

In the case of consonant stem verbs ending with **u**, the causative form can be obtained by dropping the last syllable **u** and adding **aseru**, plain form, or **asemasu**, polite form, to the stem. Therefore, the causative form of the verb **kak-u**, to write, is **kak-asemasu**, to get someone to write something. The expression **kak-aseraremasu**, to be made to write, is in the causative passive form.

In the case of consonant stem verbs ending with **u**, the potential auxiliary can be obtained by dropping the last syllable **u** and adding **emasu** to the stem, as **kak-emasu**, can write, from **kak-u**, to write.

In the case of consonant stem verbs ending with **u**, the passive voice can be obtained by dropping the last syllable **u** and adding **areru**, plain form, or **aremasu**, polite form, to the stem, as **kak-aremasu**, to be written, from **kak-u**, to write.

The irregular verbs **suru**, to do, and **kuru**, to come, can be conjugated as follows:

Irregular Verbs 1. **do** 2. **come**	Affirmative Present		Negative Present	
	Plain Form	Polite Form	Plain Form	Polite Form
Indicative mood	1. suru shi-ta (past) 2. kuru ki-ta (past)	shi-masu shi-mashita ki-masu ki-mashita	shi-nai shi-nakatta ko-nai ko-nakatta	shi-masen shi-masen deshita ki-masen ki-masen deshita
Volitional & Presumptive	1. shi-yō suru darō shita darō (past) 2. ko-yō kuru darō kita darō (past)	shi-mashō suru deshō shita deshō ki-mashō kuru deshō kita deshō	shi-mai shinai darō shinakatta darō ko-mai konai darō konakatta darō	(shi-masumai) shinai deshō shinakatta deshō (ki-masumai) konai deshō konakatta deshō
	1. shi-tai 2. ki-tai (desiderative)	shi-tai desu ki-tai desu	shi-taku nai ki-taku nai	shi-taku arimasen ki-taku arimasen
	1. saseru 2. kosaseru (causative)	sasemasu kosasemasu	sase nai kosase nai	sasemasen kosasemasen
	1. saserareru 2. ko-saserareru (causative passive)	saseraremasu ko-saseraremasu	saserare nai ko-saserare nai	saseraremasen ko-saseraremasen
	1. dekiru 2. ko-rareru (potential)	dekimasu ko-raremasu	deki nai ko-rare nai	dekimasen ko-raremasen
	1. sareru 2. ko-rareru (passive)	saremasu ko-raremasu	sare nai ko-rare nai	saremasen ko-raremasen
Connective or Participial (*te*-form)	1. shi-te shi-nagara 2. ki-te ki-nagara			
Conditional	1. sure ba 2. kure ba 1. shi-tara 2. ki-tara (past)			
Imperative	1. shi-yo 2. ko-i	shi-nasai ki-nasai	suru na kuru na	(shimasuna) (kimasuna)

The form of the continuative or participial construction is expressed by the te or de-form of consonant stem verbs, obtained by replacing the final vowel a of the plain past form by e or the second base, as kai-te or kaki, Writing or to write and . . . , from kai-ta, wrote, plain past form or kaki-masu, to write, polite present form.

An action in progress or a state of being is expressed by the te or de-form of consonant stem verbs+imasu—this form is obtained by replacing the final vowel a of the plain past form by e, as kai-te imasu, to be writing, from kai-ta, wrote.

In the case of consonant stem verbs ending with u, "while or although . . ." can be obtained by changing the last syllable u to i and adding nagara, as kak-i nagara, while writing, from kak-u, to write.

In the case of consonant stem verbs ending with u, the hypothetical subjective condition, as well as a counterhypothesis to the present facts, can be obtained by changing the last syllable u to e and adding ba, as kak-eba, if one writes, from kak-u, to write. Also, the expression nara or nara ba, and to can be applied with the plain present form of these verbs, as kak-u nara or kak-u nara ba, and kak-u to, if one writes.

In the case of consonant stem verbs, a hypothesis in opposition to past facts can be formed by the use of their plain past forms. As far as verbs in this group are concerned, a sound change is involved before adding the plain past form ta or da. The subjunctive mood becomes this ta or da+ra, nara or nara ba. The expressions kai-ta ra, kai-ta nara, and kai-ta nara ba, if one wrote, from kai-ta, wrote, are in this subjunctive mood.

The expression kak-inasai, Please write, is a complete form with an imperative meaning.

In Japanese there are two kinds of adjectives na-adjectives and i-adjectives. Here, na-adjectives are given first. Each adjective can be applied in an attributive or a predicative use. The attributive use of na-adjectives is expressed by na+a noun. The form of the predicative use can always be obtained by dropping na from these adjectives and adding the termination desu, a copula. When used predicatively, each na-adjective becomes a noun; in other words, the noun form of this class of adjectives can be induced by omitting the na of its true function. The adverbial form of na-adjectives can be obtained by replacing the final na by ni. We may also obtain its adverbial form by adding ni to the noun form.

Here, the na-adjective shinsetsu na, kind, is taken up as a model;

and this adjective in a predicative use can be conjugated as follows.
In other words, the copula (is; am; are) has the following conjugation:

Copula; *na*-adjective be kind	Affirmative Present		Negative Present	
	Plain Form	Polite Form	Plain Form	Polite Form
Indicative mood	shinsetsu-da	shinsetsu-desu	shinsetsu-de (wa) nai	shinsetsu-de (wa) arimasen
	shinsetsu-datta (past)	shinsetsu-deshita	shinsetsu-de (wa) nakatta	shinsetsu-de (wa) arimasen deshita
Volitional & Presumptive	shinsetsu-darō	shinsetsu-deshō	shinsetsu-de (wa) nai darō	shinsetsu-de (wa) nai deshō
	shinsetsu-datta darō (past)	shinsetsu-datta deshō	shinsetsu-de (wa) nakatta darō	shinsetsu-de (wa) nakatta deshō
Connective or Participial (Noun + *de*-form)	shinsetsu-de			
	shinsetsu-ni (adverb)			
Conditional	shinsetsu-nara			
	shinsetsu-dattara (past)			

I-adjectives end with either the short vowel **i** or the long vowel **ii**.
This class of adjectives, as in the case of na-adjectives, can be applied
in an attributive or a predicative use. The attributive use of i-adjectives is expressed by **i** or **ii**+a noun. When used predicatively, each
i-adjective, as it is, relates to the copula (is; am; are). The adverbial
form of i-adjectives can be obtained by replacing the final **i** by **ku**,
that is, by substituting **ku** for the short vowel **i** or by shortening the
long vowel **ii** and adding **ku**. In the case of na-adjectives, the connective particle can always be applied with them as **de**. But, the use
of the connective particle **te** in place of **de** is of equal availability to
each i-adjective. In the case of i-adjectives, the final **i** is dropped or
long **ii** shortened, this termination enabling them to suffix **ku**. This
ku then relates to the following in the form of **ku**+**te**.

Here, the i-adjective **hiroi**, wide, is taken up as a model; and this
adjective in a predicative use can be conjugated as follows:

i-adjective be wide	Affirmative Present		Negative Present	
	Plain Form	Polite Form	Plain Form	Polite Form
Indicative mood	hiro-i	hiro-i desu	hiro-ku (wa) nai	hiro-ku (wa) arimasen
	hiro-katta (past)	hiro-katta desu	hiro-ku (wa) nakatta	hiro-ku (wa) arimasen deshita
Volitional & Presumptive	hiro-i darō	hiro-i deshō	hiro-ku (wa) nai darō	hiro-ku (wa) nai deshō
	hiro-katta darō (past)	hiro-katta deshō	hiro-ku (wa) nakatta darō	hiro-ku (wa) nakatta deshō
Connective or Participial (*ku*+*te*-form)	hiro-ku te hiro-ku (adverb)			
Conditional	hiro-kere ba hiro-kattara (past)			

Copula

Rule

A は A′ です。(A *wa* A′ *desu*).　A *is* A′.

e.g.　私は大学生です。(Watakushi *wa* daigakusei *desu*)—I am a university student—は (wa) in 私は (watakushi wa), I, is used when the speaker is going to give an explanation regarding the subject, after presenting it first; that is, the particle は (wa) is the theme or topic of the sentence.　And the predicate of this sentence will be an explanation giving new information about the particular noun or pronoun presented as the theme or topic.

大学生 (daigakusei), a university student, is a noun.

です (desu) acts as a copula, connecting the two parts of a sentence as a kind of equal sign.

Note: わたし (Watashi) in familiar speech is shortened from the more formal 私 (Watakushi), I.

e.g.　あなたは勤勉です。(Anata *wa* kinben *desu*)—You are diligent—勤勉 (kinben), diligence, is the noun form derived from the な (na)-adjective 勤勉な (kinben na) diligent.

e.g.　彼は明るいです。(Kare *wa* akarui *desu*)—He is cheerful—明るいです (akarui desu), to be cheerful, is the predicative use of the attributive い (i)-adjective 明るい (akarui), cheerful.

The copula (is; am; are) has the following conjugation:

	Present/Future	Past	Present/Future Negative	Past Negative
polite form	desu	deshita	de(wa)arimasen	de(wa)arimasen deshita
plain form	da	datta	de(wa)nai	de(wa)nakatta

Drill

1. 私は外人です。　　　　I am a foreigner.
2. あなたは学生です。　　You are a student.
3. 彼は留学生です。　　　He is a foreign student.
4. 彼女はインド人です。　She is an Indian.

5. 私たちは研修生です。   We are trainees.
6. あなたたちは事務員です。   You are office workers.
7. 彼らは研究留学生です。   They are foreign research stu-
                                  dents.
8. 彼女らは先生です。   They (women) are teachers.
9. 彼女は親切です。   She is kind.
10. 彼は暗いです。   He is gloomy.
11. これは雑誌 (新聞, 週刊誌) で   This is a magazine (a newspaper;
   す。   a weekly magazine).
12. それは教科書 (日本語の本,   It is a textbook (a Japanese book;
   洋書) です。   a foreign book).
13. あれは机 (いす, 黒板) です。   That is a desk (a chair; a black-
                                  board).

Exercise

Fill in the following blanks with the nominative case "は":

√ 1. 私 (　) 店員です。   I am a salesman.
2. あなた (　) ずうずうしい   You are an awfully insolent fel-
   やつです。   low.
3. 彼 (　) 元気おう盛な人です。   He is a spirited and lively man.
4. 彼女 (　) 人妻です。   She is someone's wife.
5. 私たち (　) 警官です。   We are policemen.
6. あなたたち (　) 邦文のタイ   You are typists of Japanese.
   ピストです。
7. 彼ら (　) 本心からの悪人で   They are bad men at heart.
   す。
8. 彼女ら (　) 芸術に親しむ   They (women) are those who
   人たちです。   move freely about the world of art.
9. 彼 (　) 正直です。   He is honest.
10. 彼女 (　) 若いです。   She is young.
11. これ (　) 消しゴム (ナイ   This is an india rubber (a knife;
   フ, 定規) です。   a ruler).
12. それ (　) 鉛筆 (万年筆, ボ   It is a pencil (a fountain pen; a
   ールペン) です。   ball pen).

13. あれ（　　）教室（窓，ドア）です。 That is a classroom (a window; a door).

第 二 課　Lesson 2

Connective Particle で (de)

Rule

A は A′ で、A″ です。(A wa A′ 　　A is A′ *and* A″.
de, A″ desu).

A は A′ で、B は B′ です。(A 　　A is A′ *and* B is B′.
wa A′ *de*, B wa B′ desu).

e.g. 彼は顔見知りの映画館の支配人で、頼もしい人です。(Kare wa kao
mishiri no eigakan no shihainin *de*, tanomoshii hito desu)—He is
the manager, whom I know, of a movie theatre and a reliable
person—で (de) in 支配人で (shihainin de), the manager and . . . ,
is the connective ("and" in English) used in a compound sentence
employing the copula *desu* and may be considered to be an abbreviation of that verb. If nouns are placed before this connective
particle, they relate to the following through で (de).

e.g. 彼は床屋さんで、彼女は美容師です。(Kare wa tokoya-san *de*,
kanojo wa biyōshi desu)—He is a barber and she is a beautician.

Drill

1. あなたは邦文のタイピストで、
私は英文のタイピストです。

   You are a Japanese typist and
   I am an English typist.

2. 彼はダンスホールの支配人で、
彼女は事務員です。

   He is the manager of a dance
   hall and she is a female office
   worker.

3. あなたたちは被告で、彼らは弁
護人です。

   You are defendants and they
   are counsels.

4. 彼らは無責任な男で、彼女らは
強い女、賢い女です。

   They are irresponsible men and
   they are strong and intelligent
   women.

Exercise

Fill the blanks with the connective particle "で":

1. 彼は私の同級生（　　）、多少人
が悪いです。

   He is one of my classmates
   and has the weaknesses of most
   people.

2. 彼女と彼は同姓（　）、勤務先   She and he have the same sur-
    も同じです。   name and the same office.

3. あなたは純真（　）純朴な青   You are naive and a simple-
    年です。   hearted young man.

4. 彼らは活発（　）、元気です。   They are lively and high-
                                     spirited.

第三課 Lesson 3

The Use of も (mo), also

Rule

A も A′ です。(A *mo* A′ desu).   A *also* is A′.

e.g. 私も芸術家です。(Watakushi *mo* geijutsuka desu)—I also am an artist. After a certain fact is mentioned, a similar purport is implicated by も (mo): "also, too." も (mo), also, replaces は (wa) in the nominative case or other particles. 私も (Watakushi *mo*), I also, comes from 私は (Watakushi *wa*), I.

Drill

1. 私も常識家です。
I also am a man of common sense.

2. あなたも苦労を知らない人です。
You also are a man who knows no hardships.

3. 彼も誘惑にもろい道楽むすこです。
He also is a prodigal son easily carried away by temptations.

4. 彼女も器量は悪いです。
She also is a plain woman.

5. 私たちも煮え切らない男です。
We also are irresolute men.

6. あなたたちも良家のむすこです。
You also are the sons of good families.

7. 彼らも無為徒食者です。
They also are idlers.

8. 彼女らも十八の娘です。
They also are daughters of eighteen.

Exercise

Fill the brackets with "も":

1. 私 ( ) 若くして子を連れた未亡人です。
I also am a widow who, though young, has a child.

2. あなた ( ) にぎやかな事の好きな人です。
You also are a man who likes lively things.

3. 彼 ( ) 生活力の強い人です。
He also is a man full of vitality.

4. 彼女 （　　　） 若くて美貌な人です。 — She also is a young and beautiful woman.

5. 私たち （　　　） 清潔な紳士です。 — We also are well-groomed gentlemen.

6. あなたたち （　　　） 官僚のわからず屋どもです。 — You also are bureaucratic, irresponsible persons.

7. 彼ら （　　　） 鋭い批判をもった良い青年です。 — They also are fine young men, with keen critical minds.

8. 彼女ら （　　　） 本当の心は傍観者です。 — They (women) also are bystanders in their inner hearts.

第 四 課　Lesson 4

The Use of の (no), of

Rule

　の (no) can be rendered as "of" or "'s" in English (nouns or pronouns+の (no)+nouns)—this の (no) expresses the belongings, objects, and materials of things; means and cause; a place or whereabouts; time; the quality and conditions of things; the subjective case for an action, condition, or quality; and also serves to avoid the repetition of nouns.

　の (no) expresses the belongings of things:

e.g.　二十号室のとびらはしまっています。(Ni jū gō shitsu *no* tobira wa shimatte imasu)—The door of room No. 20 is shut—二十号室 (ni jū gō shitsu), room No. 20 and とびら (tobira), the door, are nouns.

e.g.　これは私の（あなたの；彼の；彼女の）湯のみ茶椀です。(Kore wa watakushi *no* [anata *no*; kare *no*; kanojo *no*] yunomi jawan desu) —This is my (your, his, her) cup—私の (Watakushi no), あなたの (anata no), 彼の (kare no), and 彼女の (kanojo no) are possessive pronouns.

e.g.　これは私たちの（あなたたちの；彼らの；彼女らの）財布です。(Kore wa watakushi-tachi *no* [anata-tachi *no*; kare-ra *no*; kanojo-ra *no*] saifu desu)—These are our (your, their, their) purses—私たちの (watakushi-tachi no), あなたたちの (anata-tachi no), 彼らの (kare-ra no), and 彼女らの (kanojo-ra no) are plural possessive pronouns.

e.g.　鉛筆の芯が折れました。(Enpitsu *no* shin ga oremashita)—The lead of the pencil broke—鉛筆 (enpitsu), a pencil and 芯 (shin), lead, are nouns.

　の (no) expresses the objects of things:

e.g.　日本語の学習は楽しいです。(Nihongo *no* gakushū wa tanoshii desu)—I take pleasure in the study of Japanese—日本語 (Nihongo), Japanese and 学習 (gakushū), study, are nouns.

e.g.　長い東京の旅行でした。(Nagai Tōkyō *no* ryokō deshita)—It was a long journey to Tokyo—東京 (Tōkyō), the capital of Japan and 旅行 (ryokō), journey, are nouns.

　の (no) expresses the materials of things:

e.g.　煙草の煙が回転窓から流れ出ています。(Tabako *no* kemuri ga

kaiten mado kara nagaredete imasu)—The smoke of cigarettes is
streaming from the transom window—煙草 (tabako), a cigarette
and 煙 (kemuri), smoke, are nouns.

e.g. きりのたんすがあります。(Kiri *no* tansu ga arimasu)—There is
a paulownia chest of drawers—きり (kiri), paulownia and たんす
(tansu), a chest of drawers, are nouns.

の (no) expresses means and cause:

e.g. 彼は今佐藤首相のラジオの政見放送を聞いています。(Kare wa ima
Satō shushō no rajio *no* seiken hōsō o kiite imasu)—He is now
listening to Prime Minister Sato's speech on his political views
over the radio—ラジオ (rajio), the radio and 政見放送 (seiken hōsō),
a speech on one's political views over the radio, are nouns.

e.g. 最近東京都内では自動車の事故が激増しています。(Saikin Tōkyō
tonai dewa jidōsha *no* jiko ga gekizōshite imasu)—Recently car
accidents have increased markedly in Tokyo city—自動車 (jidōsha),
a car and 事故 (jiko), an accident, are nouns.

の (no) expresses a place or whereabouts:

e.g. 東京の山の手は住宅地域です。(Tōkyō *no* Yamanote wa jūtaku
chi-iki desu)—Yamanote (the tablelands) in Tokyo is regarded as
a residential area—東京 (Tōkyō) and 山の手 (Yamanote) are nouns.

e.g. 京都のお寺はすばらしいです。(Kyōto *no* otera wa subarashii
desu)—Temples in Kyoto are magnificent—京都 (Kyōto), our
ancient capital, and お寺 (otera), a temple, are nouns.

e.g. 台所の流しがつまっています。(Daidokoro *no* nagashi ga tsumatte
imasu)—The sink in the kitchen is clogged—台所 (daidokoro), a
kitchen and 流し (nagashi), a sink, are nouns.

の (no) expresses time:

e.g. 三時のおやつに果物がでました。(San ji *no* oyatsu ni kudamono
ga demashita)—Some fruits were brought in as refreshments at
three o'clock—三時 (san ji), three o'clock and おやつ (oyatsu),
refreshments, are nouns.

e.g. 彼女は夜の星空をながめています。(Kanojo wa yoru *no* hoshi zora
o nagamete imasu)—She is looking up at the starry night sky—
夜 (yoru), night and 星空 (hoshi zora), the starry sky, are nouns.

の (no) expresses the quality or condition of things:

e.g. きのう私は路上で友だちの田中君に会いました。(Kinō watakushi
wa rojō de tomodachi *no* Tanaka-kun ni aimashita)—Yesterday I
met Mr. Tanaka, my friend, in the street—友だち (tomodachi), a
friend and 田中君 (Tanaka-kun), Mr. Tanaka, are nouns.

e.g. 彼は象牙のパイプをこすっています。(Kare wa zōge *no* paipu o

kosutte imasu)—He is rubbing his ivory pipe—象牙 (zōge), ivory and パイプ (paipu), a pipe, are nouns.

e.g. いなか臭い顔付きの男がはいってきました。(Inaka kusai kaotsuki *no* otoko ga haitte kimashita)—A man of a rustic complexion came in—いなか臭い顔付き (inaka kusai kaotsuki), a rustic complexion and 男 (otoko), a man, are nouns.

の (no) expresses the subjective case for an action, condition, or quality:

e.g. 雨の降る日は憂欝です。(Ame *no* furu hi wa yū-utsu desu)—I feel depressed on rainy days—雨の (ame *no*), rain, in the phrase of 雨の降る (ame no furu), rainy, is related to 日 (hi), a day; therefore the phrase 雨の (ame *no*) can also be written and spoken with the use of が (ga), as 雨が降る日 (ame *ga* furu hi), rainy days.

e.g. 彼の乗ったタクシーが自家用車と衝突しました。(Kare *no* notta takushii ga jikayōsha to shōtotsu shimashita)—The taxi he was in collided with a private car—the phrase 彼の (kare *no*) can also be written and spoken with the use of が (ga), as 彼が乗ったタクシー (kare *ga* notta takushii), the taxi he was in.

e.g. 彼女は花のきれいな水草を見つけました。(Kanojo wa hana *no* kirei na mizu kusa o mitsukemashita)—She discovered a water plant with a pretty flower—the phrase 花の (hana *no*) can also be written and spoken with the use of が (ga), as 花がきれいな水草 (hana *ga* kirei na mizu kusa), a water plant with a pretty flower.

の (no) serves to avoid the repetition of nouns ("one" or "ones" in English):

e.g. 私は万年筆がほしいです。緑のを見せて下さい。(Watakushi wa man-nen-hitsu ga hoshii desu. Midori *no* o misete kudasai)—I want some fountain pens. Please show me the green one—緑の (midori *no*), the green one, means "the green fountain pen."

Drill

1. 姉の夫は小さな神社の神官です。	My elder sister's husband is the Shinto priest of a small shrine.
2. 彼の会社の空気はなごやかです。	The atmosphere in his company is peaceful.
3. 彼女は子供の手を取って、歩いていきます。	She walks on, taking the child by her hand.
4. 彼女は婚家の両親がきらいです。	She dislikes her husband's parents.

5. 大売り出しの赤い幕がひらひら
   しています。

   The red hangings for the bargain sale are flitting here and
   there.

6. 高校のむすこは冬休みのスキー
   に行って，今日はいません。

   My son, in high school, is off
   for a winter skiing holiday, so
   today he is not at home.

7. 弟は父の会社の本社に勤めてい
   ます。

   My younger brother works at
   the head office of our father's
   company.

8. 彼女は田中さんの長女の雪子さ
   んです。

   She is Miss Yukiko, the eldest
   daughter of Mr. Tanaka.

9. ハモニカの音がどこからか聞こ
   えてきました。

   The sound of a harmonica came
   audibly from somewhere.

10. 衆議院の総選挙が四月の末に行
    なわれました。

    A general election for the House
    of Representatives was held at
    the end of April.

11. 日本の女の人の着物の色は大へ
    んきれいです。

    The colors of Japanese women's
    kimono are very beautiful.

12. 病の苦痛が彼を浄化しました。

    The pain of his illness has puri-
    fied him.

13. この雑誌の編集は左翼的です。

    The editing of this magazine
    has a leftist tint.

14. 彼女は目黒の高台にある実家に
    帰ってきました。

    She returned to her parents'
    home on the heights of Meguro.

15. 彼女は暇さえあれば，自分の部
    屋の机にすわっています。

    Whenever she has some leisure
    time, she sits at the desk in her
    room.

Exercise

(A) Give attention to の (no) evident in each sentence and classify
the use, pointing out as follows—の (no) expresses the belongings,
objects, and materials of things:

1. ズックのかばんはながもちしま
   せん。

   Canvas bags are not durable.

ズック (zukku), duck and かばん (kaban), a bag, are nouns.

2. 貴重品は机の引き出しにしまっ   I keep valuables in the drawer
    ておきます。   of the desk.
    机 (tsukue), a desk and 引き出し (hikidashi), a drawer, are nouns.

3. 私は電話の交換手を知っていま   I know a telephone operator.
    す。
    電話 (denwa), a telephone and 交換手 (kōkanshu), an operator, are
    nouns.

4. この子供はりんごのむき方がわ   This child doesn't know how to
    かりません。   peel apples.
    りんご (ringo), an apple, is a noun and むき方 (muki kata), how to
    peel, is a noun phrase.

5. 私はナイロンのくつ下を買いま   I bought some nylon socks.
    した。
    ナイロン (nairon), nylon and くつ下 (kutsushita), socks, are nouns.

(B) Classify the use of の (no) in each sentence and point out as
     follows—の (no) expresses means and cause, a place, and time:

1. 校庭の桜は今満開です。   The cherry blossoms in the
                                    school ground are now in full
                                    bloom.
    校庭 (kōtei), the school ground and 桜 (sakura), cherry blossoms, are
    nouns.

2. 私は新聞の広告はめったに見ま   I seldom see the advertisements
    せん。   in the newspaper.
    新聞 (shinbun), a newspaper and 広告 (kōkoku), advertisements, are
    nouns.

3. この留学生は四月の中旬，日本   This foreign student arrived in
    に着きました。   Japan in the middle of April.
    四月 (shigatsu), April and 中旬 (chūjun), the middle, are nouns.

4. 今では伝染病の死亡率は少ない   Nowadays the death rate of
    です。   infectious diseases is not striking.
    伝染病 (densenbyō), infectious diseases and 死亡率 (shibō ritsu), death
    rate, are nouns.

5. 飛行機の旅行は楽しいです。   Travelling by plane is pleasant.
    飛行機 (hikōki), a plane and 旅行 (ryokō), a trip, are nouns.

(C) Classify the use of の (no) in each sentence and point out as
     follows—の (no) expresses the quality or condition of things, the

subjective case for an action, condition, or quality, and serves to avoid the repetition of nouns:

1. 係の山田さんに話しておきま   I'll talk it over with Mr. Ya-
す。   mada, the man in charge.
   係 (kakari), the man in charge and 山田さん (Yamada-san), Mr. Yamada, are nouns.

2. 試験の終わった学生は帰宅して   Those students who have fin-
もよいです。   ished the examination are per-
                                   mitted to return home.
   試験の (shiken no), an examination, can also be written and spoken
   with the use of が (ga), as 試験が (shiken ga).

3. 絹のくつ下はナイロンのよりよ   Silk socks are better than nylon
いです。   ones.
   ナイロンの (nairon no), nylon ones, means "nylon socks."

4. きのう私はせむしの老人を見ま   Yesterday I happened to see a
した。   humpbacked old man.
   せむし (semushi), a humpback and 老人 (rōjin), an old man, are nouns.

5. ここに顔のみにくい婦人がいま   Here is an ugly woman.
す。
   顔の (kao no), one's face, can also be written and spoken with the
   use of が (ga), as 顔が (kao ga).

Answers:
(A) 1. の (no) expresses the material of a thing.
    2. の (no) expresses the belonging of a thing.
    3. の (no) expresses the object of a thing.
    4. の (no) expresses the object of a thing.
    5. の (no) expresses the material of a thing.
(B) 1. の (no) expresses a place.
    2. の (no) expresses a place.
    3. の (no) expresses time.
    4. の (no) expresses cause.
    5. の (no) expresses means.
(C) 1. の (no) expresses the quality or condition of a thing.
    2. の (no) expresses the subjective case for an action.
    3. の (no) serves to avoid the repetition of nouns.
    4. の (no) expresses the quality or condition of a thing.
    5. の (no) expresses the subjective case for condition or quality.

第五課　Lesson 5

Verb of Existence

Rule

B に A が います。(B *ni* A *ga imasu*). *There is* A (someone) B (place word).

B に A が あります。(B *ni* A *ga arimasu*). *There is* A (something) B (place word).

e.g.　社長室に六・七人の社員が います。(Shachō shitsu *ni* roku shichi nin no shain *ga imasu*)—In the director's room there are six or seven employees—社長室に (shachō shitsu ni), in the director's room, is an adverb phrase and the particle に (ni) in this phrase shows a place of existence ("in", "at", or "on" in English). The nominative case が (ga) in 六・七人の社員が (roku shichi nin no shain ga), six or seven employees, is quite closely connected to verbs of existence such as います (imasu) or あります (arimasu), there is . . . . When the nominative case is an animate object, the verb of existence います (imasu) can be used. Generally the common order in this sentence places an adverb phrase with the particle に (ni) first and then the nominative case が (ga) appears. Otherwise, we may say and write this sentence 六・七人の社員は 社長室に います。(Roku shichi nin no shain *wa* shachō shitsu *ni imasu*)—There are six or seven employees in the director's room —in this case, a rearrangement of the nominative case and adverb phrase occurs; that is, the nominative case precedes the adverb phrase. Also, this time は (wa) and not が (ga) is used as the nominative case; the restriction of a topic led by は (wa) is loose because of its function of presenting the theme; and thus, は (wa) accordingly reaches far. The feeling of approach taken by は (wa) extends over and as far as the います (imasu) or あります (arimasu) at the end of the sentence.

e.g.　鏡台の前にハンドバッグが あります。(Kyōdai no mae *ni* hando-baggu *ga arimasu*)—There is a handbag in front of the dressing table—when the nominative case is an inanimate object, the verb of existence あります (arimasu) can be used. On the other hand, we may say and write this sentence ハンドバッグは鏡台の前に あります。(Handobaggu *wa* kyōdai no mae *ni arimasu*).

Note: The verb あります (arimasu), there is . . ., is, as a rule, used with inanimate objects; but this verb is also sometimes used with animate objects as in the following:

(A) In the case of family relations (that is, making reference to those who are now alive):

私は三人の娘があります。(Watakushi wa san nin no musume ga *arimasu*)—I have three daughters.

(B) In the case of a universal fact:

私はうわ気をしないが，うわ気をする人もあります。(Watakushi wa uwaki o shinai ga, uwaki o suru hito mo *arimasu*)—I myself would not be fickle, but there are some who have secret love affairs.

(C) In the case of an old story (that is, a historical fact):

鎌倉時代に，源頼朝という人がありました。(Kamakura jidai ni, Minamoto no Yoritomo to iu hito ga *arimashita*)—There was a person named Minamoto no Yoritomo in the Kamakura era.

The verbs of existence います (imasu) and あります (arimasu), there is . . . , can be conjugated as follows:

	Present/Future	Past	Present/Future Negative	Past Negative
polite form	i-masu	i-mashita	i-masen	i-masen deshita
plain form	i-ru	i-ta	i-nai	i-nakatta
polite form	ar-imasu	ar-imashita	ar-imasen	ar-imasen deshita
plain form	ar-u	at-ta	nai	nakatta

Drill

1. 机の中に紙くずが あります。　There is some wastepaper in the desk.

2. 暗い燈火の下に二人の老人が います。　There are two old people under the dim light.

3. この部屋に青いかさのスタンド があります。　There is a desk lamp with a blue shade in this room.

4. 待合室に子供を連れた母親が います。　There is a mother with her child in the waiting room.

5. 病院に白衣の天使という看護婦　There are nurses, called angels

がいます。

in white, in the hospitals.

6. 火ばちのそばに塩せんべいのかんが あります。

There is a tin of salted rice-crackers by the brazier.

7. 広い庭のすみの 植え込みの中に 二人の人夫が います。

There are two laborers in a thicket in the corner of a large garden.

8. 松の木の下に三十ばかりの白い 切り石が積み上げてあります。

About thirty white stone slabs are piled up under a pine tree.

9. たなの上に便箋と封筒，ペンと インク，友だちからの二通の手紙 が あります。

There are writing pads and envelopes, pen and ink, and two letters from a friend on the shelf.

10. 朝日新聞社の正門に雑誌記者や 出版社の社員や映画会社，レコー ド会社の人たちが います。

There are magazine writers and the employees of publishing companies, film companies, and record companies at the front entrance of the Asahi Newspaper Office.

Exercise

Fill in the following blanks with the verbs of existence います and あります:

1. かん木の林に猟犬が（　　）。

There is a hunting dog in the shrub forest.

2. 小机の上に象牙のパイプが（　　）。

There is an ivory pipe on the small desk.

3. この会館の受付に大へん無愛想 な事務員が（　　）。

There is a most ungracious clerk at the information desk of this Association.

4. たんすの中に二・三枚の着がえ のはだ着が（　　）。

There are two or three spare sets of underwear in the chest of drawers.

5. この事務所に短いひげをはやし た嘱託の事務員が（　　）。

There is a part-time office worker with a short moustache in this office.

6. 書斎のすみに法律書が積み重ね　　Lawbooks are piled at the cor-
   て（　　）。　　　　　　　　　　ner of the study.

7. この事務所に髪をきれいに分け　　There is a typist, her hair
   たタイピストが（　　）。　　　parted neatly, in this office.

8. 日本間の刀かけにそりの強いた　　There is one strong curved
   ちが一振りのせて（　　）。　　sword laid on a sword-rack in
   　　　　　　　　　　　　　　　　the Japanese room.

9. この事務所に丸い精力的な顔を　　There is an accountant with a
   した会計係が（　　）。　　　　round energetic face in this office.

10. 食卓の上に油揚げのはいった一　　There is a bowl full of plain
    杯のうどんが（　　）。　　　　noodles with fried bean curd on
    　　　　　　　　　　　　　　　　the table.

11. 奥の部屋に中老の夫婦とお手伝　　There are the middle-aged hus-
    いさんが（　　）。　　　　　　band and wife and the maid in
    　　　　　　　　　　　　　　　　the inner room.

Answers:
1. います。 2. あります。 3. います。 4. あります。 5. います。
6. あります。 7. います。 8. あります。 9. います。 10. ありま
す。 11. います。

第六課　Lesson 6

Connective Form いて (ite) and あって (atte)

Rule

B に A がいて, B′ に A′ がいます。(B ni A ga *ite*, B′ ni A′ ga imasu).	*There is* A (someone) B (place word) *and* A′ (someone) B′ (place word).
B に A があって, B′ に A′ があります。(B ni A ga *atte*, B′ ni A′ ga arimasu).	*There is* A (something) B (place word) *and* A′ (something) B′ (place word).

The connective particle ("and" in English) is expressed by ～て (-te). This form can be obtained by changing the final vowel *a* of the plain past form to *e*. The tense of the entire sentence is determined by the tense of the final verb of the sentence. The verb いた (ita) or あった (atta), plain past form, There was . . . , changed to ～て (-te): いた (ita)──→いて (ite), There is (or: There was) . . . and . . . ; あった (atta)──→あって (atte), There is (or: There was) . . . and . . . .

e.g. 客間に父がいて，居間に母がいます。(Kyakuma ni chichi ga *ite*, ima ni haha ga imasu)—There is the father in the guest room and the mother in the living room.

e.g. むすこの部屋に携帯用のテレビがあって，娘の部屋にピアノがあります。(Musuko no heya ni keitaiyō no terebi ga *atte*, musume no heya ni piano ga arimasu)—There is a portable television in my son's room and a piano in my daughter's room.

Drill

1. 台所の流しの前に割ぽう着を着た母がいて，茶の間に不眠に疲れ果てた娘がいます。

   There is a mother in an apron standing at the kitchen sink and her daughter exhausted from lack of sleep in the living room.

2. ここに花瓶があって，そこにかさ立てがあります。

   There is a vase here and an umbrella stand there.

3. この事務所の一番奥の大テーブルに社長がいて，彼の机の向こう

   There is the director at the large desk in the extreme rear and

側に編集長がいます。　　　　　　　the chief editor opposite his desk in this office.

4. ここに鉄瓶が**あって**，あそこに暖房器具があります。

There is an iron pot here and a heater over there.

5. 日比谷交差点にほりばたが**あって**，桜田門のかどに樹木の茂みがあります。

There is a moat at the Hibiya crossing and thick trees at the corner of Sakuradamon.

Exercise

Fill in the following blanks with the connective form "いて" or "あって":

1. 調剤室に四人の男と五人の女の薬剤師が（　　　），待合室に先生を待っている二・三人の患者がいます。

There are four men and five women pharmacists in the dispensary and two or three patients, waiting for the doctor, in the waiting room.

2. ここに穴のあいたかばんが（　　　），そこに二冊外国の雑誌があります。

There is a brief case with a hole in it here and two foreign magazines there.

3. 台所に続く六畳の茶の間に着飾った若い母が（　　　），台所に夕飯のしたくをしている娘がいます。

There is an elaborately dressed young mother in the six mat living room leading off the kitchen and her daughter preparing supper in the kitchen.

4. ドアの外にそば屋のどんぶりが（　　　），狭い廊下にしるの焦げついた七輪があります。

There are bowls from a noodle shop outside the door and a small portable stove with soup burned on it in the narrow corridor.

5. 白いかやの中に子供が（　　　），淡いスタンド・ランプのかげにうちわを動かしている母がいます。

There is a child inside the white mosquito net and the mother oscillating a round fan by the dim desk lamp.

6. 横町に赤いちょうちんをつけたおでん屋が（　　　），そのまち筋に

There is an *Oden* stall, lit by a red lantern, on a side street

ポストがあります。   and a post box along that street.

Note: *Oden*, as well as *sushi* and *sukiyaki*, is a favorite dish of ours; it's fish paste, eggs, paste of the arum root, and such vegetables as radishes on skewers cooked together in tangle sauce, indispensable to the special flavor of this food. Mobile *Oden* stalls are found on side streets after dark, especially in the winter season. It has a special attraction for men and women, inducing them to drop in together to taste the food in quiet reflection.

Answers:

1. いて 2. あって 3. いて 4. あって 5. いて 6. あって

第七課 Lesson 7

The Use of "to have..."

Rule

A は B を持っています。(A wa B *o motte imasu*).

A (a person) *has* B (a thing).

A は B も持っています。(A wa B *mo motte imasu*).

A (a person) *has* B (a thing) *as well.*

A は B と C を持っています。(A wa B *to* C *o motte imasu*).

A (a person) *has* B (a thing) *and* C (a thing).

A は B や C を持っています。(A wa B *ya* C *o motte imasu*).

A (a person) *has* B (a thing), C (a thing), *and such.*

A は B や C などを持っています。(A wa B *ya* C *nado o motte imasu*).

A (a person) *has* B (a thing), C (a thing), *and so on.*

e.g. この外人は日本製の写真機を持っています。(Kono gaijin wa Nihon sei no shashinki *o motte imasu*)—This foreigner has a camera of Japanese make—を (o) in 写真機を (shashinki o), a camera, is an objective particle—を (o) follows the direct object immediately (nouns or pronouns＋を (o)＋transitive verbs).

e.g. 彼は当用漢字辞典も持っています。(Kare wa Tōyō Kanji jiten *mo motte imasu*)—He has a dictionary of current Chinese characters as well—も (mo) in 当用漢字辞典も (Tōyō Kanji jiten mo), a dictionary of current Chinese characters as well, corresponds to the English "also", "too", or "as well".

e.g. 留学生はいつも身分証明書と外人登録証を持っています。(Ryūgakusei wa itsumo mibun shōmeisho *to* gaijin tōrokushō o *motte imasu*)—A foreign student always has an identification card and a certificate of alien registration—と (to) in 身分証明書と (mibun shōmeisho to), an identification card and . . . , corresponds to the English "and"; it is the connective used between each of a series of nouns when all of the series of articles are being enumerated —と (to) is used between two or more words in a list.

e.g. この女子留学生は日本の子供の絵本や児童文学全集を持っていま

す。(Kono joshi ryūgakusei wa Nihon no kodomo no ehon *ya* jidō bungaku zenshū o *motte imasu*)—This female foreign student has Japanese picture books for children and the complete works of juvenile literature, and such—や (ya) in 日本の子供の絵本や (Nihon no kodomo no ehon ya), Japanese picture books for children . . . , and such, corresponds to the English "and such"; it is the connective used when only part of the series is being stated—や (ya) is used when the items listed do not necessarily constitute a complete list. や (*ya*)+を (o)+a transitive verb.

e.g. 彼はスポーツカーやヨットなどを持っています。(Kare wa supōtsu kā *ya* yotto *nado* o *motte imasu*)—He has a sports car, a yacht, and so on—など (nado) in ヨットなど (yotto nado), a yacht, and so on, corresponds to the English "etc." or "and so on". や (ya) +など (nado)+を (o)+a transitive verb.

The verb 持っています (motte imasu), to have, can be conjugated as follows:

	Present/ Future	Past	Present/Future Negative	Past Negative
polite form	motte imasu	motte imashita	motte imasen	motte imasen deshita
plain form	motte iru	motte ita	motte inai	motte inakatta

Drill

1. 私は和英辞書を 持っています。   I have a Japanese-English dictionary.

2. 私は兄が 両親にあてた 短い遺書を 持っています。   I have my elder brother's brief will directed to our parents.

3. 私は英和辞書も 持っています。   I have an English-Japanese dictionary as well.

4. 私は和英辞書と英和辞書を 持っています。   I have a Japanese-English and an English-Japanese dictionary.

5. 私はウィリヤー・キャザアの「ポールの場合」の和訳本やデュマの「椿姫」の英訳本を 持っています。   I have a Japanese translation of "Paul's Case" by Willa Cather, an English translation of "La Dame aux camélias" by Dumas,

6. 私は油絵や水彩画などを持っています。 — I have an oil painting, a water color painting, and so on.

and such.

Exercise

Fill in the following blanks with the particles "を", "も", "と", "や" or "など":

1. この子供は母からもらった二十円（　）そっくり紙に包んで大事に持っています。 — This child carefully keeps twenty yen he got from Mother, as it was, wrapped in paper.

2. 私（　）英文日記を持っています。 — I also have an English diary.

3. 彼女は三味線（　）ばちを持っています。 — She has a shamisen and a plectrum.

4. この操縦士は操縦法の図解や右旋回左旋回の理論を説明した航空学の本（　）を持っています。 — This pilot has a diagram of airplane controls, a book of aeronautics explaining the theory of right and left turns, and so on.

5. 私は思想家，評論家，作家，映画監督，劇作家，学者，新聞記者，あらゆる先鋭な知識人が書いた「世界史の動向と日本」と題する論文（　）雑誌を持っています。 — I have articles, magazines, and such entitled "The Movement of World History and Japan" written by thinkers, critics, writers, film directors, dramatists, scholars, journalists, and all manner of keen intellectuals.

Answers:
1. を　2. も　3. と　4. など　5. や

第 八 課　Lesson 8

The Difference of Function between
は (wa) and が (ga)

Rule

は (wa): The nominative case は (wa) indicates an essential and inevitable relationship including continuous occurrences.

e.g.　彼女の容貌はこじんまりとまとまって，どこかあかぬけしています。 (Kanojo no yōbō *wa* kojinmari to matomatte, doko ka akanuke shite imasu)—Her features are nicely proportioned, bearing some mark of refinement. は (wa) in the nominative case suggests such shading as the adverb いつも (itsumo), always; and thus, 彼女の容貌はこじんまりとまとまって, ～ (Kanojo no yōbō *wa* kojinmari to matomatte, . . .), Her features are nicely proportioned, . . . , can be understood as 彼女の容貌はいつもこじんまりとまとまって, ～ (Kanojo no yōbō wa *itsumo* kojinmari to matomatte, . . .), Her features are *always* nicely proportioned, ...

は (wa) applies similarly to sentences in the past tense.

e.g.　彼女の髪は油気がなくかさかさとかわいていました。 (Kanojo no kami *wa* aburake ga naku kasa kasa to kawaite imashita)—Her hair was ruffled for want of hair oil. は (wa) in this nominative case also includes the idea of "for a fixed period; a period of long standing, but not of short duration". And thus, 彼女の髪は油気がなくかさかさとかわいていました。 (Kanojo no kami *wa* aburake ga naku kasa kasa to kawaite imashita), Her hair was ruffled for want of hair oil, means "Her hair was ruffled *for a long time* for want of hair oil".

が (ga): The nominative case が (ga) indicates a temporary or irregular (accidental) relationship.

e.g.　正午の休み時間に，近所の事務所から出てきた勤め人や女子事務員が群れになっておほりのこいをながめています。 (Shōgo no yasumi ji-kan ni, kinjo no jimusho kara dete kita tsutomenin ya joshi jimuin *ga* mure ni natte, ohori no koi o nagamete imasu)—At the noon recess hour, the workers and office girls from the nearby offices crowd to watch the carp in the moat. が (ga) in the nominative case suggests such shading as the adverb 今，この瞬間に (ima or kono shunkan ni), now or at this moment; and thus, 近所の事務所

から出てきた勤め人や女子事務員が群れになって，～ (kinjo no jimu-sho kara dete kita tsutomenin ya joshi jimuin *ga* mure ni natte, . . .), the workers and office girls from the nearby offices crowd . . . , can be understood as 近所の事務所から出てきた勤め人や女子事務員が今（この瞬間に）群れになって，～ (kinjo no jimusho kara dete kita tsutomenin ya joshi jimuin ga *ima* [kono shunkan ni] mure ni natte, . . .), the workers and office girls from the nearby offices *now* (at this moment) crowd . . . .

が (ga) applies similarly to sentences in the past tense.

e.g. 青い陰が歩道に落ちていました。(Aoi kage *ga* hodō ni ochite imashita)—Blue shadows were cast on the pavement. が (ga) in this nominative case also includes the idea of "for a short time only, but not permanent". And thus, 青い陰が歩道に落ちていました。(Aoi kage *ga* hodō ni ochite imashita), Blue shadows were cast on the pavement, means "Blue shadows *temporarily* fell on the pavement".

Note: If you are at any time uncertain in your choice of は (wa) or が (ga), the following simple test will prove effective:

e.g. 私${は \atop が}$先生です。(Watakushi${wa \atop ga}$sensei desu)—I am an instructor.

In this sentence, the correct choice of the particle は (wa) or が (ga) can be readily determined by inserting the adverb "always" into the sentence. If inserted and found to be logical, は (wa) is quite suitable. The reason is, "I am *always* an instructor," in truth corresponds to the syntax of "The profession of teacher is one of my attributes." Thus, は (wa) indicates the subject of this sentence.

が (ga) may also be used for denoting the nominative case in this sentence. When が (ga) is inserted in this case, the meaning can be read as: I myself am an instructor *now*; I am *temporarily* taking the position of teacher in place of the regular instructor; or I myself *now* act as teacher because of the absence or illness of the regular instructor. This meaning would not be actually intended in most circumstances, making は (wa) the more logical choice.

In case you are still uncertain in your choice of は (wa) or が (ga) even after the effective mental test above mentioned, this next mental consideration will enable you to distinguish between the different functions of *wa* (with the implication of *always* or *generally*) and *ga* (with the implication of *now* or *at this moment*).

e.g. 私は先生です。(Watakushi *wa* sensei desu)—I am an instructor
—は (wa) in 私は *Watakushi wa* (I) is used when the speaker is
going to give an explanation regarding the subject, after presenting
it first; that is, the particle *wa* denotes that the word preceding
wa is the theme or topic of the sentence. And the predicate of
this sentence will be an explanation giving new information about
the particular noun or pronoun presented as the theme or topic.

e.g. 私が先生です。(Watakushi *ga* sensei desu)—I am an instructor
=It is I who am an instructor. が (ga) in 私が *Watakushi ga* (I)
is used only with subjects that identify clearly the performer or
agent of the predicate. This sentence is concerned with who is
an instructor. That is, what the speaker wants clarified is "who
is concerned with the matter described in the predicate," and the
subject should be the solution of the predicate. As can be understood from this explanation, the mechanism will become clear
with sentences in which interrogatives are used as the subject.
だれが先生ですか (*Dare ga* sensei desu ka) means "*Who* is it that
is an instructor?" In this sentence the predicate "先生 *sensei* (an
instructor)" is a fact understood by the inquirer, and the subject
だれ *dare* (who) is presented as a subject of inquiry to coincide
with the predicate. Accordingly, to coincide with the predicate
先生 *sensei* (an instructor) the answer must be a particular person
who is an instructor. So the answer will be 私が先生です。"Watakushi *ga* sensei desu." This means "It is I who am an instructor." or "I am." Thus, interrogatives used as the subject of the
sentence do not take the particle *wa* but *ga*. To sum up, the
particle *ga* has a function somewhat similar to that of identification, and is always used with the subject which is to be identified
with the facts or occurrences described in the predicate. In other
words, the particle *ga* is used in situational expressions in which
one intends to identify a matter or event he is informed of with
a particular subject.

In view of the function of the particle *wa* presenting the theme,
the use of *wa* in duplicate in one sentence is actually possible, making
no absurdity.

e.g. 私は専門は東洋史です。(Watakushi *wa* senmon *wa* Tōyō-shi
desu)—I specialize in oriental history—は (wa) in 私は *Watakushi*
wa (I) is the first topic regarding the speaker and は (wa) in 専
門は *senmon wa* (a speciality) the second topic; and lastly 東洋史

Tōyō-shi (oriental history) will become the explanation.

Likewise, the use of *ga* in duplicate in one sentence is also possible.

e.g. 象が鼻が長いのよ。(Zō *ga* hana *ga* nagai no yo)—An elephant has a long trunk—が (ga) in duplicate is also used in the interrogative structure. Take the question なにが どこが長いのですか *"Nani ga doko ga* nagai no desu ka (*What* and *which part* are long?)" Thus, interrogatives when the subjects of sentences do not take the particle *wa* but *ga*.

Drill

1.
給仕は昼食の茶を沸かしています。	An office boy is making the tea in preparation for lunch.
給仕の青年が土瓶をぶらさげたままたたずんで訪問客を見ていました。	A young office boy stood still, an earthenware tea pot in his hand, looking at a visitor.

2.
妻は急ぎ足で玄関に出てきました。	My wife, with hurried steps, came out to the entrance.
妻がきょうにかぎって美しく見えました。	My wife looked beautiful to me only on this day.

3.
父は四十を幾つかすぎた背の高い人です。	My father is a tall man of more than forty years of age.
父が八方奔走したおかげで，私はトヨタの会社に就職できました。	Thanks to my father's influence, I found employment at the Toyota Company.

4.
ボケの花は四月に咲きます。	The Japanese quince blooms in April.
ボケの花が水色のペンキ塗りの門の中に咲きそろっていました。	The Japanese quince just inside the pale blue painted gate was in full bloom.

5.
編集長はニュースにたいして敏感な性質を持っています。	The chief editor has a sensitive ear for discerning news.
編集長が1966年の3月に検挙され，神奈川県警で取り調	The chief editor was arrested in March 1966, and was ques-

べを受けました。 ... tioned at the Police Station in Kanagawa Prefecture.

Exercise

Fill in the following blanks with the nominative case "は" or "が":

1. 彼ら（　）オックスフォードで，二年の学生生活を共にしました。

They spent two years of student life at Oxford together.

2. 遠からず政変（　）あるでしょう。

A political change would soon come.

3. 彼（　）知能もすぐれ，性格もまっすぐな良い青年です。

He is a fine young man, most intelligent, and of a straightforward character.

4. 障子の骨（　）折れました。

The sliding paper door frame broke.

5. この方（　）ほとんど何事をも語らない人物です。

This person is of a nature silent on almost all matters.

6. 二人の足音（　）薄暗い廊下に堅く響きました。

The two men's heavy footsteps resounded in the gloomy corridor.

7. 池田内閣（　）総辞職しました。

The Ikeda Cabinet resigned *en bloc*.

8. 加藤家の電話（　）台所に近い廊下に取り付けてあります。

The Kato's telephone is installed in the corridor close to the kitchen.

9. ばしょうの影（　）池の面に動いています。

The shadow of a banana tree is swaying on the surface of the pond.

10. 女（　）愛情だけを信じます。

A woman believes in affection only.

11. ボーイ（　）はいってきて，私に自宅から電話がかかってきていると告げました。

A waiter came in and told me that there was a telephone call from my house.

Answers:

1. は 2. が 3. は 4. が 5. は 6. が 7. が 8. は 9. が 10. は 11. が

The Use of Place Words へ (e), に (ni), and で (de)

Rule

e.g. 私は来月関西地方へ旅行します。(Watakushi wa raigetsu Kansai chihō *e* ryokō shimasu)—I'm taking a trip to the Kansai district next month—へ (e) in 関西地方へ (Kansai chihō e), to the Kansai district, is used as a shifter in the sense of "a direction of movement". へ (e) expresses a direction and corresponds to the English "to" or "toward": the particle へ (e) is usually followed by such verbs as 来ます (kimasu), to come, 行きます (ikimasu), to go, 出かけます (dekakemasu), to go out, 上がります (agarimasu), to go up or 通います (kayoimasu), to attend. On the other hand, we may say, 私は来月関西地方に旅行します。(Watakushi wa raigetsu Kansai chihō *ni* ryokō shimasu)—I'm taking a trip to the Kansai district next month—に (ni) in 関西地方に (Kansai chihō ni), to the Kansai district, is used as a shifter in the sense of "a fixed position with the implications of the process of shift".

e.g. この教室にタイ国の留学生が三人います。(Kono kyōshitsu *ni* Tai koku no ryūgakusei ga san nin imasu)—There are three foreign students from Thailand in this classroom—に (ni) in この教室に (kono kyōshitsu ni), in this classroom, denotes a place of existence ("at" or "in" in English): に (ni)+the verb of existence います (imasu), there is . . . .

e.g. この教室に電気時計があります。(Kono kyōshitsu *ni* denki dokei ga arimasu)—There is an electric clock in this classroom—に (ni) in この教室に (kono kyōshitsu ni), in this classroom, denotes a place of existence: に (ni)+the verb of existence あります (arimasu), there is . . . .

e.g. この研修生は日立の会社で実習をします。(Kono kenshūsei wa Hitachi no kaisha *de* jisshū o shimasu)—This trainee is going to take practical training at the Hitachi Company—で (de) in 日立の会社で (Hitachi no kaisha de), at the Hitachi Company, denotes a place of action; that is, it refers to the place where an action is performed: で (de)+を (o), an objective particle+a verb (transitive).

e.g. 私は東京で勉強します。(Watakushi wa Tōkyō *de* benkyō shimasu)—I study in Tokyo. In this sentence, there is no object, possibly leading to the misuse of the particle に (ni) in place of で (de). The particle に (ni) is usually followed by verbs of existence such as あります (arimasu) or います (imasu) and thus, the use of に (ni) is, in this case, unsuitable. The sentence 私は東京で勉強します。(Watakushi wa Tōkyō *de* benkyō shimasu) may be taken as meaning "I study *some subjects* in Tokyo", the object *some subjects* being understood and omitted. When で (de) is used, を (o), an objective particle, is sometimes not explicitly evidenced in the sentence; so, in an obscure sentence like this, some objective particle should be mentally introduced into the sentence, permitting the contents to be logical with the particle で (de).

Note: The verb 寝ます (nemasu), to sleep, is an exception here; this verb can be used with either of the particles に (ni) and で (de).

e.g. 私はここに寝ています。(Watakushi wa koko *ni* nete imasu)— I am asleep here—this に (ni), emphasizing the place of being, means "I am in a state of sleep here".

e.g. 私はここで寝ています。(Watakushi wa koko *de* nete imasu)—I am asleep here—this で (de) puts emphasis on the state of action, meaning "I am engaged in the action of sleeping here".

Drill

1. 彼と彼女は連れだって電車に乗り，池袋へ出かけていきました。

He and she boarded a tram together and went off to Ikebukuro.

2. 私は明日から大阪と京都へ講演旅行に行ってきます。

I am leaving tomorrow for Osaka and Kyoto on a lecture tour.

3. ここに五人のインドの技師がいます。

There are five Indian engineers here.

4. ここに三通の航空郵便があります。

There are three air mail letters here.

5. 熱海の温泉に政府の療養所があります。

The government sanatorium is in the Atami hot spring resort.

6. 弟が来客用のいすに腰かけています。

My younger brother is seated on the chair used for visitors.

7. 私たちは山でスキーをします。

We ski in the mountains.

8. あぶない道路で遊んではいけま

Don't play in the dangerous

せん。

9. 日曜日の朝，恋人と私は川崎の ゴルフ場で落ち合いました。

On Sunday morning, my sweetheart and I met at a golf links in Kawasaki.

10. 近いうちに私は栃木県の日光へ 行くようになるだろうと思いま す。

I think I shall probably be going to Nikko in Tochigi Prefecture before long.

Exercise

Fill in the following blanks with the particles "へ", "に", and "で":

1. 是非来て下さい。箱根（　　） 会いましょう。

Please do come. I'll see you at Hakone.

2. 彼は木蔭（　　）日なたぼっこ をしていました。

He was basking in the sun in the shelter of the trees.

3. 新聞の紙面（　　）すさまじい 戦争の様子が報道されています。

There are reports of severe fighting in the newspaper.

4. 私は南方（　　）マラリヤをや りました。

I had malaria in the South.

5. 学校（　）通っている子供にと っては，日曜が一番楽しい日です。

Sunday is the most enjoyable day for children attending school.

6. 行く先の決まらないままで，彼 女は駅の方（　　）歩いていきま した。

She walked towards the station, undecided where to go.

7. 彼は洋服に着かえて外（　　） 出ようとしました。

He changed into street clothes and was getting ready to go outside.

8. 二日ばかり勤めを休み，自分の アパート（　　）ひとりきりで，寝 て暮らしました。

I stayed away from work for about two days and stayed in bed, alone in my apartment.

9. くまは穴の中（　）寝ています。

A bear is asleep in the cave.

10. この協会の理事長はせき立てら れるような気持ちで，外務省（　） 出かけていきました。

The Chief Director of this Association went off to the Foreign Office, feeling as though he were running against time.

Answers:

1. で 2. で 3. に 4. で 5. へ 6. へ 7. へ 8. で 9. に or で 10. へ

第 十 課　Lesson 10

The Use of Place Words には (niwa), and では (dewa)

Rule

 e.g.　この婦人の左ほおのくちびるのわきには，大きなほくろがあります。
(Kono fujin no hidari ho-o no kuchi biru no waki *niwa*, ōkina hokuro *ga* arimasu)—To the side of the lips on this woman's left cheek there is a large mole—には (niwa) in～くちびるのわきには (...kuchi biru no waki niwa), To the side of the lips..., is a combination of the particles に (ni) and は (wa); this には (niwa) forms an adverbial phrase and is usually followed by verbs of existence such as あります (arimasu) or います (imasu), there is .... Its usage in this case is to form contrast with a previously mentioned or understood object or condition and emphasize the subjective case in its main clause. So, ～くちびるのわきには (...kuchi biru no waki *niwa*), To the side of the lips..., is an adverbial phrase through which the subject in its main clause is particularly qualified and restricted; such a subject is ordinarily followed by the particle が (ga), as seen from 大きなほくろがあります。 (ōkina hokuro *ga* arimasu), there is a large mole. The usage of には (niwa) is rendered as "as far as...is concerned" in English; and thus, ～くちびるのわきには (...kuchi biru no waki *niwa*), To the side of the lips..., can be understood as "as far as the side of the lips is concerned". That is, there can be found a mole at least to the side of the lips; but over any other part of her body no such birth-mark may be discovered. On the other hand, we may also say, ～くちびるのわきに (...kuchi biru no waki *ni*), To the side of the lips, but ～くちびるのわきには (...kuchi biru no waki *niwa*) is more emphatic and descriptive.

 Note:　One exception to the rule is この婦人の左ほおのくちびるのわきには，大きなほくろはありますが，にきびはありません。(Kono fujin no hidari ho-o no kuchi biru no waki *niwa*, ōkina hokuro *wa* arimasu ga, nikibi *wa* arimasen)—To the side of the lips on this woman's left cheek there is a large mole, but no pimples—the は (wa) in the phrases 大きなほくろは (ōkina hokuro wa), a large mole and にきびは (nikibi wa), pimples, is used because this sentence is a contrast of two ideas.

 e.g.　男の支配している社会では，欲情の対象としての酒場の女，芸者，

ダンサーなどを高く評価しています。(Otoko no shihai shite iru sha-kai *dewa*, yokujō no taishō toshite no sakaba no on-na, geisha, dansā nado *o* takaku hyōka shite imasu)—In a society where men dominate, they value women who work in bars or as geisha and dancers only as the object of men's passions—では (dewa) in～社会では (...shakai dewa), In a society..., is a combination of the particles で (de) and は (wa); this では (dewa) forms an adverbial phrase and is usually followed by an objective particle, as seen from ダンサーなどを (dansā nado *o*), dancers.... This is because では (dewa) denotes a place of action; that is, it refers to the place where an action is performed and precedes a transitive verb. Its usage in this case is to form contrast with a previously mentioned or understood object or condition and puts emphasis on the state of action in its main clause. The usage of では (dewa) is rendered as "as far as... is concerned" in English; and thus, 男の支配している社会では (Otoko no shihai shite iru shakai *dewa*), In a society where men dominate, can be understood as "as far as a society where men dominate is concerned". That is, women commonly believed to be immoral, such as those working in bars, may be regarded as valuable in *the very* society where men dominate; but in a competitive or democratic society, in the meaning of a society of citizens, this trend is not found. On the other hand, we may also say, 男の支配している社会で (Otoko no shihai shite iru shakai *de*), In a society where men dominate, but 男の支配している社会では (Otoko no shihai shite iru shakai *dewa*) is more emphatic and descriptive.

Compare:

e.g. 庭には，水せんが咲いていました。(Niwa *niwa*, suisen ga saite imashita)—In the garden daffodils were in bloom)—には (niwa) in the adverb phrase 庭には (niwa niwa), in the garden, refers to the place where there exists a daffodil in bloom; that is, this には (niwa) shows the place where the subjective case for an action exists.

e.g. 松林のなかでは，もずが鳴いていました。(Matsu bayashi no naka *dewa*, mozu ga naite imashita)—In the pine wood butcher-birds were calling—では (dewa) in the adverb phrase 松林のなかでは (matsu bayashi no naka dewa), in the pine wood, refers to the place of an action; that is, this では (dewa) shows the place in which a butcher-bird chirps.

e.g. 遠い所で富士の峰が月光を受けて銀色に光っていました。(Tōi to-

koro *de* Fuji no mine ga gekkō o ukete gin iro ni hikatte imashita)—At a great distance, the peak of Mt. Fuji shone silver in
the rays of moonlight—で (de) in the adverb phrase (tōi tokoro
de), at a great distance, refers to the place of an action; that is,
this で (de) shows the place where the peak of Mt. Fuji in the
rays of moonlight reflects the ray.

e.g. 草の葉には，真白く霜が光っていました。(Kusa no ha *niwa*, mas-
shiroku shimo ga hikatte imashita)—The pure white frost glistened
on the blades of grass—には (niwa) in the adverb phrase 草の葉に
は (kusa no ha niwa), on the blades of grass, refers to the place
where there exists the pure white frost in brilliancy; that is,
this には (niwa) shows the place where the subjective case for
an action exists.

e.g. 京都は日本で一番の観光都市になっています。(Kyōto wa Nihon
de ichiban no kankō toshi ni natte imasu)—Kyoto has become the
most popular tourist city in Japan)—で (de) in the phrase 日本で
(Nihon de), in Japan, is used when any special animate or inanimate object is picked out, and then the nominative case under
the use of this で (de) is to be qualified and mentioned specially.
The phrase 日本で (Nihon de), in Japan, can be rendered as 日本
の都市のうちで (Nihon no toshi no uchi de), of all cities in Japan.

Drill

1. サイゴンには，華僑がおおぜい
います。

   There are many Chinese res-
   idents in Saigon.

2. 男の心には，英雄主義がありま
す。

   There is heroism in a man's
   heart.

3. 熱海では，彼は芸者を呼んで豪
遊しました。

   In Atami, he called in geisha
   and indulged in extravagant pleasures.

4. 彼女の両方のまぶたには，あふ
れるほど涙がたまって，きらきら
と光っていました。

   Both her eyes were overflowing
   with tears, making them glisten.

5. この部屋の中には，子供のおし
めがかわかされてあります。

   In this room, the baby's dirty
   diapers are drying.

6. 世間では，看護婦は白衣の天使
という美しい形容詞で呼ばれてい

   In the present world, nurses are
   known by the beautiful adjective

ます。

7. 東京都内や近郊には，光化学ス
モッグが発生します。

Photochemical smog appears in Tokyo and its suburbs.

8. この高層ホテルのエレベータ
ーには，小さな防犯用テレビカメ
ラがついています。

In elevators in this high-rise hotel, there are small crime-prevention television cameras.

9. 母をなくしたこの女子留学生
は，帰りの飛行機の中では，外と
うのえりに顔をうずめて，ずっと
泣いていました。

On the return plane journey, this female foreign student, deprived of her mother, wept all the time, smothering her face in her overcoat collar.

10. サクランボは寒い国の産が，特
においしいです。主産地の山形で
は，サクランボの八割はカン詰に
して都会にだします。

Cherries produced in cold areas taste especially good. In Yamagata Prefecture, which is the main cherry producing area, 80 percent of the cherries are canned and sent to the cities.

Exercise

Fill in the following blanks with the particles " には " or " では ":

1. 緑にかこまれたこのいなか町
（   ），公害はありません。

In this country town surrounded by green, there is no pollution.

2. 東京・大阪間の新幹線の中（
    ），座席の上に横になって三時間
を過ごしました。

In a train on the New Tokaido Line between Tokyo and Osaka, I spent three hours sprawled out along the seat.

3. 二里の沿道（   ），住民が家々
に旗をかかげて天皇・皇后両陛下
をお迎えしました。

Along the eight miles of a road, the inhabitants hung flags from their houses and welcomed the Emperor and the Empress.

4. 電燈が暗くて部屋のすみ（   ），
ゆううつな陰がよどんでいまし
た。

As the room was dimly lit, gloomy shadows hovered in the corners.

5. 私の机の中（   ），外務省から

In my desk there lay the docu-

回ってきた書類がはいっています。

6. 通り過ぎる町の店（　　），お正月の飾り付けに忙しそうでした。

The shops on the street I passed seemed to be busily engaged in their decorations for the coming New Year.

7. 北陸，新潟，東北地方 （　　），大雨が降りました。

Heavy rains fell in the Hokuriku, Niigata and Tohoku areas.

8. 東京の果物屋（　　），サクランボがではじめました。

Cherries have begun to appear in fruit stores in Tokyo.

9. 神奈川県（　　），サイクリング専用道路があります。

In Kanagawa Prefecture there is a road for the exclusive use of bicycles.

10. 月曜日の朝に，静岡県の国道（　　）土砂くずれが起こりました。

There was a landslide on a national highway in Shizuoka Prefecture on Monday morning.

11. 瀬戸内海（　　），つぎつぎに船の衝突がありました。

There were ship collisions one after the other in the Seto Inland Sea.

12. 日光街道（　　），信号待ちをしていた乗用車がトラックに追突されました。

A passenger car waiting for a traffic signal to change on the Nikko Highway was hit from behind by a truck.

Answers:
1. には　2. では　3. では　4. には　5. には　6. では　7. では
8. には　9. には　10. では　11. では　12. では

Concession

Rule

"Whenever..." in English is expressed by いつ～も (itsu...mo), "whoever..." by だれ(で)も (dare [de] mo), "wherever..." by どこへ (どこに; どこで) ～も (doko e [doko ni; doko de] ...mo), どこへも (doko e mo), どこにも (doko ni mo), or どこでも (doko de mo), "whatever..." by どんな～も (don-na...mo), なんでも (nan de mo), or 何も (nani mo), "whichever..." by どの～も (dono...mo), or どれでも (dore de mo), and "however..." by いくら～も (ikura...mo).

(A) e.g. お尋ねするのにいつがご都合よろしいですか。(Otazune suru no ni *itsu ga* gotsugō yoroshii desu ka)—When will it be convenient for me to call on you?—いつ (itsu), when, in the subjective tense always uses the particle が (ga).

e.g. 東南アジアへ出かけるのはいつですか。(Tōnan Ajia e dekakeru no wa *itsu desu* ka)—When will you start for Southeast Asia?—いつ (itsu), when, does not require any particle when followed by the copula です (desu), is, am, are.

e.g. いつかお暇の折りにいらしてください。(*Itsu ka* ohima no ori ni irashite kudasai)—Please come and see me sometime when you are free—いつか (itsu ka) means "sometime or anytime".

e.g. いつこの写真を見ても，交通事故で死んだ弟の事を思い出します。(*Itsu* kono shashin o mite *mo*, kōtsū jiko de shinda otōto no koto o omoi-dashimasu)—Whenever I look at this photograph, I remember about my younger brother who died in a traffic accident —見て (mite) comes from the plain past 見た (mita), looked at; いつ (itsu)＋て (te) or で (de)-form＋も (mo), whenever....

(B) e.g. だれがこの壁に落書きしましたか。(*Dare ga* kono kabe ni rakugaki shimashita ka)—Who scribbled on this wall?—だれが (dare ga), who, acts as the nominative case.

e.g. あれはだれの家ですか。(Are wa *dare no* ie desu ka)—Whose house is that?—だれの (dare no), whose, acts as the possessive case.

e.g. 社長はだれを解雇しましたか。(Shachō wa *dare o* kaiko shimashita ka)—Whom did the director dismiss?—だれを (dare o), whom, acts as the direct objective case.

e.g. あなたは**だれに**真珠をあげましたか。(Anata wa *dare ni* shinju o agemashita ka)—To whom did you give a pearl?—だれに (dare ni), whom, acts as the indirect objective case.

e.g. きょう欠席した生徒は**だれ** ですか。(Kyō kesseki shita seito wa *dare desu* ka)—Who is the pupil that stayed away from school today?—だれ (dare), who, does not require any particle when followed by the copula.

e.g. **だれか**見えたら，留守だと言ってください。(*Dare ka* mie tara, rusu da to itte kudasai)—If somebody should come, please tell him that I'm not at home—だれか (dare ka) means "somebody or anybody".

e.g. 家に来る人は**だれでも**歓迎します。(Ie ni kuru hito wa *dare de mo* kangei shimasu)—I welcome whoever comes to my house— だれでも (dare de mo) means "whoever, all, or not anyone".

(C) e.g. 日本では**どこが**一番景色が良いですか。(Nihon dewa *doko ga* ichiban keshiki ga yoi desu ka)—Where is the best scenic spot in Japan?—どこが (doko ga), where, acts as the nominative case.

e.g. 彼は**どこの**出身ですか。(Kare wa *doko no* shusshin desu ka)— Where does he come from?—どこの (doko no), where, acts as the possessive case.

e.g. きょうあなたは**どこへ**行きますか。(Kyō anata wa *doko e* ikimasu ka)—Where will you go today?—へ (e) in どこへ (doko e), where, expresses a direction.

e.g. **どこに**この花を置きましょうか。(*Doko ni* kono hana o okimashō ka)—Where do I put this flower?—に (ni) in どこに (doko ni), where, expresses a point (a place).

e.g. **どこで**日本人形が買えますか。(*Doko de* Nihon ningyō ga kaemasu ka)—Where can I buy a Japanese doll?—で (de) in どこで (doko de), where, denotes a place of action.

e.g. あなたの別荘は**どこ** ですか。(Anata no bessō wa *doko desu* ka) —Where is your villa?—どこ (doko), where, does not require any particle when followed by the copula.

e.g. **どこか**行く所はありませんか。(*Doko ka* iku tokoro wa arimasen ka)—Isn't there any place where we can go?—どこか (doko ka) means "somewhere or anywhere".

e.g. あなたが**どこに**いても，私は決してあなたの事は忘れません。(Anata ga *doko ni* ite *mo*, watakushi wa kessite anata no koto wa wasuremasen)—Wherever you may be, I'll never forget you—いて (ite) comes from the plain past いた (ita), existed; どこに (doko ni)+て (te) or で (de)-form+も (mo), wherever....

e.g. 私はどこへ行っても，あなたのご恩は忘れません。(Watakushi wa *doko e* itte *mo*, anata no go-on wa wasuremasen)—Wherever I may go, I'll never forget your kindness—行って (itte) comes from the plain past 行った (itta), went; どこへ (doko e)+て (te) or で (de)-form+も (mo), wherever....

e.g. どこで働いても，彼はうまくいきます。(*Doko de* hataraite *mo*, kare wa umaku ikimasu)—Wherever he may work, he will go on smoothly—働いて (hataraite) comes from the plain past 働いた (hataraita), worked; どこで (doko de)+て (te) or で (de)-form+も (mo), wherever....

e.g. 家内が病気のために，ここ当分の間どこへも旅行に行けません。(Kanai ga byōki no tame ni, koko tōbun no aida *doko e mo* ryokō ni ikemasen)—I'll be unable to take a trip anywhere for the present because of my wife's illness—どこへも (doko e mo) means "anywhere or nowhere".

e.g. このような珍品はどこにも見あたりません。(Kono yō na chinpin wa *doko ni mo* miatarimasen)—Such a rare article as this can be found nowhere—どこにも (doko ni mo) means "anywhere or nowhere".

e.g. 日本滞在中，私はどこでも見学したいです。(Nihon taizai chū, watakushi wa *doko de mo* kengaku shitai desu)—I would like to tour everywhere during my stay in Japan—どこでも (doko de mo) means "anywhere or nowhere".

(D) e.g. 何が日本で一番めずらしいと思いますか。(*Nani ga* Nihon de ichiban mezurashii to omoimasu ka)—What do you think is most unique in Japan?—何が (nani ga), what, acts as the nominative case.

e.g. これは何の本ですか。(Kore wa *nan no* hon desu ka)—What is this book?—何の (nan no), what (kind of), acts as the possessive case.

e.g. これは何ですか。(Kore wa *nan desu* ka)—What is this?—何 (nan), what, does not require any particle when followed by the copula.

e.g. 何を買うつもりですか。(*Nani o* kau tsumori desu ka)—What do you intend to buy?—何を (nani o), what, acts as the objective case.

e.g. 何か食べ物をください。(*Nani ka* tabemono o kudasai)—Please give me something to eat—何か (nani ka) means "something or anything".

e.g. 今の私の経済状態では何でも買えます。(Ima no watakushi no

keizai jōtai dewa *nan de mo* kaemasu)—I can buy anything in my present economic situation—何でも (nan de mo) means "anything".

e.g. 貧乏ぐらしの私には，何も買えません。(Binbō gurashi no watakushi niwa, *nani mo* kaemasen)—I, in destitution, can't afford to buy anything—何も (nani mo) means "nothing".

e.g. どんな本を読んでも，よく読みなさい。(*Don na* hon o yonde *mo*, yoku yominasai)—Whatever book you may read, read well—読んで (yonde) comes from the plain past 読んだ (yonda), read; どんな (don na)＋て (te) or で (de)-form＋も (mo), whatever....

(E) e.g. 洋服と和服とどれが似合いますか。(Yōfuku to wafuku to *dore ga* niaimasu ka)—Which would suit me better, foreign or Japanese clothes?—どれが (dore ga), which, acts as the nominative case.

e.g. どの色が好きですか。(*Dono* iro ga suki desu ka)—Which color do you like?—どの (dono), which, acts as the possessive case.

e.g. 朝日と毎日と，どれを取りますか。(Asahi to Mainichi to, *dore o* torimasu ka)—Which would you take, the Asahi or the Mainichi newspapers?—どれを (dore o), which, acts as the objective case.

e.g. 「いらっしゃいませ。どれにいたしましょうか。」(Irasshai mase. *Dore ni* itashimashō ka)—"Welcome! May I help you?"—どれに (dore ni), which, presents a choice.

e.g. どれか良い万年筆を見せてください。(*Dore ka* yoi man-nen-hitsu o misete kudasai)—Please show me any of your good fountain pens—どれか (dore ka) means "any one".

e.g. どの部屋を選んでも，気にいるでしょう。(*Dono* heya o erande *mo*, ki ni iru deshō)—Whichever room you may choose, you will be pleased—選んで (erande) comes from the plain past 選んだ (eranda), chose; どの (dono)＋a noun＋て (te) or で (de)-form＋も (mo), whichever....

e.g. どれでもかまいません。(*Dore de mo* kamaimasen)—Whichever will do—どれでも(dore de mo) means "any or not anyone".

(F) e.g. いくら勉強しても，東大をパスすることは彼には無理なようです。(*Ikura* benkyō shite *mo*, Tōdai o pasu suru koto wa kare niwa muri na yō desu)—However hard he may study, it seems hopeless that he will pass Tokyo University—勉強して (benkyō shite) comes from the plain past 勉強した (benkyō shita), studied; いくら (ikura)＋て (te) or で (de)-form＋も (mo), however....

Drill

1. 将来の事は何も考えてはいませ　　I haven't thought about the

future at all.

2. この部屋にはだれもいません。
There is no one else in this room.

3. 社長はこの事件を何も知りません。
The director is not acquainted with this matter at all.

4. 日本国民のだれも日泰外交の重大な転機を知っていません。
None of the Japanese people are yet acquainted with the momentous crisis in Japan's Thailand diplomatic policy.

5. 十年の米国生活のにおいは彼のどこにも感じられません。
The vestiges of his ten years of life in America can be seen nowhere.

6. だれでもそのような心配なら持っています。
Almost every one holds some such feelings of anxiety.

7. だれを恐れる必要がありますか。
Why is it necessary for anyone to be afraid?

8. 彼女の心は何かの事を考えています。
In her heart she must be thinking of something.

9. 何を言ってますか。
What are you trying to say?

10. どんな悲劇が待っていても，彼女は機械のように無神経です。
No matter what manner of tragedy might await her, she is, like a machine, insensitive.

11. いくら考えてみても，あなたがそこへ行くことはありません。
However I think about it, it's out of the question that you should go there.

12. 母はどんな事が起こっても，少しも動じません。
Mother rarely becomes excited no matter what happens.

13. いくら見ても，彼は楽天的な，物事にこだわらない性質の人です。
He is to all appearances an optimistic person with a disposition that does not pay any attention to other things.

14. だれがこの命令を出しますか。
Who issues this order?

15. 目的地がどこだかだれも知りません。
Nobody knows the destination.

Exercise

(A) Fill in each bracket with the interrogative pronoun, いつ, だれ, どこ, 何, or どれ:

1. 東大の入学試験は（　　）ですか。 — When will the entrance examination to Tokyo University be held?

2. 夕飯のおかずは（　　）ですか。 — What are the side dishes for the evening meal?

3. あなたの持ち物は（　　）ですか。 — Which are your personal effects?

4. 二階で勉強している人は（　　）ですか。 — Who is the person studying upstairs?

5. あなたの郷里は（　　）ですか。 — Where is your home town?

(B) Fill in each bracket with いつか, だれか, どこか, 何か, or どれか:

1. （　　）好みの料理をご遠慮なく注文してください。 — I hope you will order, without hesitation, any of those dishes which you like.

2. （　　）私の所へお手伝いに来てくださる人はいませんか。 — Isn't there anybody who will come to my house as a maid?

3. （　　）晴れた日に家族連れで, 湘南地方へドライブしたいと思っています。 — I think I, with my family, shall go for a drive to the Shonan district sometime when it's fine weather.

4. 外国の方に贈り物をするのに（　　）適当な物を見せてください。 — Please show me something suitable as a gift for a foreigner.

5. （　　）良い観光地へ案内していただければ, うれしいです。 — I'd be pleased if you could kindly conduct me around some worthwhile tourist sites.

(C) Fill in each bracket with such expressions of concession as いつ～も, だれでも, どこへ～も, どんな～も, どの～も, or いくら～も:

1. （　　）行って（　　）、よくふる
   まいなさい。

2. このような工芸品を見る人は
   （　　）、当時の職人の巧みさ偉大
   さを感ぜずにはいられません。

3. （　　）やめなさいと言って（
   ）、彼は聞きません。

4. （　　）道を選んで（　　）、あな
   たは成功するはずです。

5. （　　）伺って（　　）、彼は留守
   です。

6. （　　）ことがあって（　　）、私
   は必ず生きて帰ります。

Wherever you may go, behave well.

Whoever may observe works of art as these, he cannot help being impressed with the skill and greatness of the craftsmen of those days.

No matter how I may advise him to give it up, he would not listen to me.

Whichever way you may choose, you are sure to be successful.

Whenever I call on him, he is always out.

Whatever may come, I'll surely return home alive.

Answers:
(A) 1. いつ 2. 何 3. どれ 4. だれ 5. どこ
(B) 1. どれか 2. だれか 3. いつか 4. 何か 5. どこか
(C) 1. どこへ～も 2. だれでも 3. いくら～も 4. どの～も
5. いつ～も 6. どんな～も

The . . . は (wa) . . . が (ga) Construction

Rule

Some sentences in Japanese appear to have two subjects: one would serve as the subject of the entire sentence; that is, は (wa) in this pattern takes the function of presenting the theme. The other would serve as the complement of な (na)-and い (i)-adjectives in a predicative use, and the object of the auxiliary of hope such as *would like to,* the potential auxiliary such as *can,* or such verbs as *understand, need,* and *have;* that is, が (ga) in this pattern takes the role of the secondary theme under は (wa) presenting the major topic. The Japanese have a good natural command of the usage of this は (wa) . . . が (ga) contruction, but non-native speakers are sure to be faced with much difficulty in composing sentences like this. Those simple sentences and phrases which induce and bear the formation of the . . . は (wa) . . . が (ga) construction quite characteristic of the Japanese language are given first and then they are transformed into this construction.

e.g. この外人の日本語は流暢です。(Kono gaijin *no* Nihongo *wa* ryūchō desu)—This foreigner's Japanese is fluent—の (no) in the phrase of この外人の (kono gaijin no), this foreigner's, modifies the noun 日本語 (Nihongo), Japanese, as an adjective. This の (no) is changed into は (wa), as この外人は (kono gaijin wa) and は (wa) in 日本語は (Nihongo wa) under this modification is changed into が (ga), as 日本語が (Nihongo ga). This whole sentence is transformed into the following: この外人は日本語が流暢です。(Kono gaijin *wa* Nihongo *ga* ryūchō desu)—This foreigner is fluent in speaking Japanese—は (wa) in この外人は (kono gaijin wa) extends as far as . . . 流暢です (. . . ryūchō desu), to be fluent, in a predicative use, from the な (na)-adjective 流暢な (ryūchō na), fluent. The restriction of a topic by は (wa) is loose because of its function of presenting the theme; and thus, は (wa) accordingly reaches far. On the contrary, the method of limitation in both time and distance of the particle が (ga) is one that strives for more clarity; therefore, the sphere of limitation taken by が (ga) is narrower than that of は (wa). The subject in this sentence is この外人

(kono gaijin) and not 日本語 (Nihongo); that is, この外人 (kono gaijin) should be thought to be the subject for the phrase 日本語 が流暢です (Nihongo ga ryūchō desu). And also, the complement for 流暢です (ryūchō desu) is 日本語 (Nihongo); from this idea 日 本語 (Nihongo) in 日本語が (Nihongo ga) is here treated as a complement. Also, this basic sentence この外人の日本語は流暢で す。(Kono gaijin *no* Nihongo *wa* ryūchō desu) can be transformed into˙the following phrase: 日本語の流暢なこの外人 (Nihongo *no* ryūchō *na* kono gaijin), this foreigner speaking fluent Japanese.

e.g. 日本の耕地は非常に狭いです。(Nihon *no* kōchi *wa* hijōni semai desu)—The arable land of Japan is very limited—this sentence is transformed into the following: 日本は耕地が非常に狭いです。(Nihon *wa* kōchi *ga* hijōni semai desu)—Japan is very limited in its arable land. 狭いです (semai desu) from the い (i)-adjective 狭い (semai), narrow, is in a predicative use. Also, this basic sentence 日本の耕地は非常に狭いです。(Nihon *no* kōchi *wa* hijōni semai desu) can be transformed into the following phrase: 耕地の非常に狭い日 本 (kōchi *no* hijōni sema*i* Nihon), Japan with its very limited arable land.

e.g. 私の食べたいカツレツ (Watakushi *no* tabetai *katsuretsu*)—some cutlets which I would like to eat—食べたい (tabe-tai), would like to eat, in an attributive use modifies the noun カツレツ (katsu-retsu), cutlet. This phrase is transformed into the following: 私 はカツレツが食べたいです。(Watakushi *wa* katsuretsu *ga* tabe-tai desu)—I would like to eat some cutlets. が (ga) in カツレツが (katsuretsu ga) takes the same role as を (o), an objective particle, and 食べたいです (tabe-tai desu) is in a predicative use. The desiderative (would like to) is expressed by the auxiliary of hope たい (tai) attached to the second base of any verb (the verb form used with the polite -*masu* endings), as 食べたい (tabe-tai), plain form and 食べたいです (tabe-tai desu), polite form, from 食べます (tabe-masu), to eat.

e.g. 私はテニスをすることができます。(Watakushi *wa* tenisu *o* suru koto ga dekimasu)—I can play tennis—this sentence is transformed into the following: 私はテニスができます。(Watakushi *wa* tenisu *ga* dekimasu)—I can play tennis. が (ga) in テニスが (tenisu ga), tennis, takes the same role as を (o), an objective particle.

e.g. 私のわかる彼の説明 (Watakushi *no* wakaru kare no *setsumei*)— his explanation which I understand—this phrase is transformed into the following: 私は彼の説明がわかります。(Watakushi *wa* kare no setsumei *ga* wakarimasu)—I understand his explanation. が (ga) in 彼の説明が (kare no setsumei ga), his explanation, takes the same role as を (o), an objective particle. And わかります (wakar-imasu) comes from わかる (wakar-u), to understand.

e.g. 私のいる和英辞書 (Watakushi *no* iru *Wa-Ei jisho*)—a Japanese-English dictionary which I need—this phrase is transformed into the following: 私は和英辞書がいります。(Watakushi *wa* Wa-Ei jisho *ga* irimasu)—I need a Japanese-English dictionary. が (ga) in 和英辞書が (Wa-Ei jisho ga), a Japanese-English dictionary, takes the same role as を (o), an objective particle. And いります (ir-imasu) comes from いる (ir-u), to need.

e.g. 彼女のほしい指輪 (Kanojo *no* hoshii *yubiwa*)—a ring which she wants—this phrase is transformed into the following: 彼女は指輪がほしいです。(Kanojo *wa* yubiwa *ga* hoshii desu)—She wants a ring. が (ga) in 指輪が (yubiwa ga), a ring, takes the same role as を (o), an objective particle. And ほしいです (hoshii desu) comes from ほしい (hoshii), to want, a kind of 'i-adjective'.

Drill

1. この東洋人は背が高いです。
   This Oriental is tall.

2. この女学生は流行歌が好きです。
   This schoolgirl likes popular songs.

3. 彼女は洗濯がきらいです。
   She dislikes washing her clothes.

4. この私費留学生は日本語の日常会話が下手です。
   This privately supported foreign student is poor at Japanese daily conversation.

5. この小学生は作文が上手です。
   This elementary school child is good at composition.

6. 彼女は頭がいいです。
   She has a clear head.

7. このモデルは目がきれいです。
   This model has beautiful eyes.

8. 日本製の写真機はレンズがとてもすぐれています。
   A camera of Japanese make has an excellent lens.

9. 日本人形は値段が安いです。
   Japanese dolls are inexpensive.

10. このかばんはチャックがこわれています。
    This suitcase is broken in its zip fastener.

11. 私は子どもがあります。
    I have a child.

12. 彼は日本の様子がわかりませ　　He doesn't know much about
ん。　　　　　　　　　　　　　　life in Japan.

13. 私は故郷が恋しいです。　　　　I feel a longing for my home
town.

14. 私は日本語が少し話せます。　　I can speak Japanese a little.

15. あなたはおなかがすきました　　Are you hungry?
か。

Exercise

Rewrite the following sentences and phrases in the ～は～が construction:

1. 私のかわいたのど (my thirsty throat)
2. 彼の話せる**ドイツ語** (or: 彼はドイツ語を話すことができます。), the
German he can speak
3. 彼のいる**英和辞書** (an English-Japanese dictionary he needs)
4. 彼女のほしい**日本製の時計** (a watch of Japanese make she wants)
5. 私のできる**ピンポン** (or: 私はピンポンをすることができます。), the
ping-pong I can play
6. この会社の新しい**設備** (or: この会社の設備は新しいです。), this company's modern facilities
7. この洋書の高い**値段** (or: この洋書の値段は高いです。), the high price
of this foreign book
8. 彼の飲みたい**洋酒** (the foreign wine he would like to drink)
9. 日本の大へん悪い**道路** (or: 日本の道路は大へん悪いです。), Japan's
very bad roads
10. 日本の多い**雨量** (or: 日本の雨量は多いです。), Japan's heavy rainfall
11. 象の長い**鼻** (or: 象の鼻は長いです。), an elephant's long trunk
12. 私の痛い**頭** (or: 私の頭は痛いです。), my painful head
13. 日本の稠密な**人口** (or: 日本の人口は稠密です。), Japan's dense popula-
tion
14. 彼の下手な**フランス語** (or: 彼のフランス語は下手です。), his poor
French

Answers:

1. 私はのどがかわきました。(I am thirsty.)
2. 彼はドイツ語が話せます。(He can speak German.)
3. 彼は英和辞書がいります。(He needs an English-Japanese dictionary.)
4. 彼女は日本製の時計がほしいです。(She wants a watch of Japanese
make.)

5. 私はピンポンができます。(I can play ping-pong.)
6. この会社は設備が新しいです。(This company has modern facilities.)
7. この洋書は値段が高いです。(This foreign book is expensive.)
8. 彼は洋酒が飲みたいです。(He would like to drink foreign wine.)
9. 日本は道路が大へん悪いです。(Japan has very bad roads.)
10. 日本は雨量が多いです。(Japan receives heavy rain.)
11. 象は鼻が長いです。(An elephant has a long trunk.)
12. 私は頭が痛いです。(I have a headache.)
13. 日本は人口が稠密です。(Japan is densely populated.)
14. 彼はフランス語が下手です。(He is poor at French.)

第 十三 課　Lesson 13

A Comparison of は (wa), が (ga), の (no), には (niwa), and では (dewa)

Rule

e.g. 彼女の夫の戦死はほぼ確実です。(**Kanojo** no otto no senshi *wa* hobo kakujitsu desu)—That her husband died in action—that is nearly certain—the nominative case は (wa) in this sentence indicates an essential and inevitable relationship and suggests such shading as the adverb いつも (itsumo), always. That is, は (wa) in this case may be taken as meaning "an individual called a husband is counted among those killed in battle, regardless of time"; in other words, any husband or man enlisted as a soldier is *always* (or generally) destined to face death or experience death on a battlefield". And thus, は (wa) in this sentence does not imply such limitation as immediate proximity in time: "Her husband has just died". The nominative case は (wa) can be necessarily replaced by the adverbial particle も (mo) in the sentence; and also this は (wa) always requires auxiliary verbs of declaration such as だ (da), です desu, ある (aru) and ない (nai) in a complete form without certain words being included. Namely, the nominative case は (wa) is closely associated with these auxiliaries in the form of a statement.

e.g. 彼女の夫の戦死が復員省から通知されました。(Kanojo no otto no senshi *ga* Fukuinshō kara tsūchi saremashita)—She was informed by the Demobilization Bureau of her husband's death in action—the nominative case が (ga) in this sentence indicates a temporary or irregular (accidental) relationship and suggests such shading as the adverb 今 (ima), この瞬間に (kono shunkan ni), now or at this moment. That is, が (ga) in this case may be taken as meaning "The very one who fell in battle *now* is her husband". And thus, が (ga) in this sentence is related to the fact of her husband's death and her husband himself on an equal footing. The nominative case が (ga) is used to qualify or restrict a definite object and situation in such a way as to attract the listener's attention.

e.g. 私は児童心理学者です。(Watakushi *wa* jidō shinri gakusha desu) —I am a child psychologist—は (wa) in this sentence includes the idea of "The profession of child psychologist is one of my attributes".

e.g. 私は政治学を取ります。(Watakushi *wa* seiji gaku o torimasu)— I will take political science—は (wa) in this sentence places emphasis on self-speciality; that is, this は (wa) implies that consciousness which emphasizes the difference between self and others.

e.g. 風は二十九日朝から吹き続いています。(Kaze *wa* ni jū ku nichi asa kara fuki tsuzuite imasu)—The wind is still blowing since the morning of the 29th—は (wa) in this sentence places emphasis on 風 (kaze), wind; that is, this は (wa) implies that consciousness which emphasizes the difference between wind and other natural phenomena like rain and snow.

e.g. 両国の国技館はすもうをやっています。(Ryōgoku no kokugikan *wa* sumō o yatte imasu)—Wrestling is being held at Kokugikan, a national stadium, in Ryōgoku—this は (wa) refers to continuous occurrences—it is used as a fixed connection; that is, the stadium Kokugikan is temporarily expected to have games over a certain period of time; although this stadium, this nominative case, would normally require が (ga) in place of は (wa), Kokugikan is yearly repeating this performance and thus the actually intended meaning in this sentence makes は (wa) the more correct and logical choice.

e.g. 彼は共産主義者ではありません。(Kare *wa* kyōsan shugisha dewa arimasen)—He is not a communist—when the negative form is used, the subject as a rule is followed by は (wa).

e.g. 私は肉は食べました。(Watakushi wa niku *wa* tabemashita)—I ate some meat. 肉は (niku wa), meat, is an objective term which shows the receiver. The expression 肉は (niku *wa*) is more emphatic and descriptive than the expression 肉を (niku *o*).

e.g. 私はサイダーは飲みません。(Watakushi wa saidā *wa* nomimasen)—I do not drink cider—サイダーは (saidā wa), cider, is an objective term which shows the receiver. The expression サイダーは (saidā *wa*) is more emphatic and descriptive than the expression サイダーを (saidā *o*).

e.g. 米は秋田米に限ります。(Kome *wa* Akita mai ni kagirimasu)— If it's rice, there is nothing of as good quality as that in Akita Prefecture—this は (wa) can be rendered as なら (nara), If it is... or と言えば (to ie ba), Speaking of...; so, If it is rice or Speaking of rice, ...

e.g. 戦災のあとには，無数のマーケットが立ち並んでいます。(Sensai no ato *niwa*, musū no māketto ga tachi narande imasu)—Among the war scars, numerous markets stand closely side by side—には (niwa) is a combination of the particles に (ni) and は (wa); this には (niwa) forms an adverbial phrase and is usually followed by verbs of existence such as あります (arimasu) or います (imasu), there is. . . . Its usage in this case is to form contrast with a previously mentioned or understood object or condition and emphasize the subjective case in its main clause. So, 戦災のあとには (sensai no ato niwa), among the war scars, is an adverbial phrase through which the subject in its main clause is particularly qualified and restricted; so, such a subject is ordinarily followed by the particle が (ga), as seen from 無数のマーケットが立ち並んでいます。(musū no māketto *ga* tachi narande imasu). The usage of には (niwa) is rendered as "as far as. . . is concerned" in English; and thus, 戦災のあとには (sensai no ato *niwa*), among the war scars, can be understood as "as far as the war-damaged site is concerned". That is, there can be found a market at least in the war-damaged site; but in any part other than the stricken area no such barracks may be discovered. On the other hand, we may also say, 戦災のあとに (sensai no ato *ni*), among the war scars, but 戦災のあとには (sensai no ato *niwa*) is more emphatic and descriptive.

e.g. 京都では，彼は学生英語弁論大会に出場するはずです。(Kyōto *dewa*, kare wa gakusei Eigo benron taikai ni shutsujō suru hazu desu)—He is to take part in the Student English Speech Contest at Kyoto—では (dewa) is a combination of the particles で (de) and は (wa); this では (dewa) forms an adverbial phrase and denotes a place of action; that is, it refers to the place where an action is performed and precedes a transitive verb. Its usage in this case is to form contrast with a previously mentioned or understood object or condition and puts emphasis on the state of action in its main clause. The usage of では (dewa) is rendered as "as far as. . . is concerned" in English; and thus, 京都では (Kyōto *dewa*) can be understood as "as far as Kyoto is concerned". That is, I'm going to be engaged in the Student English Speech Contest at least at Kyoto; but in another area I might not have any such share. On the other hand, we may also say, 京都で (Kyōto *de*), at Kyoto, but 京都では (Kyōto *dewa*) is more emphatic and descriptive.

e.g.　父は食卓で晩酌をしていました。母は居間で刺繍をしていました。
(Chichi *wa* shokutaku de banshaku o shite imashita.　Haha *wa*
ima de shishū o shite imashita)—The father was sitting at the
table, enjoying his evening drink.　The mother was embroidering
in the living room—the は (wa) following 父 (chichi), father and
母 (haha), mother, is used because this sentence is a contrast of
two ideas and thus the subject of each idea takes special emphasis.
Namely, は (wa) is used to restrict a topic especially in a fixed
sphere.

e.g.　玄関の呼びりんが鳴りました。(Genkan no yobirin *ga* narimashita)—The doorbell rang—が (ga) in this sentence can be understood
as "The doorbell *now* rang"; that is, が (ga) indicates a temporary
or accidental relationship.

e.g.　私の会社の近くに銭湯があります。(Watakushi no kaisha no chikaku ni sentō *ga* arimasu)—There is a public bath around my
company—nouns (inanimate objects) preceding あります (arimasu),
there is..., are followed by the particle が (ga).

e.g.　私の下宿に西洋人がいます。(Watakushi no geshuku ni Seiyō-jin
ga imasu)—There is a Westerner in my lodging house—nouns
(animate objects) preceding います (imasu), there is..., are followed by the particle が (ga).

e.g.　恋人の家に猟犬がいます。(Koibito no ie ni ryōken *ga* imasu)—
There is a hunting dog at my sweetheart's house—nouns (animate
objects) preceding います (imasu), there is..., are followed by
the particle が (ga).

e.g.　官庁の数が増し，その機構が拡大されました。(Kanchō no sū *ga*
mashi, sono kikō *ga* kakudai saremashita)—The number of government offices increased and their organization enlarged.　This expression is found to be merely that in which two subjective cases,
官庁の数が (kanchō no sū ga), the number of government offices
and その機構が (sono kikō ga), their organization, in a state of
action are described in enumeration.

e.g.　彼女が音楽のなかに法悦を感じるように，彼は電気の実習に限りな
いよろこびを感じていました。(Kanojo *ga* ongaku no naka ni hōetsu
o kanjiru yō ni, kare *wa* denki no jisshū ni kagiri nai yorokobi o
kanjite imashita)—Just as she found bliss in music, he felt a limit-
less joy in his practical studies of electricity.　が (ga) in this
sentence is used to qualify her and her situation in such a way
as to attract the listener's attention.　And は (wa) in this sentence

is used in such a way as to mention him specially.

e.g. 舌はからからにかわいて, 砂ぼこりがざらざらしていました。(Shita *wa* kara kara ni kawaite, suna bokori *ga* zara zara shite imashita) —My tongue was parched; the gritty dust clung between my teeth. は (wa) in 舌は (shita wa), tongue, emphasizing the state of being, means "my tongue was in a state of being parched". が (ga) in 砂ぼこりが (suna bokori ga), the gritty dust, puts emphasis on the state of action, meaning "the gritty dust was clinging between my teeth".

e.g. 今年の春, ろく膜炎におかされて彼は東大の入学試験が受けられませんでした。(Kotoshi no haru, rokumakuen ni okasarete kare *wa* Tōdai no nyūgaku shiken *ga* ukerare masen deshita)—This spring he suffered from pleurisy, and because of this he was unable to sit for the entrance examination to Tokyo University. The subject in this sentence is 彼 (kare), he and not 入学試験 (nyūgaku shiken), the entrance examination; that is, 彼 (kare), he, should be thought to be the subject of the phrase 東大の入学試験が受けられませんでした。(Tōdai no nyūgaku shiken ga ukerare masen-deshita). And also, the object which he was unable to sit for is the entrance examination to Tokyo University; from this idea 東大の入学試験が (Tōdai no nyūgaku shiken *ga*) is treated as an objective case.

e.g. むかし, 浦島太郎という人がありました。浦島は浜べで大ぜいの子供にいじめられているかめを買いとりました。(Mukashi, Urashima Tarō to iu hito *ga* arimashita. Urashima *wa* hamabe de ōzei no kodomo ni ijimerarete iru kame o kaitori mashita)—There once was a man named Urashima Taro. Urashima bought a tortoise which was being tormented by many children at the seashore. が (ga) fixes the framework of a story and then は (wa) is used as a receiver within its framework; that is, 浦島太郎という人が (Urashima Tarō to iu hito ga), a man named Urashima Tarō—this が (ga) corresponds to the English "a" or "an" and 浦島は (Urashima wa), Urashima, to the English "the".

e.g. どれがよろしいでしょうか。(Dore *ga* yoroshii deshō ka)—Which would you prefer? いつ (itsu), When, どこ (doko), Where, だれ (dare), Who, 何 (nani), What, and どれ (dore), Which, in the subjective tense always use が (ga).

e.g. 友だちが書いた短編小説が朝日新聞に掲載されました。(Tomodachi *ga* kaita tanpen shōsetsu ga Asahi shinbun ni keisai saremashita) —The short story my friend wrote was inserted in the Asahi newspaper—as there are no relative pronouns or relative adverbs in Japanese, noun clauses are expressed through the plain present/future, plain past, plain present progressive, or plain past progressive form of any verb+the antecedent (the noun or pronoun to which these verbs refer). The nominative case in the noun clause is indicated by the particle が (ga); and 友だちが (tomodachi *ga*) in the phrase of 友だちが書いた (tomodachi ga kaita) is related to 短編小説 (tanpen shōsetsu), a short story; therefore, the phrase of 友だちが書いた短編小説 (tomodachi *ga* kaita tanpen shōsetsu), the short story my friend wrote, can also be written and spoken with the use of の (no), as 友だちの書いた短編小説 (tomodachi *no* kaita tanpen shōsetsu).

Note: は (wa) and が (ga) are equally used as the nominative case; but there is a difference between them—the feeling of approach taken by は (wa) is far-reaching and that by が (ga) is near at hand. This difference is simply pictured as follows:

私は＋　　学長です。(Watakushi wa＋　　gakuchō desu).
　　　　　　　　　　　　　　　　　I'm the school president.
私が＋学長です。　　(Watakushi ga＋gakuchō desu).
　　　　　　　　　　　　　　　　　I am the school president.

The relationship between は (wa) and が (ga) is summarized as follows:

1. は (wa) indicates an essential, inevitable relationship and is usually used with verbs of state of being.
2. が (ga) indicates a temporary, irregular relationship and is usually used with verbs of state of action.
3. The relationships in 1 and 2 are reversed when the subjective case is to be emphasized; that is, when the subjective case is to be emphasized, an essential, inevitable relationship is indicated by が (ga) while a temporary, irregular one is shown by は (wa).
4. Continuous occurrences are an inevitable relationship and thus follow the case of 1.

Drill

1. 私は政治家です。　　　　　　I am a politician.
2. 雨は今朝も降り続いています。　This morning it is still raining.
3. 看護婦がアンプルを切って，注　The nurse opens an ampule, get-

射の用意をしています。

4. 春が過ぎて，やがて梅雨でした。

Spring was gone; soon the rainy season set in.

5. 私は庶民が好きです。

I like the common people.

6. ふと彼女は彼が憎くなりました。

Hate for him unexpectedly arose within her.

7. 縁談が彼女に持ち上がっていました。

She was made a proposal of marriage.

8. 彼女のほおを涙が流れていました。

Tears flowed down her cheeks.

9. 松林のなかでは，もずが鳴いていました。

In the pine wood butcher-birds were calling.

10. 日陰には，まだ霜柱が残っていました。

In the shade the frost still remained.

11. 富士の峰が月光を受けて銀色に光りました。

The peak of Mt. Fuji shone silver in the rays of moonlight.

12. 富士は六合目あたりに雲を巻いていました。

Mt. Fuji was wrapped in clouds to about its sixth stage.

13. 翌日雨はまだ降っていました。

The following day it was still raining.

14. 私は彼の住所は知りません。

I don't know his address.

15. 「私は東京は好まないが，いよいよ東京へ行きますよ。」

"I don't like Tokyo, but I'm sure to go up to Tokyo".

16. 私はブルジョアのむすこに生まれたけれど，ブルジョアやプチブルは大きらいです。

I was born the son of a middle class family, but I myself have a great dislike for the bourgeois and petty bourgeois.

17. 前科者のむすこはどこへ行っても相手にされないでしょう。

The son of a criminal, wherever he may go, will be given no attention.

18. 外は強い風が吹き荒れて，白かばの枯葉がかさかさと揺れていました。

Outside a strong wind was blowing, rustling the withered leaves of white birch trees.

19. 冬の短い日が暮れてから，彼女
は電車に揺られながら，家に帰り
ました。

After the short days of winter were dark, she returned home, jostled in the electric tram.

20. 社長は自分の机にすわり，客は
来客用のいすに腰かけています。

The director is seated at his own desk and a visitor is seated on the chair used for visitors.

21. 国旗や団旗をかかげた群衆が列
をなして，皇居の方に向かって行
進して行きました。

A crowd of people bearing the national and party flags moved forward in a line in the direction of the Imperial Palace.

22. 夕食のあと，父と母とは火の気
の乏しい火ばちにすわっていまし
た。

After supper, my father and mother sat over the brazier in which there was no sign of fire.

23. 彼は負けぬ気の闘志の強いプレ
ーヤーであり，彼の妻はゴルフよ
りも，歩きながらうっくつした日
ごろの仕事から離れて，ともかく
ものびやかな一日を過ごすことの
方が好きなたちです。

He is a player with an unyielding and strong fighting spirit, while it is his wife's nature to prefer to spend, at any rate, one day of relaxation cut off from the gloom of her daily routine, as she walks about, rather than play golf.

Exercise

Fill in the following blanks with "は", "が", "には" and "では":

1. 彼は軍部（　　）きらいでした。

He disliked the Army authorities.

2. 秋の烈日（　　）私のほおを焼
きました。

The blazing autumn sun reddened my cheeks.

3. 丘を低く一羽のふくろう（　　）
音もなく飛び去りました。

An owl flew low over the hills, making no sound.

4. 茶の間で母の呼ぶ声（　　）聞
こえました。

I heard the voice of my mother calling from the living room.

5. 職員会議で彼（　　）いつも発
言を封じられていました。

At the teachers' conference he was always blocked from expressing his opinions.

6. 昨夜父（　　）会合があって，帰り（　　）おそかったです。

Last night my father had a meeting and returned late.

7. 富士（　　）晴れて，真白な全姿を見せていました。

The mist surrounding Mt. Fuji cleared, wholly revealing its pure whiteness.

8. 彼の左腕の夜光時計（　　）光っていました。

The luminous dial of the watch on his left hand glinted.

9. 彼女のほお（　　），微笑がただよっていました。

The shadow of a smile lingered on her cheeks.

10. 彼（　　）息（　　）止まり，目（　　）くらんで，気（　　）遠くなりました。

He gasped, grew dizzy and faint.

11. 「総理（　　）どんな人物かご存知でしょう。彼（　　）形式主義者です。」

"I think that you are aware what sort of man the prime minister is. He is a perfunctory man".

12. はとの群れ（　　）輪を描いて放送局の高い建物の上を飛んでいます。

A flock of pigeons are circling over the high buildings of a broadcasting station.

13. 彼（　　）自分の態度（　　）先輩から非難される理由はないと考えました。

He could think of no reason why his personal behaviour should be criticized by his superiors.

14. 風（　　）トタン屋根を鳴らし，ガラス窓を揺すりました。

The wind sounded on the iron roofs and shook the glass windows.

15. 雨（　　）ぱらぱらと冷たく彼のかさを打ち，白かばの木の枯葉（　　）舗道に散り乱れていました。

The cool rain pattered on his umbrella and the withered leaves of white birch trees were scattered over the pavement.

16. 彼（　　）熱のためにほお（　　）ほてって，呼吸（　　）苦しかったです。

His cheeks burned with fever and his breath was labored.

17. デパートの高い建物の屋上からたらした白布（　　），大きな文字で「大安売り」と書いてあります。

On the white pennant hanging from the roof of a tall department store building, the word "Bargain

18. 窓の外（　　）, 雨が一層強くな
り, 樹木の茂った枝が荒い風に吹
きなぶられていました。

Sale" is displayed in big letters.

Outside the windows, it began to rain more heavily, and the dense branches of the trees were bending and straining in the violent wind.

19. 夜中に母（　　）目をさますと,
娘（　　）まだ寝もしないで, 何
か書きものをしていました。その
まくら下（　　）身のまわりの物
を入れたのでしょう, リュックサ
ックが置いてありました。

When the mother awoke about midnight, she saw that her daughter was still up busily writing. Near her pillow there lay a rucksack which perhaps held her belongings.

20. 伊東温泉（　　）, 療養所と大き
な旅館があって, 何百人の患者が
朝に夕に温泉にひたっています。

There are sanatoriums and large hotels in the Ito hot spring resort —hundreds of patients are soaking in the hot springs from morning to evening.

21. 社員たち（　　）自分の部屋へ
去って, 社長室（　　）, 社長と秘
書と二人だけ（　　）手もちぶさ
たな姿でとり残されました。

The staff took leave to return to their own rooms, and only the two remained together in the director's room, the director and his secretary seeming not to know how to fill in the time.

22. 古い官僚（　　）頭からかさに
かかったものを言うかわりに, 彼
（　　）銀行家のように巧みな話術
で, 相手をあやつる術を心得てい
ます。

Unlike the old bureaucrat, speaking as a proxy for a man of power, he knows how to handle others by using his skilful art of speaking, like a banker.

23. 祖母（　　）廊下を渡ってきて,
台所をのぞきました。孫娘（　　）
かっぽう着をきて, 朝食のあと片
付けをしているところでした。

The grandmother came along the corridor and looked into the kitchen. Her granddaughter in an apron was putting things in order after breakfast.

Answers:

1. が 2. が 3. が 4. が 5. は 6. は, が 7. は 8. が 9. には 10. は, が, が, が 11. が, は 12. が 13. は, が 14. が 15. は, が 16. は, が, が 17. には 18. では 19. が, は, には 20. には 21. は, には, が 22. が, は 23. が, が

An Objective Particle

Rule

e.g. 彼はまちの公衆電話にはいって，友だちを呼び出しました。(Kare wa machi no kōshū denwa ni haitte, tomodachi *o* yobidashimashita)—Entering a public telephone booth on the street, he called up his friend—を (o) in 友だちを (tomodachi o), one's friend, is an objective particle—を (o) follows the direct object immediately: nouns or pronouns+を (o)+verbs (transitive).

e.g. 明日遠足なので，母はむすこをいつもより早目に寝かせました。(Myōnichi ensoku nano de, haha wa musuko *o* itsumo yori hayame ni nekasemashita)—There being an excursion tomorrow, the mother put her son to bed a little earlier than usual—を (o) in むすこを (musuko o), one's son, shows the object (the receiver) which alters from being worked upon.

e.g. 彼は近所に十三，四軒の貸家を持っています。(Kare wa kinjo ni jū san shi ken no kashiya *o* motte imasu)—He owns thirteen or fourteen houses for rent in the neighborhood—を (o) in 貸家を (kashiya o), houses for rent, shows the object of ownership.

e.g. 彼女は大抵神田の丸善で新刊書を買います。(Kanojo wa taitei Kanda no Maruzen de shinkansho *o* kaimasu)—She generally buys new publications at Maruzen, a bookstore, in Kanda—を (o) in 新刊書を (shinkansho o), new publications, shows the object of shift of possession.

e.g. この学生の不良化については，私は責任を感じています。(Kono gakusei no furyōka ni tsuite wa, watakushi wa sekinin *o* kanjite imasu)—As for this student's downfall, I feel responsible—を (o) in 責任を (sekinin o), responsibility, shows the object in which one's mental activities take part.

e.g. 大ぜいの人が歩道を歩いています。(Ōzei no hito ga hodō *o* aruite imasu)—Many people are walking along the footpath—を (o) in 歩道を (hodō o), along the footpath, denotes a place where or through which an action occurs and precedes a verb indicating a change of place; that is, this を (o) shows a place of shift or passage. Such verbs as 歩く (aruk-u), to walk, 走る (hashir-u), to run, and 通る (tōr-u), to pass through, are intransitive verbs but the particle を (o) here should be introduced into the sentence as if the nouns preceding these verbs were in the objective case.

Note: The particle を (o) or で (de) is of equal availability to the verb 泳ぎます (oyogimasu), to swim, but the nuance of を (o) or で (de) with this verb is as follows:

私は川を泳ぎます。(Watakushi wa kawa *o* oyogimasu)—I swim in the river—this を (o), denoting a place of shift or passage, means "I swim to move on from the upper reaches to the lower part of a river or from this shore to the opposite shore.

私は川で泳ぎます。(Watakushi wa kawa *de* oyogimasu)—I swim in the river—this で (de) shows the place of action, meaning "I am engaged in swimming, while diving into or up from the river, or moving my hands and legs in a fixed place called a river.

e.g. この留学生は東大で四年の学生生活を送りました。(Kono ryūgaku-sei wa Tōdai de yo nen no gakusei seikatsu *o* okurimashita)— This foreign student spent four years of student life at Tokyo University—を (o) in 四年の学生生活を (yo nen no gakusei seikatsu o), four years of student life, shows the elapse of time.

e.g. 長女は昨年の秋家を出ました。(Chōjo wa saku nen no aki ie *o* demashita)—My eldest daughter left home in autumn last year—を (o) in 家を (ie o), one's home, shows the starting point of an action.

Note: The phrase 家を出ました。(Ie *o* demashita), One left home, can also be written and spoken with the use of the particle から (kara), as 家から出ました。(Ie *kara* demashita), One went out of the house. The nuance of 家を (ie o) and 家から (ie kara) is as follows:

家を出ました。(Ie *o* demashita)—One left home—the meaning can be read as: One left home for some business, purposes, or errands. That is, one left a structure. On the other hand, 家から出ました。(Ie *kara* demashita)—One went out of the house—から (kara) in this case may be taken as meaning "One stepped out into the outside of a house". That is, for instance, the inside of the house is now overwhelmed by smoke from the broiling of some fish; so, one stepped out into the open air for a while.

e.g. この老婆は朝の散歩に十五キロメートルを歩きます。(Kono rōba wa asa no sanpo ni jū go kiro mētoru *o* arukimasu)—This aged woman walks fifteen kilometers for a stroll in the morning—を (o) in 十五キロメートルを (jū go kiro mētoru o), fifteen kilometers, shows quantity in space.

e.g. 彼女はこの四・五日を有意義に過ごしています。(Kanojo wa kono shi go nichi *o* yūigi ni sugoshite imasu)—She is spending her time usefully these several days—を (o) in この四・五日を (kono shi go nichi o), these several days, shows quantity in time.

Drill

1. 私はあなたを（彼を，彼女を）愛します。

    I love you (him, her).

2. 彼はエレベーターを出ました。

    He stepped out of the elevator.

3. 彼女は今門柱の間を通っています。

    She is now passing through the portal.

4. この暑さに，二人とも灰色の背広を着ています。

    In spite of the heat, the two men wear their grey lounge suits.

5. 彼らはきちんとネクタイを結んでいました。

    They wore neat ties.

6. 結婚式に行く自動車で，私は品川を通りました。

    In the car on the way to my marriage, I passed by Shinagawa.

7. 風は坂道を下から吹き上げています。

    The wind is blowing up the slope from below.

8. 風が涼しく窓のカーテンをふくらませています。

    A cool wind is billowing the curtain at the window.

9. 数十匹の大きなこいが投げこまれるえさを争っています。

    Dozens of big carp are struggling for the food dropped in.

10. 数十匹の大きなこいが魚紋を描いています。

    Dozens of big carp are forming a fish-circle.

11. 社長は女秘書にステッキと帽子を渡しました。

    The director handed his cane and hat to his female secretary.

12. 彼は借家を建てました。

    He built houses to lease.

13. 彼女は化粧を直しています。

    She is putting on fresh make-up.

14. 母はむすこの位牌の前に線香をともしました。

    Mother burned sticks of incense in front of her son's memorial tablet.

Exercise

Fill in the following blanks with the objective particle "を":

1. 彼女は玄関（　　）降りました。

    She stepped down from the entrance.

2. 彼は急いで胸のポケットから手帳（　　）出しました。

    He quickly took a notebook out of his breast pocket.

3. 彼は守衛の立っている正門（　　）ぬけました。

He passed the guard at the front entrance.

4. 女秘書が紅茶（　　）入れてきました。

The female secretary came in, bringing black tea.

5. 彼女が家（　　）出る前に，庭に咲き残ったチューリップ（　　）切りました。

Before leaving home, she cut the last remaining tulips in the garden.

6. 受付の少女が社長に面会人（　　）知らせに来ました。

A young female employee at the information desk came in to tell the director of a visitor.

7. 母は庭のしょうぶ（　　）切っています。

Mother is cutting some irises in the garden.

8. 母は娘の位牌の前に花（　　）供えました。

Mother placed some flowers in front of her daughter's memorial tablet.

9. この園児は鉛筆（　　）なめています。

This kindergarten child is licking a pencil.

10. 彼女はモツアルトの曲（　　）一生けんめいにひこうとしています。

She is trying desperately to play some music of Mozart.

11. 公園の樹木の茂みに沿った涼しい日陰の道（　　），彼はゆったりと歩いていきました。

He walked on calmly along the cool shady road adjacent to the thick trees of the park.

12. 私の乗った自動車は池袋に向かう舗装道路（　　），速力を落として走っていきました。

The car, in which I rode, ran on, reducing speed on the paved road leading to Ikebukuro.

13. 電車の線路に沿った高台の暗い通り（　　），恋人同士が話もなく歩いていました。

Along the elevated dark path following the train line, the lovers walked on, not talking.

14. 墓地への道（　　）花束（　　）かかえて歩きながら，夫とのたくさんの思い出がよみがえりました。

Holding a bunch of flowers in her arms and walking along the road leading to the cemetery, many recollections of her husband

15. 私立大学に籍 (　　) 置くよう
になってからは，彼は講義にはめ
ったに顔 (　　) 出さずに，アル
バイトによって自分の学資と小使
いと (　　) もうけ，ほとんど独
力で大学 (　　) 卒業しました。

were brought freshly to her mind.

After being enrolled at one of the private universities, he seldom attended lectures and obtained his own school expenses and pocket money through part-time jobs; in this way he graduated from university mostly by his own efforts.

第 十五 課 Lesson 15

Continuative or Participial Construction

Rule

A は B をして,... (A wa B o   A *does* B *and*...(or Doing [Hav-
shi*te*, ...)   ing done] B, A...)

て (te) or で (de) is the connective used in a compound sentence—
this connective particle corresponds to the English "and" or the
present and past participial construction. In Japanese the connective
て (te) or で (de) itself is never influenced by the tense of the main
clause in a sentence. This form can be obtained by changing the
final vowel *a* of the plain past form to *e*. The tense of the entire
sentence is determined by that of the final verb of the sentence.

In the case of vowel stem verbs ending with either of the vowels
e-ru and *i*-ru, these plain past forms can be obtained by dropping the
last syllable *ru* and adding *ta* to the stem, as 見上げた (miage-ta)
from 見上げる (miage-ru), to look up at.

- e.g. 彼の顔を見上げて (or 見上げ), 彼女は恥ずかしそうにうなずきまし
  た。(Kare no kao *o* miage-*te* [or: miage], kanojo wa hazukashi sō
  ni unazukimashita)—Looking up at his face, she nodded, with an
  air of shame—を (o) in 彼の顔を (kare no kao o), his face, is an
  objective particle, and 見上げて (miage-te) comes from the plain
  past 見上げた (miage-ta), looked up at.

- e.g. 母は友だちから三味線を借りて (or 借り), 長女の踊りにひきました。
  (Haha wa tomodachi kara shamisen *o* kari-*te* [or: kari], chōjo no
  odori ni hikimashita)—The mother borrowed a shamisen from a
  friend and played on it for her eldest daughter's dance—を (o) in
  三味線を (shamisen o), a shamisen, is an objective particle, and
  借りて (kari-te) comes from the plain past 借りた (kari-ta), borrowed.

Any verb root ending with either of the vowels *e*-ru and *i*-ru is
called a vowel stem verb. The polite form of verbs in this category
can be obtained by dropping the last syllable *ru* and adding *masu* to
the stem, as 見上げます (miage-masu) from 見上げる (miage-ru), to
look up at and 借ります (kari-masu) from 借りる (kari-ru), to borrow.
Such vowel stem verbs as 見上げる (miage-ru) and 借りる (kari-ru)
can be conjugated as follows:

Verbs		Present/Future	Past	Present/Future Negative	Past Negative
look up at	polite form	miage-masu	miage-mashita	miage-masen	miage-masen deshita
	plain form	miage-ru	miage-ta	miage-nai	miage-nakatta
borrow	polite form	kari-masu	kari-mashita	kari-masen	kari-masen deshita
	plain form	kari-ru	kari-ta	kari-nai	kari-nakatta

Any verb root ending with *u*, a consonant+*u*, is called a consonant stem verb. The polite form of vowel stem verbs can be obtained by dropping the last syllable *ru* and adding *masu* to the stem, as 食べま す (tabe-masu) from 食べる (tabe-ru), to eat. On the other hand, the polite form of consonant stem verbs can be obtained by dropping the last syllable *u* and adding *imasu* to the stem, as 書きます (kak-imasu) from 書く (kak-u), to write. In the case of vowel stem verbs, the plain past forms can be obtained by dropping the last syllable *ru* and adding *ta* to the stem, while consonant stem verbs in the plain past form involve a sound change before adding *ta* or *da*; that is, there are four euphonic changes—an *i*-euphonic change, a euphonic change to the syllabic nasal sound, a euphonic change of assimilation, and a euphonic change of friction. Rules for these sound changes are illustrated as follows:

Such a verb as さく (sa*k*-u), to spare, undergoes an *i*-euphonic change —the plain past form is さいた (sa*i*-ta). But here the verb 行く (i*k*-u), to go, is an exception; the plain past form is 行った (i*t*-ta).

Such verbs as かがみこむ (kagamiko*m*-u), to crouch and 呼ぶ (yo*b*-u), to call, undergo a euphonic change to the syllabic nasal sound—the plain past forms are かがみこんだ (kagamiko*n*-da) and 呼んだ (yo*n*-da). But here the verb 死ぬ (shi*n*-u), to die, is an exception; the plain past form is 死んだ (shi*n*-da). Note: 泳ぐ (oyo*g*-u)→泳いだ (oyo*i*-da), swam.

Such verbs as 持つ (mo*ts*-u), to carry, くぐる (kugu*r*-u), to creep, and 言う (i[*w*]-u), to say, undergo a euphonic change of assimilation— the plain past forms are 持った (mo*t*-ta), くぐった (kugu*t*-ta), and 言 った (i*t*-ta).

Such a verb as 取り出す (toridas-u), to take out, undergoes a euphonic change of friction—the plain past form is 取り出した (torida*shi*-ta).

The form of the continuative or participial construction is expressed by the て (te) or で (de)-form of consonant stem verbs, obtained by replacing the final vowel *a* of the plain past form by *e* or the second base (the verb form used with the polite -*masu* endings), as 書いて (kai-te) or 書き (kak-i), Writing or to write and..., from 書いた (kai-ta), wrote, plain past form or 書きます (kak-imasu), to write, polite present form. The expression 書いて (kai-te) can be extensively written and spoken, while the expression 書き (kak-i) is not available to conversation but chiefly used in the written language.

e.g. 彼はあわただしい時間をさいて (or さき), 先生の所へお別れのあいさつに行きました。(Kare wa awatadashii jikan *o* sai-*te* [or: sak-i], sensei no tokoro e owakare no aisatsu ni ikimashita)—He spared some of his precious time and visited the teacher to say good-bye —を (o) in 時間を (jikan o), time, is an objective particle, and さいて (sai-te) or さき (sak-i) comes from さいた (sai-ta), spared and さきます (sak-imasu), to spare.

e.g. 午後から夜まで, このこじきは軒下にかがみこんで (or かがみこみ), うつらうつらと眠っていました。(Gogo kara yoru made, kono kojiki wa noki shita ni kagamikon-*de* [or: kagamikom-i], utsura utsura to nemutte imashita)—Crouched under the eaves from afternoon to night, this beggar was dozing—かがみこんで (kagamikon-de) or かがみこみ (kagamikom-i) comes from かがみこんだ (kagamikon-da), crouched and かがみこみます (kagamikom-imasu), to crouch (intransitive verb).

e.g. 食堂へはいってくるなり, 彼は白服のボーイを呼んで (or 呼び), 食事を早くしてくれるように頼みました。(Shokudō e haitte kuru nari, kare wa shiro fuku no bōi *o* yon-*de* [or: yob-i], shokuji o hayaku shite kureru yō ni tanomimashita)—Stepping into a restaurant, he called a boy dressed in white and asked for his meal to be prepared quickly—を (o) in ボーイを (bōi o), a boy, is an objective particle, and 呼んで (yon-de) or 呼び (yob-i) comes from 呼んだ (yon-da), called and 呼びます (yob-imasu), to call.

e.g. 右手に帽子を持って (or 持ち), 社長はゆっくりと部屋を出ていきました。(Migi te ni bōshi *o* mot-*te* [or: moch-i], shachō wa yukkuri to heya o dete ikimashita)—Carrying his hat in his right hand, the director walked slowly out of the room—を (o) in 帽子を (bōshi o), one's hat, is an objective particle, and 持って (mot-te) or 持ち (moch-i) comes from 持った (mot-ta), carried and 持ちます (moch-imasu), to carry.

e.g. そっとかやをくぐって (or くぐり), 彼女は子供の床に近づき, 上から彼の顔を見ました。安らかな寝息でした。(Sotto kaya *o* kugut-*te* [or: kugur-i], kanojo wa kodomo no toko ni chikazuki, ue kara kare no kao o mimashita. Yasuraka na neiki deshita)—Quietly creeping under the mosquito net and edging near her child's bed, she looked down on his face. His breathing was peaceful—を (o) in かやを (kaya o), the mosquito net, is an objective particle, and くぐって (kugut-te) or くぐり (kugur-i) comes from くぐった (kugut-ta), crept and くぐります (kugur-imasu), to creep.

e.g. 彼は両親におやすみなさいと言って (or 言い), 大またに二階へ上がっていきました。(Kare wa ryōshin ni oyasumi nasai to it-*te* [or: ii], ōmata ni nikai e agatte ikimashita)—He strode upstairs, saying "Good-night" to his parents as he went—言って (it-te) or 言い (i-i) comes from 言った (it-ta), said and 言います (i-imasu), to say.

e.g. おばさんは茶だんすからみかんを取り出して (or 取り出し), 私に手渡してくれました。(Obasan wa chadansu kara mikan o toridashi-*te* [or: toridash-i], watakushi ni tewatashite kuremashita)—My aunt took out an orange from the tea cabinet and handed it to me—を (o) in みかんを (mikan o), an orange, is an objective particle, and 取り出して (toridashi-te) or 取り出し (toridash-i) comes from 取り出した (toridashi-ta), took out and 取り出します (toridash-imasu), to take out.

Such consonant stem verbs as さく (sa*k*-u), to spare, かがみこむ (kagamiko*m*-u), to crouch, 呼ぶ (yo*b*-u), to call, 持つ (mo*ts*-u), to carry, くぐる (kugu*r*-u), to creep, 言う (i[*w*]-u), to say, and 取り出す (toridas-u), to take out, can be conjugated as follows:

Verbs		Present/Future	Past	Present/Future Negative	Past Negative
spare	polite form	sak-imasu	sak-imashita	sak-imasen	sak-imasen deshita
	plain form	sa*k*-u	sa*i*-ta	sak-anai	sak-anakatta
crouch	polite form	kagamikom-imasu	kagamikom-imashita	kagamikom-imasen	kagamikom-imasen deshita
	plain form	kagamiko*m*-u	kagamiko*n*-da	kagamikom-anai	kagamikom-anakatta
call	polite form	yob-imasu	yob-imashita	yob-imasen	yob-imasen deshita
	plain form	yo*b*-u	yo*n*-da	yob-anai	yob-anakatta

carry	polite form	moch-imasu	moch-imashita	moch-imasen	moch-imasen deshita
	plain form	mo*ts*-u	mo*t*-ta	mot-anai	mot-anakatta
creep	polite form	kugur-imasu	kugur-imashita	kugur-imasen	kugur-imasen deshita
	plain form	kugu*r*-u	kugu*t*-ta	kugur-anai	kugur-anakatta
say	polite form	i-imasu	i-imashita	i-imasen	i-imasen deshita
	plain form	i(*w*)-u	i*t*-ta	iw-anai	iw-anakatta
take out	polite form	toridash-imasu	toridash-imashita	toridash-imasen	toridash-imasen deshita
	plain form	torida*s*-u	torida*shi*-ta	toridas-anai	toridas-anakatta

Such verbs as する (suru), to do and 来る (kuru), to come, are irregular verbs which do not belong to either vowel or consonant stem verbs.

  e.g. 途中用事をして，私は京都に着きました。(Tochū yōji o shi-*te*, watakushi wa Kyōto ni tsukimashita)—Taking care of some business on the way, I finally reached Kyoto—を (o) in 用事を (yōji o), business, is an objective particle, and して (shi-te) comes from した (shi-ta), did.

  e.g. 「肉でも買ってきて，ご馳走しなさい。」(Niku demo katte ki-*te*, gochisō shinasai)—"Go out and buy some meat and treat him to it."—きて (ki-te) comes from きた (ki-ta), came.

Such irregular verbs as する (suru), to do and 来る (kuru), to come, lacking a general principle in conjugation, must be memorized. These verbs can be conjugated as follows:

Verbs		Present/ Future	Past	Present/Future Negative	Past Negative
do	polite form	shi-masu	shi-mashita	shi-masen	shi-masen deshita
	plain form	suru	shi-ta	shi-nai	shi-nakatta
come	polite form	ki-masu	ki-mashita	ki-masen	ki-masen deshita
	plain form	kuru	ki-ta	ko-nai	ko-nakatta

Drill

1. かさを傾けて，彼は冷たい雨の中へ出ていきました。

   His umbrella at a slant, he went out into the cool rain.

2. 階段をきしませて，彼は二階から降りてきました。

   The stairs creaking, he came down from the second story.

3. 彼は外とうのポケットに両手を入れて，ゆっくり歩いていきました。

   He walked slowly, both his hands thrust into his overcoat pockets.

4. 彼は大学の法科を出て，法務省に勤めはじめたばかりで，病床に伏しました。

   He was ill in bed just after taking up his post at the Office of Attorney General upon graduation from the law department of a university.

5. 若い二人の駆け落ちが東京へ行って，無事に暮らしていけるでしょうか。

   One wonders if the young eloping couple could go up to Tokyo and could lead their lives in security.

6. 今日この芸者はお座敷を休んで，先生からお針を習ったり，手習いしたりしました。

   Today this geisha rested from her profession, and learned needlework and practised handwriting under a teacher.

7. 彼は妻が買ってきた酒を暖めて，飲みました。

   He warmed the *sake* which his wife had bought for him and drank it.

8. 彼女は紙切れを火ばちに入れて，燃やしました。

   She put a scrap of paper into the brazier and burned it.

9. 彼は上着を脱いで，ワイシャツ一枚になっていました。

   He took off his coat and wore only a shirt.

10. 彼女は新宿駅まで車を飛ばして，中央線の汽車に乗りました。

    She went directly by car to Shinjuku Station and got on a Chuo Line train.

11. 彼はアパートを追い出されて，私の宅にやってきました。

    He was driven out of his apartment and came to my house.

12. 彼女は揺れる車窓に頭をもたせ
かけて，目を閉じました。

Resting her head against the shaking train window, she closed her eyes.

13. 私はあなたのおそばを離れて，
遠い町へ来てしまいました。

Parting from you, I've come to a far away town.

14. 彼はトヨタ商会に自分で職を見
つけて，私の不在中に転居してい
きました。

He discovered a job by himself in the Toyota Firm and changed his residence during my absence.

15. これが最後になるだろうと覚悟
を決めて，彼女は夫に別れの手紙
を書きました。

Thinking that this would be the end, she wrote a parting letter to her husband.

Exercise

Fill in the following blanks with the particles "を", and "て" or "で", taking into consideration the verb given below each sentence:

1. 彼女は酒（　　）買っ（　　），主
人の帰宅を待っていました。

She bought some *sake* and waited for her husband to come home.

買った (kat-ta), bought＜買う (ka [w]-u), to buy

2. その女はたもと（　　）探っ（　　），
煙草を取り出し，すぱりと吸いつ
けました。

The woman groped in the sleeves of her kimono, took out a cigarette, and quickly lit it.

探った (sagut-ta), groped＜探る (sagur-u), to grope

3. 彼女は風呂敷包み一つ（　　）ぶ
ら下げ（　　），アパートさがしに
出ていきました。

She picked up the *furoshiki-*bundle and walked off to look for an apartment.

ぶら下げた (burasage-ta), picked up＜ぶら下げる (burasage-ru), to pick up

4. 刑事はくつ（　　）脱い（　　），
ずかずかと上がり込みました。

The detective took off his shoes and barged into the room.

脱いだ (nui-da), took off＜脱ぐ (nug-u), to take off

5. 先生がきちんとネクタイ（　　）
結ん（　　），出てきました。

The teacher, dressed neatly with a necktie, came out.

結んだ (musun-da), tied＜結ぶ (musub-u), to tie

6. 彼は電話（　　）切っ（　　），困
惑して火ばちに手をかざしまし
た。

After hanging up the phone, he, greatly perplexed, warmed his hands over the brazier.

切った (kit-ta), hung up＜切る (kir-u) to hang up

7. 彼女は両手で髪（　　）かき上　　　Combing up her hair with both
げ（　　）、嘆息しました。　　　hands, she sighed.

かき上げた (kakiage-ta), combed up＜かき上げる (kakiage-ru), to comb up

8. 彼は新聞（　　）たたん（　　）、　Folding the newspaper, he put
ポケットに入れました。　　　　it into his pocket.

たたんだ (tatan-da), folded＜たたむ (tatam-u), to fold

9. 赤ちゃんが畳の上（　　）はい　　The baby was crawling about
回っ（　　）、よだれをたらしてい　on the mats, dribbling saliva from
ました。　　　　his mouth.

はい回った (haimawat-ta), crawled about＜はい回る (haimawar-u), to crawl
about

10. 保険会社の外交員が大きなかば　　An insurance company sales-
ん（　　）かかえ（　　）、はいっ　man came in holding a big brief-
てきました。　　　　case in his arms.

かかえた (kakae-ta), held＜かかえる (kakae-ru), to hold

11. 彼は一本の煙草（　　）くわえ　　Holding a cigarette in his mouth,
（　　）、机のわきの火ばちに両手　he stretched both hands out over
をかざしました。　　　　the brazier by the desk.

くわえた (kuwae-ta), held something in one's mouth＜くわえる (kuwae-
ru), to hold something in one's mouth

12. 先生は学生の肩（　　）押し（　　Pushing the student by the
　）、職員室へ連れていきました。　shoulders, the teacher led him to
the faculty room.

押した (oshi-ta), pushed＜押す (os-u), to push

13. 彼女は生後二か月の赤ちゃん　　She is carefully holding a two-
（　　）大事そうに毛糸のケープに　month-old baby wrapped in a
包ん（　　）、抱いています。　　worsted cape in her arms.

包んだ (tsutsun-da), wrapped＜包む (tsutsum-u), to wrap

14. 彼は大学の法科（　　）出（　　）、Immediately after graduating
すぐに警察にはいりました。　　from the law department of a university, he joined the police force.

出た (de-ta), graduated from＜出る (de-ru), to graduate from

15. 大工さんが上がりかまちに腰　　The carpenter is sitting on the

(）かけ（), お茶をすすっ　　raised entrance, sipping tea.
ています。
　　かけた (kake-ta), sat＜かける (kake-ru), to sit

Answers:
1. を, て 2. を, て 3. を, て 4. を, で 5. を, で 6. を, て 7. を, て 8. を, で 9. を, て 10. を, て 11. を, て 12. を, て 13. を, で 14. を, て 15. を, て

第 十六 課 Lesson 16

な (Na)-Adjective

Rule

In Japanese there are two kinds of adjectives—な (na)-adjectives and い (i)-adjectives. Here, な (na)-adjectives are given first.

Each adjective can be applied in an attributive or a predicative use. The attributive use of な (na)-adjectives is expressed by な (na) +a noun.

e.g. 彼は池袋の広い通りを，**孤独な**気持ちで歩いていきました。(Kare wa Ikebukuro no hiroi tōri o, *kodoku na* kimochi de aruite iki-mashita)—He walked on in a solitary mood along a spacious street in Ikebukuro—孤独な (kodoku na), solitary, in an attributive use modifies the noun 気持ち (kimochi), mood.

The form of the predicative use can always be obtained by dropping な (na) of these adjectives and adding the termination です (desu), a copula. When used predicatively, each な (na)-adjective becomes a noun; in other words, the noun form of this class of adjectives can be induced by omitting the な (na) of its true function.

e.g. 生涯の不具を約束されているこの患者を待っている運命は**孤独で す**。(Shōgai no fugu o yakusoku sarete iru kono kanja o matte iru unmei wa *kodoku desu*)—The destiny which awaits this patient who has the promise of a lifetime of deformity is solitude—孤独 です (kodoku desu), to be solitude, is the predicative use of the attributive な (na)-adjective 孤独な (kodoku na), solitary; 孤独 (kodoku), solitude, is the noun form.

The adverbial form of な (na)-adjectives can be obtained by replacing the final な (na) by に (ni). Also, by adding に (ni) to the noun form we may obtain its adverbial form.

e.g. この時勢に見切りをつけて，私は故山に退き，**孤独に**生きたいです。(Kono jisei ni mikiri o tsukete, watakushi wa kozan ni shirizoki, *kodoku ni* ikitai desu)—Forsaking the times, I would like to retire to my country home and lead a solitary life—孤独に (kodoku ni), in solitary, is the adverbial form of the な (na)-adjective 孤独な (ko-doku na), solitary, and it modifies the verbal form 生きたいです (ikitai desu), would like to lead one's life.

Here, the な (na)-adjective 孤独な (kodoku na), solitary, is taken up as a model; this adjective in a predicative use can be conjugated as follows. In other words, the copula (is; am; are) has the following conjugation:

copula; *na*-adjective		Present/Future	Past	Present/Future Negative	Past Negative
be solitary	polite form	kodoku-desu	kodoku-deshita	kodoku-de (wa) arimasen	kodoku-de (wa) arimasen de-shita
	plain form	kodoku-da	kodoku-datta	kodoku-de (wa) nai	kodoku-de (wa) nakatta

Drill

1.
彼女はドレスの着こなしも上手で，どこから見ても**立派な**ダンサーです。

She wears her dress well and one can easily see she is a fine dancer.

背広の胸にネクタイがよじれていて，彼の風采は**立派では**ありません。

His appearance is untidy, with his necktie disarranged under his suit coat.

私は**立派に**生活を立てて，子供も丈夫に育てます。

I'll make a good living and bring up my child in good health.

2.
無責任な男はたよりにしない方がいいです。

You'd better not depend upon an irresponsible man.

この店の若主人はお人よしで，世間知らずで，**無責任です**。

The young master of this shop is a good-natured man, knows little of the world, and is irresponsible.

父は放蕩の味を覚えたむすこを**無責任に**責める前に，自分を責めたい気持ちでした。

The father felt he should reproach himself before he should irresponsibly blame his son who began to lead a dissipated life.

3.
この生徒は**素直な**態度で，よどみなく先生の質問に答えました。

This pupil obediently replied to the teacher's questions without hesitation.

この人は純朴で，**素直です**。

This person is simple-hearted and obedient.

この生徒はこの二・三日ひど

This pupil has become extremely

くく素直になってきました。

gentle these two or three days.

4.
私は野性的な人間を好みません。

I dislike a man with a rude nature.

彼は野性的です。

He is uncultivated.

長い軍隊生活が彼を野性的にみがきあげてしまいました。

His long army life polished him into an uncultivated manner.

5.
彼は親分はだな性格の広さもあり，金銭にこだわらない淡泊なところもあります。

He has the breadth of disposition which makes a good leader and is, to some extent, indifferent to money.

彼は何事にも淡泊です。

He is indifferent to all matters.

淡泊に言えば，あなたは野心と望みとを失っています。

To be frank with you, you have lost both ambition and hope.

6.
彼は女に対する誠実な愛情に苦しんだ経験がありません。

He has never experienced the torment of a sincere affection for a woman.

彼は自衛隊員として，生真面目で，誠実です。

As a member of the Self-Defense Force he is entirely earnest and sincere.

私はどんな事にでも，誠実にしようと思います。

I hope I'll do all things honestly.

7.
私はもうあなたに対して寛大な処置はとれません。

I can't provide you with generous treatment now.

白髪のまじった中年の官選弁護人は，深い犯罪理由がありそうに見えるこの常習窃盗犯に寛大です。

The middle-aged public defender with white hair is generous to this habitual thief who seems to have deep reasons for his criminal behavior.

私はできるだけ寛大にこの不良青年を処置します。

I'll see that this depraved youth gets treated as generously as possible.

Exercise

Fill in the following blanks with "な":

1. 彼らはなごやか（　　）雑談を
   しながら食事をしています。

   They are chatting pleasantly over a meal.

2. この小ぶとりの老人はいつも穏
   やか（　　）微笑を失いません。

   This plump, elderly man never loses his quiet smile.

3. 父はこの生真面目（　　）善良
   （　　）むすこを自慢にしています。

   The father takes pride in this earnest and good son.

4. 母の死が彼女を絶望的（　　）気
   持ちにさせました。

   The mother's death kept her in a mood of despair.

5. この学生は真剣（　　）目付き
   で，静かにうなずきました。

   This student, his eyes serious, nodded quietly.

6. この消防夫はひげもはやさず，
   髪も伸ばさない地味（　　）人です。

   This fireman is a sober man who does not cultivate a moustache or let his hair grow.

7. この歯科医は不機嫌（　　）顔
   を見せたことのない人です。

   This dentist is a man who never turns a displeasured face.

8. この小屋に孤独（　　）顔をし
   た老人と，無愛想（　　）娘がい
   ます。

   There is an aged person with an air of loneliness and an unfriendly daughter in this hut.

9. 平和（　　）家庭生活にはいるこ
   とは，何ものにもまして私の心を
   魅了します。

   To enter upon a peaceful home life appeals to my heart above anything else.

10. 彼女は真青（　　）顔になり，額
    からほおにかけて冷たい汗が流れ
    ていました。

    She became deadly pale, a cold sweat streaming down her cheeks from her forehead.

11. 彼は乱暴（　　）要求をむき出
    しにする，無秩序（　　）精神をも
    った男です。

    He is a man with a disordered spirit, exposing unreasonable demands.

12. 彼は格別に左翼的でもなく，先
    鋭（　　）自由主義者でもありませ
    ん。

    He is not outstanding as a man with left wing sympathies nor is he a keen liberalist.

13. むすこが自動車事故のために死

    Her son was killed in a car acci-

亡しました。神経質（　　）母にとっては耐えがたい悲しみでした。

dent. This was unbearable grief for the mother with her delicate nature.

14. 彼女はうつろ（　　）沈んだ表情で，庭の夏菊のあざやか（　　）黄色を見つめています。

She, silent, with downcast face, is staring vacantly at the bright yellow color of the summer-flowering chrysanthemums in the garden.

15. 彼女は東京外国語大学の食堂から校庭にあがるゆるやか（　　）通路を上って行きました。

She started out, climbing up the gentle incline leading from the cafeteria of the Tokyo University of Foreign Studies to the campus.

16. そんなのんき（　　）ことを考えていたら，あなたはめちゃくちゃになります。手を打つのは今です。

If you harbor such an irresponsible idea, you will surely go to pieces. Now is the time when you should really do something about this matter.

17. この大学生は次第にいきり立って，青年のいこじ（　　）感情から，教師と争おうとしていました。

This university student was gradually becoming excited, and was, with the perversity of youth, ready to bandy words with his instructor.

18. 悲惨（　　）生涯を生きなければならないらい病患者は，虚無的（　　）絶望的（　　）まなざしで静かに病室の天井を見つめています。

Those lepers, who must face a miserable lifetime, are staring with hopeless and despairing eyes quietly up at the ceiling in the ward.

19. 彼女は薬局のかどを曲がってから，走るのをやめ，平静（　　）足どりになって坂道を降りました。

She stopped running after turning the corner of the pharmacy, and went down the slope with quiet steps.

20. えんじ色のセーターを着た彼女は，まだ結婚前の娘かと思われる程みずみずしくて，細くくびれた胴の線に若い可憐（　　）魅力があ

She, in a crimson sweater, looks so young and fresh that she may be taken to be an unmarried girl, and at the line of her narrow

ります。

21. 彼はふなつりが好きで，夏休み
　　になると，毎日のようにかおりの
　　高いふなをとって来ては，父の酒
　　のさかなに塩をふって焼いてくれ
　　る親孝行（　　）やさしいむすこ
　　です。

He likes to fish for crucian; during the summer vacation, he would go fishing almost every day, and bring home crucian with a strong sweet smell—he is such a dutiful and gentle son as to sprinkle the fish with salt and broil it himself to go with his father's *sake*.

22. 校庭では児童たちのラジオ体操
　　の声が聞こえ，それが終わると，
　　キャッチボールのにぎやか（　　）
　　笑い声がします。

From the school ground the voice of the radio exercises for the pupils is audible, and when the exercises are finished, the noisy and cheerful laughter of those playing catch ball can be heard.

waist there is a youthful, cute charm.

Answers:

1. なごやかな (pleasant; peaceful) 2. 穏やかな (quiet) 3. 生真面目な (earnest) 善良な (good) 4. 絶望的な (desperate) 5. 真剣な (serious) 6. 地味な (sober) 7. 不機嫌な (displeasured) 8. 孤独な (lonely) 無愛想な (unfriendly) 9. 平和な (peaceful) 10. 真青な (deadly pale) 11. 乱暴な (unreasonable) 無秩序な (disordered) 12. 先鋭な (keen) 13. 神経質な (delicate) 14. うつろな (downcast; vacant) あざやかな (bright) 15. ゆるやかな (gentle) 16. のんきな (irresponsible) 17. いこじな (perverse) 18. 悲惨な (miserable) 虚無的な (hopeless) 絶望的な (despairing) 19. 平静な (quiet) 20. 可憐な (cute) 21. 親孝行な (dutiful) 22. にぎやかな (cheerful)

Connective で (de) in the case of な (na)-Adjective

Rule

で (de) is the connective ("and" in English) used in a compound sentence employing the copula です (desu) and may be considered to be an abbreviation of the verb. In the case of な (na)-adjectives, the final な (na) is dropped, this omission enabling them to be used as the noun forms. If such a noun as this is placed before this connective particle, it relates to the following through で (de).

e.g. 私はがんめいな人を好みません。(Watakushi wa *ganmei na* hito o konomimasen)—I dislike an obstinate person—がんめいな (ganmei na), obstinate, is a な (na)-adjective in an attributive use.

e.g. 彼は子供のようにがんめいです。(Kare wa kodomo no yō ni *ganmei desu*)—He is obstinate like a child—がんめいです (ganmei desu), to be obstinate, is the predicative use of the attributive な (na)-adjective がんめいな (ganmei na), obstinate; がんめい (ganmei), obstinacy, is the noun form.

e.g. 彼はがんめいで, 凶暴です。(Kare wa *ganmei de*, kyōbō desu) —He is obstinate and violent—がんめいで (ganmei de), to be obstinate and..., is the connective derived from the noun form of がんめいな (ganmei na), obstinate.

In addition, the final な (na) of almost all な (na)-adjectives can be replaced by さ (sa), also permitting the formation of the noun forms. But the な (na)-adjective ending with ～的な (...teki na), "-tic" in English such as found in the word 封建的な (hōken teki na), feudalistic, is an exception here; in other words, the noun form with さ (sa) cannot be derived from a word ending with ～的な (...teki na), "-tic".

e.g. この会社の一切の権威は, 一政治家の子供のようながんめいさのために, じゅうりんされてしまいました。(Kono kaisha no issai no ken-i wa, ichi seijika no kodomo no yō na *ganmei sa* no tame ni, jūrin sarete shimaimashita)—Because of the obstinacy of a childish politician, all the prestige of this company was treated with contempt—がんめいさ (ganmei sa), obstinacy, is also a noun form.

The negative form of the predicative use of な (na)-adjectives can always be obtained by changing the final vowel *a* of the plain present/future form to *e* and adding *nai*, as 立派でない (rippa de nai), to not be fine, from 立派だ (rippa da), to be fine. If the final vowel *i* of *nai*

is then changed to *ku*, it relates to the following through *te*, as 立派
でなくて (rippa de na *ku* te), to not be fine but . . . from 立派でない
(rippa de na*i*), to not be fine.

    e.g. この建物は**立派でなくて**，古めかしいです。(Kono tatemono **wa**
rippa de naku te, furumekashii desu)—This building is not splendid
but old-fashioned. On the other hand, we may also say, 立派で
はなくて (rippa de *wa* naku te), to not be fine but . . . —this expression is more emphatic and descriptive than 立派でなくて (rippa
de naku te).

Drill

1. 彼は子供のように**わがままで**，**わからずやで**，一本気です。	He is selfish, obstinate, and single-minded like a child.
2. この女秘書は**温和で**，的確に物事を処理していく，落ち着きはらった女です。	This female secretary has a placid nature and is a self-composed woman who can manage her affairs efficiently.
3. 彼は**無神経で**，無道徳です。	He is insensitive and immoral.
4. 彼の人柄は**穏やかで**，楽天的です。	He has a tolerant and optimistic character.
5. 彼は**温和で**，やさしいです。	He is genial and gentle.
6. 彼の顔は**平和で**，明るいです。	His face is relaxed and bright.
7. 彼女は**不純で**，**不潔で**，不道徳です。	She is impure, unclean, and immoral.
8. このおくさんは**清潔で**，**聡明で**，**活発で**，申し分のない人です。	This wife is neat, intelligent, and full of life—she is a person beyond criticism.
9. この大学生は**がむしゃらで**，不従順です。	This university student is reckless and disobedient.
10. 彼の演説は余りにも**抽象的で**，つまらないです。	His speech is much too abstract and tedious.
11. この人は**無知で**，不用心です。	This person is ignorant and careless.
12. 彼女は**純真で**，清潔です。	She is innocent and pure.
13. 彼の体格は**立派で**，色の白い美	His physique is good and he is

男子です。

14. 彼のほおは**つややかで**, 太って
います。

15. 彼は**快活で**, **行動的で**, すばら
しい青年です。

16. 彼は**冷静で**, **客観的で**, スタイ
リストです。

a fair, handsome man.

His cheeks are glossy and fat.

He is a cheerful, active, and splendid young man.

He is calm, objective, and a stylist.

Exercise

Fill the blanks with the connective particle "で":

1. 彼は甘ったれ（　　）, 自分勝手
（　　）, 気の弱い青年です。

He is a self-indulgent, selfish and weak young man.

2. 彼はこうかつ（　　）, 残酷です。

He is cunning and cruel.

3. 彼女は素直（　　）, 苦労知らず
の甘えた子供です。

She is a docile and spoiled child without knowledge of suffering.

4. この国の庶民は純真（　　）, 素
直（　　）, 疑いや反抗することを
知りません。

The common people in this country are simple and obedient, knowing neither suspicion nor resistance.

5. 彼女は大へん不用意（　　）, 無
反省です。

She is of an extremely reckless and thoughtless nature.

6. 彼らは明るくて正直（　　）, か
らっぽです。

They are cheerful, honest and guiltless.

7. 彼女は理性の勝ったという女で
はありません。しかし本能的（　　）,
直情径行的でもありません。

She is not generally a clear thinking woman; and she lacks both intuition and straightforwardness.

8. 彼女は穏やか（　　）, 調和のと
れた人です。

She has created a mild and harmonious personality.

9. 彼女は孤独（　　）, 敬虔（　　）,
真剣（　　）, 素直です。

She is lonely, pious, serious and obedient.

10. 彼は素直（　　）, 大へん気だて
のやさしいむすこです。

He is an obedient, and excessively good-tempered son.

11. 彼は無道徳（　　）, 無信仰だと
　　 いう気がします。

I feel as though he is indifferent
to ideas of morality and faith.

12. 彼はあけっぱなし（　　）, 幼稚
　　 （　　）, 純真です。

He is frank, innocent and naive.

13. 彼は無道徳（　　）, 無信仰（　　）,
　　 獣のような男であるに違いありま
　　 せん。

He must certainly be a person
like a beast with no thought of
morality or faith.

14. この支配人は口不調法（　　）,
　　 言葉を飾る技術を知らない人で
　　 す。

This manager is a poor talker
and completely lacks any artifice
in his speech.

Answers:

　1. 甘ったれで ＞ 甘ったれな (self-indulgent)　自分勝手で ＞ 自分勝手な
(selfish)

　2. こうかつで＞こうかつな (cunning)

　3. 素直で＞素直な (docile)

　4. 純真で＞純真な (simple)　素直で＞素直な (obedient)

　5. 不用意で＞不用意な (reckless)

　6. 正直で＞正直な (honest)

　7. 本能的で＞本能的な (intuitive)

　8. 穏やかで＞穏やかな (mild)

　9. 孤独で ＞ 孤独な (lonely)　敬虔で ＞ 敬虔な (pious)　真剣で ＞ 真剣な
(serious)

10. 素直で＞素直な (obedient)

11. 無道徳で＞無道徳な (immoral)

12. あけっぱなしで＞あけっぱなしな (frank)　幼稚で＞幼稚な (innocent)

13. 無道徳で＞無道徳な (immoral)　無信仰で＞無信仰な (impious)

14. 口不調法で＞口不調法な (not talkative)

第 十八 課 Lesson 18

い (I)-Adjective

Rule

　　い (i)-adjectives end with either of the short vowel い (i) or the long vowel *ii*. This class of adjectives, as in the case of な (na)-adjectives, can be applied in an attributive or a predicative use.

　　The attributive use of い (i)-adjectives is expressed by い (i) or *ii*+a noun.

　　e.g. 彼女は夜明け近くまでかかって，両親に長い手紙を書きました。 (Kanojo wa yoake chikaku made kakatte, ryōshin ni *nagai* tegami o kakimashita)—She wrote and wrote a long letter to her parents until nearly daybreak—長い (nagai), long, in an attributive use modifies the noun 手紙 (tegami), a letter.

　　e.g. この大学生はある女子医科大学の学生に激しい恋心を傾けていきました。(Kono daigakusei wa aru joshi ika daigaku no gakusei ni *hageshii* koi gokoro o katamukete ikimashita)—This university student went on giving his intense, love-filled heart to a student of a women's medical college—激しい (hageshii), intense, ending with the long vowel *ii*, in an attributive use modifies the noun 恋心 (koi gokoro), love-filled heart.

　　Some い (i)-adjectives ending with the long vowel *ii* are as follows: 大きい (ōkii), large or big, 悲しい (kanashii), sad, 美しい (utsukushii), beautiful, かわいい (kawaii), lovely, やさしい (yasashii), gentle and わびしい (wabishii), desolate.

　　When used predicatively, each い (i)-adjective, as it is, relates to the copula (is; am; are).

　　e.g. このたびの汽車の旅は長いです。 (Kono tabi no kisha no tabi wa *nagai desu*)—My journey on the train this time is long—長いです (nagai desu), to be long, is the predicative use of the attributive い (i)-adjective 長い (nagai), long.

　　e.g. 彼の芸術を愛する心は激しいです。 (Kare no geijutsu o aisuru kokoro wa *hageshii desu*)—His art-loving heart is intense—激しいです (hageshii desu), to be intense, is the predicative use of the attributive い (i)-adjective 激しい (hageshii), intense, with the long vowel *ii*.

　　The adverbial form of い (i)-adjectives can be obtained by replacing the final い (i) by く (ku), that is, by substituting く (ku) for the short vowel い (i) or by shortening the long vowel *ii* and adding く (ku).

e.g. 「長くお邪魔して済みません。私はこれで失礼させていただきます。」 ("*Nagaku* ojama shite sumimasen. Watakushi wa kore de shitsurei sasete itadakimasu")—"I'm sorry to bother you so long. I'm afraid I'll have to leave now."—長く (naga*ku*), for a long time, is the adverbial form of the い (i)-adjective 長い (naga*i*), long.

e.g. 教師はこの学生の無責任を激しくしったしました。(Kyōshi wa kono gakusei no musekinin o *hageshiku* shitta shimashita)—The instructor rated this student's irresponsibility intensely—激しく (hageshi*ku*), intensely, is the adverbial form of the い (i)-adjective 激しい (hagesh*ii*), intense, with the long vowel *ii*.

Here, the い (i)-adjectives 長い (nagai), long, ending with the short vowel *i* and 激しい (hageshii), intense, ending with the long vowel *ii*, are taken up as models; each of these adjectives in a predicative use can be conjugated as follows:

i-adjectives		Present/Future	Past	Present/Future Negative	Past Negative
be long	polite form	naga-idesu	naga-katta desu	naga-ku (wa) arimasen	naga-ku (wa) arimasen deshita
	plain form	naga-i	naga-katta	naga-ku (wa) nai	naga-ku (wa) nakatta
be intense	polite form	hagesh-ii desu	hagesh-ikatta desu	hagesh-iku (wa) arimasen	hagesh-iku (wa) arimasen deshita
	plain form	hagesh-ii	hagesh-ikatta	hagesh-iku (wa) nai	hagesh-iku (wa) nakatta

Drill

1.
先日彼は京都で珍しい民芸品を見つけました。
The other day he discovered unfamiliar works of folk art around Kyoto.

この素焼きは外人に珍しいです。
This unglazed pottery is a novelty to foreigners.

その日珍しく元気なにこにこした友人の顔を見て驚きまし
That day he was surprised to see for once a smile on his friend's

た。

私はこんな**忙**しい人に出会っ
たことがありません。

This member of the Socialist
2. この社会党員は日曜日以外は
いつも**忙**しいです。

この医者は**忙**しく自動車に乗
って往診に出ていきます。

face, indicating that he was in
high spirits.

I have never met such a busy
man.

This member of the Socialist
Party is always busy except Sun-
days.

This doctor makes his incessant
professional calls by car.

彼女に**新**しい生活方針が見つ
けられるでしょうか。

3. この四階建ての工場の建物は
新しいです。

「**新**しくお手伝いさんを雇う
と言ってもなかなか見つけられ
ません。どうかうちにいて下さ
い。」

One wonders whether or not she
could find a way by which she
could start to live a new life.

These four-storied factory buildings are new.

"It's not as easy for us to find
a new maid as a replacement for
you as it is to say it. Please do
stay with us."

これは**短**い手記です。
この鉛筆の芯は**短**いです。
4. この小学一年の子供はかばん
と帽子とを持って,「行ってきま
す」と**短**く言ったまま,家を出
ました。

These are short memoirs.
The lead of this pencil is short.
Taking his bag and cap, this
elementary school first grader left
home, calling out briefly, "I'm
going."

Exercise

Fill in the following blanks with "い":

1. 彼は平素礼儀正し（　　）人で
す。

He is by nature a courteous man.

2. 彼はいつも明る（　　）顔をし
ています。

He always wears a bright expression.

3. これは勇まし（　　）愛国の歌
です。

This is a gallant patriotic song.

4. 彼女は服装に似合わず，化粧の濃（　）顔です。

Her face is thickly covered with make-up, unsuited to her dress.

5. 白かばの木の並木に暖か（　）風が揺れています。

A warm wind is swaying the avenue of white birch trees.

6. この共産主義者は警察署で手きびし（　）拷問を受けました。

This communist was subjected to severe torture at the police station.

7. 彼の短（　）口ひげはもうほとんど真白になっています。

His short moustache has changed to almost pure white.

8. あの婦人は貧し（　）服装をしています。

That woman is dressed in tatters.

9. 彼はあまり頼もし（　）男ではありません。

He is not so reliable a person.

10. 青白（　）女の目が怒りに燃えていました。

The eyes of the pale woman were enflamed in anger.

11. 薬剤師は白（　）仕事着をきて，薬局で仕事をしています。

The pharmacist, in a white coat, has attended to the work at the pharmacy.

12. この少年はきたな（　）ノートに何か書いています。

This boy is writing something in a dirty notebook.

13. 薄暗（　）廊下を通って，彼は外務省の渡航課にはいっていきました。

Passing through the dim corridor, he went into the overseas section of the Foreign Office.

14. 私は圧迫された息苦し（　）環境から自由な世界に出たいと思います。

I think I'd like to move out from my oppressed and suffocating circumstances to the free world.

15. 彼は広（　）道を歩いて，皇居のほりに突きあたり，ゆっくりと日比谷の方へ曲がっていきました。

Walking the spacious street, he came to the moat surrounding the Imperial Palace, and then turning towards Hibiya he went slowly on.

16. この体育の教官は丸（　）精力的な顔を真赤にして，学生をにらみ，号令をかけています。

This physical instructor, his round, lively face flushed, stares at the students, giving an order to them.

17. 良（　）むすこを失ったとき
にさえも，継母は愚痴ひとつ言い
ませんでした。

Even at the loss of a good son, the stepmother would not voice a complaint.

18. 外人観光客の一人が銀座に近
（　）しやれた喫茶店にはいって
いきました。

One of the foreign tourists went into a smart tea room near the Ginza.

19. 「それはおかし（　）ね。」と
彼は心配な顔になりました。

"That's strange," he said with a worried look.

20. このお手伝いさんには主人に対
してある鋭（　）反抗の精神が
あります。

This maid has a strong spirit of resistance against her master.

21. この女の外人はきらりと青
（　）目で車内にぶら下がってあ
る横文字の広告を見ていました。

This foreign woman, with her bright blue eyes, was looking at an advertisement in foreign letters posted in the train.

22. われわれ犯罪者には，浮き世の
風は冷た（　）です。

For us criminals the wind of the world is chilly.

Answers:
1. 礼儀正しい (courteous) 2. 明るい (bright) 3. 勇ましい (gallant)
4. 濃い (thick) 5. 暖かい (warm) 6. 手きびしい (severe) 7. 短い
(short) 8. 貧しい (tattered) 9. 頼もしい (reliable) 10. 青白い (pale)
11. 白い (white) 12. きたない (dirty) 13. 薄暗い (dim) 14. 息苦
しい (suffocating) 15. 広い (spacious) 16. 丸い (round) 17. 良い
(good) 18. 近い (near) 19. おかしい (strange) 20. 鋭い (strong)
21. 青い (blue) 22. 冷たい (chilly)

Connective て (te) in the case of い (i)-Adjective

Rule

で (de) or て (te) is the connective ("and" in English) used in a compound sentence. In the case of な (na)-adjectives, the connective particle can always be applied with them as で (de). But, the use of the connective particle て (te) in place of で (de) is of equal availability to each い (i)-adjective. In the case of い (i)-adjective, the final い (i) is dropped or long *ii* shortened, this termination enabling them to suffix く (ku). This く (ku) then relates to the following in the form of く (ku)+て (te).

e.g. 彼は鋭い口舌の徒として，常に頑強な，そして誇り高い態度をしています。(Kare wa *surudoi* kuzetsu no to to shite, tsune ni gankyō na, soshite hokori takai taido o shite imasu)—As a man of sharp words, he always wears a tenacious and unbending attitude—鋭い (surudoi), sharp, is an い (i)-adjective in an attributive use.

e.g. この批評家は彼の作品を鋭く批評しました。(Kono hihyōka wa kare no sakuhin o *surudoku* hihyō shimashita)—This critic commented on his work pointedly—鋭く (surudo-ku), pointedly, is the adverbial form of the い (i)-adjective 鋭い (surudo-i), sharp.

e.g. 言葉の一つ一つが鋭くて，彼の頭の働き方がさえています。(Kotoba no hitotsu hitotsu ga *surudoku te*, kare no atama no hataraki kata ga saete imasu)—Each of his words is so piercing, he obviously has a good mind—鋭くて (surudoku te), piercing and..., is the connective derived from the adverbial form of 鋭く (surudo-ku), sharply, from 鋭い (surudo-i), sharp.

e.g. 婚約を許されない孤独のままで家出する自分の姿を考えると，彼は美しい悲劇を見るような気がしました。(Konyaku o yurusarenai kodoku no mama de ie de suru jibun no sugata o kangaeru to, kare wa *utsukushii* higeki o miru yō na ki ga shimashita)—Picturing himself as running away from home, forced into loneliness because his engagement was forbidden, he felt as though he were experiencing a great tragedy—美しい (utsukushii), beautiful, is an い (i)-adjective with the long vowel *ii* in an attributive use.

e.g. きょうは美しく晴れた秋日和です。(Kyō wa *utsukushiku* hareta aki biyori desu)—Today is a delightfully clear autumn day—美し

く (utsukush-iku), beautifully, is the adverbial form of the い (i)-adjective 美しい (utsukush-ii), beautiful.

e.g. 彼女は美しくて, 若々しくて, 元気です。(Kanojo wa *utsukushiku te*, waka waka shiku te, genki desu)—She is beautiful, young and active—美しくて (utsukushiku te), beautiful and..., is the connective derived from the adverbial form of 美しく (utsukush-iku), beautifully, from 美しい (utsukush-ii), beautiful.

The negative form of the predicative use of い (i)-adjectives can always be obtained by changing the final vowel い (i) of the plain present/future form to く (ku) and adding ない (nai), as 鋭くない (surudo-ku nai), to not be sharp, from 鋭い (surudo-i), sharp. ない (nai) being an adjective, its final vowel い (i) may also be changed to く (ku) and relate to the following through て (te), as 鋭くなくて (surudo-ku na *ku* te), to not be sharp but...from 鋭くない (surudo-ku na*i*), to not be sharp.

e.g. 彼女は鋭くなくて, 鈍感です。(Kanojo wa *surudoku naku te*, donkan desu)—She is not sharp but dull-witted.

e.g. 彼女は美しくなくて, みにくいです。(Kanojo wa *utsukushiku naku te*, minikui desu)—She is not beautiful but ugly.

On the other hand, we may also say, 鋭くはなくて (surudoku *wa* naku te) and 美しくはなくて (utsukushiku *wa* naku te)—these expressions are more emphatic and descriptive than 鋭くなくて (surudoku naku te) and 美しくなくて (utsukushiku naku te).

The noun form with さ (sa) found in な (na)-adjectives can also be derived for almost all い (i)-adjectives. The final い (i) and *ii* of the true function of this class of adjectives is replaced by さ (sa), permitting the formation of the noun forms.

e.g. 彼はどこまでも古風なものを好みます。近代的流行というものにあくまでも反抗して, 古めかしいものの美しさを愛する人です。(Kare wa doko made mo kofū na mono o konomimasu. Kindai teki ryūkō to iu mono ni akumade mo hankō shite, furu mekashii mono no *utsukushi sa* o ai suru hito desu)—In everything his taste is for the old style. He persistently resists what may be called "the latest fashion", and is a man who loves the beauty found among traditional things)—美しさ (utsukushi sa), beauty, is the noun form derived from the い (i)-adjective 美しい (utsukush-ii), beautiful.

Note: The words "large" (big) and "small" (little) in English are equally applied as both な (na)- and い (i)-adjectives in Japanese. The word "large" is rendered as 大きな (ōki na) and 大きい (ōk-ii) and the word "small" as 小さな (chiisa na) and 小さい (chiisa-i). The expressions 大

きな (ōki na) and 小さな (chiisa na) cannot be applied in a predicative use. Their adverbial forms are 大きく (ōk-iku) and 小さく (chiisa-ku) and, in addition, their connective forms are 大きくて (ōkiku te) and 小さくて (chiisaku te).

Drill

1. 秋だが, まだむし暑くて, ことに今日の日中の暑さは, 土用より暑いくらいです。

It is autumn, but still the weather is sultry; and particularly this day the heat is stronger than it is in midsummer.

2. 家がおもしろくなくて, 彼は毎日飛び出して, 遊びを求めています。

He can't find much enjoyment at home, so he goes out every day, looking for some pleasures.

3. 父親が前科者になったのは, 高利貸しにだまされたが, 貧しくて弁護士を雇えなかったためでした。

His father's having a criminal record was owing to the fact that he was deceived by a money lender and in his poverty he had no means for hiring a lawyer.

4. ふと彼女の横顔を見ると, 鼻筋がすっきりとしていて, まゆ毛が美しくて, 良家の子女らしい上品さを私は感じます。

With an unintentional glance at her profile, I discern refinement in her sharply outlined nose and shapely eyebrows, indicating she is the daughter of a good family.

5. 私のおばはもう四十を幾つか過ぎているが, 若い娘のように明るくて, もうおしろい気もほとんどないが, どこかあかぬけしていて美しく, 四・五年前と少しも変わっていません。

My aunt is now more than forty-years of age, but she is bright like a young girl and wears almost no face powder; she looks somehow naturally refined, quite as beautiful as she was several years ago

Exercise

Fill in the following blanks with the connective "て":

1. 彼女は顔色も青白く (　　), すぐれず, 全体薄よごれています。

She is of a pale and unhealthy complexion, and also her whole appearance is shabby.

2. 彼女は首筋のうぶ毛も柔らかく
（　　）, 肩の線もなめらかです。

The downy hair around her neck is soft and the line of her shoulder is smooth.

3. 「あれから寂しく（　　）, 悲しく（　　）, ごはんものどへ通りません。」

"I've felt lonely and sorrowful since then; and I can't eat."

4. この流行歌のメロディーは物悲しく（　　）, 彼はほのかな郷愁をおぼえます。

The melody of this popular song sounds doleful; and in this he can find comfort, yearning after his native home.

5. 電話の声は遠かったが, 恋人だとすぐわかり, なつかしく（　　）, 気が遠くなり, 彼は甘くしびれてしまいました。

The voice on the telephone was very distant, but he knew it to be his sweetheart's voice; and he swooned away with longing, almost losing his senses.

Answers:
1. 青白くて＞青白い (pale)
2. 柔らかくて＞柔らかい (soft)
3. 寂しくて＞寂しい (lonely)　悲しくて＞悲しい (sorrowful)
4. 物悲しくて＞物悲しい (doleful)
5. なつかしくて＞なつかしい (longing)

第 二十 課　Lesson 20

Direct and Indirect Objects

Rule

A (a person) は B (someone) に　　A does *B C* or: A does *C* to *B*.
C (something) をします。(A wa
B *ni* C *o* shimasu).
or: A は C を B にします。(A wa
C *o* B *ni* shimasu).

If two objective cases are found in one sentence, one object carries the function of "direct object"; that is, it requires the particle を (o) and is used for denoting an inanimate object in the sentence. And the other object carries the function of "indirect object"; that is, it refers to an animate object and is applied in the sentence with the particle に (ni).

　　e.g.　中小企業者団体の代表が国会へ行き，総理に面会を求めました。
　　(Chūshō kigyōsha dantai no daihyō ga kokkai e iki, sōri *ni* menkai *o* motomemashita)—Representatives from a group of medium and small entrepreneurs went to the National Diet and requested an interview with the Prime Minister—総理 (sōri), the prime minister, is a person, commonly leading to the use of the particle に (ni) as the indirect object; and 面会 (menkai), an interview, is an inanimate noun, generally permitting the use of the particle を (o) as the direct object. Generally the common order in this pattern places the indirect object first and then the direct object appears. On the other hand, we may say, 面会を総理に (menkai *o* sōri *ni*), an interview with the Prime Minister.

　　e.g.　この母は子供に乳を飲ませながら，悠然とこたつに寝そべっています。(Kono haha wa kodomo *ni* chichi *o* nomase nagara, yūzen to kotatsu ni nesobette imasu)—This mother is composedly lying beside a foot-warmer, breast feeding the baby—子供 (kodomo), the baby, is the indirect object and 乳 (chichi), breast milk, is the direct object. On the other hand, we may say, 乳を子供に (chichi *o* kodomo *ni*).

In almost all cases when two objects indicating a person and a thing are explicitly evidenced in the sentence, the use of the particles ~に (ni) ~を (o) or ~を (o) ~に (ni) should actually be intended in it.

But, the syntax of some sentences includes the objective particle and a certain place—in this case, the object, irrespective of being a human being, requires the particle を (o), while the place employs the particle に (ni) or へ (e). The difference of functions between に (ni) and へ (e) indicating a place is as follows: に (ni) is used as a shifter in the sense of "a fixed position with the implications of the process of shift"; and へ (e) is used as a shifter in the sense of "a direction of movement".

e.g. 明晩私はあなたを歌舞伎にお誘いします。(Myōban watakushi wa anata *o* Kabuki *ni* osasoi shimasu)—Tomorrow night I'll invite you to enjoy Kabuki, our ancient drama)—を (o) in あなたを (anata o), you, shows the other party or the object and に (ni) in 歌舞伎に (Kabuki ni), to enjoy Kabuki, shows a spatial point of arrival. On the other hand, we may say, 明晩私はあなたを歌舞伎へお誘いします。(Myōban watakushi wa anata *o* Kabuki *e* osasoi shimasu) —Tomorrow night I'll invite you to enjoy Kabuki, our ancient drama—あなたを (anata o), you, shows the other party or the object and 歌舞伎へ (Kabuki e), to enjoy Kabuki, shows a direction.

Note: The particle に (ni) or へ (e) indicating a place can be used rather freely without any strict direction.

e.g. このいなか娘はショー・ウィンドーに映る自分の姿を珍しそうにながめていました。(Kono inaka musume wa shōuindō *ni* utsuru jibun no sugata *o* mezurashi sō ni nagamete imashita)—This country-girl gazed in wonder at her figure reflecting from a show window —in this case the rewriting of ショー・ウィンドーへ (shōuindō e), a show window, in place of ショー・ウィンドーに (shōuindō ni), is found to be unsuitable—this is because the particle に (ni) in this sentence refers to a fixed position far from the distinct sense of a direction of movement.

e.g. 彼女は湖へ行き，湖面の結氷の下に身を沈めようと思いました。(Kanojo wa mizu umi e iki, komen no keppyō no shita *ni* mi *o* shizume yō to omoimashita)—She thought she would go to a lake and let herself sink under the iced over surface—に (ni) in 結氷の下に (keppyō no shita ni), under the iced over surface, is used in the sense of "a shift referring to a location". を (o) in 身を (mi o), oneself, indicates the object.

e.g. 私の友だちの田中さんをあなたにご紹介いたします。(Watakushi no tomodachi no Tanaka-san *o* anata *ni* goshōkai itashimasu)— Allow me to introduce my friend Mr. Tanaka to you—in this case where both objects, 田中さんを (Tanaka-san o), Mr. Tanaka and あなたに (anata ni), you, are animate, the one is followed by the particle を (o) and the other by に (ni)—the verb 紹介する (shō-kai suru), to introduce, in this sentence suggests and implies the process of shift whereby two unsituated men are lined up with each other. And thus, に (ni) in あなたに (anata ni), you, is used in the sense of a fixed position in this shift. Therefore, even in such a case as this, the use of the particle に (ni) still should actually be intended as a place or a position, while the particle を (o) in 田中さんを (Tanaka-san o), Mr. Tanaka, refers to the direct object.

e.g. そのくつ下を箱に入れてください。(Sono kutsu shita o hako *ni* irete kudasai)—Put the socks into a box—in this case where both objects そのくつ下を (sono kutsu shita *o*), the socks and 箱に (hako *ni*), a box, are inanimate, one object requires the particle を (o) and the other, indicating a place or a fixed position which is used as a shifter, is applied in the sentence with the particle に (ni).

Drill

1. 母は孫を腕に抱いてすわっています。

A mother sits down, holding her grandchild in her arms.

2. 彼女は片手にかばんを持ち，片手に子供の手を取って歩いていきます。

She walks on, holding her bag in one hand and taking the child in her other.

3. この炭焼きは兵隊ズボンにジャケツを着て，両手にまきの束をかかえています。

This charcoal maker, in army trousers and jacket, is holding fagots in both hands.

4. 彼は彼女を映画やレビューに誘ったりしていました。

He would invite her to see a film or revue.

5. 「私は若い時分の失敗をもう一度あなたにさせたくないからお話しているのです。」

"What I'm saying is that I never would want you to fail the same way I did in my younger days."

6. 彼女はまんじりともせず，腹ばいになって，まくらを胸に当てていました。夜が白みだしてきました。

She was wakeful all night, lying on her stomach with her pillow to her breast. The night began to turn to dawn.

7. 囚人護送自動車は不透明なガラスに外界の視線を避けて，裁判所を出発しました。

A patrol wagon for convicts, its opaque glass concealing its interior from the eyes of the outside world, drove away from the court.

8. 父は橋本の一族だけを重役にするという，いわば大家族主義でいきたいらしいが，私はそんなのは封建的だと思います。

Note: This に is the objective complement.

It seems to me that my father intends only members of the Hashimoto family to be directors; that is to say, it is his ambition to become principal of a great combine. I consider his idea to be quite feudal.

9. あのころ，彼女は弁護士になりたいと言って，講義録を読んでいた彼に，女学校仕込みの英語の発音を教えてやっていました。

During those days, as he read a correspondence text-book with the intention of becoming a lawyer, she would teach him English pronunciation which she had practiced in a girls' school.

10. このおじの頭に浮かんだのは，美しい孫娘を山本家の次男坊と縁組させることでした。それにはまず，当の次男坊から攻め落とすのが一番良いと思い，内々写真を彼に見せると，もう彼はころりとまいってしまいました。

It occurred to this uncle that his beautiful granddaughter and the second son of the Yamamoto family were a good match for one another. For this match, the uncle thought it best to do all he could to win over the son in question. The uncle had, on a previous occasion, shown him a photograph of his granddaughter, by which he was quite captivated.

Exercise

Fill in the following blanks with the particles "に" and "を":

1. 「あなた（　　）お手数（　　）おかけして済みません。」

"I'm sorry to have caused you trouble."

2. 私は確かに彼女（　　）愛情（　　）

It was true that I felt affection

感じておりました。

3. 「学生ストライキの首謀者（　　），
寛大な処分（　　）お願いいたし
ます。」

"I sincerely implore you to treat the ring leader of those students on strike with generosity."

4. 彼はおもむろにテーブル（　　）
ひじ（　　）つきました。

He slowly rested his elbows upon the table.

5. 彼が私の友人であること（　　），
今日まで妻（　　）知らせておき
ませんでした。

Up to now I have not told my wife that he was one of my friends.

6. 私はこの混血児（　　）生涯の
幸福（　　）保証し，平和（　　）
与えたいと思います。

I think I would like to guarantee the happiness of this half-breed child's lifetime and give peace to him.

7. 彼女は美貌で，才知があり，教
養もある女なので，彼は思わず彼
女（　　）親切（　　）示し過ぎた
かも知れません。

He may have unwittingly shown excessive kindness to her because she is a beautiful, talented, and educated woman.

8. 彼は自分の心情（　　）両親（　　）
公開することに，一種堪えられな
い気がしました。

He felt it somewhat unbearable that he was going to expose his emotions so vividly to his parents.

9. この教師はこんこんとひねくれ
た学生（　　）説諭（　　）加え，
考えの間違いを指摘して，改心を
求めました。

This instructor sincerely advised the perverse student, and pointed out the error in his thought in the hope that he would mend his ways.

10. 子供連れの友だち夫妻があまり
部屋代をためたので，アパートを
追い出され，私の宅にやってきま
した。私は別室（　　）夫妻とそ
の子供（　　）泊めてやりました。

My friend and his wife and child were driven out of their apartment because of quite a bit of back rent due and they came to my house. I put them and their child up for the night in a separate room.

Answers:
1. に，を 2. に，を 3. に，を 4. に，を 5. を，に 6. に，を，
を 7. に，を 8. を，に 9. に，を 10. に，を

Complement

Rule

A (subject) が B (direct object) 　　A *makes B C.*
を C (complement) にします。(A
ga B *o* C *ni shimasu*).

In this pattern が (ga) and not は (wa) is generally used—in this syntax the use of the particle が (ga) is more reasonable because が (ga) has a function somewhat similar to that of identification, and is always used with the subject which is to be identified with the facts or occurrences described in the predicate. In other words, the particle が (ga) is used in situational expressions in which one intends to identify a matter or event he is informed of with a particular subject.

> e.g.　絶望がかえって彼女の気持ちを安らかにしました。(Zetsubō *ga* kaette kanojo no kimochi *o* yasuraka *ni shimashita*)—Thoughts of despair somehow pacified her—が (ga) in 絶望が (zetsubō ga), despair, denotes the nominative case, を (o) in 彼女の気持ちを (kanojo no kimochi o), her mood, is the direct object and に (ni) in 安らかに (yasuraka ni), to be easy of mind, serves as a complement in this syntax; that is, に (ni) is used as a modifier in the sense of a complement for B (kanojo no kimochi o), her mood.

The construction ～を (o), direct object, ～に (ni), complement, in such a sentence as this can all be converted into the syntax ～は (wa) ～に (ni) or ～と (to) なります (narimasu), to become; and thus, the expression 彼女の気持ちを安らかにしました。(Kanojo no kimochi *o* yasuraka *ni shimashita*) can also be written as 彼女の気持ちは安らかになりました。(Kanojo no kimochi *wa* yasuraka *ni narimashita*) or 彼女の気持ちは安らかとなりました。(Kanojo no kimochi *wa* yasuraka *to narimashita*), She became easy of mind. Now in this pattern は (wa) and not が (ga) is used as the nominative case, as 彼女の気持ちは (kanojo no kimochi *wa*), her mood,—in this syntax the use of は (wa) places emphasis on self-speciality; that is, this は (wa) implies that consciousness which emphasizes the difference between self and others. Moreover, the difference between ～になります (...*ni narimasu*) and ～となります (...*to narimasu*), to become..., found in this expression is as follows: に (ni) is used in the sense of fixing a position through a shift, while と (to) of a result brought about by something or some action. Also, the expression ～は (wa) ～に (ni) or ～と (to) なります (narimasu), to become..., can be revised into the syntax using a copula as seen in 彼女の気持ちは安らかです。(Kanojo no kimochi *wa* yasuraka *desu*), She is at ease.

  e.g. 日ごろの父への不満が彼を反抗的にしました。(Higoro no chichi e no fuman *ga* kare *o* hankō teki *ni shimashita*)—His habitual dissatisfaction towards his father dragged him into a state of rebellion.

  The construction 彼を反抗的にしました。(kare *o* hankō teki *ni shimashita*) can be converted into the syntax 彼は反抗的になりました。(Kare *wa* hankō teki *ni narimashita*), He became rebellious, and then revised into the syntax 彼は反抗的です。(Kare *wa* hankō teki *desu*), He is rebellious.

Drill

1. あきらめが彼女の感情を鈍感に
   しました。

   Thoughts of abandonment came to blunt her emotions.

   彼女の感情を鈍感にしました。→ {
   彼女の感情は鈍感になりました。(Her emotions became blunt.)
   彼女の感情は鈍感です。(Her emotions are blunt.)

2. 彼の生命の本質的な要求が、彼
   を自由主義者にしました。

   The essential demands of his life encouraged him to be a liberalist.

   彼を自由主義者にしました。→ {
   彼は自由主義者になりました。(He became a liberalist.)
   彼は自由主義者です。(He is a liberalist.)

3. 英国留学が、彼をユーモアを楽
   しむたちの紳士にしました。

   His study in England made him a gentleman with a nature that enjoyed humor.

彼をユーモアを楽しむたちの
紳士にしました。 → {
彼はユーモアを楽しむたちの紳士
になりました。(He became a gen-
tleman with a nature that enjoyed
humor.)

彼はユーモアを楽しむたちの紳士
です。(He is a gentleman with
a nature that enjoys humor.)
}

Exercise

Fill in the following blanks with "が" "を" and "に"; and also revise them, using the syntax ～は～になります and ～は～です。

1. 衆愚政治（　　）彼（　　）孤独 な自由主義者（　　）しました。

   Mob administration led him to be a solitary liberalist.

2. この男のわがままや一時の感情 （　　）一人の女性（　　）不幸 （　　）しました。

   This man's selfishness and his momentary emotion brought un-happiness to a woman.

3. 愛する二人だけの堅い約束（　 ），二人の将来（　　）悲運（　 ）しました。

   A firm promise between the two lovers affected the future ill-luck of the two.

4. 愛する二人だけの堅い約束のひ そかな勝利（　　），彼（　　）有 頂天（　　）しました。

   The secret victory of a firm promise between the two lovers intoxicated him.

Answers:

1. が，を，に　彼は孤独な自由主義者になりました。彼は孤独な自由 主義者です。

2. が，を，に　一人の女性は不幸になりました。一人の女性は不幸で す。

3. が，を，に　二人の将来は悲運になりました。二人の将来は悲運で す。

4. が，を，に　彼は有頂天になりました。彼は有頂天です。

第 二十二 課　Lesson 22

The Syntax "to become"

Rule

A (subject) は B (a noun) に　　　A *becomes* B (a noun).
なります。(A *wa* B *ni narimasu*).

A (subject) は B (*na*-adj.) に　　A *becomes* B (*na*-adj.).
なります。(A *wa* B *ni narimasu*).

A (subject) は B (*i*-adj.) く な　　A *becomes* B (*i*-adj.).
ります。(A *wa* B *ku narimasu*).

In this pattern は (wa) and not が (ga) is used as the nominative case (the theme)—in this syntax the use of は (wa) is more reasonable because は (wa) places emphasis on self-speciality; that is, this は (wa) implies that consciousness which emphasizes the difference between self and others. And the predicate of this sentence will be an explanation giving new information about the particular noun or pronoun presented as the theme or topic.

e.g. 彼は自分で私の保証人に なりました。(Kare *wa* jibun de watakushi no hoshōnin *ni narimashita*)—He offered himself as my guarantor—保証人 (hoshōnin), a guarantor, is a noun and に (ni) in になりました (ni narimashita), became, is used in the sense of fixing a position in both space and time; that is, this に (ni) is used from such a point of view as to fix a position through shifting.

In the case of な (na)-adjectives, the noun form of this class of adjectives can be induced by omitting the な (na) of its true function. This noun+になります (ni narimasu), to become.

e.g. 彼女はまた孤独に なりました。(Kanojo *wa* mata kodoku *ni narimashita*)—She again became lonely—孤独 (kodoku), loneliness, is the noun form derived from the な (na)-adjective 孤独な (kodoku na), lonely, in an attributive use.

In the case of い (i)-adjectives, the final い (i) or *ii* is dropped, this termination enabling them to suffix く (ku). This く (ku) relates to なります (narimasu), to become.

e.g. 彼女は心弱く なりました。(Kanojo *wa* kokoro yowa*ku narimashita*)—Her mind grew weak—弱く (yowa*ku*), weakly, is the adverbial form of the い (i)-adjective 弱い (yowai), weak.

The verb なる (nar-u), to become, in the category of the consonant stem verb, undergoes a euphonic change of assimilation—this connective form is なって (nat-te), to become and...from the plain past なった (nat-ta), became or なり (nar-i) from the polite present/future なります (nar-imasu).

In the case of both nouns and noun forms from な (na)-adjectives, they always relate to the following in the form of ～になって (...ni natte) or ～になり (...ni nari).

e.g. 彼は私の保証人になって (or になり), いろいろ面倒をみてくださいました。(Kare wa watakushi no hoshōnin ni natte [or ni nari], iro iro mendō o mite kudasaimashita)—He became my guarantor and kindly looked after me in many ways—保証人 (hoshōnin), a guarantor, is a noun.

e.g. 彼女は孤独になって (or になり), 考え込みました。(Kanojo wa kodoku ni natte [or ni nari], kangae komimashita)—She became lonely, lost in thought—孤独 (kodoku), loneliness, is the noun form of the な (na)-adjective 孤独な (kodoku na), lonely.

Also, in the case of い (i)-adjectives, the connective always relates to the following in the form of く なって (ku natte) or く なり (ku nari).

e.g. 彼女は心弱く なって (or く なり), 涙が流れました。(Kanojo wa kokoro yowaku natte [or ku nari], namida ga nagaremashita)—Her heart grew weak and tears flowed from her eyes.

The negative connective is as follows:

e.g. 彼自身私の保証人に (は) ならなくて (or に [は] ならないで), 彼の身内の方がなってくださいました。(Kare jishin watakushi no hoshōnin ni [wa] naranaku te [or ni (wa) naranai de], kare no miuchi no kata ga natte kudasaimashita)—He himself did not become my guarantor but one of his relatives acted for me.

e.g. 彼女は孤独に (は) ならなくて, (or に [は] ならないで), 生気を取りもどしました。(Kanojo wa kodoku ni [wa] naranaku te [or ni (wa) naranai de], seiki o torimodoshimashita)—She did not become lonely but regained animation.

e.g. 彼女は心弱く (は) ならなくて, (or く [は] ならないで), 活気づいてきました。(Kanojo wa kokoro yowaku [wa] naranaku te [or ku (wa) naranai de], kakki zuite kimashita)—Her heart did not grow weak but became spirited.

Drill

1. 彼女は幸福に なりました。　　　　She became happy.

2. 何もかも無駄に なりました。 　　It was all in vain.

3. この子は少しかれた声に なりま
 した。 　　This child's voice became a little
 hoarse.

4. 彼女は大へん悪い女に なりまし
 た。 　　She became a very bad woman.

5. 何も思い過ごすことなんか無く
 なりました。 　　I had nothing more to worry
 about.

6. あなたは私には関係の無い人に
 なりました。 　　You became indifferent to me.

7. 彼女の顔の表情は以前よりも柔
 らかく なりました。 　　The expression on her face became more softened.

8. 私の目から見ると，あなたは寂
 しい方に なりました。 　　In my eyes, you became a lonely
 person.

9. 私は心の中をすっかり冷たい水
 で洗ったような気持ちに なりまし
 た。 　　I felt refreshed, as if I had my
 heart washed clean with cold
 water.

10. 近づくことのできなくなったあ
 なたの面影を私はなつかしく なり
 ます。 　　I will yearn after your figure
 which I've become unable to approach.

11. 一度生活を踏みはずしたあとは，
 生きて行くことが困難に なりまし
 た。 　　After once having made a false
 step in life, I found it hard to
 make a living.

Exercise

Fill in the following blanks with "に", "く", and "なり":

1. 八時（　　）なりました。 　　The clock struck eight.

2. 彼は困ったこと（　　）なりまし
 た。 　　He had a problem.

3. 彼は働く気（　　）なりました。 　　He had the intention to work.

4. この女性は美容師（　　）なりま
 した。 　　This woman became a beautician.

5. 床をのべてもらって，彼は横
 （　　）なりました。 　　After he had a bed prepared, he
 lay down.

6. 彼女は自分の運命がわびし（ 　　She felt wretched for her destiny.

）なりました。

7. 旧師の忠告に従って，彼はきら
っていた務めをもする気（　）な
りました。

Heeding his former teacher's admonition, he became willing to work, which he had previously refused to do.

8. 一昨日の夜六時ごろから娘はぷ
いといな（　）なりました。

The daughter suddenly disappeared about six o'clock the night before last.

9. 彼女は安らかな気持ちに（　），
ゆっくりと昼近くまで眠りました。

She was relieved, and slept leisurely until nearly noon.

10. この会社は昔よりももっと景気
がよく（　），事務室も一室だけ
ひろ（　）なっていました。

This company became much more prosperous than in former days. One more room had been added to the offices.

11. 彼は一等車の窓から暮れていく
早春の郊外風景をながめました。
だんだんと家の数が少なく（　），
点々とした村の家々にひがつきは
じめていました。

Through the windows in the first class car, he gazed at the suburban scenery of the early spring as dusk neared. The number of homes in sight gradually became fewer and in the houses in the villages lights began to shine here and there.

Answers:

1. に 2. に 3. に 4. に 5. に 6. く 7. に 8. く 9. なり
10. なり，く 11. なり

第 二十三 課　Lesson 23

The Conjectural Form (1)

Rule

The conjectural form is used when the speaker relates in conjecture the state or condition of an object which is obscure. The expression だろう (darō), plain form, or でしょう (deshō), polite form, is used to indicate the conjectural form. This でしょう (deshō) is related to verbs, nouns, and adjectives quite freely.

In the case of verbs, でしょう (deshō) is put after the plain present/future form of any verb.

e.g. 彼はあなたのご希望に添うような方針を立てるでしょう。(Kare wa anata no gokibō ni sou yō na hōshin o tateru *deshō*)—He'll form a policy in accordance with your wishes—方針を立てる (hōshin o tate-ru) means "to form a policy".

e.g. 彼女は生物を食べないでしょう。(Kanojo wa nama mono o tabe-nai *deshō*)—She will not eat uncooked food—食べない (tabe-nai), to not eat, is a verb in the plain present/future negative form.

e.g. 彼女のご主人は遠からずなくなるでしょう。(Kanojo no goshujin wa tōkarazu nakunaru *deshō*)—Her husband would soon die—なくなる (nakunar-u) means "to die".

e.g. 彼はあなたの忠告を聞かないでしょう。(Kare wa anata no chūko-ku o kikanai *deshō*)—He'll not listen to your advice—聞かない (kik-anai), to not listen to, is a verb in the plain present/future negative form.

In the case of nouns, each noun, as it is, relates to だろう (darō), plain form, or でしょう (deshō), polite form.

e.g. 彼は運転手でしょう。(Kare wa untenshu *deshō*)—He will be a driver—運転手 (untenshu), a driver, is a noun.

e.g. 彼は軍人ではないでしょう。(Kare wa gunjin dewa nai *deshō*)—He will not be a military man—軍人 (gunjin), a military man, is a noun.

The form of conjecture of な (na)-adjectives can always be obtained by dropping な (na) and adding the termination だろう (darō), plain form, or でしょう (deshō), polite form. When the final な (na) is dropped, the noun form is obtained, which, placed before だろう (darō) or でしょう (deshō), provides its form of conjecture.

e.g. 早く見切りをつける方が利口でしょう。(Hayaku mikiri o tsukeru hō ga rikō *deshō*)—You'd be smart to give up this matter soon—利口 (rikō), cleverness, is the noun form of the な (na)-adjective 利口な (rikō na), clever.

e.g. 彼女は勤勉ではないでしょう。(Kanojo wa kinben dewa nai *deshō*) —She will not be diligent—勤勉 (kinben), diligence, is the noun form of the な (na)-adjective 勤勉な (kinben na), diligent.

In the case of the formation of conjecture of い (i)-adjectives, each い (i)-adjective, as it is, relates to だろう (darō), plain form, or でしょう (deshō), polite form. い (i)-adjectives end with either the short vowel い (i) or the long vowel *ii*.

e.g. きょうは二日酔いで苦しいでしょう。(Kyō wa futsuka yoi de kurushii *deshō*)—Today you'll suffer a hang-over)—苦しい (kurushii), to feel oppressed, is an い (i)-adjective ending with a long vowel.

e.g. 彼女は若くないでしょう。(Kanojo wa wakaku nai *deshō*)—She will not be young—若くない (wakaku nai), to not be young, comes from the い (i)-adjective 若い (wakai), young.

The form of conjecture in the case of verbs in a compound sentence is expressed by the plain present/future form of any verb+だろう (darō) or でしょう (deshō); and し (shi) as its connective particle is put after だろう (darō) or でしょう (deshō). In the normal polite style, the ending of a sentence employs the polite form whereas all other verbs, adjectives, and copulas within the sentence are in the plain form. Therefore, the use of だろう (darō) is quite common in this compound sentence.

e.g. 彼女は板ばさみになって困るだろうし，親戚づきあいも気づまりになるでしょう。(Kanojo wa itabasami ni natte komaru *darō shi*, shinseki zukiai mo kizumari ni naru deshō)—She would be in a dilemma with worry, and also associations with her relatives would possibly be awkward—困るだろうし (komaru darō shi) means "will be in a dilemma and..."

e.g. 彼は酒も飲まないだろうし，かけごとにも興味がないらしいです。(Kare wa *sake* mo nomanai *darō shi*, kakegoto ni mo kyōmi ga nai rashii desu)—He will not drink *sake*, and also will probably have no interest in gambling—飲まないだろうし (nomanai darō shi) means "will not drink and..."

In the case of the irregular verbs する (suru), to do and 来る (kuru), to come, the conjectural expression will be するだろう (suru darō), and するでしょう (suru deshō); 来るだろう (kuru darō) and 来るでしょ

う (kuru deshō) as in the following:

e.g. この少年はどんな仕事でも喜んでするでしょう。(Kono shōnen wa don na shigoto de mo yorokon de *suru deshō*)—This boy will willingly do any kind of work.

e.g. 彼はこのようなつまらない仕事をしないでしょう。(Kare wa kono yō na tsumaranai shigoto o *shinai deshō*)—He will not do such an odd job as this.

e.g. この学生は勉強もよくするだろうし，運動も達者らしいです。(Kono gakusei wa benkyō mo yoku *suru darō shi*, undō mo tassha rashii desu)—This student will study hard, and also will perhaps be good at sports.

e.g. この生徒は勉強もしないだろうし，両親のお使いもしないようです。(Kono seito wa benkyō mo *shinai darō shi*, ryōshin no otsukai mo shinai yō desu)—This pupil will not study, and also will not likely go on errands for his parents.

e.g. アメリカにいる叔父は桜の咲く季節に日本へ来るでしょう。(Amerika ni iru oji wa sakura no saku kisetsu ni Nihon e *kuru deshō*)—My uncle in America will come to Japan at the cherry-blossom season.

e.g. 今年友だちは日光見物に来ないでしょう。(Kotoshi tomodachi wa Nikkō kenbutsu ni *konai deshō*)—This year my friend will not come to Nikko for sightseeing.

e.g. 遠からず弟は実家へも来るだろうし，私の方へも来るはずです。(Tōkarazu, otōto wa jikka e mo *kuru darō shi*, watakushi no hō e mo kuru hazu desu)—Before long my younger brother will go to our parents' house, and also will come to my house.

e.g. 彼女は東京にも来ないだろうし，私の所にも顔を出さないでしょう。(Kanojo wa Tōkyō ni mo *konai darō shi*, watakushi no tokoro ni mo kao o dasanai deshō)—She will not come to Tokyo, and also will make no appearance at my house.

Drill

1. 明日らんが咲くでしょう。　　　　Tomorrow orchids will bloom.

2. 何かの間違いでしょう。　　　　　There could be some mistake.

3. 間違いないでしょう。　　　　　　There can't be any mistake.

4. 「南方へいらっしゃるんでしょう。」　"You'll be going South, won't you?"

5. だれが責任をもってくれるでしょうか。　Who would willingly be responsible for this?

6. 反抗すれば，左翼だというでしょう。

If they protest, they would surely be called leftwing.

7. すぐに答えるのが恥ずかしいのでしょう。

She might be ashamed of too prompt a reply.

* のでしょう (no deshō) is more emphatic and descriptive than でしょう (deshō).

8. 「私は明日から東芝の会社の顧問になるんだ。愉快でしょう。」

"I'll be an adviser to the Toshiba Company from tomorrow. It will be interesting, won't it?"

9. 彼の活躍すべき時代は生涯に二度と来ないでしょう。

The time would not come again in his lifetime when he would play an active role.

10. 進歩のかわりに後退が来ないだろうか，科学の代わりに破滅が来ないでしょうか。

One wonders whether retreat would not come instead of progress; wonders whether ruin would come to take the place of science!

11. 日がたつにつれて，私の言葉の意味も理解されるだろうし，自分の軽率をも自覚するに違いありません。

As the days pass, he will come to understand the significance of my words and will even be made conscious of his own rashness.

Exercise

Fill in each bracket with the conjectural form でしょう:

1. 多分そう（　　）。

Probably you're right.

2. しかられたの（　　）。

You were scolded, weren't you?

3. 何を言うことがある（　　）。

What could be said.

4. 私には何もできない（　　）。

There would be nothing more I could do.

5. みんな反戦論者になる（　　）。

Everybody would become anti-war advocates.

6. この国は独立運動を起こす（　　）。

This country would make a move for independence.

7. 今ごろは多分彼は名古屋に行ってる（　　）。

Now he has probably gone to Nagoya.

8. 彼女はまだ帰ってないんです。 どうしたん（　　）。

She is not back yet. I wonder what has happened to her.

9. 彼は社会主義者になってしまう（　　）。

He would become a socialist.

10. 無事では済まない（　　）。いずれ身辺に危険がある（　　）。

You can't escape trouble. You'll be in personal danger.

11. 町民は町長に恨みを持っているし，彼の圧制を憎んでいるから，一斉にほうきする（　　）。

Since the townspeople hold a grudge against the town headman, and they detest his oppression, they would simultaneously rise in revolt.

第 二十四 課 Lesson 24

The Conjectural (Appearance) Form (2)

Rule

In the case of verbs, the expression らしいです (rashii desu) or よ
うです (yō desu), to seem, is put after the plain present/future form
of any verb. Now, the expression らしいです (rashii desu) or ようで
す (yō desu) is in a shift, permitting itself to be used as the auxiliary
showing conjecture.

- e.g. 雨が降るらしいです (or ようです)。(Ame ga furu *rashii desu*
  [or: *yō desu*])—It seems likely to rain—降る (fur-u) means "to rain".
- e.g. 彼は九州へ出かけないらしいです (or ようです)。(Kare wa Kyū-
  shū e dekake nai *rashii desu* [or: *yō desu*])—He seems not to be
  going off to Kyushu—出かけない (dekake-nai) comes from 出かけ
  る (dekake-ru), to go off.
- e.g. 彼の収入がふえたらしいです (or ようです)。(Kare no shūnyū ga
  fueta *rashii desu* [or: *yō desu*])—His income seems to have increased
  —ふえた (fue-ta) comes from ふえる (fue-ru), to increase.
- e.g. 彼は会社に遅れなかったらしいです (or ようです)。(Kare wa kai-
  sha ni okure nakatta *rashii desu* [or: *yō desu*])—He seems not to
  have been late for the company—遅れなかった (okure-nakatta)
  comes from 遅れる (okure-ru), to be late.

In the case of nouns, らしいです (rashii desu) or のようです (no yō
desu) as the predicative use is put after them.

- e.g. 彼は消防士らしいです (or のようです)。(Kare wa shōbōshi *rashii
  desu* [or: *no yō desu*])—He seems to be a fireman—消防士 (shōbōshi), a fireman, is a noun.
- e.g. 彼は理学士ではないらしいです (or ようです)。(Kare wa rigaku-
  shi dewa nai *rashii desu* [or: *yō desu*])—He seems not to be a
  bachelor of science—理学士 (rigakushi), a bachelor of science, is
  a noun.
- e.g. 彼女は栄養士だったらしいです (or ようです)。(Kanojo wa eiyōshi
  datta *rashii desu* [or: *yō desu*])—She seems to have been a nutritionist—栄養士 (eiyōshi), a nutritionist, is a noun.
- e.g. 彼は旅芸人で(は)なかったらしいです (or ようです)。(Kare wa
  tabi geinin de [wa] nakatta *rashii desu* [or: *yō desu*])—He seems
  not to have been an itinerant actor—旅芸人 (tabi geinin), a strol-

ling player, is a noun.

In the case of な (na)-adjectives, らしいです (rashii desu) as the predicative use is put after their noun forms. Also, each な (na)-adjective, as it is, relates to ようです (yō desu).

- e.g. 東京の郊外は静からしいです (or 静かなようです)。(Tōkyō no kō-gai wa shizuka *rashii desu* [or: shizuka *na yō desu*])—The outskirts of Tokyo seem to be quiet—静か (shizuka), quietness, is the noun form of the な (na)-adjective 静かな (shizuka na), quiet, in an attributive use.

- e.g. 彼は親切で (は) ないらしいです (or ようです)。Kare wa shinsetsu de [wa] nai *rashii desu* [or: *yō desu*])—He seems not to be kind—親切で (は) ない (shinsetsu de [wa] nai) comes from the な (na)-adjective 親切な (shinsetsu na), kind, in an attributive use.

- e.g. その当時彼女は陽気だったらしいです (or ようです)。(Sono tōji kanojo wa yōki datta *rashii desu* [or: *yō desu*])—She seems to have been cheerful at that time—陽気だった (yōki datta) comes from the な (na)-adjective 陽気な (yōki na), cheerful, in an attributive use.

- e.g. この裁判官の判決は正当で (は) なかったらしいです (or ようです)。(Kono saiban kan no hanketsu wa seitō de [wa] nakatta *rashii desu* [or: *yō desu*])—This judge's decision seems not to have been reasonable—正当で (は) なかった (seitō de [wa] nakatta) comes from the な (na)-adjective 正当な (seitō na), reasonable, in an attributive use.

In the case of い (i)-adjectives, らしいです (rashii desu) or ようです (yō desu) as the predicative use is put after the い (i) of their true functions.

- e.g. この金ペンは高いらしいです (or ようです)。(Kono kin pen wa takai *rashii desu* [or: *yō desu*])—This gold pen seems expensive—高い (takai), expensive, is an い (i)-adjective.

- e.g. この通りは広く (は) ないらしいです (or ようです)。(Kono tōri wa hiroku [wa] nai *rashii desu* [or: *yō desu*])—This street seems not to be wide—広く (は) ない (hiroku [wa] nai) comes from the い (i)-adjective 広い (hiroi), wide.

- e.g. この全集は安かったらしいです (or ようです)。(Kono zenshū wa yasukatta *rashii desu* [or: *yō desu*])—This complete collection seems to have been inexpensive—安かった (yasukatta) comes from the い (i)-adjective 安い (yasui), inexpensive.

- e.g. この井戸は深く (は) なかったらしいです (or ようです)。(Kono ido wa fukaku [wa] nakatta *rashii desu* [or: *yō desu*])—This well seems not to have been deep—深く(は)なかった (fukaku [wa] nakatta) comes from the い (i)-adjective 深い (fukai), deep.

Drill

1. 彼女は詩人ではないらしいです (or ようです)。

She seems not to be a poet.

2. 彼は孤児ではなかったらしいです (or ようです)。

He seems not to have been an orphan.

3. 彼は北海道へ行ったらしいです (or ようです) ね。

I hear that it seems certain he has gone to Hokkaido.

4. 彼は友だちの間ではなかなか人気があるらしいです (or ようです)。

It seems that he is very popular among his friends.

5. 彼女の父が二人の結婚に反対しているらしいです (or ようです)。

Her father seems to disapprove of the marriage between the two.

6. 彼は京都で旅館に泊まらなかったらしいです (or ようです)。

He seems not to have stayed at a hotel in Kyoto.

7. NHK では，時どき日本語の放送をやっているらしいんです (or ようなんです)。

It seems that NHK sometimes takes on such work as broadcasting a Japanese language study.

　　* らしいんです (rashiin desu) is more colloquial than らしいです (rashii desu).

8. 彼は自動車事故の痛手から，もはやたちなおってきたらしいです (or ようです)。

He seems to have already recovered from his serious injuries in a car accident.

Exercise

Fill in each bracket with the conjectural form ようです:

1. 彼は何か一つ大きく欠けている ( )。

There seems to be a large deficiency in his nature.

2. 医者は今患者をみている ( )。

The doctor seems to be attending to a patient right now.

3. 彼女の予感が的中してきた ( )。

Her premonition seems to have come true.

4. 彼は無為徒食の自分を責めてい

He seemed to blame himself for

る（　　）。

his being idle.

5. 何かしらほのぼのとした思いが
わいてくる（　　）。

Somehow she felt a faint warmness surging up in her heart.

6. 娘は何かそわそわと落ち着かな
い（　　）。

The daughter somehow seemed to be even more restless than usual.

7. 政局は安定し，不動の政治体制
は整った（　　）。

The political situation gave cause for optimism, and the invincible political organization seemed established.

8. 彼女の寂しげな姿は捨てた一人
の男への憎しみに要約される（
　　）。

Her lonely figure seemed to be concentrated into a resentment of the man who deserted her.

Answers:
1. ようです　2. ようです　3. ようです　4. ようでした　5. ようでした　6. ようでした　7. ようでした　8. ようでした

The Conjectural (Appearance) Form (3)

Rule

The expression そうです (sō desu), to seem, in place of the expressions らしいです (rashii desu) and ようです (yō desu), is also used to indicate the conjectural form. This そうです (sō desu) is related to verbs, and adjectives.

In the case of verbs, this expression そうです (sō desu) is expressed by dropping ます (masu) of the polite present/future form of any verb and adding そうです (sō desu) to the second base (the verb form used with the polite -*masu* endings).

 e.g. 雪が降りそうです。(Yuki ga furi *sō desu*)—It seems likely to snow—降り (fur-i) comes from 降ります (fur-imasu), to fall.

In the case of な (na)-adjectives, そうです (sō desu) as the predicative use is put after their noun forms.

 e.g. 彼女は幸福そうです　(Kanojo wa kōfuku *sō desu*)—She seems to be happy—幸福 (kōfuku), happiness, is the noun form of the な (na)-adjective 幸福な (kōfuku na), happy.

In the case い (i)-adjectives, the final い (i) of these words as the predicative use may be dropped and そうです (sō desu) added.

 e.g. この井戸は浅そうです。(Kono ido wa asa *sō desu*)—This well seems to be shallow—浅 (asa) comes from the い (i)-adjective 浅い (asai), shallow.

 * The expression そうです (sō desu) is applied to such words as よい (yoi), good and ない (nai), be not; have not, both い (i)-adjectives, the final い (i) of these words may be dropped and さ (sa) added.

 e.g. この辞書はよさそうです。(Kono jisho wa yosa *sō desu*)—This dictionary seems good—よさ (yosa) comes from よい (yoi), good.

 e.g. この辺には，子供たちの広い遊び場がなさそうです。(Kono hen niwa, kodomo tachi no hiroi asobiba ga nasa *sō desu*)—There seem to be no spacious areas for children around here—なさ (nasa) comes from ない (nai), be not; have not.

The expression らしいです (rashii desu), ようです (yō desu), or そうです (sō desu) is used as the auxiliary showing conjecture. On the other hand, the expression らしい (rashii) or ような (yō na), like or seeming in English, acts in an attributive use and signifies conjecture.

In the case of verbs, the expression ような (yō na) is put after their plain present, plain past, plain present progressive, or plain past progressive forms.

   e.g.　彼女は両親にわびる**ような**気持ちになっています。(Kanojo wa ryō-shin ni wabiru *yō na* kimochi ni natte imasu)—She feels as though she owes an apology to her parents—わびる (wabi-ru), to apologize, is a verb.

The expression らしい (rashii) is primarily specified as an abstract adjective—this らしい (rashii) is connected to a noun or an adjective.

In the case of a noun, the expression らしい (rashii) is put after it.

   e.g.　学生**らしい**服装をした男の人が歩いてきました。(Gakusei *rashii* fukusō o shita otoko no hito ga aruite kimashita)—A man dressed as a student came walking—学生 (gakusei), a student, is a noun.

When the expression ような (yō na) is similarly used, the sentence is formed by inserting の (no) between the noun and ような (yō na) —in other words, in the case of a noun, the expression ような (yō na) cannot, as it is, be used; a noun can always be applied with it as の ような (no yō na).

   e.g.　彼は学生のような帽子をかぶっています。(Kare wa gakusei *no yō na* bōshi o kabutte imasu)—He wears a cap like a student's—学生 (gakusei), a student, is a noun.

In the case of the attributive use of な (na)-adjectives, the final な (na) may be dropped, this omission enabling them to be used as the noun forms. Such a noun as this relates to the following through そうな (sō na), seeming.

   e.g.　私はこの喫茶店の陽気そうなおばさんが好きです。(Watakushi wa kono kissaten no yōki *sō na* obasan ga suki desu)—I like the seemingly cheerful mistress of this coffee-shop—陽気 (yōki), cheerfulness, is the noun form of the な (na)-adjective 陽気な (yōki na), cheerful.

In the case of the attributive use of い (i)-adjectives, the final い (i) or ii may be dropped, this termination enabling them to add らし い (rashii).

   e.g.　彼女は橋の上にしょんぼりとたたずんでいる，きたならしい男の顔を見て驚きました。(Kanojo wa hashi no ue ni shonbori to tatazunde iru, kitana *rashii* otoko no kao o mite odorokimashita)—She happened to see the face of a shabby man standing alone on the bridge and was quite startled—きたな (kitana) comes from the い (i)-adjective きたない (kitanai), shabby.

The expression ような (yō na), like, is connected to a noun and the plain present/future, plain past, plain present progressive, or plain past progressive form of any verb. But, the expression ように (yō ni), as if (as though)..., serves as an adverb—that is, this expression modifies a verb.

　　e.g. 彼は鬼の首でも取ったように得意がっています。(Kare wa oni no kubi de mo totta *yō ni* tokui gatte imasu)—He is proud of himself as if he boldly took hold of a demon's neck—ように (yō ni) is an adverb, not an adjective.

Drill

1. 悪魔が通り過ぎたような気がし
ました。

There arose a feeling as though demons had passed by.

2. 彼女はうめくように言いました。

She murmured, half to herself.

3. 彼はほとんど毎日のように私の
家へ来ました。

He came to my house almost every day.

4. 子供らしい乱暴な大きな字をな
ぐり書きしたような手紙です。

The letter is scribbled the big, rough characters one might expect of a child.

5. 私の仕事からみれば，彼の仕事
は遊んでるようなもんです。

Compared with my work, his would seem to be pure pleasure.

　　* もんです (mon desu) is more colloquial than ものです (mono desu).

6. 彼はアパートを自分ひとりで建
ててみせるようなことを言ってい
ます。

He represents himself as a person who will, unaided, construct an apartment house.

7. 彼はむちゃな生活を悔いるよう
な気持ちになっています。

He feels something of regret for his messed up life.

8. 彼には，他人の利益をそねむよ
うな気持ちがひそんでいます。

There is concealed a feeling in him of envy of others' advantages.

9. この先生は宿題をなまける生徒
を大目にみるようになりました。

This teacher has come to overlook those pupils who neglect their homework.

10. 彼は足もとをすくわれたような
気持ちでいます。

He feels unsure of his footing.

11. 彼女は緊張した心配そうな姿を
しています。

She wears a strained and worried appearance.

12. 彼女は絶望的な孤独に目がくら

She feels as if she were about

むような気がしています。

to faint at the hopeless solitude.

13. 彼女は医者に電話をかけて，なるべく早く往診してくれるように頼みました。

She telephoned a doctor, and asked him to come as quickly as possible.

14. 国民の深刻な生活難の風景が町のいたる所にみられるようになりました。

The spectacle of the people's great living difficulties was to be seen everywhere on the streets.

15. 中小企業者の廃業や倒産が行なわれるようになりました。

The closing of medium and small enterpreneurs or their bankruptcy came to be enforced.

Exercise

Fill in the following blanks with ような，ように，そうな, or そうに:

1. 私は婚約が出来ない（　　）なります。

I can't become engaged.

2. 彼女は涙があふれ（　　）気がしました。

She knew that the tears were welling inside her.

3. 気が変になる（　　）暑さです。

The heat is oppressive enough to exhaust everybody in both mind and body.

4. 何か彼の服装が軽薄（　　）気がします。

I feel that his dress is somehow a mark of fickleness.

5. 彼女は心が青ざめてくる（　　）気持ちでした。

She felt as though her mind was filled with sudden terror.

6. 彼は新しい勇気がわいてくる（　　）気がしました。

He felt as though new vigor were surging up inside him.

7. 彼はわざと冷やかす（　　）彼女を呼びました。

He called her in, with an air of deliberate teasing.

8. 彼女はじっと恋人の顔を見つめました。燃える（　　）目でした。

She stared at the face of her lover. Her eyes were gleaming.

9. 彼は何かにせき立てられる（　　），上京しました。

He went up to Tokyo, as if urged on by something beyond himself.

10. 借金取りを見ると，彼は毛虫を

Looking at the debt collector,

かんだ（　　）顔になりました。

his face suddenly changed color as if he had bitten into a hairy caterpillar.

11. 両親に無断でこっそり逃げる（　　）、彼は家を出て上京しました。

He went up to Tokyo by slipping out of the house, avoiding telling his parents of his departure.

12. 何ごともなかった（　　）表情で，彼女は家の玄関へはいっていきました。

With no expression on her face to betray that anything unusual had transpired, she entered the gate of her house.

13. この子供はころがる（　　），母親のまくらもとににじり寄りました。

This child hastened nervously to his mother's bedside.

14. 生徒の気持ちを察して，先生はわざとなだめる（　　）話をしていたようでした。

The teacher, considering the pupil's feelings, seemed to be relating the stories, on purpose, in a soothing voice.

15. 彼女は恋人の顔を見上げて，恥ずかし（　　）うなずきました。耳のつけ根まで赤かったです。

She nodded with an air of shame, looking up at the face of her lover —a blush spreading to the base of her ears.

Answers:

1. ように　2. そうな　3. ような　4. そうな　5. ような　6. ような　7. ように　8. ような　9. ように　10. ような　11. ように　12. ような　13. ように　14. ような　15. そうに

The Volitional Form

Rule

The expression らしい (rashii) or ような (yō na), "like" or "seeming" in English, signifies conjecture about the present object. On the other hand, the expression よう (yō), う (ō), plain form and ましょう (mashō), polite form, "shall", "will", or "Let's" in English, refers rather to the future connection. The expression よう (yō), う (ō), or ましょう (mashō) refers to the will of the speaker or the speaker's sounding out the other party. Moreover, the use of the volitional form is pursued through the grouping of three forms—*the simple volitional form* (verbs+よう [yō], う [ō], or ましょう [mashō]) is commonly translated as "will", "shall", or "Let's"; *the imminent volitional form* (verbs+ようとする [yō to suru], plain form and ようとします [yō to shimasu], polite form and ようと思う [yō to omo(w)-u], plain form and ようと思います [yō to omoimasu], polite form; verbs+うとする [ō to suru], plain form and うとします [ō to shimasu], polite form or うと思う [ō to omo(w)-u], plain form and うと思います [ō to omoimasu], polite form) is well expressed by "be going to", "be about to", "be ready to", or "to try to"; and *the interrogative volitional form* (verbs+ようかと思う [yō ka to omo(w)-u], plain form and ようかと思います [yō ka to omoimasu], polite form or verbs+うかと思う [ō ka to omo(w)-u], plain form and うかと思います [ō ka to omoimasu], polite form) is commonly translated as "(I) think (I) might".

In the case of vowel stem verbs ending with either of the vowels *e*-ru and *i*-ru, the volitional form can be obtained by dropping the last syllable *ru* and adding ましょう (mashō), ようとします (yō to shimasu), ようと思います (yō to omoimasu), or ようかと思います (yō ka to omoimasu) to the stem.

e.g.　自分でなんとか道を見つけ**ましょう**。(Jibun de nan to ka michi o mitsuke *mashō*)—I myself will manage to seek for some way—見つけ (mitsuke) in 見つけましょう (mitsuke mashō) comes from 見つける (mitsuke-ru), to seek for.

e.g.　いすに腰掛け**ましょう**。(Isu ni koshikake *mashō*)—Let's sit on the chair—腰掛け (koshikake) in 腰掛けましょう (koshikake mashō) comes from 腰掛ける (koshikake-ru), to sit.

e.g.　彼は車を玄関に乗りつけ**ようとします**。(Kare wa kuruma o genkan ni noritsuke *yō to shimasu*)—He is ready to ride up to the entrance in his car—乗りつけ (noritsuke) in 乗りつけようとします (noritsuke yō to shimasu) comes from 乗りつける (noritsuke-ru), to ride up.

e.g. 私は和服になって，羽織を着ようと思います。(Watakushi wa wafuku ni natte, haori o ki *yō to omoimasu*)—I'm going to wear a haori (Japanese style jacket) over my kimono—着 (ki) in 着よう と思います (ki yō to omoimasu) comes from 着る (ki-ru), to wear.

e.g. 今から私はシャワーを浴びようかと思います。(Ima kara watakushi wa shawā o abi *yō ka to omoimasu*)—I think I might take a shower from now—浴び (abi) in 浴びようかと思います (abi yō ka to omoimasu) comes from 浴びる (abi-ru), to pour water over the body.

e.g. 私は酢の物は食べまい。(Watakushi wa su no mono wa tabe *mai*)—I'll not eat pickled dishes—食べ (tabe) comes from 食べる (tabe-ru), to eat. The negation of the volitional form is expressed by まい (mai), plain form or ますまい (masu mai), polite form; but the expression ますまい (masu mai) is not commonly used.

In the case of consonant stem verbs ending with *u*, the volitional form can be obtained by changing the last syllable *u* to *i* and adding ましょう (mashō). Also, in the case of these verbs, the volitional form can be obtained by dropping the last syllable *u* and adding うとします (ō to shimasu), うと思います (ō to omoimasu), or うかと思います (ō ka to omoimasu).

e.g. 私がそこへ行きましょう。(Watakushi ga soko e iki *mashō*)—I'll go there—行き (ik-i) in 行きましょう (iki mashō) comes from 行く (ik-u), to go.

e.g. 講義を聞きましょう。(Kōgi o kiki *mashō*)—Let's listen to a lecture—聞き (kik-i) in 聞きましょう (kiki mashō) comes from 聞く (kik-u), to listen to.

e.g. 彼はくつをかかとで脱ごうとします。(Kare wa kutsu o kakato de nugō *to shimasu*)—He is about to push off his shoes with his heels —脱ごう (nug-ō) in 脱ごうとします (nugō to shimasu) comes from 脱ぐ (nug-u), to take off.

e.g. 私は子供を里子に出して，働こうと思います。(Watakushi wa kodomo o satogo ni dashite, hatarakō *to omoimasu*)—I'm going to leave my child with a nurse and go to work—働こう (hatarak-ō) in 働こうと思います (hatarakō to omoimasu) comes from 働く (hatarak-u), to work.

e.g. 私は睡眠剤で自殺を計ろうかと思います。(Watakushi wa suimin

zai de jisatsu o hakarō *ka to omoimasu*)—I think I might attempt
suicide with sleeping drugs—計ろう (hakar-ō) in 計ろうかと思いま
す (hakarō ka to omoimasu) comes from 計る (hakar-u), to attempt.

  e.g. 私は強いアルコール性の飲み物は飲むまい。(Watakushi wa tsuyoi
  arukōru sei no nomimono wa *nomu mai*)—I'll not drink strong
  alcoholic drinks—飲む (nom-u) means "to drink" and まい (mai)
  is the negation of the volitional form.

  In the case of the irregular verb する (suru), to do, this expression
will be しましょう (shimashō), しようとします (shiyō to shimasu), し
ようと思います (shiyō to omoimasu), or しようかと思います (shiyō ka
to omoimasu) as in the following:

  e.g. 夕飯のしたくをしましょう。(Yūhan no shitaku o *shimashō*)—
  I'll prepare supper.

  e.g. どこまでもこの研究をしましょう。(Doko made mo kono kenkyū
  o *shimashō*)—Let's carry on this research to the last.

  e.g. 彼は私のおかれている立場を理解しようとします。(Kare wa wata-
  kushi no okarete iru tachiba o rikai *shiyō to shimasu*)—He will
  try to understand the present situation in which I am placed.

  e.g. この件につき，あなたのお話を聞くことにしようと思います。(Ko-
  no ken ni tsuki, anata no ohanashi o kiku koto ni *shiyō to omoimasu*)—I'm going to hear your decision about this matter.

  e.g. 私は婚約を延期しようかと思います。(Watakushi wa konyaku o
  enki *shiyō ka to omoimasu*)—I think I might put off my engagement.

  e.g. もうこんなかわいそうな事はしまい。(Mō kon na kawaisō na
  koto wa *shimai*)—I'll never do such an awful thing again.

  In the case of the irregular verb 来る (kuru), to come, this expression will be きましょう (kimashō), こようとします (koyō to shimasu),
こようと思います (koyō to omoimasu), or こようかと思います (koyō
ka to omoimasu).

  Also, う (ō) or よう (yō) is sometimes used in the conjectural form.

  e.g. 不良品もあろう。(Furyō hin mo arō)—There also would be some
  articles of inferior quality.

  e.g. この試合では，恐らく日本が勝とう。(Kono shiai dewa, osoraku
  Nihon ga katō)—In this match, Japan would probably be victori-
  ous.

  The expression 不良品もあろう。(furyō hin mo arō) may be said
as 不良品もあるであろう。(furyō hin mo aru *de arō*) and 恐らく日本が
勝とう。(osoraku Nihon ga katō) as 恐らく日本が勝つであろう。(osoraku Nihon ga katsu *de arō*). The expression であろう (de arō) con-

sists of the three words で～あろ～う (de-ar-ō); at present this で～あろ～う (de-ar-ō) is united into one word, leading to the formation of the expression だろう (darō).

Drill

1. 両親の言葉を無視して駆け落ちしましょう。

Ignoring the words of my parents, I'll run away with her.

2. 「あなたの言うことはよくわかりました。私も考えておきましょう。」

"I well understand what you say. Also, I'll think about the matter."

3. 彼は星空を仰ぐようにして、「もう少し歩きましょう。」と彼女に言いました。

Apparently gazing at the starry sky, he said to her, "Let's walk for a little."

4. この野党議員は政府の方針にけちをつけようとします。

This assemblyman of the Opposition is ready to throw cold water on the Government's policy.

5. この旅行者はかばんを駅に預けようとします。

This passenger is ready to leave his bag in the station.

6. 私はひびの感想を書こうと思います。

I'm going to write my daily impressions.

7. 私は主役を演じようかと思います。

I think I might play the principal role.

8. 子供が道ばたに倒れようとします。

A child is about to fall down on the roadside.

9. 私は彼と手を切ろうかと思います。

I think I might sever my friendship with him.

10. 私は所持品をまとめようとします。

I'm going to gather my belongings.

11. 社長はいすの背から上着をとろうとします。

The director is about to take his coat from the back of the chair.

12. 私は雨合羽を着ようと思います。

I'm going to wear a raincoat.

13. 彼女は人差し指で目をぬぐおう

She is about to wipe her eyes

とします。   with her forefinger.

14. 母はむすこのシャツにボタンを   Mother is ready to sew buttons
    つけようとします。   on her son's shirt.

15. 彼女は応接間の掃除をしようと   She is about to clean the draw-
    します。   ing room.

Exercise

Fill in the following blanks with the volitional forms, using the verbs given below the sentences:

1. とにかく, この研究を（   ）。   At any rate, I'll continue per-
                                    forming this research.
   続けて行く (tsuzukete ik-u), to continue performing

2. 私は日本語の勉強に（   ）。   I'll devote myself to the study
                                    of Japanese.
   専念する (sen-nen suru), to devote oneself to...

3. 彼はもう（   ）。   He is now ready to go home.
   帰る (kaer-u), to go home

4. 主人はお手伝いさんの手から受   The master is about to take the
   話機を（   ）。   receiver from the maid's hand.
   受け取る (uketor-u), to take

5. 私は一日中働き口をさがしにぶ   I think I might scout around
   らぶら（   ）。   all day long to find work.
   歩きまわる (arukimawar-u), to scout around

6. 私は良い配偶者を（   ）。   I'm going to find a good partner.
   さがす (sagas-u), to find

7. 私は一つ覚えの流行歌を（   ）。 I'm going to sing one of the
                                    popular songs I know by heart.
   歌う (uta[w]-u), to sing

8. 彼は食後のコーヒーを（   ）。   He is about to have his after-
                                    dinner coffee.
   飲む (nom-u), to drink

9. 私は端役を（   ）。   I think I might play a meager
                                    role.
   努める (tsutome-ru), to play

10. 私は今度はこの仕事に（   ）。 I think I might set about this
                                    work in real earnest this time.

本腰を入れる (hongoshi o ire-ru), to set about...in real earnest

11. この学生は先生の質問を（　　）。 This student is ready to parry the teacher's question.

そらす (soras-u), to parry

12. 私はこの数カ月昼夜兼行で（
　　）。 I think I might work both day and night these several months.

働く (hatarak-u), to work

13. 彼女は悪い境遇に（　　）。 She is about to stand against hard circumstances.

耐える (tae-ru), to stand against

14. 彼女は洗面所へ（　　）。 She is ready to rush to the wash room.

かけつける (kaketsuke-ru), to rush

15. 私は皮をむかないりんごを（
　　）。 I think I might bite into an unpeeled apple.

丸かじりする (marukajiri suru), to bite into

Answers:
1. 続けて行きましょう　2. 専念しましょう　3. 帰ろうとします　4. 受け取ろうとします　5. 歩きまわろうかと思います　6. さがそうと思います　7. 歌おうと思います　8. 飲もうとします　9. 努めようかと思います　10. 本腰を入れようかと思います　11. そらそうとします　12. 働こうかと思います　13. 耐えようとします　14. かけつけようとします　15. 丸かじりしようかと思います

第 二十七 課　Lesson 27

The Progressive Form

Rule

An action in progress or a state of being is expressed by the て (te) or で (de)-form of any verb+います (imasu)—this form is obtained by replacing the final vowel *a* of the plain past form by *e*.

In the case of vowel stem verbs, these plain past forms can be obtained by dropping the last syllable る (ru) and adding た (ta) to the stem. This た (ta) is then changed to て (te). This て (te)-form, derived from this stem verb in the plain past form, relates to います (imasu). For instance, the form 見て (mi-te) comes from 見た (mi-ta) from 見る (mi-ru), to see. Also, the form 食べて (tabe-te) comes from 食べた (tabe-ta) from 食べる (tabe-ru), to eat. The polite present progressive form will be 見ています (mite-imasu), to be looking at and 食べています (tabete-imasu), to be eating.

In the case of consonant stem verbs in the plain past form, a sound change is involved before adding た (ta) or だ (da). Then the た (ta) or だ (da) is changed to て (te) or で (de). This て (te) or で (de)-form, derived from this stem verb in the plain past form, relates to います (imasu). That is, there are four euphonic changes—an *i*-euphonic change, a euphonic change to the syllabic nasal sound, a euphonic change of assimilation, and a euphonic change of friction. Rules for these sound changes are illustrated as follows: such a verb as 書く (ka*k*-u), to write, undergoes an *i*-euphonic change—the plain past form is 書いた (ka*i*-ta); the polite present progressive form is 書いています (kaite-imasu). But here the verb 行く (i*k*-u), to go, is an exception; the plain past form is 行った (i*t*-ta) and the polite present progressive form is 行っています (itte-imasu)—the progressive form in this case denotes a state or condition of the object, not an action in progress. Such verbs as 読む (yo*m*-u), to read, and 遊ぶ (aso*b*-u), to play, undergo a euphonic change to the syllabic nasal sound—the plain past forms are 読んだ (yo*n*-da) and 遊んだ (aso*n*-da) and the polite present progressive forms are 読んでいます (yonde-imasu) and 遊んでいます (asonde-imasu). Such verbs as 立つ (ta*ts*-u), to stand up, 乗る (no*r*-u), to get on, and 買う (ka[*w*]-u), to buy, undergo a euphonic change of assimilation—the plain past forms are 立った

(ta*t*-ta), 乗った (no*t*-ta), and 買った (ka*t*-ta) and the polite present progressive forms are 立っています (tatte-imasu), 乗っています (notte-imasu), and 買っています (katte-imasu). Such a verb as 話す (hanas-u), to speak, undergoes a euphonic change of friction—the plain past form is 話した (hana*shi*-ta) and the polite present progressive form is 話しています (hanashite-imasu).

- e.g. 母は二人の子供の話を楽しそうに聞いています。(Haha wa futari no kodomo no hanashi o tanoshi sō ni *kiite imasu*)—The mother is listening amusedly to her two children's conversation—聞いて (kii-te) comes from 聞いた (kii-ta) from 聞く (kik-u), to listen to. This progressive form denotes an action in progress.

- e.g. おばあさんはゆっくりお茶を飲んでいます。(Obāsan wa yukkuri ocha o *nonde imasu*)—The aged woman is sipping tea slowly—飲んで (non-de) comes from 飲んだ (non-da) from 飲む (nom-u), to drink. This progressive form denotes an action in progress.

- e.g. 彼女はつまようじを使っています。(Kanojo wa tsumayōji o *tsukatte imasu*)—She is picking her teeth with a toothpick—使って (tsukat-te) comes from 使った (tsukat-ta) from 使う (tsuka[w]-u), to use. This progressive form denotes an action in progress.

- e.g. 彼は黒い縁のめがねをかけています。(Kare wa kuroi fuchi no megane o *kakete imasu*)—He wears black rimmed eyeglasses—かけて (kake-te) comes from かけた (kake-ta) from かける (kake-ru), to wear. This progressive form denotes a state or condition of the object.

- e.g. 私は本当に日本語の勉強に飽きています。(Watakushi wa hontō ni Nihongo no benkyō ni *akite imasu*)—I've indeed lost interest in the study of Japanese—飽きて (aki-te) comes from 飽きた (aki-ta) from 飽きる (aki-ru), to lose interest in. This progressive form denotes a state or condition of the object.

- e.g. 家族が夕飯の食卓を囲んでいます。(Kazoku ga yūhan no shokutaku o *kakonde imasu*)—A family group is sitting around the supper table—囲んで (kakon-de) comes from 囲んだ (kakon-da) from 囲む (kakom-u), to sit around. This progressive form denotes a state or condition of the object.

- e.g. 恋人が桜の木の下の日陰で私を待っています。(Koibito ga sakura no ki no shita no hikage de watakushi o *matte imasu*)—In the shadow of the cherry trees my fiancée is waiting for me—待って (mat-te) comes from 待った (mat-ta) from 待つ (mats-u), to wait for. This progressive form denotes a state or condition of the object.

e.g. 私は子供を三人持っています。(Watakushi wa kodomo o san nin *motte imasu*)—I have three children—持って (mot-te) comes from 持った (mot-ta) from 持つ (mots-u), to have. This progressive form denotes a state or condition of the object. On the other hand, we may say, 私は子供が三人います。(Watakushi wa kodomo ga san nin imasu), 私は三人の子供がいます。(Watakushi wa san nin no kodomo ga imasu), or 私は三人子供がいます。(Watakushi wa san nin kodomo ga imasu). The nominative case 私は (Watakushi wa) in these sentences can be understood as 私には (Watakushi niwa), as for me, ...; and thus, it may be concluded that "three" and "children" are in apposition. So, in these three sentences, the nominative case for the verb います (imasu), to have; there is, is 子供 (kodomo), children. Also, in this case the verb あります (arimasu) in place of the verb います (imasu) can be used as 私は子供が三人あります。(Watakushi wa kodomo ga san nin arimasu), 私は三人の子供があります。(Watakushi wa san nin no kodomo ga arimasu), or 私は三人子供があります。(Watakushi wa san nin kodomo ga arimasu).

The progressive form signifies an action in progress or a state of being—besides this, it shows the condition brought about by some action, a gathering of the action, the repetition of the action, or a previously performed action in the way of experience and record.

e.g. もう何もかもあなたの意図は**わかっています**。(Mō nani mo kamo anata no ito wa *wakatte imasu*)—I've already fully perceived your intention—わかって (wakat-te) comes from わかった (wakat-ta) from わかる (wakar-u), to perceive. This progressive form denotes the condition brought about by some action.

e.g. このごろは，自動車事故で一日四人から八人ずつ人が**死んでいます**。(Kono goro wa, jidōsha jiko de ichi nichi yo nin kara hachi nin zutsu hito ga *shinde imasu*)—Recently four or eight persons per day have been killed in car accidents—死んで (shin-de) comes from 死んだ (shin-da) from 死ぬ (shin-u), to die. This progressive form denotes a gathering of action; that is, the subjectivity is in the case of plurality—the whole of each subjective action is, in this case, shown as one state in progress.

e.g. 私は毎朝七時に起きています。(Watakushi wa mai asa shichi ji ni *okite imasu*)—I get up at seven o'clock every morning—起きて (oki-te) comes from 起きた (oki-ta) from 起きる (oki-ru), to get up. This progressive form denotes the repetition of the action.

e.g. 私は「春の踊り」は東京の浅草の国際劇場でなんかいも**見ています**。

(Watakushi wa 'Haru no Odori' wa Tōkyō no Asakusa no Koku-sai gekijō de nan kai mo *mite imasu*)—I've enjoyed seeing "A Dance of Spring" many times at the Kokusai Theatre in Asakusa in Tokyo—見て (mi-te) comes from 見た (mi-ta) from 見る (mi-ru), to see. This progressive form refers to a previously performed action as one's experience or record.

The progressive form can be conjugated as follows:

	Present/Future	Past	Present/Future Negative	Past Negative
polite form	te de +imasu	imashita	imasen	imasen deshita
plain form	te de +iru	ita	inai	inakatta

The progressive forms of such irregular verbs as する (suru), to do and 来る (kuru), to come, are しています (shite imasu) and 来ています (kite imasu).

e.g.　彼は今宿題をしています。(Kare wa ima shukudai o *shite imasu*) —He is now doing homework.

e.g.　彼女は私宅に来ています。(Kanojo wa shitaku ni *kite imasu*)— She has come to my house—This progressive form denotes a state or condition of the object.

The conjugation of such irregular verbs as する (suru), to do and 来る (kuru), to come, in the progressive form is illustrated as follows:

Verbs		Present/Future	Past	Present/Future Negative	Past Negative
to be doing	polite form	shite-imasu	shite-imashita	shite-imasen	shite-imasen deshita
	plain form	shite-iru	shite-ita	shite-inai	shite-inakatta
to be coming	polite form	kite-imasu	kite-imashita	kite-imasen	kite-imasen deshita
	plain form	kite-iru	kite-ita	kite-inai	kite-inakatta

Drill

1. 寮生は毛布をたたんでいます。

The boarders are folding up their blankets.

2. この警官は服装を整えています。

This policeman is adjusting his uniform.

3. 子供が板のとびらをたたいてい ます。

A child is knocking at the wooden door.

4. 刑事は彼の所持品を検査してい ます。

The detective is examining his belongings.

5. 彼女はげたを脱いでいます。

She is slipping off her wooden clogs.

6. 本当にきょうは私は疲れていま す。

I'm indeed tired today.

7. 彼女は微笑をもらしています。

She is letting a smile escape.

8. 彼は自分の走る足数をかぞえて いました。

He kept counting his steps as he ran.

9. 教授は校庭をぶらぶら歩き回っ ています。

The professor is walking lei- surely around the campus.

10. この老人は寝る前に庭をひとま わり歩いています。

This aged man is taking a round in the garden before he goes to bed.

11. 社長は机にすわって，食後の煙 草をふかしています。

The director is seated at his desk, enjoying an after-dinner smoke.

12. お寺が竹やぶに囲まれて，屋根 だけ見せています。

A temple is surrounded by groves of bamboo, with only its roof showing.

13. 彼はあついするめを裂き，ウイ スキーと一緒にかじっていまし た。

Tearing the heated dried cuttle- fish, he was nibbling at it alter- nately over sips of whisky.

14. この会社の重役連中は毎晩ご馳 走を食べて酒をくらっています。

Those who are directors in this company have enjoyed delicious food and given themselves over to drinking every night.

15. 母は電気コンロでするめを焼い　　The mother was roasting dried
ていました。　　　　　　　　cuttlefish over an electric cooker.

16. 彼女はある公務員と結婚するま　　Until she married a public of-
での間，おじさんの仕事を手伝っ　ficial, she had lent a hand in her
ていました。　　　　　　　　uncle's work.

Exercise

Fill in the following blanks with the progressive form, using the
verbs given below the sentences:

1. 彼女は窓に立って，金魚を（　　Leaning against the window,
）。　　　　　　　　　　　she watched the goldfish.

見た (mi-ta), watched＜見る (mi-ru), to watch

2. 電話の妻の声は（　　）。　　The voice of my wife over the
telephone sounds agitated.

せきこんだ (sekikon-da), sounded agitated＜せきこむ (sekikom-u), to sound
agitated

3. 彼女は悲痛な顔を（　　）。　　She has adopted an expression
of great sorrow.

悲痛な顔をした (hitsū na kao o shi-ta), looked sad＜悲痛な顔をする (hitsū
na kao o suru), to look sad

4. 彼は今重大問題に（　　）。　　He is now facing an important
problem.

立ち向かった (tachimukat-ta), faced＜立ち向かう (tachimuka[w]-u), to face

5. 彼は机の中の紙くずを（　　）。　He is disposing of the wastepaper in his desk.

かたづけた (katazuke-ta), disposed＜かたづける (katazuke-ru), to dispose

6. 妻は夫の愛情の深さに（　　）。　The wife is satisfied with the
depth of her husband's affection.

満足した (manzoku shi-ta), was (were) satisfied＜満足する (manzoku suru),
to be satisfied

7. 彼女はデリケートな感情を（　　She does not possess any delicate
）。　　　　　　　　　　　feelings.

持った (mot-ta) possessed＜持つ (mots-u), to possess

8. 彼は人生にもっとほかのものを　　He expected something more of
（　　）。　　　　　　　　life.

期待した (kitai shi-ta), expected＜期待する (kitai suru), to expect

9. 彼女は外出のしたくを（　　）。　　　She is dressed for going out.

したくをした (shitaku o shi-ta), got ready＜したくをする (shitaku o suru), to get ready

10. 彼は早口にしゃべりながら，ビ　　　Speaking rapidly, he is drinking
　　　ールをがぶがぶと（　　）。　　　　his beer in great drafts.

飲んだ (non-da), drank＜飲む (nom-u), to drink

11. 彼は意味深いつぶやきを（　　）。　He is murmuring with deep
　　　　　　　　　　　　　　　　　　meaning.

もらした (morashi-ta), let out＜もらす (moras-u), to let out

12. 友だちは私の部屋の中を（　　）。　My friend is looking about my
　　　　　　　　　　　　　　　　　　room.

見まわした (mimawashi-ta), looked about＜見まわす (mimawas-u), to look about

13. 日本軍部はヒトラー主義を理想　　　The Japanese military authori-
　　　と（　　）。　　　　　　　　　ties were adopting Hitler's prin-
　　　　　　　　　　　　　　　　　　ciples as their ideal.

した (shi-ta), did; adopted＜する (suru), to do

14. 彼女は夫にゆかたを出し，脱い　　　She took out a *yukata*, and put
　　　だものを（　　）。　　　　　　his clothes in order as he un-
　　　　　　　　　　　　　　　　　　dressed.

始末した (shimatsu shi-ta), put...in order＜始末する (shimatsu suru), to put...in order

15. 電車の中の人は，談笑し，雑誌　　　The people in the electric tram
　　　を読み，（　　）。　　　　　　are chatting, reading magazines,
　　　　　　　　　　　　　　　　　　and dozing.

いねむりした (inemuri shi-ta), dozed＜いねむりする (inemuri suru), to doze

16. 五人の人夫が汗を流しながら，　　　Five laborers, sweating heavily,
　　　引っ越し荷物をトラックの上に　　are heaving removal things onto
　　　（　　）。　　　　　　　　　　a truck.

押し上げた (oshiage-ta), heaved＜押し上げる (oshiage-ru), to heave

Answers:
　　1. 見ていました　2. せきこんでいます　3. しています　4. 立ち向かっています　5. かたづけています　6. 満足しています　7. 持っていません　8. 期待していました　9. しています　10. 飲んでいます　11. もらしています　12. 見まわしています　13. していました　14. 始末していました　15. いねむりしています　16. 押し上げています

Common Courtesy in Requests

Rule

ください (kudasai), please, くださいませんか (kudasaimasen ka),
Won't you...?, or いただきたいのです (itadakitai no desu) and いた
だきたいです (itadakitai desu), I would like to ask you a favour...is
expressed after て (te) or で (de)-form of any verb.

The expression くださいませんか (kudasaimasen ka) is more polite
request than ください (kudasai). いただきたいのです (itadakitai *no*
desu) is more emphatic and descriptive than いただきたいです (itadakitai desu). The expression いただきたいのです (itadakitai no desu)
and いただきたいです (itadakitai desu) are used when the speaker or
the subject of a sentence is requesting of a superior or a customer,
but never towards an equal, a subordinate, or a friend. Such an expression as いただきたいのです (itadakitai no desu) is regarded as the
delicate basis for good speech in humbling oneself before any man
of higher status.

e.g. コーヒーとお菓子を持ってきてください。(Kōhī to okashi o motte
kite *kudasai*)—Please bring some coffee and cookies—持ってきて
(motte kite) comes from the plain past 持ってきた (motte kita),
brought in.

e.g. 砂糖を取ってくださいませんか。(Satō o totte *kudasaimasen ka*)
—Would you mind passing the sugar?—取って (tot-te) comes from
the plain past 取った (tot-ta), took.

e.g. 新宿駅へ行く道を教えてください。(Shinjuku eki e iku michi o
oshiete *kudasai*)—Please show me the way to Shinjuku Station—
教えて (oshie-te) comes from the plain past 教えた (oshie-ta), taught.

e.g. この紙に地図を書いてくださいませんか。(Kono kami ni chizu o
kaite *kudasaimasen ka*)—Won't you draw a map on this paper?—
書いて (kai-te) comes from the plain past 書いた (kai-ta), wrote.

e.g. 来週から自動車の実習を始めさせていただきたいのです。(Raishū
kara jidōsha no jisshū o hajimesasete *itadakitai no desu*)—I would
like to be permitted to start my practical studies of cars from
next week—始めさせて (hajimesase-te) comes from 始めさせた (ha-
jimesase-ta), allowed one to start. Viewed from the use of the
expression いただきたいのです (itadakitai no desu), it can be under-

stood that the speaker of this sentence is asking a favor of a superior or the man in charge at the company where he is going to get practical training.

e.g. 三十分ほど待っていただきたいのです。(San juppun hodo matte *itadakitai no desu*)—You'll have to wait about thirty minutes—待って (mat-te) comes from 待った (mat-ta), waited. The speaker of this sentence is asking a favor of a visitor or a customer, suggesting that the speaker himself or the person being asked for has his hands full or the customer is obliged to await his turn. The idea of this sentence is "I expect you'll be kind enough to wait".

In the negative form of this expression, the plain present/future negative of vowel stem verbs can always be obtained by dropping the final る (ru) of the plain present/future form and adding ない (nai) to this root. This ない (nai) directly relates to でください (de kudasai), でくださいませんか (de kudasaimasen ka), でいただきたいのです (de itadakitai no desu), or でいただきたいです (de itadakitai desu).

e.g. 学校に遅れないでください。(Gakkō ni okurenai *de kudasai*)— Please don't be late for school—遅れない (okure-nai) comes from 遅れる (okure-ru), to be late.

e.g. そのような事を子供に教えないでくださいませんか。(Sono yō na koto o kodomo ni oshienai *de kudasaimasen ka*)—Won't you please not tell the child about such things?—教えない (oshie-nai) comes from 教える (oshie-ru), to teach.

e.g. 私の新しい住所は，彼に知らせないでいただきたいのです。(Watakushi no atarashii jūsho wa, kare ni shirasenai *de itadakitai no desu*)—As for my new address, I would like to ask you a favor and keep it from him—知らせない (shirase-nai) comes from 知らせる (shirase-ru), to inform.

In the negative form of this expression, the plain present/future negative of consonant stem verbs can always be obtained by changing the final *u* of the plain present/future form to *a* and adding ない (nai) to this root. This ない (anai) directly relates to でください (de kudasai), でくださいませんか (de kudasaimasen ka), でいただきたいのです (de itadakitai no desu), or でいただきたいです (de itadakitai desu).

e.g. この小包を書留便で送らないでください。(Kono kozutsumi o kakitome bin de okuranai *de kudasai*)—Please don't send this parcel by registered mail—送らない (okur-anai) comes from 送る (okur-u), to send.

e.g. 木の枝を折らないでくださいませんか。(Ki no eda o oranai *de*

kudasaimasen ka)—Won't you please not break off the branches of the trees?—折らない (or-anai) comes from 折る (or-u), to break off.

e.g. 両親の事は聞かないでいただきたいのです。(Ryōshin no koto wa kikanai *de itadakitai no desu*)—As for my parents, I would like to ask you not inquire about them—聞かない (kik-anai) comes from 聞く (kik-u), to ask.

Drill

1. そのくつ下を箱に入れてください。

Please put the socks into a box.

2. おつりを調べてくださいませんか。

Won't you check your change?

3. お酒を二本までにして，二時間ぐらいしてむすこを帰らせていただきたいのです。

I hope you will make my son leave after two hours; don't give him any more than two bottles of *sake*, will you?

4. 娘を監督してくださいませんか。

Won't you take my daughter under your supervision?

5. よくいらしてくださいました。お楽にしてください。

Thank you for your cordial visit. Please make yourself comfortable.

6. えらい野暮なことをおたずねにならないでください。

Please don't ask such a silly thing.

7. この別れ話を承諾しないでください。

Please don't agree to the idea of this separation.

8. あんなたよりない男はやめてください。

Please give up such an unreliable man.

9. すずり箱を取ってきてくださいませんか。

Would you mind fetching an inkstone case?

10. 氷水を二つください。

Please, two glasses of ice water.

11. 何から何まで彼の言いなりにならないでください。

Please don't always act according to all of his advice.

12. 情けないお世辞を言わないでください。

Please don't give me your pity.

13. 娘の事をあきらめてくださいま

Won't you please abandon your

せんか。

affair with my daughter?

14. 彼女の素行を調べさせていただ
きたいのです。

I would like to be permitted to
check up on her behaviour.

15. 彼女に金銭的な援助をさせてい
ただきたいのです。

I would like to be permitted to
give her financial support.

16. もう少し彼女に親切にしてやっ
てください。

Please show a little more kindness to her.

Exercise

Fill in the following blanks with ください, くださいませんか, or
いただきたいのです:

1. きょうのうちにどこかアパート
をさがして，引き移って（　　）。

Please find an apartment somewhere today and move there.

引き移って (hiki utsut-te)＜引き移った (hiki utsut-ta)＜引き移る (hiki utsur-
u), to move

2. この紙切れを火ばちに入れて，
燃やして（　　）。

Please put this scrap of paper
into the brazier and burn it.

燃やして (moyashi-te)＜燃やした (moyashi-ta)＜燃やす (moyas-u), to burn

3. 食器を買ってきて（　　）。

Please go and purchase some
tableware.

買ってきて (katte kite)＜買ってきた (katte kita)＜買ってくる (katte kuru),
to go and purchase

4. 私にあなたの新しいアパートの
名を知らせて（　　）。

Please let me know the name
of your new apartment house.

知らせて (shirase-te)＜知らせた (shirase-ta)＜知らせる (shirase-ru), to let
one know

5. 電燈を引きおろして（　　）。

Please pull down the electric
lamp.

引きおろして (hikioroshi-te)＜引きおろした (hikioroshi-ta)＜引きおろす (hiki-
oros-u), to pull down

6. 彼女の複雑な心理について，ご
理解をして（　　）。

I would like to ask you to understand her complicated mental state.

理解をして (rikai o shite)＜理解をした (rikai o shita)＜理解をする (rikai o
suru), to understand

7. この手紙を読んでみて（　　）。

Please try and read this letter.

読んでみて (yonde mi-te)＜読んでみた (yonde mi-ta)＜読んでみる (yonde
mi-ru), to try to read

8. 真情を吐露して（　　）。   Would you mind laying bare your true feelings?

    吐露して (toro shite)＜吐露した (toro shita)＜吐露する (toro suru), to lay bare

9. 一日も早く彼と関係の無い人に   I want you to become indifferent
なって（　　）。   to him as quickly as possible.

    なって (nat-te)＜なった (nat-ta)＜なる (nar-u), to become

10. せめてあなただけに私の気持ち   I would like to make my heart
をすっかりわかって（　　）。   understood completely at least by you.

    わかって (wakat-te)＜わかった (wakat-ta)＜わかる (wakar-u), to understand

11. 彼女と結婚させて（　　）。   I would like to be permitted to marry her.

    結婚させて (kekkon sase-te)＜結婚させた (kekkon sase-ta)＜結婚させる (kekkon sase-ru), to get one married

12. 新家庭の準備をさせて（　　）。   I would like to be allowed the time to make preparations for my new home.

    準備をさせて (junbi o sase-te)＜準備をさせた (junbi o sase-ta)＜準備をさせる (junbi o sase-ru), to get one to make preparations

13. 机の中から洋書を取り出して（　　）。   I would like to ask you to take out the foreign book from inside the desk.

    取り出して (toridashi-te)＜取り出した (toridashi-ta)＜取り出す (toridas-u), to take out

14. 支配人を電話へ呼び出して（　　）。   I would like to ask you a favor and call the manager over the telephone.

    呼び出して (yobidashi-te)＜呼び出した (yobidashi-ta)＜呼び出す (yobidas-u), to call up

15. なるべくならば，この学生を許してあげて（　　）。   If circumstances allow, I would like to ask you to let this student go.

    許してあげて (yurushite age-te)＜許してあげた (yurushite age-ta)＜許してあげる (yurushite age-ru), to let one go

16. 私は夜勤をしないで，帰らせて（　　）。   I would like to be permitted to go home without having night

duty.

帰らせて (kaerase-te)＜帰らせた (kaerase-ta)＜帰らせる (kaerase-ru), to get one to go home

Answers:

1. ください 2. ください 3. ください 4. ください 5. ください 6. いただきたいのです 7. ください 8. くださいませんか 9. いただきたいのです 10. いただきたいのです 11. いただきたいのです 12. いただきたいのです 13. いただきたいのです 14. いただきたいのです 15. いただきたいのです 16. いただきたいのです

Common Courtesy in Giving and Receiving

Rule

やります (yarimasu) or あげます (agemasu), to give, is used when the speaker or the subject of the sentence does some favor for somebody else. The subsidiary verb あげます (agemasu) from あげる (age-ru) is the term of humility of the subsidiary verb やります (yarimasu) from やる (yar-u). やります (yarimasu) is used when doing a favor for a subordinate or an equal—one of your own family members, close friends, or children. あげます (agemasu) is used when doing a favor for an equal or a superior. Such subsidiary verbs as やります (yari-masu) and あげます (agemasu) are put after the て (te) or で (de)-form of any verb, this form being obtained by replacing the final vowel *a* of the plain past form by *e*.

In the case of vowel stem verbs, these plain past forms can be obtained by dropping the last syllable る (ru) and adding た (ta) to the stem. This た (ta) is then changed to て (te).

In the case of consonant stem verbs in the plain past form, a sound change is involved before adding た (ta) or だ (da). Then the た (ta) or だ (da) is changed to て (te) or で (de). This て (te) or で (de)-form, derived from these two stem verbs in the plain past form, relates to やります (yarimasu) or あげます (agemasu).

e.g. 彼女は妹にレコードをかけてやりました。(Kanojo wa imōto ni rekōdo o *kakete yarimashita*)—She played a record for her younger sister—かけてやりました (kakete yarimashita) consists of the two verbs かけて (kake-te) from the plain past かけた (kake-ta), played and やりました (yar-imashita) from やる (yar-u), to give.

e.g. この学生は病床の先生に花束の贈り物をしてあげました。(Kono gakusei wa byōshō no sensei ni hana taba no *okurimono o shite agemashita*)—This student gave a gift of a bunch of flowers to the teacher on his sickbed—贈り物をして (okurimono o shi-te) comes from the plain past 贈り物をした (okurimono o shi-ta), made a present and あげました (age-mashita) from あげる (age-ru), to give.

Besides, the subsidiary verbs やろう (yarō) and あげよう (ageyō) are used when the speaker has the intention of performing some acts positively.

e.g. 株の売買によって，これを学資にして**勉強して やろう**。(Kabu no baibai ni yotte, kore o gakushi ni shite *benkyōshite yarō*)—I'll surely study by obtaining my own school expenses through the purchase and sale of stocks—勉強して (benkyōshi-te) comes from 勉強した (benkyōshi-ta), studied.

e.g. 先生のこの研究を**手伝って あげよう**。(Sensei no kono kenkyū o *tetsudatte ageyō*)—I'll help my teacher with this research—手伝って (tetsudat-te) comes from 手伝った (tetsudat-ta) helped.

もらいます (moraimasu) or いただきます (itadakimasu), to obtain; here loosely "kindly" is used when the subject of the sentence is given some help from somebody else. The subsidiary verb いただきます (itadakimasu) from いただく (itadak-u) is the term of humility of the subsidiary verb もらいます (moraimasu) from もらう (mora[w]-u). もらいます (moraimasu) is used when being given some help or gift from a subordinate or an equal. いただきます (itadakimasu) is used when being given some help or gift from an equal or a superior. Such subsidiary verbs as もらいます (moraimasu) and いただきます (itadakimasu) are put after the て (te) or で (de)-form of any verb.

e.g. 友だちに誘われて，銀座で夕食を**ご馳走して もらいました**。(Tomodachi ni sasowarete, Ginza de yūshoku o *gochisōshite moraimashita*)—My friend took me to Ginza to treat me to dinner)—ご馳走してもらいました (gochisōshite moraimashita) consists of the two verbs ご馳走して (gochisōshi-te) from the plain past ご馳走した (gochisōshi-ta), treated A to B and もらいました (moraimashita) from もらう (mora[w]-u), to receive; ご馳走してもらいました (gochisōshite moraimashita) literally means "was kindly treated".

e.g. 私は両親から柔らかく**なだめて いただきました**。(Watakushi wa ryōshin kara yawarakaku *nadamete itadakimashita*)—I was gently calmed by my parents—なだめて (nadame-te) comes from なだめた (nadame-ta), calmed and なだめていただきました (nadamete itadakimashita) literally means "was kindly calmed".

Besides, the subsidiary verb もらいます (moraimasu) or いただきます (itadakimasu) in the case of the present form sometimes expresses the subject's strong resolution or the mood of giving an order to others.

e.g. きょうの英語の試験が六十点以下の生徒には，放課後もう一度試験を**受けて もらいます**。(Kyō no Eigo no shiken ga roku jutten ika no seito niwa, hōkago mō ichido shiken o *ukete moraimasu*)—Those pupils who have gotten below 60 points on today's English examination are requested to sit for the examination once more after school—受けて (uke-te) comes from 受けた (uke-ta), sat for.

e.g. バスが故障したので，ここで降りて いただきます。(Basu ga koshō shita node, koko de *orite itadakimasu*)—There being a breakdown in the bus, passengers are requested to get off here—降りて (ori-te) comes from 降りた (ori-ta), got off.

くれます (kuremasu) or くださいます (kudasaimasu), to give; here loosely "kindly" is used when the subject of the sentence does some favor for the speaker. The subsidiary verb くださいます (kudasaimasu) from くださる (kudasaru) is the term of respect of the subsidiary verb くれます (kuremasu) from くれる (kure-ru). くれます (kuremasu) means that a subordinate or an equal does a favor, in almost all cases, for those whom he is closely connected with. くださいます (kudasaimasu) is used when a superior or an equal does some favor for someone. Such subsidiary verbs as くれます (kuremasu) and くださいます (kudasaimasu) are put after the て (te) or で (de)-form of any verb.

e.g. 親友が病院にわたしを見舞って くれました。(Shinyū ga byōin ni watashi o *mimatte kuremashita*)—My close friend came to inquire after me at the hospital—見舞ってくれました (mimatte kuremashita) consists of the two verbs 見舞って (mimat-te) from the plain past 見舞った (mimat-ta), inquired after and くれました (kure-mashita) from くれる (kure-ru), to give; 見舞ってくれました (mimatte kuremashita) literally means "kindly inquired after; was kind enough to inquire after; was so kind as to inquire after".

e.g. 主治医が朝に夕に妻の容体を電話で知らせて くださいました。 (Shuji-i ga asa ni yū ni tsuma no yōtai o denwa de *shirasete kudasaimashita*)—Every morning and evening the physician in charge reported my wife's condition over the telephone—知らせて (shirase-te) comes from 知らせた (shirase-ta), reported and 知らせてくださいました (shirasete kudasaimashita) literally means "kindly reported".

The negative forms of やります (yarimasu) or あげます (agemasu), もらいます (moraimasu) or いただきます (itadakimasu), and くれます (kuremasu) or くださいます (kudasaimasu) are やりません (yarimasen) or あげません (agemasen), もらいません (moraimasen) or いただきません (itadakimasen), and くれません (kuremasen) or くださいません (kudasaimasen).

e.g. 私はこのカメラを友だちに貸して (or 貸しては) やりません。(Watakushi wa kono kamera o tomodachi ni *kashite* [or: kashite wa] *yarimasen*)—I'll not lend this camera to my friend—貸して (kashite) comes from 貸した (kashi-ta), lent.

*貸しては (kashite *wa*) is more emphatic than 貸して (kashite).

e.g. お手伝いさんに私の身のまわりの品をかばんに**入れて** (or 入れては)
もらいませんでした。(Otetsudaisan ni watakushi no mi no mawari
no shina o kaban ni *irete* [or: irete wa] *moraimasen deshita*)—
The maid did not put my personal effects into my suitcase—入
れて (ire-te) comes from 入れた (ire-ta), put in.

e.g. 兄嫁はわたしに心を**砕いて** (or 砕いては) **くれません**。(Ani yome
wa watashi ni kokoro o *kudaite* [or: kudaite wa] *kuremasen*)—My
elder brother's wife does not break her heart over me—砕いて
(kudai-te) comes from 砕いた (kudai-ta), broke.

In the case of the subsidiary verb やります (yarimasu) within the
sentence, the form of やって (yatte) or やり (yari) is used.

e.g. 家内がお菓子を新聞紙で**包んでやって** (or 包んでやり),「これ，あ
なたにおみやげよ」と言いました。(Kanai ga okashi o shinbunshi de
tsutsunde yatte [or: tsutsunde yari], "Kore, anata ni omiyage yo"
to iimashita)—My wife wrapped some cookies in a piece of newspaper and said, "This is a present for you".—包んで (tsutsun-de)
comes from 包んだ (tsutsun-da), wrapped.

The subsidiary verb もらいます (moraimasu) used within the sentence is in the form of もらって (moratte) or もらい (morai).

e.g. 毎晩この子供は母親に服を**脱がせてもらって** (or 脱がせてもらい),
床にはいります。(Maiban kono kodomo wa haha oya ni fuku o
nugasete moratte [or: nugasete morai], toko ni hairimasu)—Every
night this child is undressed by the mother, and put into bed—
脱がせて (nugase-te) comes from 脱がせた (nugase-ta), made one
take off.

The subsidiary verb くれます (kuremasu) used within the sentence
is in the form of くれて (kurete) or くれ (kure).

e.g. 家庭教師が**来てくれて** (or 来てくれ), むすこの宿題を見てくれます。
(Katei kyōshi ga *kite kurete* [or: kite kure], musuko no shukudai
o mite kuremasu)—The tutor comes and helps my son with homework—来て (kite) comes from 来た (kita), came.

Drill

1. 政府は国産の新鋭旅客機を国民
の目の前に**見せてくれました**。

The government demonstrated
a new, domestic, passenger plane
directly before the peoples' eyes.

2. この教授が私に日本語を**教えて**

This professor taught me Japa-

くださいました。

3. 叔父が私にこの時計を買って
   くださいました。

My uncle bought me this watch.

4. 私は弟におもちゃを買ってや
   りました。

I bought a toy for my younger brother.

5. 私は彼を廊下へ呼び出しても
   らいました。

I asked for someone to call him out into the corridor.

6. 彼が私に花束と本とを送って
   くれました。

He sent a bunch of flowers and a book to me.

7. 彼女は黙ってみかんをむいて
   くれました。

She remained silent, peeling the orange for me.

8. 彼女が私のお米の配給を取って
   来てくれました。

She went out and came back with my ration of rice.

9. この子供は救護所で懇切な手当
   をしていただきました。

This child got careful treatment at a first-aid station.

10. 彼女は針を取り上げて，私のく
    つ下を繕ってくれました。

She took up the needle and darned my socks.

11. 病気の間，隣の部屋の人が食事
    をこしらえてくださいました。

The person in the next apartment made me some meals since I had become ill.

12. 彼のワイシャツも洋服もよごれ
    ていました。彼女に洗濯してもら
    いました。

His white shirt and clothes were soiled. She had his clothes washed for him.

13. この店の主人は私を親切にいた
    わってくださいました。

The master of this shop was kind and took good care of me.

14. 私が身動きもできずに病床にふ
    していると，看護婦さんがみかん
    をしぼって飲ませてくださいま
    した。

The nurse would squeeze oranges and treat me to drinks of juice when I could not move an inch on my sickbed.

15. 人形の内職をやっている隣室の
    子を連れた未亡人が，病気の私に
    おかゆを煮てくださいました。

The widow with one child in the next room, who works at making dolls there, cooked rice gruel for me in my illness.

Exercise

Change each verb given below the sentences into the て or で-form and fill in each bracket with the verb:

1. 医者が食餌についての注意を（　　）くださいました。

   The doctor gave me instructions about my diet.

   与えた (atae-ta), gave＜与える (atae-ru), to give

2. ごらんのとおりの風来坊で，だれも（　　）くれません。

   I'm a wanderer as you can see, and nobody would care to join me.

   来た (kita), came＜来る (kuru), to come

3. 彼女はめったに（　　）くれませんでした。

   She seldom troubled to visit me.

   来た (kita), came

4. 手紙をやっても，叔父はなかなか（　　）くださいませんでした。

   My uncle would not appear, even in spite of the letters.

   来た (kita), came

5. 数日前に，父が（　　）くれて，えびの罐詰をくださいました。

   My father came to see me several days ago, and he brought some canned lobster.

   来た (kita), came

6. 社長が愛想よくいすを（　　）くださいました。

   The director hospitably offered a chair to me.

   勧めた (susume-ta), offered＜勧める (susume-ru), to offer

7. 彼は父に手紙を書いて，妻を実家に（　　）もらいました。

   He wrote to his father and demanded his wife be returned to her parents' home.

   帰した (kaeshi-ta), made one return home＜帰す (kaes-u), to make one return home

8. 友だちは四日たっても五日たっても，おしゃべりに（　　）くれませんでした。

   Four, then five days passed by and my friend did not come to chat.

   来た (kita), came

9. 彼女は遊びに（　　）くれませんでした。

   She did not come to spend some time with me.

   来た (kita), came

10. 感情の細やかな優しい夫で，い

    My husband is a gentle one who

| つも柔らかく私を（　）くれます。 | understands the delicacy of emotion, and in his kindness he always enfolds me tenderly. |

包んだ (tsutsun-da), wrapped up＜包む (tsutsum-u), to wrap up

| 11. この出版社は政府から用紙の特別（　）もらいました。 | This publishing company obtained a special distribution of paper from the government. |

配給をした (haikyū o shita), distributed＜配給をする (haikyū o suru), to distribute

| 12. 英米の事情に精通している人に私たちの仕事を（　）いただきました。 | In our work we got the help of a person who is familiar with the situation in England and America. |

助けた (tasuke-ta), helped＜助ける (tasuke-ru), to help

| 13. 極寒の夜気が冷えてくると，お手伝いさんが火ばちに炭を（　）くれます。 | When it grows cold in the depth of the winter night, the maid adds charcoal to a brazier. |

つぎ足した (tsugitashi-ta), added＜つぎ足す (tsugitas-u), to add

| 14. 妻は真青な顔になってうめいていました。夫はすぐに医師の来診を求めて応急の（　）もらいました。 | The wife was pale, and moaning. The husband at once called a doctor, who gave her emergency treatment. |

手当をした (teate o shita), treated＜手当をする (teate o suru), to treat

| 15. 街燈を消した暗い道を私は足でさぐるようにして帰ってくると，玄関で母が私を（　）くださいました。 | I returned home picking my way along the dark road with its unlit street lamps; I was met at the vestibule by my mother. |

迎えた (mukae-ta), met＜迎える (mukae-ru), to meet

Answers:
1. 与えて 2. 来て or 来ては 3. 来て or 来ては 4. 来て or 来ては 5. 来て 6. 勧めて 7. 帰して 8. 来て or 来ては 9. 来て or 来ては 10. 包んで 11. 配給をして 12. 助けて 13. つぎ足して 14. 手当をして 15. 迎えて

True Compound Verb (1)

Rule

The form of approach and that of divergence can be explicitly evidenced in the sentence through the use of て (te) or で (de)+such subsidiary verbs as きます (kimasu), to come and いきます (ikimasu), to go. The form denoting approach can be applied in the sentence as て (te) or で (de)+the subsidiary verb きます (kimasu), to come—this carries the meaning of action coming towards the speaker or subject, the beginning of the action and the progress of the action. On the other hand, the form denoting divergence can be applied in the sentence as て (te) or で (de)+the subsidiary verb いきます (iki-masu), to go—this carries the meaning of action receding in the distance and the progress of the action. This form is made up of two verbs; that is, compound verbs. Any verb, preceding the final verb such as きます (kimasu), to come and いきます (ikimasu), to go, can be expressed with て (te) or で (de). The final vowel *a* of the plain past form of any verb which is placed before either of these two verbs used as a shifter is changed to *e*, permitting the formation of the compound verbs.

e.g. つい四・五日前に南ベトナムのサイゴン大使の田中さんが帰ってきました。(Tsui shi go nichi mae ni Minami Betonamu no Saigon taishi no Tanaka-san ga *kaette kimashita*)—Just several days ago Mr. Tanaka, the Ambassador to Saigon in South Viet Nam, returned home—帰ってきました (kaette kimashita) consists of the two verbs 帰って (kaet-te) from the plain past 帰った (kaet-ta), returned and きました (kimashita), came.

e.g. 不意に涙が浮かんできました。(Fui ni namida ga *ukande kimashita*)—Suddenly tears came into her eyes—浮かんで (ukan-de) comes from the plain past 浮かんだ (ukan-da), came up to the surface.

e.g. かさを半びらきにして，彼女は建物の陰を歩いていきました。(Kasa o hanbiraki ni shite, kanojo wa tatemono no kage o *aruite ikimashita*)—With her umbrella half opened, she walked under the eaves of the building—歩いていきました (aruite ikimashita) consists of the two verbs 歩いて (arui-te) from the plain past 歩いた (arui-ta), walked and いきました (ikimashita), went.

e.g. 羽田空港から二人の政府高官が泰国に飛んで いきました。(Haneda kūkō kara futari no seifu kōkan ga Taikoku ni *tonde ikimashita*) —Two high government officials left Haneda Airport by plane for Thailand—飛んで (ton-de) comes from the plain past 飛んだ (ton-da), flew.

Drill

1. 彼女は絵を見て きました。

   She came back after looking at some paintings.

2. 彼は廊下を歩いて いきました。

   He kept on walking down the corridor.

3. したくして出て きなさい。

   Get dressed and come on.

4. 彼女はこつこつとうつ向きがちに歩いて いきました。

   She trudged off with her head down.

5. まもなく，彼女から新しい住所を知らせて きました。

   Before long, she informed me of her new address.

6. 後悔に似た涙が流れて きました。

   Tears of regret came flowing from her eyes.

7. 明日私はあなたを上野動物園へ連れて いきます。

   Tomorrow I'll take you to the Ueno Zoo.

8. さっき警官は貧民くつからみなしごを本署に連れて きました。

   Only a short while ago a policeman brought in an orphan from a slum to the police headquarters.

9. 私は家に子供一人きり留守番に置いて きました。

   I came here, leaving my child alone to take care of the house.

10. 彼は獄吏になってから，世間の暗黒面をずいぶん見て きました。

    He has seen the dark side of the world ever since becoming a jailer.

11. 弟はオーバーのえりを立てて，はいって きました。

    My younger brother, the collar of his overcoat turned up, came in.

12. 彼は手を引こうとするように，彼女に近づいて きました。

    He came near, as if he were going to take her by the hand.

13. 車が急なカーブを描くと，彼女が私の方へ倒れて きました。

    When the car took a sudden curve, she came falling toward me.

14. 彼女は子供をかかえて，帰って

    She left, holding the child in her

いきました。   arms.

15. 夜十一時を少しまわったころ、   A little after eleven at night, he
彼は下宿へ帰ってきました。   returned to his lodging house.

Exercise

Change each verb given below the sentences into the て or で-form
and fill in each bracket with the verb:

1. 彼女はぐっと不快が（　）きま   Displeasure began to surge up
した。   with a jerk inside her.
   こみ上げた (komiage-ta), welled up＜こみ上げる (komiage-ru), to well up

2. 彼女はどこかへ行ってしまった   It is apparent that she has gone
ようです。親戚か知人かを（　）   somewhere. She's probably gone
いったのでしょう。   to some of her relatives or ac-
                           quaintances.
   たよった (tayot-ta), relied upon＜たよる (tayor-u), to rely upon

3. 表の格子戸が開きました。彼女   The latticed door at the front
は（　）きたのでした。   opened—she had come back.
   帰った (kaet-ta), returned＜帰る (kaer-u), to return

4. 彼女はそっと部屋に（　）き   She quietly came into the room.
ました。
   はいった (hait-ta), entered＜はいる (hair-u), to enter

5. 彼は暖房のあるビルディングか   He stepped out of the heated
ら寒風の町に（　）きました。   building and into the cold wind
                           of the street.
   出た (de-ta), stepped out＜出る (de-ru), to step out

6. 十一時になっても、十二時にな   Though the clock struck—elev-
っても、主人は（　）きません   en, twelve—the husband did not
でした。   return.
   帰った (kaet-ta), returned＜帰る (kaer-u), to return

7. この本を読んでいるうちに、彼   While reading this book, she
女は甘美な物語のなかに（　）い   herself became involved in its
きました。   sweet story.
   おぼれた (obore-ta), indulged＜おぼれる (obore-ru), to indulge

8. 二人の流しが（　）きました。   Two street singers came in.
   はいった (hait-ta), entered＜はいる (hair-u), to enter

9. 台風が次第に（　）きました。   The typhoon was approaching.

近づいた (chikazui-ta), approached＜近づく (chikazuk-u), to approach

10. 彼は大またに足音も荒く（　　）
きました。　　　　　　　　　He came striding into his home
with big heavy footsteps.

帰った (kaet-ta), returned＜帰る (kaer-u), to return

11. 彼女は新宿駅の南口の階段を足
早に（　　）いきました。　She ran quickly down the steps
at the south exit of Shinjuku Station.

降りた (ori-ta), got down＜降りる (ori-ru), to get down

12. 食事が（　　）きました。　The meal was brought in.

運ばれた (hakobare-ta), was carried＜運ばれる (hakobare-ru), to be carried

13. お手伝いさんが，友人の来訪を
告げるために（　　）きました。　The maid came in to announce
the arrival of my friend.

はいった (hait-ta), entered＜はいる (hair-u), to enter

14. 高層建築や住宅が新宿から代々
木一帯に日ごとに（　　）いきま
した。　　　　　　　　　　Lofty buildings and residences
increased day after day through-
out the whole area extending from
Shinjuku to Yoyogi.

ふえた (fue-ta), increased＜ふえる (fue-ru), to increase

15. 彼は立ち上がると，忙しそうに
（　　）いきました。　　He rose to his feet, and bustled
out.

出た (de-ta), went out＜出る (de-ru), to go out

Answers:

1. こみ上げて　2. たよって　3. 帰って　4. はいって　5. 出て　6.
帰って　7. おぼれて　8. はいって　9. 近づいて　10. 帰って　11. 降
りて　12. 運ばれて　13. はいって　14. ふえて　15. 出て

True Compound Verb (2)

Rule

The forms of solution, conclusion, and consequence can be explicitly evidenced in the sentence through the use of て (te) or で (de)+such subsidiary verbs as おきます (okimasu), to keep, しまいます (shimaimasu), had+the past participle, and あります (arimasu), to be; there have (has) been. The form denoting solution can be applied in the sentence as て (te) or で (de)+the subsidiary verb おきます (okimasu), to leave; to keep—this carries the meaning of one's volitional action; that is, this form expresses that action which is preparatory for the subsequent items that would naturally follow. The form denoting conclusion can be expressed with the て (te) or で (de)-form+the subsidiary verb しまいます (shimaimasu), had+the past participle—this carries such meaning that an action is to be performed up to the last moment. The form denoting consequence can be expressed with the て (te) or で (de)-form+the subsidiary verb あります (arimasu), to be; there have (has) been—this carries the meaning of a state or condition resulting from a previously performed action; that is, the form of consequence can be used with only transitive verbs because it expresses the condition of an object effected by an action.

e.g. この問題については，私は当事者の気持ちに任せておきます。(Kono mondai ni tsuite wa, watakushi wa tōjisha no kimochi ni *makasete okimasu*)—I'll leave this problem to the feelings of the persons concerned—任せておきます (makasete okimasu) consists of the two verbs 任せて (makase-te) from the plain past 任せた (makase-ta), entrusted and おきます (okimasu), to leave.

e.g. この大学生は個人の理想を無くしてしまいました。(Kono daigakusei wa kojin no risō o *nakushite shimaimashita*)—This university student had lost his personal ideal—無くしてしまいました (nakushite shimaimashita) consists of the two verbs 無くして (nakushi-te) from the plain past 無くした (nakushi-ta), lost and しまいました (shimaimashita), ended.

e.g. 寮内はみな消燈して，長い廊下にはほの暗い電燈が二つ三つつけてあります。(Ryōnai wa mina shōtō shite, nagai rōka niwa hono gurai dentō ga futatsu mittsu *tsukete arimasu*)—Inside the dormitory lights are all out, and along the long corridor there are two or three dim lights—つけてあります (tsukete arimasu) is a transitive verb; this consists of the two verbs つけて (tsuke-te) from the plain past つけた (tsuke-ta), switched on and あります (arimasu), there exists.　The phrase 電燈が二つ三つつけてあります (dentō *ga* futatsu mittsu *tsukete arimasu*) is induced from the following construction—(だれかが) 電燈を二つ三つつけました ([Dare ka ga] dentō *o* futatsu mittsu *tsukemashita*), *Someone* switched on two or three lights.　The form denoting consequence nearly corresponds in meaning to the form denoting continuance used with an intransitive verb; the difference is that the former is effected by the third person pronoun but the latter has no such nuance.

* 電燈がつけてあります。(Dentō ga *tsukete arimasu*)—The electric light is on—つけてあります (tsukete arimasu) is a transitive verb.

* 電燈がついています。(Dentō ga *tsuite imasu*)—The electric light is on—ついています (tsuite imasu) is an intransitive verb.

Drill

1. 彼は行って しまいました。 　　He had gone.

2. 私は彼女をもう少しそっとして おきます。 　　I'll see her left undisturbed for a little while longer.

3. 一昨日, 彼はおじさんに手紙を 出して しまいました。 　　He sent a letter to his uncle the day before yesterday.

4. 彼は忙しいので, 食事をあとま わしにして しまいました。 　　He was so busy that he left his meal till later.

5. 元気な男はみんな自衛隊に行っ て しまいました。 　　All able men have been drafted into the Self-Defense Force.

6. むすこには私からこの件をよく 話して おきます。 　　I'll make this matter very clear to my son.

7. 彼はちぐはぐな成長をしてし まいました。 　　His growth was stunted.

8. 昨夜私は寝苦しい一夜を過ごし て しまいました。 　　I spent a sleepless night last night.

9. 私の言ったことを覚えて おい てください。 　　Please bear what I said in mind.

10. 彼女は応接間の掃除をして お 　　She had cleaned the drawing

きました。   room.

11. 日泰の外交交渉は絶望に**陥って**しまいました。

Japanese - Thailand diplomatic negotiations had been plunged into despair.

12. この歩哨は銃を抱いたまま**いね**むりしてしまいました。

This sentry had taken a nap, his gun still clutched in his arms.

13. 衣料は昨年から切符制に**なって**しまいました。

From last year the coupon system was adopted for clothing.

14. 家内は病みやつれて，すっかりやせてしまいました。

My wife was quite thin in ill health.

15. 夜通しの子供の看護に母は**疲れ切って**しまいました。

The mother was tired out from nursing her child the whole night.

Exercise

Change each verb given below the sentences into the て or で-form and fill in each bracket with the verb:

1. 私はあなたの提案を（   ）おきます。

I'll think over your proposal.

考えた (kangae-ta), thought＜考える (kangae-ru), to think

2. 彼は共産主義をただ一筋に（   ）しまいました。

He had a straightforward faith in communism.

信じ切った (shinjikit-ta), fully believed＜信じ切る (shinjikir-u), to fully believe

3. 彼女は自分を（   ）しまいました。

She had lost herself.

見失った (miushinat-ta), lost＜見失う (miushina[w]-u), to lose

4. 一人むすこが北海道へ行っていなくなると，この家は年老いた両親二人きりに（   ）しまいました。

There were only aged parents left in this family now that their only son had gone to Hokkaido.

なった (nat-ta), became＜なる (nar-u), to become

5. この大学生は父から手紙を受け取って，将来の方針を（   ）しまいました。

This university student resolved to change the course of his future on receipt of a letter from his father.

変更した (henkō shita), changed＜変更する (henkō suru), to change

6. 私は社長に会ってあなたの就職

I'll see the company director and

のことを（　　）おきます。 — talk to him about your employment.

話した (hanashi-ta), talked＜話す (hanas-u), to talk

7. 彼に会って身辺に気をつけるように（　　）おきます。 — I'll see him and advise him to take care of the uncertainty of his position.

忠告した (chūkoku shita), advised＜忠告する (chūkoku suru), to advise

8. 会社の上層部がいだいている偏見と独裁的な驕慢とを（　　）おけません。 — There can be no toleration of the prejudices and dictatorial arrogance entertained by the upper stratum of the company.

許した (yurushi-ta), permitted＜許す (yurus-u), to permit

9. あなたのご忠告を肝に銘じて（　　）おきます。 — I'll keep your advice in mind.

記憶した (kioku shita), remembered＜記憶する (kioku suru), to remember

10. 部屋のすみには，短波のラジオが（　　）あります。 — In a corner of the room a short-wave radio is set up.

おいた (oi-ta), placed＜おく (ok-u), to place

11. 彼の勉強部屋の壁には，奇妙な漫画が（　　）あります。 — A quaint cartoon is stuck on the wall of his study.

はりつけた (haritsuke-ta), stuck＜はりつける (haritsuke-ru), to stick

12. この作家は原稿を（　　）しまいました。 — This writer finished writing up his manuscripts.

書き上げた (kakiage-ta), finished writing up＜書き上げる (kakiage-ru), to finish writing up

13. 彼女は不遇な（　　）しまいました。 — She had died in unfortunate circumstances.

死に方をした (shini kata o shita), died＜死に方をする (shini kata o suru), to die

14. 前もって係りの者にあなたの実習の件を（　　）おきます。 — I'll talk over your practical training beforehand with the man in charge.

話した (hanashi-ta), talked＜話す (hanas-u), to talk

15. 首相の人命救助の感謝状が額にはめられて，彼の部屋の壁に（　　）あります。 — A letter of thanks from the prime minister for his saving a life is framed and hung on the wall in his room.

かけた (kake-ta), hung＜かける (kake-ru), to hang

Answers:

1. 考えて　2. 信じ切って　3. 見失って　4. なって　5. 変更して　6. 話して　7. 忠告して　8. 許して or 許しては　9. 記憶して　10. おいて　11. はりつけて　12. 書き上げて　13. 死に方をして　14. 話して　15. かけて

第 三十二 課　Lesson 32

True Compound Verb (3)

Rule

The form denoting trial can be expressed with the て (te) or で (de)-form+the subsidiary verb みます (mimasu), to try to—this carries the meaning that an action is to be done on trial.

e.g.　私は彼女に電話をかけて，ちょっと様子を**聞いて みます**。(Wataku-shi wa kanojo ni denwa o kakete, chotto yōsu o *kiite mimasu*)— I'll telephone her, and try to find out just what the situation is —聞いてみます (kiite mimasu) consists of the two verbs 聞いて (kii-te) from the plain past 聞いた (kii-ta), asked and みます (mi-masu), to try to.

e.g.　近いうちに教授になって，北大へ赴任する伊藤氏に彼は**会って みました**。(Chikai uchi ni kyōju ni natte, Hokudai e funin suru Itō-shi ni kare wa *atte mimashita*)—He had an interview with Mr. Ito who is about to start for his post at the Hokkaido University as a professor—会ってみました (atte mimashita) consists of the two verbs 会って (at-te) from the plain past 会った (at-ta), met and みました (mimashita), tried.

Drill

1. 彼は以前勤めたことのある日産自動車会社を**たずねて みました**。

He called at the Nissan Auto-mobile Company where he had worked before.

2. また一つ仕事を**さがして みましょう**。

I'll try to search for work again.

3. 彼はあくる日の午後，また民族学研究所へ**行って みました**。

The next afternoon he again went to the Folklore Research Institute.

4. 彼はさっきポケットに突っこんだ紙片を**出して みました**。

He took out the piece of paper which he had thrust into his pocket just a while before.

5. この未亡人は一生懸命になって子供を**育てて みました**。

This widow tried and brought up the child properly.

6. 彼女は彼ににっこり**笑いかけて**
   みました。

She beamed upon him.

7. 彼は彼女のアパートを**たずねて**
   みました。

He called at her apartment.

8. 彼は家に帰って，自分の机にす
   わってみました。

He returned home and sat down
at his desk.

9. 父は煙草をくわえて，子供部屋
   を**のぞいて みました。**

Holding a cigarette in his mouth,
the father peered into the nursery.

10. 博物館がおわかりになりません
    でしたら，どなたにでもその場所
    を**おたずねになって みてくださ**
    い。

If you can't find the museum,
please ask anyone the place.

11. 私は彼女の人生観を変えるよう
    に**説得して みました。**

I tried to persuade her to change
her view of life.

12. 私は顔見知りの映画館の支配人
    をたずね，友だちを映写技師に雇
    ってくれるように**頼んで みまし**
    た。

I called on the manager, whom
I know, of a movie theatre and
asked him to employ my friend as
a projectionist.

13. 久しぶりで，彼女は伊藤家を**た**
    ずねて みました。

She visited the Ito family after
a long absence.

14. 彼は二階の勉強部屋の壁に泰国
    の地図を**はりつけて みました。**

He attached a map of Thailand
to the wall in his study upstairs.

15. 彼は政党政治について解説を
    書いて みました。

He made an effort to write his
own commentary on party politics.

Exercise

Change each verb given below the sentences into the て or で-form
and fill in each bracket with the verb:

1. インターンはこの患者の病状を
   （　　　）**みました。**

An intern tried to examine the
condition of this patient.

   診察した (shinsatsu shita), diagnosed＜診察する (shinsatsu suru), to diag-
   nose

2. 彼は煙草を十本か十五本に（
   　　　）**みました。**

He tried to cut down on ten or
fifteen cigarettes.

減らした (herashi-ta), cut down＜減らす (heras-u), to cut down

3. この貴族は庶民の生活に（　）みました。 This aristocrat tried to touch the lives of the common people.

触れた (fure-ta), touched＜触れる (fure-ru), to touch

4. 今のところ暇ですから，そのうちに（　）みます。 Since I'm quite free at present, I'll call on you one day.

おたずねした (otazune shita), visited＜おたずねする (otazune suru), to visit

5. そのうちお宅へ（　）みます。 I'll call at your home some day.

どうぞお元気で... Well, I wish you good health...

うかがった (ukagat-ta), called at (on)＜うかがう (ukaga[w]-u), to call at (on)

6. 食事が終わるとすぐ，彼女は妹の部屋へ（　）みました。 When the meal was over, she went at once to her younger sister's room.

行った (it-ta), went＜行く (ik-u), to go

7. もう一度彼女はこの探偵小説を（　）みました。 She read this detective story once more.

読んだ (yon-da), read＜読む (yom-u), to read

8. 東外大に（　）みると，学長はきょうは会えないから明日にしてほしいという返事でした。 When he telephoned the Tokyo University of Foreign Studies to make an appointment with the president, he was informed that he could not see the president before the next day.

電話をかけた (denwa o kake-ta), telephoned＜電話をかける (denwa o kake-ru), to telephone

9. 都電の停留場の前から曇り空の下をゆっくり歩いて，西ケ原の友人の家に（　）みました。 He walked slowly under a cloudy sky from in front of the streetcar stop, and dropped in at his friend's house in Nishigahara.

寄った (yot-ta), dropped in at＜寄る (yor-u), to drop in at

10. 彼は社長室のとびらを（　）みました。 He pushed open the door of the director's room.

押しあけた (oshiake-ta), pushed open＜押しあける (oshiake-ru), to push open

11. 朝方医者は重症の入院患者を（　）みました。 Towards morning the doctor examined the seriously ill inpatient.

見た (mi-ta), examined＜見る (mi-ru), to examine

12. 娘はたんすの小戸だなから母の
写真を（　　）みました。

The daughter fetched her mother's photograph from a small drawer in her wardrobe.

出した (dashi-ta), took out＜出す (das-u), to take out

13. 昼の食事のあと，彼女は庭に
（　　）みました。

After lunch, she went out into the garden.

出た (de-ta), went out＜出る (de-ru), to go out

14. 「本当に独身で通すのですか」と
彼女は彼にわざと（　　）みまし
た。

"Will you really always live alone?", she asked him pointedly.

聞いた (kii-ta), asked＜聞く (kik-u), to ask

15. 彼女は早く過去を忘れて，新し
い生活にはいるように（　　）み
ました。

She was mindful of entering upon a peaceful life, forgetting the past as quickly as possible.

心掛けた (kokoro gake-ta), was mindful of＜心掛ける (kokoro gake-ru), to be mindful of

Answers:
1. 診察して 2. 減らして 3. 触れて 4. おたずねして 5. うかがって 6. 行って 7. 読んで 8. 電話をかけて 9. 寄って 10. 押しあけて 11. 見て 12. 出して 13. 出て 14. 聞いて 15. 心掛けて

Some Auxiliary Verbs

(may be; must be; to be+infinitive; to intend to)

Rule

Such expressions as かもしれない (kamoshirenai), plain form, かもしれません (kamoshiremasen), polite form, may be; にちがいない (ni chigai nai), plain form, にちがいありません (ni chigai arimasen), polite form, must be; はずだ (hazu da), plain form, はずです (hazu desu), polite form, the copula+infinitive; and つもりだ (tsumori da), plain form, つもりです (tsumori desu), polite form, to intend to, are used as an auxiliary verb in the sentence.

In the case of verbs, each of these expressions かもしれません (kamoshiremasen), にちがいありません (ni chigai arimasen), はずです (hazu desu), and つもりです (tsumori desu) is put after the plain present/future or past form of any verb.

e.g. もしかしたら、彼女は未亡人になる（の）**かもしれません**。(Moshika shitara, kanojo wa mibōjin ni naru [no] *kamoshiremasen*)—If worst came to worst, she might be plunged into widowhood—なる (nar-u), to become, is a verb in the plain present/future form.

* のかもしれません (*no* kamo shiremasen) is more emphatic and descriptive than かもしれません (kamoshiremasen).

e.g. 彼は食事に行った（の）**かもしれません**。(Kare wa shokuji ni itta [no] *kamoshiremasen*)—He might have gone to his meal—行った (itta), went, is a verb in the plain past form.

The negative form of the auxiliary verb かもしれません (kamoshiremasen) in the case of verbs can always be expressed by the plain present/future or past negative form of any verb+かもしれません (kamoshiremasen).

e.g. 彼は今年外務省を退職しない**かもしれません**。(Kare wa kotoshi gaimushō o taishoku shinai *kamoshiremasen*)—He might not retire from the Foreign Ministry this year—退職しない (taishoku shinai), to not retire from, is a verb in the present/future negative form

e.g. 彼は家族と熱海へ避暑に行かなかった**かもしれません**。(Kare wa kazoku to Atami e hisho ni ikanakatta *kamoshiremasen*)—He and his family might not have gone to pass the summer in Atami—行かなかった (ikanakatta), did not go, is a verb in the plain past negative form.

In the case of nouns, かもしれません (kamoshiremasen) is put after them.

   e.g. 彼女は流行歌手かもしれません。(Kanojo wa ryūkō kashu *kamo-shiremasen*)—She may be a popular singer—流行歌手 (ryūkō kashu), a popular singer, is a noun.

In the negative form of the auxiliary verb かもしれません (kamo-shiremasen) in the use of the copula, ではない (dewa nai) or ではなかった (dewa nakatta), the copula in the plain present/future or past negative form, is used. This ではない or ではなかった relates to かもしれません (may).

   e.g. 彼は国費留学生ではないかもしれません。(Kare wa kokuhi ryūga-kusei dewa nai *kamoshiremasen*)—He may not be a foreign student on government support—ではない (dewa nai), to not be, is the copula in the plain present/future negative form.

   e.g. 彼女は私費留学生ではなかったかもしれません。(Kanojo wa shihi ryūgakusei dewa nakatta *kamoshiremasen*)—She may not have been a foreign student at her own expense—ではなかった (dewa nakatta), was not, is the copula in the plain past negative form.

In the predicative use of な (na)-adjectives, かもしれません (kamo-shiremasen) follows the same form as nouns. That is, the final な (na) of each な (na)-adjective true function may be dropped, this omis-sion enabling it to be used as the noun form. This noun form is put before かもしれません。

   e.g. この工員は勤勉かもしれません。(Kono kōin wa kinben *kamoshi-remasen*)—This factory hand may be diligent—勤勉 (kinben), dili-gence, is the noun form of the な (na)-adjective 勤勉な (kinben na), diligent.

In the nagative form of the auxiliary verb かもしれません (kamo-shiremasen) in the use of な (na)-adjectives, ではない (dewa nai) or ではなかった (dewa nakatta) is used. This ではない (dewa nai) or ではなかった (dewa nakatta) relates to かもしれません。

   e.g. この女工は正直ではないかもしれません。(Kono jokō wa shōjiki dewa nai *kamoshiremasen*)—This factory girl may not be honest —正直 (shōjiki), honesty, is the noun form of the な (na)-adjective 正直な (shōjiki na), honest.

   e.g. このたびの私のボーナスは十分ではなかったかもしれません。(Kono tabi no watakushi no bōnasu wa jūbun dewa nakatta *kamoshire-masen*)—My bonus this time may not have been sufficient—十分 (jūbun), sufficiency, is the noun form of the な (na)-adjective 十

分な (jūbun na), sufficient.

In the case of い (i)-adjectives, each い (i)-adjective ending with either the short vowel い (i) or the long vowel *ii*, as it is, relates to かもしれません (kamoshiremasen).

e.g. この庭園は狭いかもしれません。(Kono teien wa semai *kamoshiremasen*)—This garden may be narrow—狭い (semai), narrow, is an い (i)-adjective ending with a short vowel.

e.g. この噴水は大きいかもしれません。(Kono funsui wa ōkii *kamoshiremasen*)—This fountain may be big—大きい (ōkii) is an い (i)-adjective ending with a long vowel.

In the negative form of the auxiliary verb かもしれません (kamoshiremasen) in the use of い (i)-adjectives, the final vowel い (i) of the plain present/future form is changed to く (ku) and ない (nai), plain present/future negative form, or なかった (nakatta), plain past negative form, added. This くない (ku nai) or くなかった (ku nakatta) relates to かもしれません。

e.g. この湖は浅くないかもしれません。(Kono mizu-umi wa asaku nai *kamoshiremasen*)—This lake may not be shallow—浅くない (asaku nai) is the plain present/future negative form in the predicative use of the い (i)-adjective 浅い (asai), shallow.

e.g. あのとき彼女は悲しくなかったかもしれません。(Ano toki kanojo wa kanashiku nakatta *kamoshiremasen*)—She may not have been sad at that time—悲しくなかった (kanashiku nakatta) is the plain past negative form in the predicative use of the い (i)-adjective 悲しい (kanashii), sad.

In the case of verbs, にちがいありません (ni chigai arimasen), must be, is put after the plain present/future or past form of any verb and conveys the sense of probability.

e.g. 彼は私の過失を非難するにちがいありません。(Kare wa watakushi no kashitsu o hinan suru *ni chigai arimasen*)—He must blame me for my fault—非難する (hinan suru), to blame, is a verb in the plain present/future form.

e.g. 彼の家に何かおもしろくないことがあったにちがいありません。(Kare no ie ni nani ka omoshiroku nai koto ga atta *ni chigai arimasen*)—Something untoward must have occurred at his home—あった (atta), there occurred, is a verb in the plain past form.

In the case of nouns, にちがいありません (ni chigai arimasen) is put after them.

e.g. 彼は一流の作家にちがいありません。(Kare wa ichiryū no sakka *ni chigai arimasen*)—He must be a first rate writer—作家 (sakka), a writer, is a noun.

In the predicative use of な (na)-adjectives, にちがいありません (ni chigai arimasen) follows the same form as nouns. That is, the final な (na) may be dropped, this omission enabling it to be used as the noun form. This noun form is put before にちがいありません。

e.g. 今彼女は幸福にちがいありません。(Ima kanojo wa kōfuku *ni chigai arimasen*)—Now she must be happy—幸福 (kōfuku), happiness, is the noun form of the な (na)-adjective 幸福な (kōfuku na), happy.

In the case of い (i)-adjectives, each い (i)-adjective, as it is, relates to にちがいありません。

e.g. この建物は新しいにちがいありません。(Kono tatemono wa atarashii *ni chigai arimasen*)—This building must be new—新しい (atarashii), new, is an い (i)-adjective.

はずです (hazu desu), to be+infinitive, is put after the plain present/future form of any verb.

e.g. 今日は土曜日だから，私は叔父さんに会うはずです。(Kyō wa doyōbi dakara, watakushi wa ojisan ni au *hazu desu*)—As today is Saturday, I'm to meet my uncle—会う (a[w]-u), to meet, is a verb in the plain present/future form.

e.g. 来年には，彼は独立して法律事務所を持つことができるはずでした。(Rai nen niwa, kare wa dokuritsu shite hōritsu jimusho o motsu koto ga dekiru *hazu deshita*)—In the following year, he was to stand on his own feet and have his own law office—はずでした (hazu deshita) is the polite past form of はずです。

The negative form of the auxiliary verb はずです in the case of verbs can always be expressed by the plain present/future or past negative form of any verb+はずです。

e.g. 彼女は今池袋の映画館で上映している「戦争と平和」というソビエト映画をまだ見ないはずです。(Kanojo wa ima Ikebukuro no eigakan de jōei shite iru 'Sensō to Heiwa' to iu Sobieto eiga o mada minai *hazu desu*)—She is not yet supposed to see the Soviet film entitled "War and Peace" which is now on at a movie theatre in Ikebukuro—見ない (minai), to not see, is a verb in the plain present/future negative form. On the other hand, we may say, まだ見ていないはずです (mada mite inai hazu desu), is not yet supposed to see. Compared with the expression 見ない (minai), to not see, the expression 見ていない (mite inai) denotes the condition or state of the object.

e.g. 彼は関西旅行へ行かなかったはずです。(Kare wa Kansai ryokō e

ikanakatta *hazu desu*)—He was not to have made a trip to the Kansai district—行かなかった (ikanakatta), did not go, is a verb in the plain past negative form.

In the case of な (na)-adjectives, each な (na)-adjective, as it is, relates to はずです。

e.g. この都市の交通機関は旅行者に便利なはずです。(Kono toshi no kōtsūkikan wa ryokōsha ni benri na *hazu desu*)—Traffic facilities in this city are to be convenient for travellers—便利な (benri na), convenient, is a な (na)-adjective.

The negative form of the predicative use of な (na)-adjectives can always be obtained by changing the final vowel *a* of the plain present/future form to *e* and adding ない (nai). Thus, for example, the plain present/future predicative form of 便利な (benri na), convenient, described in the previous sentence is 便利だ (benri da), to be convenient; and this plain present/future negative form is 便利で(は)ない (benri de [wa] nai), to not be convenient. That is, this で(は)ない (de [wa] nai) relates to はずです, as 便利で(は)ないはずです (benri de [wa] nai hazu desu), is not to be convenient. On the other hand, we may say, 不便なはずです (fuben na hazu desu), is to be inconvenient —this time the prefix with the adjective 便利な (benri na), convenient, being 不便な (*fu*ben na), inconvenient. This prefix is exemplified as follows:

親切な	(shinsetsu na), kind	幸福な	(kōfuku na), happy
不親切な	(*fu*shinsetsu na), unkind	不幸な	(*fu*kō na), unhappy
正直な	(shōjiki na), honest	幸運な	(kōun na), fortunate
不正直な	(*fu*shōjiki na), dishonest	不運な	(*fu*-un na), unfortunate
正当な	(seitō na), reasonable	十分な	(jūbun na), sufficient
不当な	(*fu*tō na), unreasonable	不十分な	(*fu*jūbun na), insufficient
正確な	(seikaku na), accurate	必要な	(hitsuyō na), necessary
不正確な	(*fu*seikaku na), inaccurate	不必要な	(*fu*hitsuyō na), unnecessary
完全な	(kanzen na), complete		
不完全な	(*fu*kanzen na), incomplete		

e.g. いなかの生活は便利ではないはずです (or 不便なはずです)。(Inaka no seikatsu wa benri dewa nai *hazu desu* [or: fuben na *hazu desu*])—Life in the rural districts is not supposed to be convenient (or: is to be inconvenient).

In the case of い (i)-adjectives, each い (i)-adjective, as it is, relates to はずです。

e.g. 政治家の中には左翼系統の人が相当に多いはずです。(Seijika **no** naka niwa sayoku keitō no hito ga sōtō ni ōi *hazu desu*)—There are likely to be plenty of left-wing people among the politicians —多い (ōi), many, is an い (i)-adjective.

The negative form of the predicative use of い (i)-adjectives can always be obtained by changing the final vowel い (i) of the plain present/future form to く (ku) and adding ない (nai). Thus, for example, the plain present/future predicative form is described in the previous sentence as 多い (ōi), many; and the plain present/future negative form is 多く(は)ない (ōku [wa] nai), not many. That is, this くない (ku nai) relates to はずです, as 多く(は)ないはずです (ōku [wa] nai hazu desu), is not to be many.

e.g. 西洋諸国に比べると、日本への留学生は多くはないはずです。(Seiyō shokoku ni kuraberu to, Nihon e no ryūgakusei wa ōku wa nai *hazu desu*)—Compared with Western countries, those foreign students who would come to Japan and study are not supposed to be numerous.

つもりです (tsumori desu), to intend to; to be going to, is put after the plain present/future form of any verb.

e.g. 私は四年間東京の大学で電気の勉強をするつもりです。(Watakushi wa yo nen kan Tōkyō no daigaku de denki no benkyō o suru *tsumori desu*)—I'm going to study electricity at a university in Tokyo for four years—勉強をする (benkyō o suru), to study, is a verb in the plain present/future form.

e.g. 来年は彼女は芸大を受験するつもりでした。(Rai nen wa kanojo wa geidai o juken suru *tsumori deshita*)—She intended to sit for the entrance examination to the University of Art in the following year—つもりでした (tsumori deshita), intended to, is the polite past form of つもりです。

The negative form of the auxiliary verb つもりです in the case of verbs can always be expressed by the plain present/future negative form of any verb+つもりです or つもりでした。

e.g. 今度の土曜日には、私は上野国立西洋美術館の展覧会を見に行かないつもりです。(Kondo no doyōbi niwa, watakushi wa Ueno kokuritsu seiyō bijutsukan no tenrankai o mi ni ikanai *tsumori desu*)—Next Saturday I'm not going to go see the exhibition at the Ueno National Western Art Gallery—見に行かない (mi ni ikanai), to not go to see, is the plain present/future negative form of the verb 見に行く (mi ni ik-u), to go to see.

e.g. あの時私は彼に協力しないつもりでした。(Ano toki watakushi wa

kare ni kyōryoku shinai *tsumori deshita*)—I did not intend to co-operate with him at that time—協力しない (kyōryoku shinai), to not co-operate, is the plain present/future negative form of the verb 協力する (kyōryoku suru), to co-operate.

Drill

1. この雑誌は社会主義**かもしれません**。

This magazine might even be socialistic.

2. 私は内面的にあなたに協力して いる**つもりです**。

I am trying to co-operate with you in an indirect way.

3. そのくらいの心配ならだれでも 持っている**はずです**。

Almost every one ought to hold some feelings of such anxiety.

4. 私のいとこは来年の春東大を卒 業する**はずです**。

My cousin is to graduate from Tokyo University in the spring of the next year.

5. 彼は黙って主人のおしかりを受 ける**つもりでした**。

He intended to take the master's rebukes without a word on his part.

6. この店は営業不振に悩んでいた **にちがいありません**。

This shop must have been worried about the slackness of business.

7. おそらく彼の論説に耳を傾ける 知識人は激減した**にちがいありま せん**。

Probably it was that intelligent listeners to his views had remarkably decreased.

8. この哲学者は時には生活の変化 を楽しむこともある**かもしれませ ん**。

This philosopher might enjoy a change in his life sometime.

9. 「あなたは自衛隊の幹部候補生 の試験を受ける**つもりですか**。」

"Do you intend to sit for the cadet officer's examination of the Self-Defence Force?"

10. 厳粛な校長の訓戒は生徒たちの 胸にひびいた**かもしれません**。

The principal's admonitions in solemn tones would have sounded a response in the pupils' hearts.

11. この人は社会主義だか共産主義

This man would unmistakably

だかにかぶれているにちがいあり
ません。

be infected by socialism or communism or something of the sort.

12. 当局は相当の決意をもって，思
想と言論の弾圧に乗りだして来る
にちがいありません。

The authorities would un-
doubtedly undertake oppression of
thought and speech with absolute
resolution.

13. あなたは自分の軽率を自覚する
にちがいありません。

You will even become conscious
of your own rashness.

14. 彼は宗教に対しては，恐らく頭
から軽蔑してかかるにちがいあり
ません。

He would probably fight against
religion with unsparing contempt.

15. 八時間働けば，現在では相当の
収入はあるはずです。

If one were to work for eight
hours, he could expect quite a
good income at present.

16. 日本電気会社は，さがせばすぐ
にわかるにちがいありません。

If one inquired, he could soon
find out where the Japan Electric
Company was.

17. わずか一カ月ののちに，彼は大
使館員となって泰国に行くはずで
す。

Within only one month, he is
going to Thailand as a member
of the embassy staff.

18. 子供の養育そのものが，彼女の
生きがいであるかもしれません。

Bringing up a child itself would
make her life worth-while.

19. 彼は近いうちに自衛隊にはいる
はずです。

It seems that before long he will
be in the Self-Defence Force.

20. やはり彼女は本性からゆがんで
しまった女であったかもしれませ
ん。

She might really have been evil
at heart as everyone thought.

21. 店の主人はこの使用人を解雇し
なかったにちがいありません。

The master of the shop would
certainly not have dismissed this
employee from duty.

22. このような問題は私が解決しな
くても，父が自然に解決してくれ
るにちがいありません。

Though I could not possibly
solve a problem like this, my
father would certainly create a

23. 犯罪者のむすことして，彼もまた世間から白い目で見られる**にちがいありません**。

As the son of a criminal, he too would be, without doubt, ostracized by society.

24. このむすこは両親の言葉を無視して，駆け落ちしようとします。これが今世間でいわれている「自由」というもの**かもしれません**。

Ignoring the words of his parents, this son is ready to run away with his fiancée—this may be the "freedom" now spoken of in society.

25. 私の親友が危機に立っています。彼自身か，それとも私か，だれかしらの怠慢によるものである**にちがいありません**。

The crisis must be faced by my close friend—that must have been due to carelessness on his own part, or on my own, or on someone else's.

26. 夫婦げんかをして彼女は家を飛び出しました。彼女はもうどこかの鉄道線路で子供を抱いたまま死んでいるの**かもしれません**。

She had a quarrel with her husband and rushed out of the house. Holding a baby in her arms, she already might have lost her life on a railway track somewhere.

27. この身体障害者はそりかえっていすの背に頭をのせ，漠然と天井をながめているのは絶望の表情**かもしれません**。

This physically handicapped person threw his head back against the chair, looking vaguely up at the ceiling; perhaps his expression showed despair.

28. 本当にすぐれた政治は国民を苦しめる形ではなくて，国民をよろこばせる形であるべき**はずです**。

Really excellent administration does not oppress the people but ought to form its policy in such a way as to please the people.

29. 医師会と医学界との共同主催の医師大会があります。いまのところ私は内科と小児科の二つに参加することになる**はずです**。

There is a physician's meeting, under the co-auspices of the medical association and the medical academy. As far as I know, I'll be participating in both internal

natural solution.

medicine and pediatrics.

Exercise

Fill in the following blanks with "かもしれません", "にちがいあり
ません", "はずです" and "つもりです":

1. 彼女は私の友人のおくさんで
ある（　　）。

She must be my friend's wife.

2. 友だちを現在の貧しさから救い
出してやる方法がある（　　）。

There must be some way to
saving my friend from his present
poverty.

3. 私は親不幸（　　）。

I might be unfilial.

4. レストランには，二人の友人が
待っている（　　）。

My two friends ought to be
waiting for me to arrive at the
restaurant.

5. 私はいつまでもこの敗北を続け
て行かない（　　）。

I don't intend to accept this
defeat indefinitely.

6. 私はあなたの今後の論文を十分
に注意して見る（　　）。

I will be watching your future
articles with great care.

7. 私自身の方が主人より先に死ぬ
（　　）。

Perhaps I myself might die
before my husband.

8. 私は二年ほど日本に滞在する
（　　）。

I intend to stay in Japan for
about two years.

9. 宗教は自由であるべき（　　）。

Perhaps there ought to be freedom of religion.

10. 言ったって，あなたにはわから
ない（　　）。

Even if I told you, you might
not understand me.

11. 半年そこらで，日本語をマスタ
ーすることは困難（　　）。

It might be difficult to master
the Japanese language in half a
year or so.

12. 私は辞職しなくてはならない
（　　）。

I may have to resign my post.

13. 彼女は今彼に腹を立てている
（　　）。

Now she may be filling with
anger at him.

14. あなたは多少考え違いをしてい

You must be more or less mis-

る（　　）。

taken in your thinking.

15. この学生を先に罰すべき（　　）。

This student might, first, be punished.

16. 彼は軍隊のなかでは，尊敬されていた（　　）。

He must have been respected within the army.

17. 物価騰貴は国民の生活を脅かす（　　）。

A rise in prices of commodities would undoubtedly threaten the people's very lives.

18. 彼女は私の親切を誤解して，私が彼女を愛しているのだと思った（　　）。

She misunderstood my kindness and might have thought I was attached to her.

19. あなたが腹を立てているのも当然（　　）。

I think it might also be quite natural that you're angry.

20. 彼は今日も私の家へ顔を出す（　　）。

He ought to make his appearance at my house today as usual.

21. この食糧難では，米一合手に入れるのさえわずらわしいことをわかっている（　　）。

In this food crisis even one measure of rice is difficult to come by,—this ought to have been fully understood by you.

22. 彼女の覚悟も彼の理想も結局はかない夢に終わってしまう（　　）。

One wonders if her resolution and his ideal might be just a dream in the long run.

23. この青年を本当に改心させるためには，宗教につかせるのがいい（　　）。

To make this young man truly mend his ways, it might be desirable to direct him toward religion.

24. 彼は無道徳で無信仰で，獣のような男である（　　）。

He must certainly be like a beast with no thought of morality or faith.

25. 娘の顔がいくらか青ざめて見えたのは，長い旅行の疲れであった（　　）。

That the daughter was looking a little pale might be the result of her fatigue from the long journey.

26. 彼が詩を書き始めたというのは

He began to write poetry—this

落ちぶれた姿の自分を自嘲する気
持ちなの（　）。

27. 私の青春を踏みにじったのは，
郷里の古い因習といってもいい
（　）。

28. へたにこの若主人を一人歩きさ
せると，店ののれんに傷がついて
しまう（　）。

29. お店のために自分の幸福を犠牲
にすることが，この支配人にとっ
ては幸福だと思っているの（　）。

might be due to a feeling of self-
derision at his fallen status.

It might be said that it is an
old tradition of my home town
that trampled down my young
days.

If we would let this young
master go his own way unguarded,
he might bring harm to the good
name of the shop.

The very act of sacrificing his
own happiness for the shop may
have been happiness to this
manager.

Answers:

1. にちがいありません　2. にちがいありません　3. かもしれません
4. はずです　5. つもりです　6. つもりです　7. かもしれません　8. つ
もりです　9. かもしれません　10. かもしれません　11. かもしれません
12. かもしれません　13. かもしれません　14. にちがいありません　15.
かもしれません　16. にちがいありません　17. にちがいありません　18.
かもしれません　19. かもしれません　20. はずです　21. はずです
22. かもしれません　23. かもしれません　24. にちがいありません　25.
かもしれません　26. かもしれません　27. かもしれません　28. かもし
れません　29. かもしれません

第 三十四 課　Lesson 34

The Form of Necessity or Obligation (must)

Rule

Necessity or obligation is expressed by なければなりません (nake-reba narimasen), or なければいけません (nakereba ikemasen), or なければだめです (nakereba dame desu), a negative conditional meaning "must" or "should".

In the case of vowel stem verbs ending with either *e*-ru or *i*-ru, this form can be obtained by dropping the last syllable *ru* and adding なければなりません, or なければいけません, or なければだめです to the stem.

    e.g. あなたは彼に運転免許証を与えなければなりません (or なければいけません; なければだめです)。(Anata wa kare ni unten menkyoshō o atae *nakereba narimasen* [or: *nakereba ikemasen*; *nakereba dame desu*])—You have to give a driver's license to him—与え (atae) comes from 与える (atae-ru), to give.

    e.g. あなたはあなた自身を信じ，あなたの考えを信じなければなりません (or なければいけません; なければだめです)。(Anata wa anata jishin o shinji, anata no kangae o shinji *nakereba narimasen* [or: *nakereba ikemasen*; *nakereba dame desu*])—You have to believe in yourself and your opinions—信じ (shinji) comes from 信じる (shinji-ru), to believe.

In the case of consonant stem verbs ending with *u*, this form can be obtained by dropping the last syllable *u* and adding *a* to the stem. This *a* relates to なければなりません, or なければいけません, or なければだめです。

    e.g. ともかく，ご両親を安心させるために，あなたは妹さんの結婚問題に骨折らなければなりません (or なければいけません; なければだめです)。(Tomokaku, goryōshin o anshin saseru tame ni anata wa imōtosan no kekkon mondai ni honeora *nakereba narimasen* [or: *nakereba ikemasen*; *nakereba dame desu*])—At any rate you have to take much trouble over your younger sister's matrimonial matters in order to relieve your parents' anxiety—骨折ら (honeor-a) comes from 骨折る (honeor-u), to take trouble.

    e.g. あなたはまじめに働かなければなりません(or なければいけません; なければだめです)。(Anata wa majime ni hataraka *nakereba nari-*

masen [or: *nakereba ikemasen*; *nakereba dame desu*])—You must work honestly—働か (hatarak-a) comes from 働く (hatarak-u), to work.

This form of such irregular verbs as する (suru), to do and 来る (kuru), to come, is しなければなりません (shinakereba narimasen), or しなければいけません (shinakereba ikemasen), or しなければだめです (shinakereba dame desu); こなければなりません (konakereba narimasen), こなければいけません (konakereba ikemasen), こなければだめです (konakereba dame desu).

e.g. あなたは危険な仕事をしなければなりません (or しなければいけません；しなければだめです)。(Anata wa kiken na shigoto o *shinakereba narimasen* [or: *shinakereba ikemasen*; *shinakereba dame desu*])—You have to do a dangerous task.

e.g. 夕食のはじまる前に，帰ってこなければなりません (or こなければいけません；こなければだめです)。(Yūshoku no hajimaru mae ni, kaette *konakereba narimasen* [or: *konakereba ikemasen*; *konakereba dame desu*])—You have to come home before dinner is ready.

The negative of *must* is expressed by なくてもいいです (nakute mo ii desu), なくても結構です (nakute mo kekkō desu), or なくてもかまいません (nakute mo kamaimasen).

In the case of vowel stem verbs, this form is as follows—the root ending with either *e* or *i*+なくてもいいです，なくても結構です，なくてもかまいません。

e.g. あなたは彼の見解を確かめなくてもいいです (or なくても結構です；なくてもかまいません)。(Anata wa kare no kenkai o tashikame *nakute mo ii desu* [or: *nakute mo kekkō desu*; *nakute mo kamaimasen*])—You need not ascertain his outlook—確かめ (tashikame) comes from 確かめる (tashikame-ru), to ascertain.

e.g. あなたは彼の支配に甘んじなくてもいいです (or なくても結構です；なくてもかまいません)。(Anata wa kare no shihai ni amanji *nakute mo ii desu* [or: *nakute mo kekkō desu*; *nakute mo kamaimasen*])—You need not be content with his control—甘んじ (amanji) comes from 甘んじる (amanji-ru), to be content with.

In the case of consonant stem verbs, this negative form is as follows—なくてもいいです，なくても結構です，or なくてもかまいません follows *a* after replacing the final *u* with *a*.

e.g. あなたは彼女の詩集の序文を書かなくてもいいです (or なくても結構です；なくてもかまいません)。(Anata wa kanojo no shishū no jobun o kak*a nakute mo ii desu* [or: *nakute mo kekkō desu*; *nakute mo kamaimasen*])—You need not write a preface for her collection of poems—書か (kak-a) comes from 書く (kak-u), to write.

e.g. ここではくつを脱がなくてもいいです (or なくても結構です；なく
てもかまいません)。(Koko dewa kutsu o nug*a nakute mo ii desu*
[or: *nakute mo kekkō desu*; *nakute mo kamaimasen*])—You need
not take off your shoes here—脱が (nug-a) comes from 脱ぐ (nug-
u), to take off.

In the case of such irregular verbs as する (suru), to do and 来る
(kuru), to come, this negative form is as follows:

e.g. あなたは東京見物をしなくてもいいです (or しなくても結構です；
しなくてもかまいません)。(Anata wa Tōkyō kenbutsu o *shinakute
mo ii desu* [or: *shinakute mo kekkō desu*; *shinakutemo kamaimasen*])
—You need not go sightseeing around Tokyo.

e.g. 私宅へあいさつにこなくてもいいです (or こなくても結構です；こ
なくてもかまいません)。Shitaku e aisatsu ni *konakute mo ii desu*
[or: *konakute mo kekkō desu*; *konakute mo kamaimasen*])—You
need not come to my house to pay your respects.

In the case of nouns, they relate to なければなりません, or なけれ
ばいけません, or なければだめです through で (de).

e.g. 命をかけて女を愛する人で なければなりません (or なければいけま
せん；なければだめです)。(Inochi o kakete on-na o aisuru hito *de
nakereba narimasen* [or: *nakereba ikemasen*; *nakereba dame desu*])
—You must be a person who can love a woman at the risk of
your life—人 (hito), a person, is a noun.

In the case of な (na)-adjectives, the final な (na) is dropped, this
omission enabling them to be used as the noun forms. Such a noun
as this relates to なければなりません, or なければいけません, or なけ
ればだめです through で (de).

e.g. 警察官は市民に親切で なければなりません (or なければいけませ
ん；なければだめです)。(Keisatsukan wa shimin ni shinsetsu *de
nakereba narimasen* [or: *nakereba ikemasen*; *nakereba dame desu*])
—A policeman must be kind to the citizens—親切 (shinsetsu),
kindness, is the noun form of the な (na)-adjective 親切な (shinsetsu na), kind.

This negative form in the case of nouns and the noun forms
derived from the な (na)-adjectives is similarly as follows: nouns+で
(de)+なくてもいいです (nakute mo ii desu)；なくても結構です (nakute
mo kekkō desu)；なくてもかまいません (nakute mo kamaimasen).

e.g. 夕食のおかずは肉で なくてもいいです (or なくても結構です；な
くてもかまいません)。(Yūshoku no okazu wa niku *de nakute mo
ii desu* [or: *nakute mo kekkō desu*; *nakute mo kamaimasen*])—The

side dishes for dinner need not be meat—肉 (niku), meat, is a noun.

e.g. 年末の大売り出しの装飾は華美で なくてもいいです (or なくても結
構です；なくてもかまいません)。(Nen matsu no ōuridashi no sōsho-
ku wa kabi *de nakute mo ii desu* [or: *nakute mo kekkō desu*; *nakute mo kamaimasen*])—Decorations for the year-end bargain sales
need not be gorgeous—華美 (kabi), gorgeousness, is the noun form
of the な (na)-adjective 華美な (kabi na), gorgeous.

In the case of い (i)-adjectives, the final い (i) is dropped, this
termination enabling them to suffix く (ku). This く (ku) directly
relates to なければなりません, or なければいけません, or なければだめ
です。

e.g. 一本のペンに身を託する自由なる論客は自己を信ずる心が強く なけ
ればなりません (or なければいけません；なければだめです)。(Ippon
no pen ni mi o taku suru jiyū naru ronkaku wa jiko o shinzuru
kokoro ga tsuyo*ku nakereba narimasen* [or: *nakereba ikemasen*;
nakereba dame desu])—A free lance journalist, depending for his
livelihood only on the pen, has to be strong in self-confidence—
強く (tsuyoku), strongly, is the adverbial form of the い (i)-adjec-
tive 強い (tsuyoi), strong.

This negative form in the case of い (i)-adjectives is as follows: い
(i)-adj. ＋く (ku)＋なくてもいいです (or なくても結構です；なくてもか
まいません)。

e.g. 大売り出しの幕は赤く なくてもいいです (or なくても結構です；な
くてもかまいません)。(Ōuridashi no maku wa aka*ku nakute mo ii
desu* [or: *nakute mo kekkō desu*; *nakute mo kamaimasen*])—The
hangings for the bargain sale need not be red—赤く (akaku) is
the adverbial form of the い (i)-adjective 赤い (akai), red.

Note: In the case of verbs, necessity or obligation can also be written and
spoken with the use of such expressions as ねばなりません (neba narimasen), or ねばいけません (neba ikemasen), or ねばだめです (neba dame
desu) and なくてはなりません (nakute wa narimasen), or なくてはいけま
せん (nakute wa ikemasen), or なくてはだめです (nakute wa dame desu).

In addition, nouns, noun forms and い (i)-adjectives in the form of
necessity or obligation can also be used with such an expression as な
くてはなりません (nakute wa narimasen), or なくてはいけません (nakute
wa ikemasen), or なくてはだめです (nakute wa dame desu).

Drill

1. 苦しい思いを我慢しなければな　　You must bear tormented
りません。　　　　　　　　　　　　thoughts.

2. すすんで級友の模範とならなくてはなりません。

You must take the leadership and a model for the other classmates.

3. 兵隊は物を考えなくてもいいです。兵隊は戦争する機械です。

A soldier need not think of anything. A soldier is a machine for carrying out a war.

4. 「なぜ私がそこへ行かなくてはなりませんか。」

"Why must I go there?"

5. 彼女は自分でこの問題を解決しなくてはなりません。

She herself has to solve this problem.

6. 私は積極的に彼と協力しなければなりません。

I must actively co-operate with him.

7. 彼女は自分の不幸に耐え，自分の身を守っていかなければなりません。

She has to defend herself, bearing her unhappiness.

8. 国民ことごとく奮起してこの国難を突破しなくてはなりません。

The whole nation has to bestir itself and tide itself over this national crisis.

9. 文部省を退職する彼は，事務の引きつぎをしなくてはなりません。

He, who will retire from the Ministry of Education, must surrender his duties to another.

10. 彼は今失業中で，何とかして自分の身の処置をつけなくてはなりません。

He is now unemployed, and has to manage to find some solution for himself.

11. 先生は急がずにゆっくりと学生を指導していかなくてはなりません。

The teacher has to guide the students slowly and steadily.

12. 全体のためにはあくまで自己を放棄して公につくさなくてはなりません。

One must abandon himself completely, and serve the public.

13. あの連中に気に入られるような体裁を整えなくてもいいです。

You need not keep up an appearance to please that bunch.

14. あした自衛隊に入隊だというか

Since I'm enlisting in the Self-

ら，今日のうちに出立しなきゃな
らんです。

Defence Force in one day from
now, I have to leave sometime
today.

* しなきゃならんです is more colloquial than しなくてはなりません。

15. 夫に死別したこの婦人は，自分
の生きて行く新しい道をどこかに
見つけ出さ**なくてはなりません**で
した。

This woman who was bereaved
of her husband had to discover a
new way of carrying on her life
somewhere else.

16. 彼はこの二週間ぶらぶらと遊ん
でしまいました。失われたこの貴
重な日々をとりもどさ**なくてはな
らない**ような，せき立てられる気
持ちでした。

He had spent all these two weeks
in idleness. He felt hard-pressed
to regain each separate precious
day which had been lost.

17. 会社の壁には，運転成績表のジ
グザグな線が描いてあります。運
転手にとっては，一人でも多く乗
客を乗せ**なくてはなりません**。

On the wall of the company is
drawn a zigzag line recording the
progress of the drivers. To them,
even one extra passenger should
be picked up.

18. 彼女は出かせぎに行った夫がど
こにいるかも知らず，どの地方で
働いているかも知らずに待ってい
なくてはならないのです。

Without knowing the whereabouts of her husband who has
gone to far distant places to work
or in what part of the country he
is working, she is forced to wait
for him.

* なくてはならないのです is more emphatic and descriptive than なくては
ならないです。

Exercise

Fill in the following blanks with なければなりません or なくてもい
いです, using the verbs, adjectives, and nouns given below the sentences:

1. あらゆる事を（   ）。

You must bear all kinds of hard-
ship.

忍ぶ (shinob-u), to bear

2. カーテンの色は白（   ）。

The color of a curtain need not

be white.

白 (shiro), white, a noun

3. 防波堤は（　　）。　　　　　　A breakwater must be high.

高い (takai), high, an *i*-adjective

4. 学者は（　　）。　　　　　　A scholar need not be sociable.

社交的な (shakōteki na), sociable, a *na*-adjective

5. 彼のご機嫌とりを（　　）。　　You need not flatter him.

ご機嫌とりをする (gokigen tori o suru), to flatter

6. 彼は彼女との愛情をひた向きに　He has to defend his affections
（　　）。　　　　　　　　　　for her blindly.

守る (mamor-u), to defend

7. あなたは彼女に対して道義的任　You must carry out your moral
務を遂行（　　）。　　　　　　duty toward her.

遂行する (suikō suru), to carry out

8. 自分の悲劇は自分で解決（　　）。　One will have to solve his own
tragedies for himself.

解決する (kaiketsu suru).　to solve

9. 両親との別離という事実に直面　He has to face the fact of separa-
（　　）。　　　　　　　　　　tion between his parents.

直面する (chokumen suru), to face

10. 新聞記者は命をとして言論を　Journalists must protect free
（　　）。　　　　　　　　　　speech at the sacrifice of their
lives.

守る (mamor-u), to protect

11. あなたは彼女との恋にもっと強　You'll have to be strong enough
く（　　）。　　　　　　　　　to respond adequately to your love
for her.

生きる (iki-ru), to respond; to live.

12. 言論機関に携わるものはどこま　Those in charge of the organs
でも厳正（　　）。　　　　　　of public communication must be
strict to the last.

厳正 (gensei), strictness, is the noun form of the *na*-adjective 厳正な
(gensei na), strict

13. 彼は身に降りかかる労苦をはね　He has to lead his life, pushing
のけながら生きて（　　）。　　aside the hardships which hang
over him.

生きていく (ikite ik-u), to lead one's life

14. 私は彼に反抗（　　）。 I have to raise an objection to him.

反抗する (hankō suru), to raise an objection

15. この件につき，あなたは彼を（　　）。 You have to convince him about this matter.

納得させる (nattoku sase-ru), to convince

16. 歴史家は古めかしいものの美しさを愛する人（　　）。 A historian must be a person who loves the beauty found among traditional things.

人 (hito), a person, a noun

17. 賠償金について，日本政府は泰側と折衝して（　　）。 As to reparations, the Japanese government must continue to negotiate with Thailand.

折衝していく (sesshōshite ik-u), to continue to negotiate

18. たとえ政府にさからい法律にさからっても，守るべき自己の心はただ一筋に（　　）。 Even if they should disobey the government and the law, they should straightforwardly fulfill the demands of their own hearts.

守り通す (mamoritōs-u), to fulfill

Answers:

1. 忍ばなければなりません 2. でなくてもいいです 3. 高くなければなりません 4. 社交的でなくてもいいです 5. しなくてもいいです 6. 守らなければなりません 7. しなければなりません 8. しなければなりません 9. しなければなりません 10. 守らなければなりません 11. 生きなければなりません 12. でなければなりません 13. いかなければなりません 14. しなければなりません 15. 納得させなければなりません 16. でなければなりません 17. いかなければなりません 18. 守り通さなければなりません

The Form of Permission and Prohibition
(may; should not)

Rule

　　...もいいです (...mo ii desu), permission, is used after the て (te) or で (de)-form of any verb. て (te) or で (de) is the connective particle which corresponds to the English "and" and this form can be obtained by changing the final vowel *a* of the plain past form to *e*. This て (te) or で (de)-form＋もいいです (mo ii desu) can be rendered as "may" or "can" in English. The negative form is as follows: て (te) or で (de)＋はいけません (wa ikemasen), or はなりません (wa narimasen), or はだめです (wa dame desu), must not; should not.

e.g.　はっきりと，あなたがおとうさんと反対の立場に立ってもいいです。 (Hakkiri to, anata ga otōsan to hantai no tachiba ni tatte *mo ii desu*)—You may take a definite stand in opposition to your father —立って (tat-te) comes from 立った (tat-ta), stood, in the plain past form.

e.g.　あの国会議員の支持をしてもいいです。(Ano kokkai gi-in no shiji o shite *mo ii desu*)—You may support that member of the Diet —支持をして (shiji o shite) comes from 支持をした (shiji o shita), supported, in the plain past form.

e.g.　日本酒を飲んでもいいです。(Nihon shu o nonde *mo ii desu*)— You may drink Japanese *sake*—飲んで (non-de) comes from 飲んだ (non-da), drank, in the plain past form.

e.g.　亨楽的生活を続けてはいけません (or はなりません；はだめです)。 (Kyōraku teki seikatsu o tsuzukete *wa ikemasen* [or: *wa narimasen*; *wa dame desu*])—You should not continue your gay life—続けて (tsuzuke-te) comes from 続けた (tsuzuke-ta), continued, in the plain past form.

e.g.　戦争を望んではいけません (or はなりません：はだめです)。(Sensō o nozonde *wa ikemasen* [or: *wa narimasen*; *wa dame desu*])—One should not long for war—望んで (nozon-de) comes from 望んだ (nozon-da), longed for, in the plain past form.

e.g.　おとうさんを非難してはいけません (or はなりません；はだめです)。(Otōsan o hinan shite *wa ikemasen* [or: *wa narimasen*; *wa dame desu*])—You should not find fault with your father—非難し

て (hinan shite) comes from 非難した (hinan shita), found fault with, in the plain past form.

Drill

1. 政府のやり方に反対してもいい
   です。

   You may have objections to the policy of the government.

2. ストーブに石炭を入れてもいい
   ですか。

   May I put several pieces of coal into the stove?

3. 先生を恨んではだめです。

   You must not feel hatred toward your teacher.

4. 足を投げ出してすわってはいけ
   ません。

   You should not sit down with your legs stretched out.

5. なんでもやれるような錯覚を起
   こしてはいけません。

   You must not delude yourself into thinking that you can do anything.

6. 授業中に友だちに話しかけては
   いけません。

   You should not speak to your friends during the lesson.

7. 孤独を誇ってもいいです。

   You may take pride in your solitude.

8. 二人の間の感情がくいちがって
   はいけません。

   The emotions between the two should not be at cross-purposes.

9. この問題を未解決のまま放置し
   てはだめです。

   You should not leave this problem unsolved.

10. 戦争に行くためには、婚約なん
    かしてはなりません。

    You must not become engaged if you propose going to the war.

11. 彼のような冷静な自由主義者が
    排斥されてはなりません。

    An unemotional liberalist like him should not be ousted.

12. 彼に積極的援助をしてもいいで
    す。

    You may give positive assistance to him.

13. 彼女が何を考えているかという
    ことを気にしてはなりません。

    You must not pay any attention to what she thinks.

14. 今から友人を見舞いに行って来
    てもいいですか。

    May I go and inquire after my friend now?

15. 型通りの文句でこの工員をほめたり激励したりしてはだめです。

You must not give praise and encouragement to this worker in the conventional phrases.

16. 他人の手ぬぐいで自分の顔をふいてはだめです。

You should not wipe your face with an other's handkerchief.

17. 早急に愛情の問題を処理してはいけません。

You should not arrange your love affairs so promptly.

18. 欠点を指摘されるのを恐れてはだめです。

You should not be afraid of having your shortcomings pointed out.

19. 友人を危機に追い込んではいけません。

You must not plunge your friend into crisis.

20. 他人に警戒され憎まれてはなりません。

You should not be watched and hated by others.

21. 夢につかれてはなりません。

You should not be obsessed by a dream.

22. 自分を狭くして生きてはいけません。

You should not lead a life confined within a narrow circle.

23. あなたの考えは拘束されてはなりません。

Your opinions should not be suppressed.

24. 世の中は理論通りには行きません。今の世界の動き，社会全体の有様，各自の家庭の都合，それらの条件をも無視してはいけません。

The world does not proceed according to theory. The present movement of the world and the conditions of the whole of society, the family circumstances of every person—these factors also must not be ignored.

Exercise

Fill in each bracket with a verbal form suitable for these expressions, taking into consideration the verb given below each sentence:

1. 夜遊びに（　）もいいですか。　　May I have the night out?
行った (it-ta), went＜行く (ik-u), to go

2. 彼女と並んで（　）もいいです。　　You may sit down beside her.

すわった (swat-ta), sat down＜すわる (swar-u), to sit down

3. 主人に恨みを（　　）はなりま　　You must not hold a grudge
せん。　　　　　　　　　　　　　　against your master.
持った (mot-ta), held; had＜持つ (mots-u), to hold; to have

4. 英雄主義に（　　）もいいです。　You may yearn after heroism.
あこがれた (akogare-ta), yearned＜あこがれる (akogare-ru), to yearn

5. あんなやつに（　　）はだめで　　You must not go against such
す。　　　　　　　　　　　　　　　fellows.
逆らった (sakarat-ta), went against＜逆らう (sakara[w]-u), to go against

6. （　　）もいいですか。　　　　　May I have my evening drink?
晩酌した (banshaku shita), had one's evening drink＜晩酌する (banshaku
suru), to have one's evening drink

7. 彼女を（　　）はなりません。　　You should not make her unhappy.
不幸にした (fukō ni shita), made someone unhappy＜不幸にする (fukō ni
suru), to make someone unhappy

8. 両親に（　　）はいけません。　　You should not be indulged in
by your parents.
甘やかされた (amayaka sare-ta), was indulged in＜甘やかされる (amayaka sare-ru), to be indulged in

9. 弟さんと（　　）はなりません。　You should not quarrel with
your younger brother.
けんかした (kenka shita), quarrelled＜けんかする (kenka suru), to quarrel

10. 友人の支持を（　　）はなりま　You should not lose the support
せん。　　　　　　　　　　　　　of your friends.
失った (ushinat-ta), lost＜失う (ushina[w]-u), to lose

11. 級友の人望を（　　）はなりま　You should not lose your popu-
せん。　　　　　　　　　　　　　larity among your classmates.
失った (ushinat-ta), lost＜失う (ushina[w]-u), to lose

12. この話は（　　）はだめです。　This discussion should not be
deferred.
保留にした (horyū ni shita), deferred＜保留にする (horyū ni suru), to defer

13. 相手の人を（　　）はいけませ　You should not restrict the per-
ん。　　　　　　　　　　　　　　sonality of the partner.
拘束した (kōsoku shita), restricted＜拘束する (kōsoku suru), to restrict

14. 朝早い汽車で（　　）もいいで　May I go up to Tokyo by the

すか。   early train?

上京した (jōkyō shita), went up to Tokyo＜上京する (jōkyō suru), to go
up to Tokyo

15. 自分の不運を（　　）はいけま   You should not lament your bad
　　せん。   fortune.

嘆いた (nagei-ta), lamented＜嘆く (nagek-u), to lament

16. 火を（　　）もいいですか。   May I stoke up the fire?

かき回した (kakimawashi-ta), stoked＜かき回す (kakimawas-u), to stoke

17. 現在の自分の立場だけを（　　）   You must not consider only your
　　はだめです。   present situation.

考えた (kangae-ta), considered＜考える (kangae-ru), to consider

18. 煙草を（　　）はいけません。   You should not toss away your
                                cigarette.

投げ捨てた (nagesute-ta), tossed＜投げ捨てる (nagesute-ru), to toss

19. 当局に（　　）はいけません。   You should not crawl to the
                                Authorities.

あゆした (ayu shita), crawled to; flattered＜あゆする (ayu suru), to crawl
to; to flatter

20. 女性を（　　）はいけません。   You should not stare at a lady.

じろじろ見た (jirojiro mi-ta), stared at＜じろじろ見る (jirojiro mi-ru), to
stare at

21. 権力を（　　）はだめです。   You should not brandish your
                                authority.

振りまわした (furimawashi-ta), brandished＜振りまわす (furimawas-u), to
brandish

22. 総理との面会を（　　）もいい   You may request an interview
　　です。   with the prime minister.

申し込んだ (mōshikon-da), requested＜申し込む (mōshikom-u), to request

23. 明日（　　）もいいですか。   May I leave the hospital tomor-
                                row?

退院した (tai-in shita), left the hospital＜退院する (tai-in suru), to leave
the hospital

24. 彼の失敗を（　　）はだめです。   You must not jeer at his failure.

ののしった (nonoshit-ta), jeered at＜ののしる (nonoshir-u), to jeer at

25. 授業中教室のガラス窓を通して   You should not gaze absent-
　　外をぼんやり（　　）はいけませ   mindedly outside through the

ん。   classroom's glass windows during
the lesson.

ながめた (nagame-ta), gazed＜ながめる (nagame-ru), to gaze

Answers:

1. 行って　2. すわって　3. 持って　4. あこがれて　5. 逆らって
6. 晩酌して　7. 不幸にして　8. 甘やかされて　9. けんかして　10. 失
って　11. 失って　12. 保留にして　13. 拘束して　14. 上京して　15. 嘆
いて　16. かき回して　17. 考えて　18. 投げ捨てて　19. あゆして　20.
じろじろ見て　21. 振りまわして　22. 申し込んで　23. 退院して　24.
ののしって　25. ながめて

第 三十六 課　Lesson 36

Some Auxiliary Verbs Denoting "Judgement",
"Criticism", "Emotion", and "Suggestion"

Rule

　The expression 方がいいです (hō ga ii desu), had better, is put after the plain present/future form of any verb.

e.g.　このたびの修学旅行をあきらめる**方がいいです**。(Kono tabi no shū-gaku ryokō o akirameru *hō ga ii desu*)—You had better give up the school excursion this time—あきらめる (akirame-ru), to give up, is a vowel stem verb in the plain present/future form.

e.g.　明朝は早めに起きる**方がいいです**。(Myōchō wa hayame ni okiru *hō ga ii desu*)—You had better get up a little earlier tomorrow morning—起きる (oki-ru), to get up, is a vowel stem verb in the plain present/future form.

e.g.　もうおふろから上がる**方がいいです**。(Mō ofuro kara agaru *hō ga ii desu*)—You had better get out of the bath now—上がる (agar-u), to get out of; to go up, is a consonant stem verb in the plain present/future form.

e.g.　ズボンをはく**方がいいです**。(Zubon o haku *hō ga ii desu*)—You had better slip on trousers—はく (hak-u), to slip on; to put on, is a consonant stem verb in the plain present/future form.

　In the negative form of this expression the plain present/future negative of vowel stem verbs can always be obtained by dropping the final る (ru) of the plain present/future form and adding ない (nai) to this root.　This ない (nai) directly relates to 方がいいです.

e.g.　借家を建てない**方がいいです**。(Shakuya o tatenai *hō ga ii desu*)—You had better not build houses to lease—建てない (tate-nai), to not build, comes from 建てる (tate-ru), to build.

e.g.　日本語の勉強にあきない**方がいいです**。(Nihongo no benkyō ni akinai *hō ga ii desu*)—You had better not lose interest in the study of Japanese—あきない (aki-nai), to not lose interest in, comes from あきる (aki-ru), to lose interest in.

　In the negative form of this expression the plain present/future negative of consonant stem verbs can always be obtained by changing the final *u* of the plain present/future form to *a* and adding *nai*. This *anai* directly relates to 方がいいです.

e.g. 通俗な威厳をつくらない方がいいです。(Tsūzoku na igen o tsu-kuranai *hō ga ii desu*)—You had better not make a common show of decorum—つくらない (tsukur-anai), to not make, comes from つくる (tsukur-u), to make.

e.g. タクシーを呼ばない方がいいです。(Takushii o yobanai *hō ga ii desu*)—You had better not call a taxi—呼ばない (yob-anai), to not call, comes from 呼ぶ (yob-u), to call.

Note: The expression 方がいいでしょう (hō ga ii deshō) in place of 方がいいです (hō ga ii desu) can also be used; でしょう (deshō) in 方がいいでしょう (hō ga ii deshō) is a form of です (desu), am; is; are, denoting probability.

The expression 必要があります (hitsuyō ga arimasu), to be neces-sary, is put after the plain present/future form of any verb and its negative form is 必要はありません (hitsuyō wa arimasen), to not be necessary.

e.g. 彼女の言に耳を傾ける必要があります。(Kanojo no gen ni mimi o katamukeru *hitsuyō ga arimasu*)—It is necessary for you to pay special attention to what she has said—耳を傾ける (mimi o kata-muke-ru), to listen to, is a vowel stem verb in the plain present /future form.

e.g. 留学生は邦画を見る必要があります。(Ryūgakusei wa hōga o miru *hitsuyō ga arimasu*)—It is necessary for foreign students to see Japanese films—見る (mi-ru), to see, is a vowel stem verb in the plain present/future form.

e.g. 彼に毎月若干の生活費を送る必要があります。(Kare ni maitsuki jakkan no seikatsuhi o okuru *hitsuyō ga arimasu*)—It is necessary for you to give him a small retainer every month for his living expenses—送る (okur-u), to send, is a consonant stem verb in the plain present/future form.

e.g. 米国の事情を知る必要があります。(Beikoku no jijō o shiru *hi-tsuyō ga arimasu*)—It is necessary for you to have some know-ledge of America's conditions—知る (shir-u), to know, is a con-sonant stem verb in the plain present/future form.

e.g. めがねをかける必要はありません。(Megane o kakeru *hitsuyō wa arimasen*)—It is not necessary for you to put on your eyeglasses —かける (kake-ru), to put on, is a vowel stem verb in the plain present/future form.

e.g. 最後まで抵抗する必要はありません。(Saigo made teikō suru *hitsu-yō wa arimasen*)—It is not necessary for you to resist stoutly to the last—抵抗する (teikō suru), to resist, is an irregular verb in the plain present/future form.

The expression なくてもいいです (nakute mo ii desu), need not, can also be used as the negative form of the expression 必要がありま す (hitsuyō ga arimasu), to be necessary. In this case, the final る (ru) of vowel stem verbs is dropped and なくてもいいです (nakute mo ii desu) added to this root or the final *u* of consonant stem verbs is changed to *a* and なくてもいいです (nakute mo ii desu) added to this *a*.

e.g. 彼に笑顔を向け**なくてもいいです**。(Kare ni egao o muke *nakute mo ii desu*)—You need not turn a smiling face to him)—向け (muke) comes from 向ける (muke-ru), to turn.

e.g. 右翼団体で顔を売ら**なくてもいいです**。(Uyoku dantai de kao o ur*a nakute mo ii desu*)—You need not gain popularity under the rightist wing—売ら (ur-a) comes from 売る (ur-u), to gain.

In the case of nouns, such an expression as が必要です (ga hitsuyō desu), to be necessary, can also be used. In this case, the expression らしさ (rashisa) is put before が必要です (ga hitsuyō desu); that is, a noun+らしさ (rashisa) relates to が必要です (ga hitsuyō desu).

e.g. 良縁に恵まれるには女らしさが**必要です**。(Ryōen ni megumareru niwa on-na rashisa *ga hitsuyō desu*)—It is necessary for you to be womanly to be blessed with a good match—女 (on-na), a woman, in 女らしさ (on-na rashisa), womanly, is a noun.

In the case of both な (na)-adjectives and い (i)-adjectives, such an expression as が必要です (ga hitsuyō desu), to be necessary, can also be used. The final な (na) of な (na)-adjectives and the final い (i) of い (i)-adjectives may both be dropped and さ (sa) added. This さ (sa), the noun form derived from these adjectives, is used before が必要で す (ga hitsuyō desu).

e.g. 彼には生活力の強さが**必要です**。(Kare niwa seikatsuryoku no tsuyosa *ga hitsuyō desu*)—It is necessary for him to hold strong in his manner of living—強さ (tsuyo-sa), strength, is the noun form derived from the い (i)-adjective 強い (tsuyo-i), strong.

e.g. 屈託のない明朗さが**必要です**。(Kuttaku no nai meirōsa *ga hitsuyō desu*)—It is necessary for you to have a carefree brightness—明 朗さ (meirō-sa), brightness, is the noun form derived from the な (na)-adjective 明朗な (meirō-na), bright.

Drill

1. そういう言い方を**しなくてもい いです**。

No need to speak like that.

2. 早く将校になった**方がいいでし**

It's better for you to become

ょう。

3. はっきり言う**必要はありませ
ん**。

No need to speak frankly about
it.

4. 左翼的な雑誌は持たない**方がい
い**です。

It's better for you not to keep
those left-leaning journals.

5. 矢継ぎ早に質問を浴びせる**方が
いい**です。

You had better fire questions in
rapid succession.

6. あなたは彼の支配に甘んじない
方がいいです。

You had better not be content
with his control.

7. 彼との関係を正常な軌道にもど
す**方がいい**です。

You had better put your relations with him back in the right
direction.

8. 言葉を和らげる**方がいいでしょ
う**。

You had better soften your
words.

9. 彼女に憎悪をたぎらかさない**方
がいい**です。

You had better not stir hatred
in her.

10. 彼の行動を非難しない**方がいい**
です。

You had better not revile his
actions.

11. あなたは世論を惑わすような論
説を発表しない**方がいい**です。

You had better not publish an
article that will mislead public
opinion.

12. 日本語の勉強のみに大部分の精
力を注ぎこむ**方がいい**です。

You had better devote most of
your energy only to the study of
Japanese.

13. 自衛隊に入隊の前に婚約を取り
決める**方がいい**です。

You had better settle your engagement before going into the
Self-Defence Force.

14. 日本を視察する**必要がありま
す**。

It is necessary for you to make
an inspection tour of Japan.

15. この事については，妻に相談す
る**必要があります**。

It would be necessary for you
to ask your wife's advice about
this matter.

16. この事を彼に知らせておく**べき**

One wonders whether or not it

だろうか知らせない**方がいい**でしょうか。

17. 彼にちゃんと返事をする**方がい**いでしょう。

18. 急が**なくてもいい**です。

19. すぐ婚約を結ぶ**必要があります**。

20. 彼の軽率をとがめる**必要があります**。

21. この問題については当事者の気持ちに任せる**方がいい**です。

22. 彼の考えもよく聞いておく**方がいい**です。

23. 行動を決定するまでは冷静さが**必要**です。

24. 私が一切責任をもつから，あなたは何も考え**なくてもいい**です。

25. 組合の力でもって資本家の生産をうんときびしく監督する**必要があります**。

26. 父は言論活動をやめる**方がいい**です。

27. 彼女との問題を解決する**必要があります**。

28. 彼女を安心させる**必要があります**。

29. 何日も同じことを思い続ける**必要はありません**。

would be better to acquaint him with this matter.

It would be better for you to give him a legitimate reply.

There's no need for you to be too hasty.

It's necessary for you to get engaged right now.

It's necessary for you to blame him for his thoughtlessness.

It would be best to leave this problem to the feelings of the persons concerned.

His ideas as well are worth listening to.

Composure is necessary before you decide how to act.

Since it's all my responsibility, there's no need for you to think about it.

It is necessary to utilize the union's strength and forcibly control capitalist production.

It would be better for the father to give up airing his opinions.

It is necessary to solve the problem he has with her.

It is necessary for you to give her a sense of security.

It is not necessary to ponder over the same thing for many days.

Exercise

Fill in the following blanks with "方がいいです", "なくてもいいです", "必要があります", "必要はありません", and "が必要です":

1. 自分の感情を押える（　　）。　　　　She had better control her emotions.

押える (osae-ru), to control

2. 気を晴らす（　　）。　　　　It is necessary to clear your mind.

気を晴らす (ki o haras-u), to clear one's mind

3. 憂うつにならない（　　）。　　　　You had better not become despondent.

憂うつにならない (yūutsu ni nar-anai), to not become despondent＜憂うつになる (yūutsu ni nar-u), to become despondent

4. 家族を養うだけの給料をもらう　　　It is necessary for you to obtain （　　）。　　　　sufficient salary to provide for your family.

給料をもらう (kyūryō o mora[w]-u), to obtain salary

5. 左翼思想に傾か（　　）。　　　　You need not lean towards the left wing.

傾く (katamuk-u), to lean

6. 責任をのがれない（　　）。　　　　You had better not avoid any responsibility.

のがれない (nogare-nai), to not avoid＜のがれる (nogare-ru), to avoid

7. 火ばちに炭をつぎ足さ（　　）。　　You need not add charcoal to a brazier.

つぎ足す (tsugitas-u), to add

8. 皮肉めかして言わ（　　）。　　　　You need not speak cynically to her.

言う (i[w]-u), to speak

9. いつも穏やかな微笑を失わない　　　You had better not lose your （　　）。　　　　constant quiet smile.

失わない (ushinaw-anai), to not lose＜失う (ushina[w]-u), to lose

10. 低い声で話す（　　）。　　　　It is not necessary for you to speak in a low voice.

話す (hanas-u), to speak

11. 彼女の気持ちを察する（　　）。　　It is necessary for you to con-

...sider her feelings.

察する (sassuru), to consider

12. 彼女を絶望的な気持ちにさせな You had better not keep her in
い（ ）。   a mood of despair.

気持ちにさせない (kimochi ni sase-nai), to not keep one in a mood of...
＜気持ちにさせる (kimochi ni sase-ru), to keep one in a mood of...

13. 文化程度の高い人間になる It is necessary to become a
（ ）。   highly cultivated man.

なる (nar-u), to become

14. この子供をやさしくなだめる It is necessary for you to coax
（ ）。   this child gently.

なだめる (nadame-ru), to coax

15. 友人や先輩からきびしく非難さ It is not necessary for you to
れる（ ）。   be severely reproached by your
                  friends and seniors.

非難される (hinan sare-ru), to be reproached

16. ほとんど毎晩酒色のもてなしを You had better not receive the
受けない（ ）。   entertainment of drinking parties
                  and women almost every night.

受けない (uke-nai), to not receive＜受ける (uke-ru), to receive

17. 性急さ（ ）。   It is necessary for you to be
                  quick-tempered.

性急さ (seikyū-sa) is the noun form derived from the な (na)-adjective 性
急な (seikyū-na), quick-tempered

18. 婚約を延期する（ ）。   It is not necessary to put off
                  your engagement.

延期する (enki suru), to put off

19. あの問題を思いつめ（ ）。   You need not brood over the
                  problem.

思いつめる (omoi tsume-ru), to brood over

20. おとうさんと争わない（ ）。   You had better not bandy words
                  with your father.

争わない (arasow-anai), to not bandy words with＜争う (araso[w]-u), to
bandy words with

21. 離婚し（ ）。   You need not resort to divorce.

離婚する (rikon suru), to divorce—in the case of the irregular verb する

(suru), to do, the expression *nakute mo ii desu*, need not, will be しなくてもいいです (*shinakute mo ii desu*), need not do.

22. 愛情の問題を形式的に解決しない（　　）。

    You had better not solve a problem of affection in a formal way.

解決しない (kaiketsu shinai), to not solve＜解決する (kaiketsu suru), to solve

23. 彼の気持ちを少し和らげる（　　）。

    It is necessary for you to soften him a little.

和らげる (yawarage-ru), to soften

24. 友人をせん望する（　　）。

    It is not necessary for you to envy your friend.

せん望する (senbō suru), to envy

25. 私の兄を見舞いにこ（　　）。

    You need not come to inquire after my elder brother.

来る (kuru), to come—in the case of the irregular verb 来る (kuru), to come, the expression *nakute mo ii desu*, need not, will be こなくてもいいです (*ko*nakute mo ii desu), need not come.

26. 別れの悲しみを理解する（　　）。

    It is necessary to understand the sadness of separation.

理解する (rikai suru), to understand

27. 自分のことは自分で責任を持つ（　　）。

    It is necessary to accept the responsibility for your own affairs.

責任を持つ (sekinin o mots-u), to accept the responsibility

28. 先生にそむかない（　　）。

    You had better not disobey your teacher.

そむかない (somuk-anai), to not disobey＜そむく (somuk-u), to disobey

29. 自分の観念にからまれない（　　）。

    You had better not be bound by your own ideas.

からまれない (karamare-nai), to not be bound＜からまれる (karamare-ru), to be bound

Answers:

1. 方がいいです　2. 必要があります　3. 方がいいです　4. 必要があります　5. なくてもいいです　6. 方がいいです　7. なくてもいいです　8. なくてもいいです　9. 方がいいです　10. 必要はありません　11. 必要があります　12. 方がいいです　13. 必要があります　14. 必要があります　15. 必要はありません　16. 方がいいです　17. が必要です　18. 必要はありません　19. なくてもいいです　20. 方がいいです　21. なく

てもいいです　22.　方がいいです　23.　必要があります　24.　必要はあり
ません　25.　なくてもいいです　26.　必要があります　27.　必要がありま
す　28.　方がいいです　29.　方がいいです

The Form of an Auxiliary which Suggests a Rumor

The Form of an Auxiliary which Suggests a Rumor

Rule

The expression そうだ (sō da), plain form; そうです (sō desu), polite form, I hear...; They say...; People say..., is used as an auxiliary verb to suggest a rumor in the sentence.

e.g. この留学生はよく日本語の授業をなまける**そうです**。(Kono ryūga-kusei wa yoku Nihongo no jugyō o namakeru *sō desu*)—I hear that this foreign student often neglects Japanese lessons—なまける (namake-ru), to neglect, is a vowel stem verb in the plain present/future form.

e.g. 彼は文部省に勤めない**そうです**。(Kare wa Monbushō ni tsutome nai *sō desu*)—I hear that he will not be in the service of the Ministry of Education—勤めない (tsutome-nai), to not be in the service of, comes from 勤める (tsutome-ru), to serve.

e.g. この女子留学生は日本滞在中こけし人形を千個集めた**そうです**。(Kono joshi ryūgakusei wa Nihon taizai chū *Kokeshi* ningyō o senko atsumeta *sō desu*)—I hear that this female foreign student, during her stay in Japan, collected a thousand *Kokeshi* dolls (a doll made of wood and decorated with various designs)—集めた (atsume-ta), collected, comes from 集める (atsume-ru), to collect.

e.g. ビルマの留学生は新入留学生の歓迎会でえびのてんぷらを食べなかった**そうです**。(Biruma no ryūgakusei wa shin-nyū ryūgakusei no kangeikai de ebi no tenpura o tabenakatta *sō desu*)—I hear that a Burmese foreign student did not touch the fried lobster at the reception for new foreign students—食べなかった (tabe-nakatta), did not eat, comes from 食べない (tabe-nai), to not eat, from 食べる (tabe-ru), to eat.

e.g. 彼は業務一切を長男に譲る**そうです**。(Kare wa gyōmu issai o chōnan ni yuzuru *sō desu*)—People say that he'll hand over all his business to his eldest son—譲る (yuzur-u), to transfer, is a consonant stem verb in the plain present/future form.

e.g. 彼はまだ郷里に引きこもらない**そうです**。(Kare wa mada kyōri ni hikikomoranai *sō desu*)—People say that he'll not yet shut himself up in his birthplace—引きこもらない (hikikomor-anai), to not shut oneself up, comes from 引きこもる (hikikomor-u), to shut oneself up.

e.g. 彼は子供のときに実母を失った**そうです**。(Kare wa kodomo no toki ni jitsubo o ushinatta *sō desu*)—They say that he lost his real mother in his boyhood—失った (ushinat-ta), lost, comes from 失う (ushina[w]-u), to lose.

e.g. あの未亡人は不貞と不道徳の泥沼に足を踏みこまなかった**そうで す**。(Ano mibōjin wa futei to fudōtoku no doro numa ni ashi o fumikomanakatta *sō desu*)—They say that the widow did not step into the mire of unchastity and immorality—足を踏みこまなかっ た (ashi o fumikom-anakatta), did not step into, comes from 足を 踏みこまない (ashi o fumikom-anai), to not step into, from 足を踏 みこむ (ashi o fumikom-u), to step into.

In the case of nouns, だ (da), plain form, is; am; are, which acts as a copula, is put after the noun. The noun+だ (da) or だった (dat-ta) relates to そうです。

e.g. 彼らはハワイからの観光客だ**そうです**。(Karera wa Hawai kara no kankōkyaku da *sō desu*)—I hear that they are sightseers from Hawaii—観光客 (kankōkyaku), sightseers, is a noun.

e.g. 彼はスパイだった**そうです**。(Kare wa supai datta *sō desu*)—I hear that he was a spy—スパイ (supai), a spy, is a noun.

The negative form of そうです in the case of nouns is as follows: a noun+で(は)ない (de [wa] nai) or で(は)なかった (de [wa] nakatta) +そうです。

e.g. 彼は僧侶で(は)ない**そうです**。(Kare wa sōryo de [wa] nai *sō desu*) —I hear that he is not a Buddhist priest)—僧侶 (sōryo), a Bud- dhist priest, is a noun.

e.g. 彼は刑事で(は)なかった**そうです**。(Kare wa keiji de [wa] nakatta *sō desu*) —I hear that he was not a detective—刑事 (keiji), a detec- tive, is a noun.

In the case of the predicative use of な (na)-adjectives, な (na) of these adjectives is dropped and だ (da), plain form, copula, added. When used predicatively, each な (na)-adjective becomes a noun; this noun form+だ (da) or だった (datta) relates to そうです。

e.g. 彼は粗野だ**そうです**。(Kare wa soya da *sō desu*)—I hear that he is rude—粗野 (soya), rudeness, is the noun form of the な (na)- adjective 粗野な (soya na), rude.

e.g. 彼の両親は貧乏だった**そうです**。(Kare no ryōshin wa binbō datta *sō desu*)—I hear that his parents were poor—貧乏 (binbō), poverty, is the noun form of the な (na)-adjective 貧乏な (binbō na), poor.

The negative form of そうです in the case of the predicative use of な (na)-adjectives is as follows: this noun form+で(は)ない (de [wa] nai) or で(は)なかった (de [wa] nakatta)+そうです。

e.g. 彼は仕事に怠慢で(は)ないそうです。(Kare wa shigoto ni taiman de [wa] nai *sō desu*)—I hear that he is not inattentive to his work)—怠慢 (taiman), inattention, is the noun form of the な (na)-adjective 怠慢な (taiman na), inattentive.

e.g. 彼女の要求は正当で(は)なかったそうです。(Kanojo no yōkyū wa seitō de [wa] nakatta *sō desu*)—I hear that her demands were not reasonable—正当 (seitō), reasonableness, is the noun form of the な (na)-adjective 正当な (seitō na), reasonable.

In the case of the predicative use of い (i)-adjectives, the い (i) of these adjectives, as it is, relates to そうです。

e.g. この店の商品は高いそうです。(Kono mise no shōhin wa takai *sō desu*)—I hear that commodities in this shop are expensive—高い (takai), expensive, is an い (i)-adjective.

e.g. 父は以前私に甘かったそうです。(Chichi wa izen watakushi ni amakatta *sō desu*)—I hear that Father used to be lenient toward me—甘かった (amakatta) is the plain past form of the い (i)-adjective 甘い (amai), lenient, in a predicative use.

The negative form of そうです in the case of the predicative use of い (i)-adjectives is as follows: the negative form of these adjectives can always be obtained by changing the final vowel い (i) of the plain present/future form to く (ku) and adding ない (nai) or なかった (nakatta). This くない (ku nai) or くなかった (ku nakatta) relates to そうです。

e.g. 東京を貫流する隅田川は深く(は)ないそうです。(Tōkyō o kanryū suru Sumida gawa wa fukaku [wa] nai *sō desu*)—I hear that the Sumida River flowing through Tokyo City is not deep)—深くない (fukaku nai), to not be deep, is the plain present/future negative form of the い (i)-adjective 深い (fukai), deep, in a predicative use.

e.g. 叔母は私にきびしく(は)なかったそうです。(Oba wa watakushi ni kibishiku [wa] nakatta *sō desu*)—I hear that my aunt was not strict with me—きびしくなかった (kibishi ku nakatta) is the plain past negative form of the い (i)-adjective きびしい (kibishii), strict, in a predicative use.

Drill

1. 彼女は勝気だそうです。   I hear that she is spirited.
2. 日本製の時計は安いそうです。   I hear that watches of Japanese

make are inexpensive.

3. 彼女は戦争未亡人だそうです。

I hear that she is a war widow.

4. 彼は積極的な活動的な人だそう
です。

I hear that he is a positive and active person.

5. 彼女は過去には何の興味も持た
ない人だそうです。

I hear that she is a person having no interest in the past.

6. 彼はどこかに大きな孤独を背負
った人だそうです。

I hear that he is a person somehow burdened with a great loneliness.

7. 彼は軍人ずれのした荒っぽい男
だそうです。

I hear that he is a rude man who has been strongly influenced by his long career as a soldier.

8. 彼は結婚がめんどう臭いそうで
す。

I hear that he feels some uncertainty about marriage.

9. 彼女は良い機会に再婚するそう
です。

I hear that she will marry again when the opportunity arises.

10. なにごとにも彼はこだわること
のきらいな男だそうです。

I hear that in everything he is a man who dislikes storing things up.

11. 彼女は離婚の手続をするそうで
す。

I hear that she'll press divorce proceedings.

12. 彼女は縁談を断わったそうで
す。

I hear that she refused a proposal of marriage.

13. この未亡人は良縁に見向きもし
ないそうです。

I hear that this widow pays no attention to a good match.

14. 彼女は自分をささえる力を失っ
たそうです。

I hear that she lost the power to support herself.

15. 彼は朝刊を長い時間かかって読
むそうです。

I hear that he takes much time to read the morning paper.

16. 彼女は理性の勝った女だそうで
す。

People say that she is a clear thinking girl.

17. 彼女は愛情のためには，あらゆ
るものを犠牲にしても悔いないそ

People say that she is not repelled even by the sacrifice of

うです。

18. 彼はよく目上の者と対立するそうです。

People say that he often disagrees with his seniors.

19. 彼女は未来のあらゆる希望を捨てたそうです。

I hear that she abandoned all hope for her future.

20. 彼は一種の唯物主義者だそうです。

They say that he is somewhat materialistic.

21. 彼は自分のぜいたくを捨てたそうです。

People say that he gave up his own luxuries.

22. 彼は自分の仕事のおもしろさに没頭し，女を愛するだけの暇も惜しがる人だそうです。

I hear that he is a man absorbed in the pleasure of his own work, even begrudging sufficient time to love a woman completely.

23. 彼は腕ずくで人生を押し渡って行くようなふてぶてしい男だそうです。

I hear that he is an impudent man who would push and carry out his life by sheer strength.

Exercise

Fill in the following blanks with そうです:

1. 彼女は陽気ではない（　　）。

I hear that she is not cheerful.

2. この地方は冬でも寒くない（　　）。

I hear that in this district it is not cold even in winter.

3. 彼女は将来の方針を変更することに決めた（　　）。

I hear that she resolved to change the course of her future.

4. 彼は職業につく希望を捨てた（　　）。

People say that he relinquished his hopes of taking on some profession.

5. 彼女は未知の青年から手紙を受け取った（　　）。

They say that she received a letter from an unknown young man.

6. この会社は世界的に優秀な仕事をしている（　　）。

People say that this company is carrying on its universally acknowledged splendid work.

7. 彼は権威に屈する人だ（　　）。

People say that he is a man who submits to authority.

8. 尼僧は孤独に耐える力を持っている（　　）。

People say that a nun has the strength to bear the solitude.

9. この記者はきぜんと自分の考えを立て通す（　　）。

They say that this journalist presses forward his viewpoint with resolution.

10. 彼は敏腕な政治家だ（　　）。

I hear that he is a capable politician.

11. 彼は新官僚の筆頭だ（　　）。

I hear that he is at the head of the new bureaucracy.

12. 彼は人の顔を見ながら，その心を推察する（　　）。

People say that he looks at a person's face to read his heart.

13. この作家は執筆禁止になった（　　）。

They say that this author was banned from writing.

14. 彼はこうかつな話しぶりをする（　　）。

People say that he handles conversation in a crafty way.

15. 彼は有名な軍事評論家だ（　　）。

People say that he is a famous military critic.

16. アメリカは有り余るほどの石油資源を持っている（　　）。

People say that America possesses extensive petroleum resources.

17. 日本はメキシコと石油協定を結んだ（　　）。

People say that Japan signed a petroleum agreement with Mexico.

18. 彼は辞職せざるを得ない（　　）。

People say that he is obliged to resign his post.

19. 彼は自信を回復した（　　）。

People say that he regained his confidence.

20. 彼女は心がくずれかかっている（　　）。

I hear that her heart is on the brink of collapse.

21. 彼は自分と妻子との安全だけを考える人だ（　　）。

I hear that he is a person who gives thought to the safety of himself and his wife and children only.

22. 彼はなんとなく独身でいく（
　　）。

I hear that he is going on being a bachelor aimlessly.

23. この国には，旅行の自由もなく，居住の自由もなく，職業の自由もなければ，選挙の自由もない（
　　）。

People say that in this country there is neither freedom to travel nor to reside; and there is no freedom in the choice of a profession or even freedom in elections.

The Use of Purpose, Parallel, and Paradox

Rule

In the case of vowel stem verbs ending with *e*-ru or *i*-ru, an infinitive indicating purpose ("to...", "in order to...", or "so as to ..." in English) can be obtained by dropping the last syllable *ru* and adding に (ni) to the stem. Otherwise, the purpose of an action is expressed by vowel stem verbs in the plain present/future form+ ために (tame ni).

e.g. 今晩私は洋食を食べに (or 食べるために) 駒込の一流の食堂へ行きます。(Konban watakushi wa yōshoku o tabe *ni* [or: taberu *tame ni*] Komagome no ichiryū no shokudō e ikimasu)—Tonight I'm going to a first-class restaurant in Komagome to eat some European food—食べ (tabe) in 食べに (tabe ni) comes from 食べる (tabe-ru), to eat; and 食べる (tabe-ru) in 食べるために (taberu tame ni) is a vowel stem verb in the plain present/future form.

e.g. 明晩私は演劇を見に (or 見るために), 友だちと新宿のコマ劇場へ行きます。(Myōban watakushi wa engeki o mi *ni* [or: miru *tame ni*], tomodachi to Shinjuku no Koma gekijō e ikimasu)—Tomorrow evening I'm going to the Koma Theatre in Shinjuku with a friend to see some drama—見 (mi) in 見に (mi ni) comes from 見る (mi-ru), to see; and 見る (mi-ru) in 見るために (miru tame ni) is a vowel stem verb in the plain present/future form.

In the case of consonant stem verbs ending with *u*, a consonant +*u*, the purpose of an action can be obtained by changing the last syllable *u* to *i* and adding に (ni). Otherwise, the purpose of an action is expressed by consonant stem verbs in the plain present/future form+ために (tame ni).

e.g. 近い内に, 私は音楽を聞きに (or 聞くために), 上野の音楽堂へ行くつもりです。(Chikai uchi ni, watakushi wa ongaku o kiki *ni* [or: kiku *tame ni*] Ueno no ongakudō e iku tsumori desu)—In a few days I intend to go to a music hall in Ueno to listen to some music—聞き (kik-i) in 聞きに (kiki ni) comes from 聞く (kik-u), to listen to; and 聞く (kik-u) in 聞くために (kiku tame ni) is a consonant stem verb in the plain present/future form.

する (suru), to do, in the irregular verb group, is put after those

nouns in which a sense of action is inherent. And thus, here exist
verbal forms through the use of the noun+する (suru), to do. In the
case of these verbal forms, an infinitive indicating purpose is rendered
as the noun+に (ni), the noun+のために (no tame ni), and the verb
(plain present/future form)+ために (tame ni).

e.g. この留学生は日本文学の勉強に (or 日本文学の勉強のために；日本
文学を勉強するために), 日本へ来ました。(Kono ryūgakusei wa Ni-
hon bungaku no benkyō *ni* [or: Nihon bungaku no benkyō *no
tame ni*; Nihon bungaku o benkyō suru *tame ni*], Nihon e kimashita)—This foreign student came to Japan to study Japanese
literature—勉強 (benkyō), study, in 勉強に (benkyō ni) and in 勉強
のために (benkyō no tame ni) is a noun; and 勉強する (benkyō
suru), to study, is a verb in the plain present/future form.

"While (or although). . ." is expressed by ながら (nagara). ながら
(nagara) is a connective particle expressing an action or condition
parallel to another, and it also expresses paradox.

In the case of vowel stem verbs ending with *e*-ru and *i*-ru, "while
or although. . ." can be obtained by dropping the last syllable *ru*
and adding ながら (nagara) to the stem.

e.g. この少年はテレビを見ながら, お菓子をおいしそうに食べています。
(Kono shōnen wa terebi o mi *nagara*, okashi o oishi sō ni tabete
imasu)—This boy is enjoying some cookies while watching television—見 (mi) in 見ながら (mi nagara) comes from 見る (mi-ru), to
see; and this ながら (nagara) expresses an action or condition
parallel to another.

e.g. この事をよく知っていながら, 彼は私に告げようとはしません。
(Kono koto o yoku shittei *nagara*, kare wa watakushi ni tsuge
yō to wa shimasen)—Though he was quite aware of this matter,
he would not inform me of it—知ってい (shittei) in 知っていなが
ら (shittei nagara) comes from 知っている (shittei-ru), to be aware
of; and this ながら (nagara) expresses paradox.

In the case of consonant stem verbs ending with *u*, "while or
although. . ." can be obtained by changing the last syllable *u* to *i*
and adding ながら (nagara).

e.g. 私は歩きながら, いつも考えます。(Watakushi wa aruki *nagara*,
itsumo kangaemasu)—I always think of something while walking
—歩き (aruk-i) in 歩きながら (aruki nagara) comes from 歩く
(aruk-u), to walk; and this ながら (nagara) expresses an action
or condition parallel to another.

e.g. 彼は相当の給料をもらいながら, 今なお両親から金銭的援助を受け

ています。(Kare wa sōtō no kyūryō o morai *nagara*, ima nao ryōshin kara kinsenteki enjo o ukete imasu)—Although he receives a respectable salary, he is still getting financial support from his parents—もらい (mora-i) in もらいながら (morai nagara) comes from もらう (mora[w]-u), to receive; and this ながら (nagara) expressess paradox.

"...ing and ...ing" is expressed by ...たり (...tari) ...たりして (...tari shite)—this expression indicates parallelism.

In the case of vowel stem verbs ending with *e*-ru or *i*-ru, a parallel can be obtained by dropping the last syllable *ru* and adding ...たり (...tari) to the stem and ...たりして (...tari shite) to the following verb stem.

e.g. 陶工はかまのふたをあけ**たり**，しめ**たりして**仕事をしています。

(Tōkō wa kama no futa o ake *tari*, shime *tari shite* shigoto o shite imasu)—A potter is engaged in work, opening the lid of a kiln and shutting it—あけ (ake) in あけたり (ake tari) comes from あける (ake-ru), to open, and しめ (shime) in しめたりして (shime tari shite) comes from しめる (shime-ru), to shut.

A parallel can be formed with consonant stem verbs in the plain past form. In the case of consonant stem verbs ending with *u*, a sound change is involved before adding た (ta) or だ (da). Then the た (ta) or だ (da) in these plain past forms relates to ...り (...ri) ...りして (...ri shite).

e.g. お手伝いさんは朝部屋を掃い**たり**，ふい**たりして**大へん忙しいです。

(Otetsudai san wa asa heya o hai*ta ri*, fui*ta ri shite* taihen isogashii desu)—The maid is quite busy in the morning, sweeping and wiping the room—掃いた (hai-ta), swept, in 掃いたり (haita ri) comes from 掃く (hak-u), to sweep and ふいた (fui-ta), wiped, in ふいたりして (fuita ri shite) comes from ふく (fuk-u), to wipe.

Drill

1. 今日の午後私は池袋へ買い物に行きます。

This afternoon I'll go shopping at Ikebukuro.

2. 今日私は恋人への贈り物を買いに，池袋のデパートへ行きます。

Today I'm going to a department store in Ikebukuro to buy some gifts for my fiancée.

3. この母は子供に乳を飲ませ**なが**ら，こたつに寝そべっています。

This mother is lying beside a foot-warmer, breast feeding the baby.

4. 彼はコーヒーをかきまわし**なが**
ら，友だちの驚いた表情を見てい
ました。

He watched his friend's face
turn pale while stirring a cup of
coffee.

5. 父は手をふき**ながら**，はいって
来ました。

The father came in wiping his
hands.

6. 電車はきしり**ながら**，坂をくだ
って行きます。

An electric car, creaking, runs
down the slope.

7. 夫人は茶の間に客を迎え**ながら**，
つぶやきました。

The wife muttered to herself as
she led a visitor into the living
room.

8. お手伝いさんは部屋を出て行き
ながら，歌を歌っていました。

Leaving the room, the maid
sang a song.

9. 彼は東京で給仕を**しながら**，夜
学へ通っています。

He is attending a night school
while working as an office boy in
Tokyo.

* In the case of the irregular verb する (suru), to do, the expression "While
..." is しながら (shi nagara), while doing....

10. てれ**ながら**，ふと彼女は彼の方
を見ました。

Feeling awkward, she involun-
tarily turned toward him.

11. 彼は東京へ行くと言い**ながら**，
しかしそれから一月も郷里でぐず
ぐずしていました。

Although saying that he was
going up to Tokyo, he loitered in
his home town for more than a
month.

12. ラッシュアワーの物すごい雑踏
にもまれ**ながら**，母は子供の手を
しっかり握っていました。

The mother was holding firmly
to her child while jostled in the
throng of the early morning rush
hour.

13. 起き上がり**ながら**，彼女は「さ
あ，お上がりください」と言いま
した。

As she rose up, she said, "Please
come in."

14. 目白の方へ逃げ**ながら**，ひょい
と振りかえると，ちょうど橋は二
つに割れて，燃え落ちようとする

While running in the direction
of Mejiro I turned back,—I then
noticed that the bridge was break-

ところでした。

15. 親子二代にわたって押しかかっ
ている「この社会」の重さを背中
に感じながら，娘は母の言葉を聞
いていました。

16. プリンス自動車会社に勤めてい
る四・五年の間に，私宅のパーテ
ィに招かれたり，夕飯に呼ばれた
りして，いつとなしに彼女はダン
スを覚えました。

ing apart and in a blaze it was
going to collapse into the river.

Feeling the heavy burden of
"this society" hung upon both
mother and daughter over two
generations, the daughter was
taking heed of her mother's words.

Over a period of several years
at the Prince Automobile Company, she naturally learned to
dance by being invited to parties
or to dinner in private homes.

Exercise

Fill in the following blanks with ながら，たり...たりして，ため
に, or に:

1. この日を予想しており（　），
彼は何の対策も考えてはいません
でした。

2. 小説を読みふけっているむすこ
をながめ（　），父は一本の煙草
をくゆらしていました。

3. 心のどこかでは社長に無視され
たような空虚を感じ（　），彼は
社長室を出ました。

4. むすこがズボンのバンドを引き
しめ（　），「今から行って来ま
す」と言いました。

5. 娘は多少赤くなり（　），「ち
ょっと彼の所へ行ってみます」と
言いました。

6. 狭い廊下にそば屋のどんぶりが

While things had been working
toward this time, he did nothing
to estimate, to plan ahead any
needed measures.

The father puffed a cigarette as
he looked at his son absorbed in
reading a novel.

He stepped out of the director's
room, feeling a vacuum in his
heart as if he had been ignored
by the director.

Tightening the belt of his trousers, the son said, "I'm going
now."

The daughter, her face redden-
ing a little, said, "I'll go and see
him."

Bowls of a noodle-shop and dirty

出てい（　　），よごれたスリッパ
が脱いであっ（　　），悪臭を放っ
ていました。

slippers were lying in the narrow
corridor, giving off quite an odor.

7. 彼は兄と二人で酒を飲み（
），恋人に手を焼いた話をしま
した。

Drinking *sake* with his elder
brother, he talked about his bitter
experience with his sweetheart.

8. 社長は紅茶を私にすすめ（
），にこやかに「サラリーはいく
らほしいですか」と言いました。

While offering me a cup of black
tea, the director smilingly said,
"How much do you want for your
salary?"

9. 自分の不幸からのがれる（
），彼女は尼さんになりました。

To escape from her own un-
happiness, she became a nun.

10. 彼はこれから戦場へ，死に（
）行くのです。

He is now to go off to the battlefield to die.

11. あくる日の午後，彼女は東京ま
で見送る（　　），夫と一緒に汽車
に乗りました。

The next afternoon she rode the
train as far as Tokyo in company
with her husband to see him off.

12. 彼女は昔の友人にみとられ（
），次第に虫の息になっていきま
した。

She gradually lapsed into difficult breathing while being cared
for by her old friend.

13. 彼は恋人と一緒に大名行列を見
（　　）行く約束をし（　　），それ
をすっぽかして，ひとり自分の部
屋に閉じこもっていました。

In spite of the fact that he had
promised his sweetheart to go
together to see a feudal lord pro-
cession, he fell down on it and
shut himself up in his room.

14. 「私の店は小さくなってしまい
ましたよ」と，彼女は笑い（　　）
言いました。

"You see my shop has become
smaller," said she, laughing.

15. 浅草の国際劇場へ「春の踊り」
を見（　　）行って娘が帰って来
たので，「おもしろかった」と母
が聞きました。

When the daughter returned
home after seeing "A Dance of
Spring" at the Kokusai Theatre
in Asakusa, the mother asked her,

"Did you enjoy it?"

16. 舞台では今あんなに花やかに踊
　　っ（　　）歌っ（　　），昔とちっ
　　とも変わりありません。

On the stage the dancing and
singing is so colorful, just as it
used to be.

Answers:

1. ながら　2. ながら　3. ながら　4. ながら　5. ながら　6. たり
...たりして　7. ながら　8. ながら　9. ために　10. に　11. ために
12. ながら　13. に，ながら　14. ながら　15. に　16. たり...たり
して

第 三十九 課　Lesson 39

Expressions Denoting "an Experience in the Past" and "Immediate Proximity in Time"

Rule

The expression ことがあります (koto ga arimasu), once, and ばかりです (bakari desu), just, can be applied with vowel and consonant stem verbs in the plain past form.

In the case of vowel stem verbs, these plain past forms can be obtained by dropping the last syllable *ru* and adding た (ta) to the stem.

In the case of consonant stem verbs in the plain past form, a sound change is involved before adding た (ta) or だ (da). Then the た (ta) or だ (da) in these plain past forms relates to the expressions ことがあります (koto ga arimasu) and ばかりです (bakari desu).

- e.g.　この青年は共産主義にかぶれたことがあります。(Kono seinen wa kyōsanshugi ni kabureta *koto ga arimasu*)—This young man was once infected by communism—かぶれた (kabure-ta) comes from かぶれる (kabure-ru), to be infected.

- e.g.　私はニュース映画で幾多の戦場場面を見たことがあります。(Watakushi wa nyūsu eiga de ikuta no senjō bamen o mita *koto ga arimasu*)—I once watched many scenes of battlefields in the newsreel)—見た (mi-ta) comes from 見る (mi-ru), to watch.

- e.g.　私は鉄血宰相ビスマルクの伝記を読んだことがあります。(Watakushi wa tekketsu saishō Bisumaruku no denki o yonda *koto ga arimasu*)—I once read a biography of Bismarck, the Iron Chancellor—読んだ (yon-da) comes from 読む (yom-u), to read.

- e.g.　私は彼に宗教書を貸したことがあります。(Watakushi wa kare ni shūkyōsho o kashita *koto ga arimasu*)—I once lent some religious books to him—貸した (kashi-ta) comes from 貸す (kas-u), to lend.

- e.g.　この夫は妻の心をいたわるというデリケートな感情をもったことがありません。(Kono otto wa tsuma no kokoro o itawaru to iu derikēto na kanjō o motta *koto ga arimasen*)—This husband has never possessed any delicate feelings to console his wife's heart—もった (mot-ta) comes from もつ (mots-u), to possess, and ことがありません (koto ga arimasen) is the negative form of ことがあります。

e.g. 彼は彼女の東京行きを引き留めた**ばかりです**。(Kare wa kanojo no Tōkyō yuki o hikitometa *bakari desu*)—He has just detained her going up to Tokyo—引き留めた (hikitome-ta) comes from 引き留める (hikitome-ru), to detain.

e.g. 橋は二つに割れて燃え落ちた**ばかりです**。(Hashi wa futatsu ni warete moeochita *bakari desu*)—The bridge has just broken apart in a blaze—燃え落ちた (moeochi-ta) comes from 燃え落ちる (moe-ochi-ru), to collapse in a blaze.

e.g. 胸をわずらっていた母が息を引き取った**ばかりです**。(Mune o wa-zuratte ita haha ga iki o hikitotta *bakari desu*)—The mother, who had developed a lung disease, breathed her last just now—息を引き取った (iki o hikitot-ta) comes from 息を引き取る (iki o hi-kitor-u), to breathe one's last.

e.g. 彼は喫茶店を開いた**ばかりです**。(Kare wa kissaten o hiraita *bakari desu*)—He has just opened a coffee-house—開いた (hirai-ta) comes from 開く (hirak-u), to open.

*Besides, the expression ばかりの (bakari no) is used as a noun phrase and clause, which shows extent. And the expression ばかりいます (bakari imasu) shows emphasis; it is used after the て (te) or で (de)-form of any verb—this form is obtained by replac-ing the final vowel *a* of the plain past form by *e*.

e.g. 彼は日本へ来たばかりの留学生です。(Kare wa Nihon e kita *ba-kari no* ryūgakusei desu)—He is a foreign student who has just come to Japan—来た (kita) comes from 来る (kuru), to come, and the expression ばかりの (bakari no), which shows extent, relates to the noun 留学生 (ryūgakusei), a foreign student.

e.g. 彼は遊んでばかりいます。(Kare wa asonde *bakari imasu*)—He is doing nothing but play—遊んで (ason-de) comes from 遊んだ (ason-da), played, and the expression ばかりいます (bakari imasu) shows emphasis.

e.g. 彼は勉強ばかりしています。(Kare wa benkyō *bakari shite imasu*)—He is doing nothing but study—勉強 (benkyō), study, a noun＋ばかりしています (bakari shite imasu).

Drill

1. 彼女は悲痛な顔をしたことがあります。

   She once adopted an expression of great sorrow.

2. 彼女はさむざむとした心で町に出たばかりです。

   She has just stepped out into the street, feeling listless.

3. 彼は警察から白い目で見られた
   ことがあります。
   He was once frowned upon by the police.

4. 日仏交渉が始まったばかりで
   す。
   Japanese-French negotiations have just begun.

5. この学生は先生にひどくしぼら
   れたばかりです。
   This student has just been strongly reproached by the teacher.

6. 日本は東洋の諸国を侵略したこ
   とがあります。
   Japan once invaded various countries in the East.

7. この外人は日露戦史を二・三冊
   読み終わったばかりです。
   This foreigner has just finished reading two or three volumes of the history of the Russo-Japanese War.

8. 父は多摩川へつりに行ったばか
   りです。
   My father has just gone fishing at the Tama River.

9. 彼は東大から私大へ変わったば
   かりです。
   He has just transferred from Tokyo University to a private university.

10. 彼は彼女を日光へ案内したこと
    があります。
    He once conducted her around Nikko for sightseeing.

11. 彼女は初恋の男と再会したばか
    りです。
    She has just been re-united with her first lover.

12. この不良少年は大阪駅で見つか
    って，引きもどされたばかりで
    す。
    This delinquent boy was intercepted at Osaka Station and taken back just now.

13. 彼女は羽田空港に着いたばかり
    のアメリカ観光団の一人です。
    She is one of the American tourist party which has just arrived at Haneda Airport.

14. この受験生は朝から晩まで勉強
    ばかりしています。
    This examinee has been employed only in study from morning till night.

15. 彼女はたまらない孤独に襲われ
    たことがあります。
    She was once attacked by an unbearable solitude.

Exercise

Fill in each bracket with a verbal form suitable for such expressions as an experience in the past and immediate proximity in time, taking into consideration the verb given below each sentence:

1. 私はぎりぎり一杯の時間に縛られたあわただしい食事を（　　）ことがあります。

   I once took hasty meals thrown together in the minimum of time.

   食事をする (shokuji o suru), to take a meal

2. この人は同情という感情を（　　）ことがありません。

   This person has never had any feeling that can be called sympathy.

   感情をもつ (kanjō o mots-u), to have a feeling

3. 妻はきれいに私のくつの手入れを（　　）ばかりです。

   The wife has just nicely attended to the cleaning of my shoes.

   手入れをする (teire o suru), to care for

4. 彼女は学生時代に山を歩いたり、水泳をしたり（　　）ことがあります。

   She once rambled about the hills and went swimming during her school days.

   A をしたり B をしたりする (A o shitari B o shitari suru), to do A and B

5. 彼は家を増築（　　）ばかりです。

   He has just extended his house.

   増築する (zōchiku suru), to extend a house

6. 彼は何を聞いても正直に返事を（　　）ことがありません。

   He has never given an honest answer to any question.

   返事をする (henji o suru), to reply

7. この予備校生は自棄的な気持ちに（　　）ことがあります。

   This student of a preparatory school once felt sad and despondent.

   気持ちになる (kimochi ni nar-u), to feel

8. 刑事はすりの所持品を検査（　　）ばかりです。

   The detective has just examined a pickpocket's belongings.

   検査する (kensa suru), to examine

9. 支店長は本社から来た書類を開（　　）ばかりです。

   The branch manager has just opened the documents that came from the head office.

   開く (hirak-u), to open

10. 朝ごとにこの老婆は足腰が痛
（　　）ことがあります。
痛む (itam-u), to ache

Every morning this aged woman awoke with aching legs and hips.

11. この寮生は所持品をまとめてた
なに上（　　）ばかりです。

上げる (age-ru), to put up

This boarder has just gathered his belongings and put them up on the shelf.

12. この下級生は上級生に一種の反
抗を感（　　）ことがあります。

感じる (kanji-ru), to feel

This lower-class student once felt some resistance in an upper-class student.

13. この社員の要点を回避した答え
方が社長をいらいらさ（　　）こ
とがあります。

いらいらさせる (ira ira sase-ru), to irritate

The manner of this staff member's answer, avoiding the main point, once irritated the company director.

14. この教授は雑談めいた話の中か
ら，学生の思想傾向を探（　　）こ
とがあります。

探る (sagur-u), to probe

This professor, under the guise of idle chatter, once attempted to draw out a student's turn of thought.

15. むすこは会社へ出勤するしたく
を（　　）ばかりです。
したくをする (shitaku o suru), to get ready

The son has just got ready to go out to company.

Answers:
1. 食事をした 2. 感情をもった 3. 手入れをした 4. 水泳をした
りした 5. 増築した 6. 返事をした 7. 気持ちになった 8. 検査した
9. 開いた 10. 痛んだ 11. 上げた 12. 感じた 13. いらいらさせた
14. 探った 15. したくをした

Some Idiomatic Expressions

Rule

The expressions たがります (tagarimasu), to become eager to...,
始めます (hajimemasu), to begin to..., 終わります (owarimasu), to
finish...ing, 過ぎます (sugimasu), to exceed, 方 (kata), how to...
(a noun phrase), and やすいです (yasui desu), to be easy to ..., and
にくいです (nikui desu), to be difficult to... (i-adjectives), can be
used after the second base of verbs (the verb form used with the
polite -*masu* endings).

e.g.　デパートのおもちゃ売り場へ連れて行くと，この子はどのおもちゃ
でもいじり**たがります**。(Depāto no omocha uriba e tsurete iku to,
kono ko wa dono omocha demo ijiri *tagarimasu*)—This child becomes eager to finger all of the toys when he is taken to the toy
counter at a department store—いじり (ijir-i) comes from いじり
ます (ijir-imasu), to finger.

e.g.　この作家は夜ふけに構想を練り**始めます**。(Kono sakka wa yofuke
ni kōsō o neri *hajimemasu*)—This writer begins to work over a
plot late at night—練り (ner-i) comes from 練ります (ner-imasu),
to work over.

e.g.　この大学生は今月の下旬ごろ卒論を書き**終わります**。(Kono daigakusei wa kongetsu no gejun goro sotsuron o kaki *owarimasu*)—
This university student will finish writing his graduation thesis
about the end of this month—書き (kak-i) comes from 書きます
(kak-imasu), to write.

e.g.　この工員は働き**過ぎます**。(Kono kōin wa hataraki *sugimasu*)—
This factory hand overworks—働き (hatarak-i) comes from 働き
ます (hatarak-imasu), to work.

e.g.　この日本語の教師の日本語の教え**方**は実に上手です。(Kono Nihon-
go no kyōshi no Nihongo no oshie *kata* wa jitsu ni jōzu desu)—
The method of teaching Japanese taken by this teacher of the
Japanese language is quite excellent—教え (oshie) comes from 教
えます (oshie-masu), to teach.

e.g.　私はかぜを引き**やすいです**。(Watakushi wa kaze o hiki *yasui
desu*)—I am susceptible to colds—引き (hik-i) comes from 引きま
す (hik-imasu), to catch.

e.g. この人は扱いにくいです。(Kono hito wa atsukai *nikui desu*)—
It's hard to handle this person—扱い (atsuka-i) comes from 扱い
ます (atsuka-imasu), to handle.

Drill

1. ペンキ屋さんは今応接間の壁を
塗り 終わりました。

The house painter has just finished painting the wall in the
drawing room.

2. この煙草はすい やすいです。

It's easy to smoke this cigarette.

3. 高校を出たばかりの青年のくせ
に，彼は酒を飲み たがります。

Though a young man barely
out of high school, he is eager to
drink *sake*.

4. 漢方薬は飲み にくいです。

It's hard to take Chinese medicine.

5. ちょっと前，むすこは日本語読
本を読み 始めました。

Just a moment ago my son began
to read a Japanese reader.

6. この学校には，泳ぎ 方の知らな
い生徒がおおぜいいます。

In this school there are many
pupils who do not know how to
swim.

7. この留学生は遊び 過ぎます。

This foreign student is given too
much to pleasure.

Exercise

Fill in each bracket with a verbal form suitable for these expressions, taking into consideration the verb given below each sentence:

1. 私はあなたの（   ）方には賛
成できません。

I can't go with your way of
thinking.

考えます (kangae-masu), to think＜考える (kangae-ru)

2. 私には漢字は（   ）やすいで
す。

It's easy for me to memorize
Chinese characters.

覚えます (oboe-masu), to memorize＜覚える (oboe-ru)

3. こんな小さな活字は（   ）に
くいです。

Such small type is difficult to
read.

読みます (yom-imasu), to read＜読む (yom-u)

4. 彼は（   ）過ぎます。

He studies too hard.

勉強します (benkyō shimasu), to study＜勉強する (benkyō suru)

5. 彼は彼女に（　　）たがります。　　He longs to see her.
   会います (a-imasu), to see or to meet＜会う (a[w]-u)

6. あかちゃんは乳がほしくて（　　The baby began to cry for its
   ）始めました。　　　　　　　　milk.
   泣きます (nak-imasu), to cry＜泣く (nak-u)

7. 学生は先生が黒板に書いた字を　The students finished copying
   帳面に（　　）終わりました。　in their notebooks the letters the
   　　　　　　　　　　　　　　　teacher wrote on the blackboard.
   写します (utsush-imasu), to copy＜写す (utsus-u)

Answers:
1. 考え　2. 覚え　3. 読み　4. 勉強し　5. 会い　6. 泣き　7. 写し

第 四十一 課　Lesson 41

Hypothetical Subjunctive Condition (1)

Rule

Conditions ("if" in English) denote uncertain terms or supposition concerning the present and future, including supposition contrary to the present and past facts. Here, uncertain conditions or supposition connected with the present and future, as well as a counterhypothesis to the present facts, is taken up; in the next chapter a counter-hypothesis to the past facts is presented.

Such expressions as れば (reba), なら (nara) or ならば (nara ba), and と (to) indicating hypothetical subjunctive conditions can be used with vowel stem verbs.

In the case of vowel stem verbs ending with e-ru or i-ru, the hypothetical subjunctive condition can be obtained by dropping the last syllable ru and adding れば (reba) to the stem.

e.g.　彼がさじを投げれば、もうだれも政府にたてついて火中のくりを拾う者はいません。(Kare ga saji o nage reba, mō dare mo seifu ni tatetsuite kachū no kuri o hirou mono wa imasen)—If he gives up all hope of doing anything, there is no longer any man who would run the risk of pitting himself against the government—投げ (nage) in 投げれば (nage reba) comes from 投げる (nage-ru), to give up.

The negative form to which the hypothetical subjunctive condition is attached is as follows: in the case of vowel stem verbs ending with e-ru or i-ru, the verb is first negated by dropping the last syllable ru and adding ない (nai) to the stem. Then the final い (i) of this ない (nai) is replaced by ければ (kereba), as なければ (nakereba).

e.g.　人じんを食べなければ，栄養不良になります。(Ninjin o tabe nakereba, eiyō furyō ni narimasu)—If you don't eat carrots, you will be undernourished—食べなければ (tabe-nakereba) comes from 食べない (tabe-nai), to not eat.

When using such expressions as なら (nara) or ならば (nara ba) and と (to), they are similarly placed after any vowel stem verb in the plain present/future form.

e.g.　この女子学生の態度を子細に注意して見るなら（or 見るならば；見ると）、彼女の家庭環境がよくわかります。(Kono joshi gakusei no taido o shisai ni chūishite miru *nara* [or: miru *nara ba*; miru *to*], kanojo no katei kankyō ga yoku wakarimasu)—If one takes care to notice the details of this female student's behaviour, he will be quite aware of her family circumstances—見る (mi-ru), to notice, in 見るなら (miru nara) or in 見るならば (miru nara ba) and in 見ると (miru to) is a vowel stem verb in the plain present/future form.

e.g. 早く寝ないなら (or 寝ないならば; 寝ないと), 明朝の早い汽車に間に合うように起きられません。(Hayaku nenai *nara* [or: nenai *nara ba*; nenai *to*], myōchō no hayai kisha ni maniau yō ni okiraremasen)—If you don't go to bed early, you might not wake up in time for the early train the next morning—寝ない (ne-nai), to not go to bed, comes from 寝る (ne-ru), to sleep. Any vowel stem verb in the plain present/future negative form, as it is, relates to なら (nara), ならば (nara ba), and と (to).

* The difference in nuance between ...れば (reba), なら (nara) and ならば (nara ba), and と (to) is as follows:

e.g. 雨降りに外へ出れば, ぬれてしまいます。(Ame furi ni soto e de *reba*, nurete shimaimasu)—If one goes outside on a rainy day, he will get wet in the rain—the use of れば (reba) shows a simple theory. There is no statement concerning whether or not one will really go out; this れば (reba) refers to the fact that one gets wet if he merely steps out into the rain. Here exists the reason for him to be wet. This theory is arrived at from knowledge obtained through past experience; but it refers to only the result of a simple induction, being independent of any process of induction and any source of actual experience.

e.g. あなたが外へ出るなら (or 出るならば), 私は家にいます。(Anata ga soto e deru *nara* [or: deru *nara ba*], watakushi wa ie ni imasu)—If you go outside, I'll stay at home—なら (nara) or ならば (nara ba) indicates a mere subjunctive clause which exerts no directing or restricting, no guiding or limiting influence over the principal clause.

e.g. こんな日に外へ出ると, ぬれてしまいます。(Kon-na hi ni soto e deru *to*, nurete shimaimasu)—When one goes outside on such a day as this, he will get wet in the rain—the statement with と (to) refers to actuality, far from theory. Here exists another story about the existence or non-existence of the reason for one's being wet—such a reason as this stands apart; one really gets wet. Statements led by the particle と (to) denote the result of experience; nevertheless it is not freed from any experience itself, but rather operates on a background of that experience.

In cases where the same subject continues to perform certain acts, the expression と (to) is used; in this case the expression ば (ba) and なら (nara) cannot be replaced by と (to).

e.g. 彼はポケットからハンカチを出すと，それで額の汗をぬぐいました。
(Kare wa poketto kara hankachi o dasu *to*, sore de hitai no ase o nuguimashita)—Taking a handkerchief out of his pocket, he wiped the perspiration on his forehead with it.

The expression ば (eba), なら (nara) or ならば (nara ba), and と (to) can be applied with consonant stem verbs.

In the case of consonant stem verbs ending with *u*, the hypothetical subjunctive condition can be obtained by changing the last syllable *u* to *e* and adding ば (ba).

e.g. 彼と手を切れば，あなたはやりにくくなります。(Kare to te o kir-*eba*, anata wa yariniku ku narimasu)—If you sever your friendship with him, you might be in a difficult situation—切れば (kir-eba) comes from 切る (kir-u), to sever.

The negative form to which the hypothetical subjunctive condition is attached is as follows: in the case of consonant stem verbs ending with *u*, the verb is first negated by dropping the last syllable *u* and adding ない (anai) to the stem. Then the final い (i) of this ない (anai) is replaced by ければ (kereba), as なければ (anakereba).

e.g. この本を読まなければ，日本文化の論文は書けません。(Kono hon o yom*a nakereba*, Nihon bunka no ronbun wa kakemasen)—If you don't read this book, you will be unable to write an article on Japan's culture—読まなければ (yom-anakereba) comes from 読まない (yom-anai), to not read.

When using such expressions as なら (nara) or ならば (nara ba) and と (to), they are similarly placed after any consonant stem verb in the plain present/future form.

e.g. まじめに働くなら (or 働くならば)，あなたは社長に深く信用されます。(Majime ni hataraku *nara* [or: hataraku *nara ba*], anata wa shachō ni fukaku shinyō saremasu)—If you work diligently, you will be deeply trusted by the director—働く (hatarak-u), to work, in 働くなら (hataraku nara) and in 働くならば (hataraku nara ba) is a consonant stem verb in the plain present/future form.

e.g. 生活を正さないなら (or 正さないならば；正さないと)，私はあなたを罷免します。(Seikatsu o tadasanai *nara* [or: tadasanai *nara ba*; tadasanai *to*], watakushi wa anata o himen shimasu)—If you don't reform your way of living, I might discharge you—正さない (tadas-anai), to not reform, comes from 正す (tadas-u), to reform.   Any consonant stem verb in the plain present/future negative form, as it is, relates to なら (nara) or ならば (nara ba), and と (to).

* The difference in nuance between ば (eba), なら (nara) or ならば (nara ba), and と (to) is as follows:

e.g. だれでも酒を飲めば，酔います。(Dare demo 'sake' o nom-*eba*, yoimasu)—If anybody drinks *sake*, he will get drunk—the relationship between 飲む (nom-u), to drink and 酔う (yo[w]-u), to get drunk, is an inevitable theory common to the public at large. This proposition with ば (eba) denotes a theory.

e.g. 酒を飲む**なら**，飲んでください。('Sake' o nomu *nara*, nonde kudasai)—If you drink *sake*, please have some—なら (nara) or ならば (nara ba) indicates a mere subjunctive clause which exerts no restricting influence over the principal clause.

e.g. 私は酒を飲む**と**，眠くなります。(Watakushi wa 'sake' o nomu *to*, nemuku narimasu)—If I drink *sake*, I'll become sleepy—the relationship between 飲む (nom-u), to drink and 眠くなる (nemuku nar-u), to become sleepy, is a matter of fact which acts upon the single person "I"; that is, the phrase with と (to) preceding the principal clause suggests a shading like "in such a case as when ..." or "whenever...".

In the case of the irregular verbs する (suru), to do and 来る (kuru), to come, this expression will be すれば (sure ba), するなら (suru nara), するならば (suru nara ba), and すると (suru to); 来れば (kure ba), 来るなら (kuru nara), 来るならば (kuru nara ba), and 来ると (kuru to) as in the following:

e.g. この仕事を**すれば**，お駄賃をあげます。(Kono shigoto o *sure ba*, odachin o agemasu)—If you do this work, I'll give you some reward.

e.g. 私に抵抗**すれば**，処罰を受けるばかりです。(Watakushi ni teikō *sure ba*, shobatsu o ukeru bakari desu)—If you stand against me, you are but to be punished—抵抗すれば (teikō sure ba) comes from 抵抗する (teikō suru), to resist. 抵抗 (teikō), resistance, in 抵抗する (teikō suru), to resist, is a noun and those nouns in which a sense of action is inherent can all be converted into verbal forms by the noun+する (suru), to do. する (suru), to do, itself is an irregular verb; therefore, such a verbal form as this assumes the grammatical changes of the irregular verb group.

e.g. 今晩私の所へ**来れば**，日本食を御馳走します。(Konban watakushi no tokoro e *kure ba*, Nihon shoku o gochisō shimasu)—If you'll come and see me tonight, I'll treat you to some Japanese foods.

The negative form of this expression will be しなければ (shinakere ba), しないなら (shinai nara), しないならば (shinai nara ba), and しないと (shinai to); 来なければ (konakere ba), 来ないなら (konai nara), 来ないならば (konai nara ba), and 来ないと (konai to) as in the following:

- e.g. 今日中にこの仕事をしなければ (or しないなら；しないならば；しないと), お金を払いません。(Kyōjū ni kono shigoto o *shinakere ba* [or: *shinai nara*; *shinai nara ba*; *shinai to*], okane o haraimasen)—If you don't finish up this work within today, I'll not pay you.

- e.g. 明後日来なければ (or 来ないなら；来ないならば；来ないと), 当分あなたにお会いできません。(Myōgonichi *konakereba* [or: *konai nara*; *konai nara ba*; *konai to*], tōbun anata ni oai dekimasen)—If you don't come the day after tomorrow, I'll be unable to see you for a while.

In the case of nouns, such expressions as であれば (de areba), なら (nara), ならば (nara ba), and だと (da to) can be used; these expressions are similarly put after the noun.

- e.g. 御希望であれば (or 御希望なら；御希望ならば) 私の知っている点をお話ししましょう。(Gokibō *de areba* [or: gokibō *nara*; gokibō *nara ba*], watakushi no shitte iru ten o ohanashi shimashō)—If you want to listen to me, I'll tell you the facts as I know them—御希望 (gokibō) is a noun from 御 (go), an honorific prefix and 希望 (kibō), hope.

The negative form of this expression is the noun＋でなければ (de nakereba), でないなら (de nai nara), でないならば (de nai nara ba), and でないと (de nai to).

- e.g. 東洋人でなければ (or 東洋人でないなら；東洋人でないならば), この放送局はアナウンサーに採用しません。(Tōyō-jin *de nakereba* [or: Tōyō-jin *de nai nara*; Tōyō-jin *de nai nara ba*], kono hōsōkyoku wa anaunsā ni saiyō shimasen)—If not Orientals, this broadcasting station would not employ anybody as an announcer.

In the case of な (na)-adjectives, the final な (na) may be dropped, this omission enabling them to be used as the noun forms. Such a noun as this relates to であれば (de areba), なら (nara), ならば (nara ba), and だと (da to), as in the case of a noun.

- e.g. 陽気であれば (or 陽気なら；陽気ならば), みんなに好かれます。(Yōki *de areba* [or: yōki *nara*; yōki *nara ba*], min-na ni sukaremasu)—If one is cheerful, he will be liked by everybody—陽気 (yōki), cheerfulness, is the noun form of the な (na)-adjective 陽

気な (yōki na), cheerful.

The negative form of this expression is the noun derived from the な (na)-adjective＋でなければ (de nakereba), でないなら (de nai nara), でないならば (de nai nara ba), and でないと (de nai to).

e.g. 誠実でなければ (or 誠実でないなら；誠実でないならば), 何事にも成功しません。(Seijitsu *de nakereba* [or: seijitsu *de nai nara*; seijitsu *de nai nara ba*], nani goto nimo seikō shimasen)—If one is not sincere, he will not succeed in anything—誠実 (seijitsu), sincerity, is the noun form of the な (na)-adjective 誠実な (seijitsu na), sincere.

Such expressions as ければ (kereba), なら (nara), ならば (nara ba), and と (to) can be applied with い (i)-adjectives. In the case of い (i)-adjectives ending with either the short vowel い (i) or the long vowel *ii*, the hypothetical subjunctive condition can be obtained by replacing the final い (i) by ければ (kereba).

e.g. 暗ければ，電燈を付けなさい。(Kura *kereba*, dentō o tsuke nasai) —If it's too dark, please switch on the light—暗 (kura) in 暗ければ (kura kereba) comes from 暗い (kurai), dark.

The negative form of this expression can be formed as follows: the negative form of the predicative use of い (i)-adjectives can always be obtained by changing the final vowel い (i) of the plain present/future form to く (ku) and adding ない (nai). Then the final い (i) of this くない (kunai) is replaced by ければ (kereba), as くなければ (kunakereba).

e.g. おかずは甘くなければ，食べる気にはなりません。(Okazu wa a-ma*ku nakereba*, taberu ki niwa narimasen)—If the side dishes are not sweet, I don't feel inclined to have any of them—甘くなければ (amaku nakereba) comes from 甘くない (amaku nai), to not be sweet.

Each い (i)-adjective, as it is, may be put before the expressions なら (nara), ならば (nara ba), and と (to).

e.g. 寒いなら (or 寒いならば), 火をたきなさい。(Samui *nara* [or: samui *nara ba*], hi o taki nasai)—If you feel chilly, please make a fire—寒い (samui), cold, is an い (i)-adjective.

e.g. 安くないなら (or 安くないならば), 買いません。(Yasu*ku nai nara* [or: yasu*ku nai nara ba*], kaimasen)—If not cheap, I'll not buy anything—the predicative use of any い (i)-adjective in the plain present/future negative form, as it is, relates to なら (nara), ならば (nara ba), and と (to).

Drill

1. この国に**進駐すれば**，世界戦争
が起こるでしょう。

   If we march into this country, we will awaken a world war.

2. 事件が重大化され**複雑化すれば**，
彼は興奮します。

   If an affair is important and complex, he will become excited.

3. あなたと**比べれば**，彼はほとん
ど何事をも語らない人です。

   As compared with you, he is a man silent on almost all matters.

4. 私に書くなと**おっしゃるなら**，
書きません。

   If you order me to stop writing, I'll not write.

   * おっしゃる (ossharu) is more polite than 言う (i[w]-u), to say.

5. 政府の方針通りのものを書けと
おっしゃるなら，こちらからお断
わりします。

   If I am to be ordered to write only favorably of the government's policy, I myself must refuse to do so.

6. あなたが一つ二つの論文を**発表
すれば**，読者があなたのお説に共
鳴するでしょう。

   If you publish one or two articles, the readers will be all of the same mind as you.

7. **あなたなら**，何でもお返事しま
す。

   I'll answer any of your own questions.

8. 彼女に金銭的な**援助ができれ
ば**，いいのですが。

   If I could give her financial support, that'd be fine.

9. **働く気になれば**，良い所をさが
してあげます。

   If you intend to work, I'll find a good place for you.

10. あなたが**そういう気になるなら**，
会社の社長の方はよいように話を
つけてやります。

    If you yourself have such a will, I'll do my best to talk with the director at the company.

11. あなたが本当に**賢い女ならば**，
彼のような無責任な男のことは忘
れられるはずです。

    If you were really an intelligent woman, you'd be able to forget an irresponsible man like him.

12. 一日も早く彼女の就職口を**さが
さなければ**，災難が自分の身に降
りかかりそうです。

    Misfortune would rain down me if I didn't find her a position as quickly as possible.

13. トヨタの会社は，**さがせばすぐ**

    If you inquired, you could soon

にわかります。

The truth is that she is waiting anxiously for him.

14. 実を**言えば**，彼女は彼を心待ちにしています。

15. 自由な言論を**封じられてしまえば**，口舌の徒は虫けらのような無力な自分を自覚しなくてはなりません。

find out where the Toyota Company is.

The truth is that she is waiting anxiously for him.

If freedom of speech should be forbidden, a man of words would be obliged to realize that he himself is as powerless as an insect.

Exercise

Fill in the following blanks with なら(ば), ないと, すれば, ば, れば, or と, taking into consideration each term given below the sentences:

1. 改悛の情顕著（　　），この犯人は執行猶予の恩典が得られます。

If this criminal showed a sincere repentance, he might be able to receive a special favor such as probation.

　　顕著 (kencho) is the noun form derived from the な (na)-adjective 顕著な (kencho na), marked

2. 彼の生涯をこの浮沈の際に，救い上げることができる（　　），私は彼にできるだけの援助をしたいです。

If I can save his life at this crossroad, I am willing to support him as much as possible.

　　救い上げることができる (sukui ageru koto ga deki-ru) means "can save"

3. 本当の事を言（　　），あなたと友だちになりたいです。

To tell you the truth, I want to be a friend with you.

　　言う (i[w]-u), to say

4. 彼女の舞台姿を見（　　），彼はもうどんな女にも振り向きもしないでしょう。

If he should witness her stage performance, he would no longer take an interest in any other of woman.

　　見る (mi-ru), to witness

5. はたで聞いている（　　），まるで先生が講義をしているような彼の言い方です。

If anyone were near, listening, his way of talking would sound just as if the teacher were making a lecture himself.

聞いている (kiitei-ru) means "to be listening to"

6. この川に斜めにかかった橋の東
づめを，南へ二丁，川に沿って行
く（   ），伊吹屋という瀬戸物問
屋があります。

If you proceed a few hundred yards south along the river from the east side of the bridge slanting over it, you will find a wholesale china shop called "Ibukiya".

行く (ik-u), to go

7. へたに若主人を一人歩きさせる
（   ），この店ののれんをつぶし
てしまうかもしれません。

If we would let the young master go his way unguarded, he might dishonor this shop.

一人歩きさせる (hitori aruki sase-ru), to let one go his way unguarded

8. 彼と行きたいと思う（   ），行
ってもいいです。

If you want to go along with him, you may go.

思う (omo[w]-u), to think

9. この兵器さえあ（   ），もう大
丈夫です。

If we can obtain this weapon, we will be free from any fear.

ある (ar-u), to have; there is

10. この酵素肥料さえあ（   ），し
ろうとでも自給自足は可能です。

If we can provide this fermented fertilizer, even amateurs will be able to produce food.

ある (ar-u), to have; there is

11. 彼が青年らしく夢中になってい
るのを見（   ），冷やかしては済
まない気がします。

Observing his youthful excitement, I feel sorry for teasing him.

見る (mi-ru), to observe

12. 自分が絵を描いて一生を送れる
（   ），出世も栄達もほしくない
気がします。

If I myself could live my whole life by painting, I feel I would desire for nothing else—neither success nor advancement.

送れる (okure-ru), can lead

13. 彼女が本当に改心して，仕事に
はげむ（   ），私は大へんうれし
いです。

If she should mend her ways in a true sense, work hard, I'd be quite happy.

仕事にはげむ (shigoto ni hagem-u), to work hard

14. 彼女を避け（　　）、私自身の気
持ちが傾いていきそうです。
避けない (sake-nai), to not avoid＜避ける (sake-ru), to avoid

If I didn't avoid her, I might give way to her in my mind.

15. しあわせでありさえ（　　）、人
は悪い事はしません。
しあわせでありさえする (shiawase de arisae suru), to be always happy

If one is always happy, he will never do anything wrong.

Answers:
1. 顕著ならば　2. 救い上げることができるならば　3. 言えば　4. 見れば　5. 聞いていると　6. 行くと　7. 一人歩きさせると　8. 思うなら　9. あれば　10. あれば　11. 見れば　12. 送れるならば　13. 仕事にはげむならば　14. 避けないと　15. しあわせでありさえすれば

Hypothetical Subjunctive Condition (2)

Rule

A counterhypothesis to the past facts is given here. Such a hypothesis as evident in Japanese is quite different from that in English; in other words, in Japanese there is found no distinct difference between the indicative mood and the subjunctive mood. However, a hypothesis in opposition to past facts is indicated, in its if-clause, by such conditional suffixes as たら (tara), たなら (ta nara), and たなら ば (ta nara ba). And, in this main clause there are no exact verbal expressions and rules of concord which relate to the conditional mood —style and wording in the main clause can be preferably varied, closely associated with the speaker's subjective feelings and the scene of conversation through the medium of him.

The lack of an explicit method and usage in the subjunctive mood in the Japanese language often causes the subject of conversation to be such that the Japanese people find it impossible to create any hypothetical way of thinking.

In the case of vowel stem verbs ending with *e*-ru or *i*-ru, this hypothetical subjunctive condition can be obtained by dropping the last syllable *ru* and adding たら (tara), たなら (ta nara), and たならば (ta nara ba) to the stem. た (ta), found in such suffixes as たら (tara), たなら (ta nara), and たならば (ta nara ba), is derived from the plain past form of any vowel stem verb. Therefore; another clue for the formation of this subjunctive condition is found in the plain past form of vowel stem verbs: that is, this plain past form＋ら (ra), なら (nara), and ならば (nara ba).

e.g.　父がかつてのむすこの様子を見たら (or 見たなら；見たならば)，何 と言うだろうか。(Chichi ga katsute no musuko no yōsu o mi *tara* [or: mi *ta nara*; mi *ta nara ba*], nan to iu darō ka)—What if the father had seen the condition of his son in former times. What would he have said?—見 (mi) in 見たら (mi tara), in 見たなら (mi ta nara) or 見たならば (mi ta nara ba), comes from 見る (mi-ru), to see. The expression 何と言うだろうか (nan to *iu* darō ka) in the main clause should reasonably be replaced by the phrase 何 と言っただろうか (nan to *itta* darō ka) or 何と言ったでしょうか

(nan to *itta* deshō ka), these probably being the more grammatical, logical, and standard expressions in the subjunctive mood. But such an expression as 何と言っただろうか (nan to *itta* darō ka) or 何と言ったでしょうか (nan to *itta* deshō ka) is still removed from the common spoken Japanese. Instead, in this case 何と言うだろうか (nan to *iu* darō ka) or 何と言うでしょうか (nan to *iu* deshō ka) is preferably expressed. In other words, in a sentence like this we seldom use, in the main clause, any expression with a verb in the past form, rather and mainly permitting the use of the conjectural form だろう (darō), でしょう (deshō), or the simple volitional form ましょう (mashō) or some auxiliary verbs かもしれません (kamoshiremasen), may, にちがいありません (ni chigai arimasen), must be, はずです (hazu desu), to be+infinitive; to be supposed to, to be introduced into the sentence.

In the case of vowel stem verbs, the negative form can be obtained by dropping the last syllable *ru* and adding なかったら (nakatta ra), なかったなら (nakatta nara), and なかったならば (nakatta nara ba) to the stem. Otherwise, this negative form is obtained by the vowel stem verbs in the plain past negative form+ら (ra), なら (nara), and ならば (nara ba).

    e.g. 部屋をきちんとかたづけ**なかったら** (or かたづけ**なかったなら**：か
たづけ**なかったならば**), 両親にしかられるかもしれません。(Heya o kichinto katazuke *nakatta ra* [or: katazuke *nakatta nara*; katazuke *nakatta nara ba*], ryōshin ni shikarareru kamoshiremasen) —If I had not put my room in order, I might have been scolded by my parents—かたづけ (katazuke) comes from かたづける (katazuke-ru), to put in order. しかられる (shikarare-ru), to be scolded, in this main clause can not be replaced by the expression しかられた (shikarare-ta), was scolded, since it would not be actually spoken.

In the case of consonant stem verbs, this subjunctive mood can be formed by the use of their plain past forms. As far as verbs in this group are concerned, a sound change is involved before adding the plain past form た (ta) or だ (da). The subjunctive mood becomes this た (ta) or だ (da)+ら (ra), なら (nara), and ならば (nara ba). A clue for the formation of this subjunctive mood with consonant stem verbs is to be acquainted with their conjugations along with rules for the sound change.

    e.g. 私が念願の英国留学試験にパスしたと聞いた**ら** (or 聞いた**なら**；聞
いた**ならば**), よろこんでください。(Watakushi ga nengan no Eikoku

ryūgaku shiken ni pasu shita to kiita *ra* [or: kiita *nara*; kiita *nara ba*], yorokonde kudasai)—If you should hear that I have passed the examination to study in England, my heart's desire, please rejoice in it—聞いた (kiita), heard, in 聞いたら (kiita ra) is the plain past form; such a verb as 聞く (ki*k*-u), to hear, undergoes an *i*-euphonic change as 聞いた (ki*i*-ta).

e.g. このセーターを編んだ**ら** (or 編んだ**なら**；編んだ**ならば**), いくら かお金になります。(Kono sētā o anda *ra* [or: anda *nara*; anda *nara ba*], ikuraka okane ni narimasu)—If you had knitted this sweater, it would have profited you something—編んだ (anda), knitted, in 編んだら (anda ra) is the plain past form; such a verb as 編む (a*m*-u), to knit, undergoes a euphonic change to the syllabic nasal sound, as 編んだ (a*n*-da).

e.g. 彼を級長に選んだ**ら** (or 選んだ**なら**；選んだ**ならば**), 級友は彼に従 うべきです。(Kare o kyūchō ni eranda *ra* [or: eranda *nara*; eranda *nara ba*], kyūyū wa kare ni shitagau beki desu)—If the classmates had picked him out as a monitor, they ought to have taken his advice—選んだ (eranda), chose, in 選んだら (eranda ra) is the plain past form; such a verb as 選ぶ (era*b*-u), to choose, undergoes a euphonic change to the syllabic nasal sound, as 選んだ (era*n*-da).

e.g. この勝負に勝った**ら** (or 勝った**なら**；勝った**ならば**), 相当の賞金が もらえます。(Kono shōbu ni katta *ra* [or: katta *nara*; katta *nara ba*], sōtō no shōkin ga moraemasu)—If you had won this match, you might have gotten quite a large prize—勝った (katta), won, in 勝ったら (katta ra) is the plain past form; such a verb as 勝つ (ka*ts*-u), to win, undergoes a euphonic change of assimilation, as 勝った (ka*t*-ta).

e.g. 部屋をきれいに飾った**ら** (or 飾った**なら**；飾った**ならば**), 気分も良 くなります。(Heya o kirei ni kazatta *ra* [or: kazatta *nara*; kazatta *nara ba*], kibun mo yoku narimasu)—If you had arranged your room neatly, you would have also felt better—飾った (kazatta), decorated, in 飾ったら (kazatta ra) is the plain past form; such a verb as 飾る (kaza*r*-u), to decorate, undergoes a euphonic change of assimilation, as 飾った (kaza*t*-ta).

e.g. テレビを買ったら (or 買った**なら**；買った**ならば**), 私は毎日見よ うと思っています。(Terebi o katta *ra* [or: katta *nara*; katta *nara ba*], watakushi wa mainichi miyō to omotteimasu)—If I had bought a television set, I think I would have watched it every day—買った (katta), bought, in 買ったら (katta ra) is the plain past form; such a verb as 買う (ka[*w*]-u), to buy, undergoes a euphonic change of assimilation, as 買った (ka*t*-ta).

e.g. 貸間をよごしたら (or よごしたなら；よごしたならば)，間借り人が家主に弁償しなければならないのです。(Kashima o yogoshita *ra* [or: yogoshita *nara*; yogoshita *nara ba*], magari-nin ga yanushi ni benshō shinakereba naranai no desu)—If the room to lease had been spoiled, the roomer would have been obliged to compensate the landlord for it—よごした (yogoshita), spoiled, in よごしたら (yogoshita ra) is the plain past form; such a verb as よごす (yogo*s*-u), to spoil, undergoes a euphonic change of friction, as よごした (yogo*shi*-ta).

In the case of consonant stem verbs, the negative form is expressed by the use of their plain past negative forms＋ら (ra), なら (nara), and ならば (nara ba).

e.g. 彼が私の協力を断わらなかったら (or 断わらなかったなら；断わらなかったならば)，うまく商売をやっていけます。(Kare ga watakushi no kyōryoku o kotowa*ra nakatta ra* [or: kotowa*ra nakatta nara*; kotowa*ra nakatta nara ba*], umaku shōbai o yatte ikemasu)—If he had not refused my cooperation, he would have been able to carry on his business well—断わらなかった (kotowara nakatta), did not refuse, in 断わらなかったら (kotowara nakatta ra) is the plain past negative form.

In the case of the irregular verbs する (suru), to do and 来る (kuru), to come, the subjunctive mood will be したら (shita ra), したなら (shita nara), and したならば (shita nara ba); 来たら (kita ra), 来たなら (kita nara), and 来たならば (kita nara ba) as in the following:

e.g. この仕事を念入りにしたら (or したなら；したならば)，あなたを昇級させます。(Kono shigoto o nen-iri ni *shita ra* [or: *shita nara*; *shita nara ba*], anata o shōkyū sasemasu)—If you had done this work conscientiously, I would have had you promoted.

e.g. 一緒について来たら (or 来たなら；来たならば)，ご両親に申し訳ありません。(Issho ni tsuite *kita ra* [or: *kita nara*; *kita nara ba*], goryōshin ni mōshiwake arimasen)—If you had come with me, I could not have faced your father and mother again.

The negative form of such irregular verbs as する (suru), to do and 来る (kuru), to come, in this subjunctive mood will be しなかったら (shinakatta ra), しなかったなら (shinakatta nara), and しなかったならば (shinakatta nara ba); 来なかったら (konakatta ra), 来なかったなら (konakatta nara), and 来なかったならば (konakatta nara ba).

e.g. この仕事を期限内にしなかったら (or しなかったなら；しなかったならば)，取り消します。(Kono shigoto o kigen nai ni *shinakatta ra* [or: *shinakatta nara*; *shinakatta nara ba*], torikeshimasu)—If you had not done this work within the time limit, I would have cancelled it.

e.g. もうちょっと早く来なかったら (or 来なかったなら；来なかったならば), 私は留守にしているところでした。(Mō chotto hayaku *konakatta ra* [or: *konakatta nara*; *konakatta nara ba*], watakushi wa rusu ni shite iru tokoro deshita)—If you had not come a moment earlier, I would have been just out.

In the case of a noun, the expression in the subjunctive mood is the noun+であったら (de atta ra), だったら (datta ra), だったなら (datta nara), and だったならば (datta nara ba).

e.g. 私が悪女であったら (or だったら；だったなら；だったならば), このような事には良心が痛まないでしょう。(Watakushi ga akujo *de atta ra* [or: *datta ra*; *datta nara*; *datta nara ba*], kono yō na koto niwa ryōshin ga itamanai deshō)—If I had been a slut, I would not have felt a pang of conscience about such a matter as this —悪女 (akujo), a slut, is a noun.

The negative form with nouns is the noun+でなかったら (de nakatta ra), でなかったなら (de nakatta nara), and でなかったならば (de nakatta nara ba).

e.g. 妻帯者でなかったら (or でなかったら；でなかったならば), 今ごろはブラジルのような国でコーヒーの栽培をしているでしょう。(Saitaisha *de nakatta ra* [or: *de nakatta nara*; *de nakatta nara ba*], ima goro wa Burajiru no yō na kuni de kōhī no saibai o shite iru deshō)—If I had not been a married man, I would have been engaged in coffee growing in Brazil or some such country by this time—妻帯者 (saitaisha), a married man, is a noun.

In the case of な (na)-adjectives, the final な (na) may be dropped, this omission enabling them to be used as the noun forms. Such a noun as this relates to であったら (de atta ra), だったら (datta ra), だったなら (datta nara), and だったならば (datta nara ba), as in the case of a noun.

e.g. 交通が便利であったら (or だったら；だったなら；だったならば), そこへ引っ越します。(Kōtsū ga benri *de atta ra* [or: *datta ra*; *datta nara*; *datta nara ba*], soko e hikkoshimasu)—If traffic facilities had been convenient, we would have moved there—便利 (benri), convenience, is the noun form of the な (na)-adjective 便利な (benri na), convenient.

The negative form of this expression is nouns derived from な (na)-adjective+でなかったら (de nakatta ra), でなかったなら (de nakatta nara), and でなかったならば (de nakatta nara ba).

e.g. 外国語に堪能でなかったら (or でなかったなら；でなかったならば),
外交官にはなれません。(Gaikokugo ni tan-nō *de nakatta ra* [or: *de nakatta nara*; *de nakatta nara ba*], gaikōkan niwa naremasen)—
If one had not been good at foreign languages, he could not have
become a diplomat—堪能 (tan-nō) is the noun form of the な (na)-
adjective 堪能な (tan-nō na), good at.

Such expressions as かったら (katta ra), かったなら (katta nara),
and かったならば (katta nara ba) can be applied with い (i)-adjectives.
In the case of い (i)-adjectives ending with either the short vowel い
(i) or the long vowel *ii*, the hypothetical subjunctive condition can
be obtained by replacing the final い (i) by かったら (katta ra).

e.g. 彼女が思慮深かったら (or かったなら；かったならば), 横道にそれ
ることはないでしょう。(Kanojo ga shiryobuka *katta ra* [or: *katta
nara*; *katta nara ba*], yokomichi ni soreru koto wa nai deshō)—
If she had been a little more prudent, she would not have digressed
into wrong ways—思慮深 (shiryobuka) comes from the い (i)-
adjective 思慮深い (shiryobukai), prudent.

The negative form of this expression can be obtained by replacing
the final い (i) by くなかったら (ku nakatta ra), くなかったなら (ku
nakatta nara), and くなかったならば (ku nakatta nara ba).

e.g. まま母がやさしくなかったら (or くなかったなら；くなかったなら
ば), 今ごろは私はぐれていたにちがいありません。(Mama-haha ga ya-
sashi*ku nakatta ra* [or: *ku nakatta nara*; *ku nakatta nara ba*], ima
goro wa watakushi wa gurete ita ni chigai arimasen)—If my
stepmother had not been gentle, I ought to have strayed from
the right path by this time—やさし (yasashi) comes from the い
(i)-adjective やさしい (yasashii), gentle.

"Even if ..." in English is expressed by たとえ～ても (tatoe...
temo) or たとえ～たにしても (tatoe...ta ni shitemo). The pattern た
とえ～ても (tatoe...temo) indicates the present or future tense and
たとえ～たにしても (tatoe...ta ni shitemo) indicates the past tense.

e.g. たとえ雨が降っても, 私はそこへ行きます。(*Tatoe* ame ga fut*temo*,
watakushi wa soko e ikimasu)—Even if it rains, I'll go there—
降って (fut-t*e*) in 降っても (futtemo) comes from 降った (fut-t*a*),
fell, a verb in the plain past form.

e.g. たとえ彼女の理想が夢でも, 私はこの夢を信じたいです。(*Tatoe*
kanojo no risō ga yume *demo*, watakushi wa kono yume o shinji
tai desu)—Even if her ideal were a dream, I myself would like to
believe in *this* dream—夢 (yume), a dream, in 夢でも (yume demo)

is a noun.

e.g. たとえこの寮生活が不便でも，下宿する気にはなれません。(*Tatoe kono ryō seikatsu ga fuben demo*, geshuku suru ki niwa naremasen)—Even if my life in this dormitory were inconvenient, I would have no intention of taking up private lodgings—不便 (fuben), inconvenience, in 不便でも (fuben demo) is the noun form of the な (na)-adjective 不便な (fuben na), inconvenient.

e.g. たとえこの品物が高くても，友だちの結婚のお祝いに買って送ってあげたいです。(*Tatoe kono shinamono ga takaku temo*, tomodachi no kekkon no oiwai ni katte okutte age tai desu)—Even if this article were expensive, I'd like to get and send it to my friend as a wedding gift—高 (taka) in 高くても (takaku temo) comes from the い (i)-adjective 高い (takai), expensive.

e.g. たとえその映画を見たにしても，私はそれほど感動はしないでしょう。(*Tatoe sono eiga o mita ni shitemo*, watakushi wa sore hodo kandō wa shinai deshō)—Even if I had seen the film, I would not have been so deeply moved by it—見た (mi-ta), saw, in 見たにしても (mita ni shitemo), is a verb in the plain past form.

e.g. たとえ不良少年であったにしても，更生することができます。(*Tatoe furyō shōnen de atta ni shitemo*, kōsei suru koto ga dekimasu)—Even if he had been a depraved boy, he would have been able to start his life afresh—不良少年 (furyō shōnen), a bad boy, in 不良少年であったにしても (furyō shōnen de atta ni shitemo), is a noun.

e.g. たとえ政府からの奨学金が十分であったにしても，この物価高では留学生の生活も楽ではありません。(*Tatoe seifu kara no shōgakukin ga jūbun de atta ni shitemo*, kono bukka daka dewa ryūgakusei no seikatsu mo raku dewa arimasen)—Even if the scholarship from the government had been sufficient, foreign students would also have found it difficult to carry on their lives under this rise in commodity prices—十分 (jūbun) in 十分であったにしても (jūbun de atta ni shitemo) is the noun form of the な (na)-adjective 十分な (jūbun na), sufficient.

e.g. たとえ道路が広かったにしても，このような交通事故は起こりそうです。(*Tatoe dōro ga hiro katta ni shitemo*, kono yō na kōtsū jiko wa okori sō desu)—Even if the road had been wider, such a traffic accident as this might probably have taken place—広 (hiro) in 広かったにしても (hiro katta ni shitemo) comes from the い (i)-adjective 広い (hiroi), wide.

Drill

1. たとえ試験管洗いでも，私は張り切ってやります。

2. あなたに**会**ったら，事情一切を告白します。

3. あなたに良い考えでもあったら，聞きたいと思って出てきました。

4. **たとえ やせても**，かまいません。

5. 彼がまともに暮らしたら，私は大へんしあわせです。

6. 世論が**間違**っていたら，訂正しなければなりません。

7. たとえ今この囚人を**釈放**しても，暮らしに困るようです。

8. この学生を**放校**したら，それで済むことはこの先生にはわかっていました。

9. 彼女のおかげで，飢え死にが**免れたら**，こんなにうれしいことはありません。

10. たとえ官職を**捨て**たにしても，この女性の生涯を救い出してやりたいです。

11. あなたにその気があったら，私はいつでも英語を教えていただきます。

Even though I do such small jobs as washing test-tubes, I'll carry them out in high spirits.

I might have confessed everything if I had met you.

I came here, thinking that you'd perhaps have had a good idea.

I don't mind even if I do become thin.

If he had led a sincere life, I'd have been quite happy.

If public opinion had been misguided, it should have been corrected.

Even if we should release this prisoner now, we think he'd find it hard to make a living.

This teacher was quite aware that had this student been expelled from school, no further annoyance would have arisen.

If we could have been relieved of starvation through her help, we would have been able to find greater happiness than we have now.

Even though I might have given up my official duties, I would have saved this woman's life.

If you had wished it, I'd have been glad to let you teach me English anytime.

12. もうちょっとおそかったら，橋 と一緒に彼も私も川へ落ちたとこ ろでした。

If we had been a moment later, he and I both would have gone down into the river with the bridge.

Exercise

Fill in the following blanks with the subjunctive mood, taking into consideration each term given below the sentences:

1. 竹みたいに（ ），お嫁に行か なくてもいいでしょう。

If I had become as thin as a bamboo rod, then perhaps there would have been an excuse for me not to get married.

やせる (yase-ru), to become thin

2. （ ），あきらめようと彼女は 思っていました。

If she had had to resign herself, she felt she could have reconciled herself.

あきらめなければならなかった (akirame-nakereba naranakatta), had to resign＜あきらめなければならない (akirame-nakereba naranai), to have to resign

3. この地価が（ ），手に入れた いです。

If the price of this land had been inexpensive, I'd have liked to gain possession of it.

安い (yasui), inexpensive

4. あなたのような情熱を（ ）， 私はきっと素直な良い女に生まれ 変わるはずでした。

If I had had a passion similar to yours, I surely could have been reborn into an obedient and good woman.

もっている (mottei-ru), to have

5. 他人の目から（ ），清潔で聡 明で，はつらつとした申し分のな い妻でした。

As she would have appeared to others she was neat, intelligent, and full of life—she was a wife beyond criticism.

見る (mi-ru), to see

6. 衰えをみせない体格の良さを （ ），彼を引退させておくのは もったいない気がしました。

Looking at his good physique which showed little decline, one would have felt that it was a waste for him to keep retired from active life.

見る (mi-ru), to look at

7. あの時（　　）, 昔のお客さんの顔も見られませんし, インフレや食糧やなんやかんやといっても, 生きているほどありがたいことはありません。

If I had died then, I would not have been able to see the faces of my former customers; and moreover, even if grumbling over inflation, or food, or what have you, it's happiness enough for me to be still alive.

死んでいた (shinde i-ta), was dead＜死んでいる (shinde i-ru), to be dead

8. 兵役は国民の義務であると一言（　　）, あらゆる青年はそれだけで納得したものでした。

With the single phrase "military service is the compulsory duty of the people"—all young men would have been convinced simply by this slogan.

言った (it-ta), said＜言う (i[w]-u), to say

9. 共産主義者のこの社長のむすこの嫁に（　　）, この女は共産主義かにかぶれるにちがいありません。

If this woman had become the bride of the son of this director, a communist, she would surely have been infected by communism or something of the sort.

なった (nat-ta), became＜なる (nar-u), to become

10. 彼女のことを（　　）, 東京へ出て弁護士になる勉強をすることが私に残されたただ一つの道です。

If I had abandoned my affair with her, then for me to go to Tokyo to study to be a lawyer would have been the only prudent thing to do.

あきらめる (akirame-ru), to abandon

11. ちゃんと筋道の通った理屈を（　　）, 自分の立場は納得できます。

If I had been given to understand a clear and reasonable argument, I would have accepted my situation.

聞かされる (kikasare-ru), to be made to listen to

12. 右か左か，白か黒かはっきりし
た色彩を（　　），彼は五分間も安
心しておられない人でした。

He was a person who could not
have felt relaxed even for five
minutes without having been given
a definite position and a clear
distinction of right from left, or
white from black.

与えられなかった (ataerare-nakatta), was not given＜与えられない (atae-
rare-nai), to not be given

Answers:

1. やせたら 2. あきらめなければならなかったら 3. 安かったら 4.
もっていたら 5. 見たら 6. 見たら 7. 死んでいたら 8. 言ったら
9. なったら 10. あきらめたら 11. 聞かされたら 12. 与えられなか
ったら

Intransitive and Transitive Verbs

Rule

Those verbs which do not take the objective particle を (o) are called intransitive verbs whereas transitive verbs usually take the direct object. There are some rules concerning the transformation from the intransitive to the transitive state, but in almost all cases no definite rule may be adopted between the two verbs.

Such intransitive verbs as 流れる (nagare-ru), to flow, 落ちる (ochi-ru), to fall, and 冷える (hie-ru), to get cold, are converted by dropping the last syllable る (ru), this termination enabling them to suffix す (s-u); and thus, these transitive verbs run as follows: 流す (nagas-u), to let flow, 落とす (otos-u), to drop, and 冷やす (hiyas-u), to cool.

Type 1. Morphemic contrast:

Intransitive		Transitive	
-re	(ru)	-s	(u)
-i	(ru)	-os	(u)
-e	(ru)	-as	(u)

e.g.

涙が彼女の目から**流れ**ました。(Namida ga kanojo no me kara *nagaremashita*)—The tears flowed from her eyes—流れました (nagare-mashita), flowed, comes from 流れる (nagare-ru), to flow.

彼は燈籠を川に**流し**ました。(Kare wa tōrō o kawa ni *nagashi-mashita*)—He let flow a lantern on the river—流しました (nagash-imashita), let flow, comes from 流す (nagas-u), to let flow.

e.g.

この子供は窓から**落ち**ました。(Kono kodomo wa mado kara *ochimashita*)—This child fell out of the window—落ちました (ochi-mashita), fell, comes from 落ちる (ochi-ru), to fall.

彼女は卵の一杯はいったかごを路上に**落と**しました。(Kanojo wa tamago no ippai haitta kago o rojō ni *otoshimashita*)—She dropped a basket full of eggs on the street—落としました (otosh-imashita), dropped, comes from 落とす (otos-u), to drop.

e.g.
気温が冷えます。(Kion ga *hiemasu*)—The temperature is chilly —冷えます (hie-masu) comes from 冷える (hie-ru), to get cold.

私はビールを氷で冷やしました。(Watakushi wa bīru o kōri de *hiyashimashita*)—I cooled beer on the ice—冷やしました (hiyash-imashita), cooled, comes from 冷やす (hiyas-u), to cool.

Such intransitive verbs as 広がる (hirogar-u), to spread, 高まる (takamar-u), to raise, and 隔たる (hedatar-u), to become estranged, are converted by dropping the last syllable *ar-u*, this termination enabling them to suffix *e-ru*; and thus, these transitive verbs run as follows: 広げる (hiroge-ru), to spread out, 高める (takame-ru), to promote, and 隔てる (hedate-ru), to estrange.

Type 2. Morphemic contrast:

Intr.	-a (ru)
Tr.	-e (ru)

e.g.
彼の名声は国中に広がりました。(Kare no meisei wa kuni jū ni *hirogarimashita*)—His fame spread all over the country—広がりました (hirogar-imashita), spread, comes from 広がる (hirogar-u), to spread.

彼は朝刊を広げました。(Kare wa chōkan o *hirogemashita*)—He spread out the morning paper—広げました (hiroge-mashita), spread out, comes from 広げる (hiroge-ru), to spread out.

e.g.
彼の地位が高まりました。(Kare no chi-i ga *takamarimashita*)—His position raised—高まりました (takamar-imashita), raised, comes from 高まる (takamar-u), to raise.

彼女は興奮して，声を高めました。(Kanojo wa kōfun shite, koe o *takamemashita*)—She got excited, elevating her voice—高めました (takame-mashita), elevated, comes from 高める (takame-ru), to elevate.

e.g.
私は彼と隔たりました。(Watakushi wa kare to *hedatarimashita*)—I've become estranged from him—隔たりました (hedatar-imashita), became estranged, comes from 隔たる (hedatar-u), to become estranged.

感情がもつれて，私は彼女を隔てました。(Kanjō ga motsurete, watakushi wa kanojo o *hedatemashita*)—I estranged her by an entangled impulse—隔てました (hedate-mashita), estranged, comes from 隔てる (hedate-ru), to estrange.

Such intransitive verbs as 近づく (chikazuk-u), to come near, くっ
つく (kuttsuk-u), to stick, and ちぢむ (chijim-u), to shrink, are converted by dropping the last syllable *u*, this termination enabling them
to suffix *e-ru*; and thus, these transitive verbs run as follows: 近づけ
る (chikazuke-ru), to allow one to come near, くっつける (kuttsuke-ru),
to fix, and ちぢめる (chijime-ru), to shorten.

Type 3. Morphemic contrast:

Intr.	-	(u)
Tr.	-e	(ru)

e.g.

冬休みが**近づきました**。(Fuyu yasumi ga *chikazukimashita*)—
The winter vacation is near at hand—近づきました (chika-
zuk-imashita), came near, comes from 近づく (chikazuk-u),
to come near.

彼はえさで鹿を**近づけました**。(Kare wa esa de shika o *chika-
zukemashita*)—He drew the deer close with food—近づけま
した (chikazuke-mashita), drew, comes from 近づける (chikazuke-ru), to allow one to come near.

e.g.

どろがくつに**くっつきました**。(Doro ga kutsu ni *kuttsukima-
shita*)—The mud adhered to my shoes—くっつきました
(kuttsuk-imashita), adhered, comes from くっつく (kuttsuk-
u), to stick.

アルバムに京都の写真をのりで**くっつけました**。(Arubamu ni
Kyōto no shashin o nori de *kuttsukemashita*)—I stuck a
picture of Kyoto in the album with paste—くっつけました
(kuttsuke-mashita), stuck, comes from くっつける (kuttsuke-
ru), to fix.

e.g.

セーターは洗濯すると**ちぢみます**。(Sētā wa sentaku suru to
chijimimasu)—A sweater shrinks in the wash—ちぢみます
(chijim-imasu) comes from ちぢむ (chijim-u), to shrink.

彼は過労のために，命を**ちぢめました**。(Kare wa karō no tame
ni, inochi o *chijimemashita*)—He shortened his life from
excessive labor—ちぢめました (chijime-mashita), shortened,
comes from ちぢめる (chijime-ru), to shorten.

With intransitive verbs as 飛ぶ (tob-u), to fly, and 動く (ugok-u),
to move, *as* is inserted before the last syllable *u*; and thus, these
transitive verbs run as follows: 飛ばす (tobas-u), to let fly, and 動か
す (ugokas-u), to move.

Type 4. Morphemic contrast:

Intr.	-	(u)
Tr.	-as	(u)

e.g.
すずめが低く飛びました。(Suzume ga hikuku *tobimashita*)—
A sparrow flew low in the air—飛びました (tob-imashita),
flew, comes from 飛ぶ (tob-u), to fly.

生徒は校庭でたこを飛ばしました。(Seito wa kōtei de tako o
tobashimashita)—The pupils flew kites in the playground—
飛ばしました (tobash-imashita), let fly, comes from 飛ばす
(tobas-u), to let fly.

e.g.
この機械は電気で動きます。(Kono kikai wa denki de *ugokimasu*)
—This machine goes by electricity—動きます (ugok-imasu),
comes from 動く (ugok-u), to move.

私はこの機械を動かしました。(Watakushi wa kono kikai o
ugokashimashita)—I've set this machine in motion—動かし
ました (ugokash-imashita), moved, comes from 動かす (ugokas-u), to move.

Such verbs as 増す (mas-u), to increase, and 減じる (genji-ru), to
fall off, take the same form in both the intransitive and transitive
states; and in the sentence the role of the transitive of each of these
verbs can be discriminated by the use of the objective particle; otherwise, the intransitive of these verbs has no objective particle を (o).

e.g.
川の水が増しました。(Kawa no mizu ga *mashimashita*)—The
river has risen—増しました (mash-imashita), rose, comes
from 増す (mas-u), to rise, an intransitive verb.

社長は彼の俸給を増しました。(Shachō wa kare no hōkyū o
mashimashita)—The director increased his salary—増しまし
た (mash-imashita), increased, comes from 増す (mas-u), to
increase, a transitive verb.

e.g.
タイ国からの米の輸入が減じました。(Taikoku kara no kome no
yunyū ga *genjimashita*)—The import of rice from Thailand
has fallen off—減じました (genji-mashita), fell off, comes
from 減じる (genji-ru), to fall off, an intransitive verb.

日本政府は英国への輸出品を減じました。(Nihon seifu wa Eikoku
e no yushutsuhin o *genjimashita*)—The Japanese Government has decreased exports to England—減じました (genjimashita), decreased, comes from 減じる (genji-ru), to decrease, a transitive verb.

The phrase 窓が あけてあります。(Mado *ga akete arimasu*), The window is open, is induced from the following construction—(だれか が) 窓を あけました。([Dareka ga] mado *o akemashita*), *Someone* opened the window. The form denoting consequence nearly corresponds in meaning to the form denoting continuance used with an intransitive verb; the difference is that the former is effected by the third person pronoun but the latter has no such nuance.

* 窓が あけてあります。(Mado *ga akete arimasu*)—The window is open—あけてあります (akete arimasu) is a transitive verb.

* 窓が あいています。(Mado *ga aite imasu*) or 窓が あきます。(Mado *ga akimasu*)—The w ndow opens—あいています (aite imasu) and あきます (akimasu) are intransitive verbs.

Drill

1. ごみ箱のごみが燃えました。	Trash in a trash box burned.
彼はごみ捨て場のごみを燃やしました。	He burned the trash in a refuse-heap.
2. 彼は今朝六時に起きました。	He woke up at six o'clock this morning.
母は私を七時に起こしました。	Mother called me at seven o'clock.
3. お湯が沸きました。	The water has boiled.
彼女は牛乳を沸かしました。	She scalded milk.
4. この部屋は先月ふさがりました。	This room was occupied last month.
私はねずみがあけた穴をふさぎました。	I stopped up the hole a rat had gnawed open.
5. 戸がしまりました。	The door shut.
彼は戸をばたんとしめました。	He banged a door.
6. この子供の命が助かりました。	The life of this child was saved.
彼はおぼれている人を助けました。	He saved a person from drowning.
7. この本はよく出ます。	This book sells well.
彼は二・三カ月前に神田に店を出しました。	He set up a shop in Kanda a few months ago.

Exercise

Fill each bracket with the transitive verb given below each sentence:

1. {
時計が**止まりました**。   The clock has stopped.
私はラジオを（   ）。   I turned off the radio.
}
The transitive of 止まる (tomar-u), to stop, is 止める (tome-ru).

2. {
梅雨期が**始まりました**。   The rainy season has set in.
私は今日から日本語の勉強を（   I began to study Japanese from
   ）。   today.
}
The transitive of 始まる (hajimar-u), to begin, is 始める (hajime-ru).

3. {
桜の花が**散りました**。   The cherry blossoms have fallen.
太陽は雲を（   ）。   The sun dispelled the clouds.
}
The transitive of 散る (chir-u), to dispel, is 散らす (chiras-u).

4. {
私は教会のそばを**通りました**。   I passed by the church.
私は客を二階へ（   ）。   I showed a guest upstairs.
}
The transitive of 通る (tōr-u), to pass, is 通す (tōs-u).

5. {
口ひげが**はえました**。   The mustache has grown.
口ひげを（   ）。   I've cultivated a mustache.
}
The transitive of はえる (hae-ru), to grow, is はやす (hayas-u).

6. {
川水が**ふえました**。   The river has risen.
彼は残業して収入を（   ）。   He increased his income with
     overtime work.
}
The transitive of ふえる (fue-ru), to increase, is ふやす (fuyas-u).

Answers:
   1. 止めました   2. 始めました   3. 散らしました   4. 通しました
5. はやしました   6. ふやしました

The Use of the Potential Auxiliary "Can"

Rule

"Can" in English is expressed by ことができる (koto ga dekiru), plain form, or ことができます (koto ga dekimasu), polite form. The expression ことができます (koto ga dekimasu) is put after any verb in the plain present/future form.

e.g. 彼は情勢を客観的に見ることができます。(Kare wa jōsei o kyak-kan teki ni miru *koto ga dekimasu*)—He can observe the situation objectively—見る (mi-ru), to see, is a vowel stem verb in the plain present/future form.

e.g. 彼は超然と一切を耐えることができます。(Kare wa chōzento issai o taeru *koto ga dekimasu*)—He can bear everything with a detached air—耐える (tae-ru), to bear, is a vowel stem verb in the plain present/future form.

e.g. この留学生は大へん熱いお風呂にはいることができます。(Kono ryūgakusei wa taihen atsui ofuro ni hairu *koto ga dekimasu*)—This foreign student can get into a bath which is very hot—はいる (hair-u), to get into, is a consonant stem verb in the plain present/future form.

e.g. この少年はナイフでりんごの皮を上手にむくことができます。(Kono shōnen wa naifu de ringo no kawa o jōzu ni muku *koto ga dekimasu*)—This boy can peel an apple expertly with a knife—むく (muk-u), to peel, is a consonant stem verb in the plain present/future form.

Otherwise, this potential auxiliary is expressed by られる (rareru), plain form and られます (raremasu), polite form, or る (eru), plain form and ます (emasu), polite form.

In the case of vowel stem verbs ending with either *e*-ru or *i*-ru, this potential auxiliary can be obtained by dropping the last syllable *ru* and adding られます (raremasu) to the stem.

e.g. 彼は私に漢字の筆順が教えられます。(Kare wa watakushi ni *Kanji* no hitsujun ga oshie *raremasu*)—He can teach me the stroke order of *Kanji*—教えられます (oshie-raremasu), can teach, comes from 教える (oshie-ru), to teach. When using the expression られます (raremasu), the potential is preceded by が (ga); that is,

が (ga) in this case is treated as an objective case. Quoting the previous sentence, the phrase 漢字の筆順が (*Kanji* no hitsujun *ga*), the stroke order of *Kanji*—this が (ga) takes the same role as を (o), an objective particle.

Note: As far as vowel stem verbs are concerned, there is no difference in form between the potential and passive voice.

e.g. 私はあなたに日本語が教えられます。(Watakushi wa anata ni Nihongo *ga* oshie *raremasu*)—I can teach you Japanese—教えられます (oshie-raremasu), can teach, is in the potential form. In this case, the object for this verb is used with the particle が (ga), as seen from 日本語が (Nihongo *ga*), the Japanese language.

e.g. 私はあなたに日本語を教えられます。(Watakushi wa anata ni Nihongo *o* oshie *raremasu*)—I am taught Japanese by you—教えられます (oshie-raremasu), to be taught, is in the passive voice. In this case, the object for this verb is used with the particle を (o), as seen from 日本語を (Nihongo *o*), the Japanese language.

Thus, the clue for discrimination in the choice of the potential and the passive voice is in those particles が (ga) and を (o) which precede the last words.

e.g. 私はスキヤキが食べられます。(Watakushi wa *Sukiyaki* ga tabe *raremasu*)—I can eat *Sukiyaki*, a dish of meat, Chinese onion, and roast bean curd cooked together—食べられます (tabe-raremasu), can eat, is in the potential form. The passive voice of this sentence is as follows: スキヤキは私に食べられます。(*Sukiyaki* wa watakushi ni tabe *raremasu*)—*Sukiyaki* is eaten by me—食べられます (tabe-raremasu), to be eaten, is in the passive voice. But *Sukiyaki* is an inanimate object, not an animate object; so, such a subject as *Sukiyaki* in the passive voice would not be actually evident in Japanese sentences. Thus, the formation of the passive voice such as this can be wholly ignored.

e.g. 西の方に遠く富士山が見られます。(Nishi no hō ni tōku Fuji-san ga mi *raremasu*)—We can see Mt. Fuji far to the west—見られます (mi-raremasu), can see, is in the potential form. The passive voice of this sentence is as follows: 西の方に遠く富士山が見られます。(Nishi no hō ni tōku Fuji-san ga mi *raremasu*)—Mt. Fuji can be seen far to the west—見られます (mi-raremasu), can be seen; to be visible, is in the passive voice. Otherwise, this sentence can also be expressed as follows: 西の方に遠く富士山が見えます。(Nishi no hō ni tōku Fuji-san ga mi*emasu*)—Mt. Fuji can be seen far to the west—見えます (mie-masu), to be able to see; to be visible, is in the spontaneous voice. The use of such a nominative case as Mt. Fuji, an inanimate object, is quite possible; and the expressions 見られます (mi-raremasu) and 見えます (mie-masu) evident in these two sentences have respectively such shading as: られます (raremasu) in 見られます (mi-raremasu) is the auxiliary of possibility and this expression is used in the sense that something is in sight if one has a desire to observe it. On the other hand, the expression 見えます (mie-masu), an intransitive verb, is used in the sense that something exists there, irrelevant to the will of an observer.

In the case of consonant stem verbs ending with *u*, a consonant +*u*, the potential auxiliary can be obtained by dropping the last syllable *u* and adding ます (emasu) to the stem.

e.g. この外人はきわめて自由に日本語が話せます。(Kono gaijin wa kiwamete jiyū ni Nihongo ga hanas*emasu*)—This foreigner can speak Japanese quite freely—話せます (hanas-emasu), can speak, comes from 話す (hanas-u), to speak.

e.g. この園児は一人で使いに行けます。(Kono enji wa hitori de tsukai ni ik*emasu*)—This kindergartener can go on an errand alone—行けます (ik-emasu), can go, comes from 行く (ik-u), to go.

In the case of the irregular verbs する (suru), to do and 来る (kuru), to come, the potential form will be することができます (suru koto ga dekimasu), and ができます (ga dekimasu); 来ることができます (kuru koto ga dekimasu), and 来られます (koraremasu) as in the following:

e.g. この女生徒はししゅうをすることができます。(Kono joseito wa shishū o *suru koto ga dekimasu*)—This schoolgirl can do embroidery—ししゅうをする (shishū o suru), to embroider, belongs to the verb する (suru), to do, an irregular verb. This can also be expressed as: この女生徒はししゅうができます。(Kono joseito wa shishū *ga dekimasu*)—ししゅう (shishū), embroidery, is one of those nouns in which a sense of action is inherent; every noun form such as this relates to ができます (ga dekimasu).

e.g. あなたは来週私の寮へ来ることができますか。(Anata wa raishū watakushi no ryō e *kuru koto ga dekimasu* ka)—Will you be able to come to my dormitory next week?—this can also be expressed as: あなたは来週私の寮へ来られますか。(Anata wa raishū watakushi no ryō e *koraremasu* ka).

e.g. 今夜は同窓会の者で新年会をやる予定になっています。あなたは駒場の会場へ来られますか。(Konya wa dōsōkai no mono de shin-nen-kai o yaru yotei ni natte imasu. Anata wa Komaba no kaijō e *koraremasu* ka)—Tonight our alumni association is planning a New Year's Party. Will you be able to come to the meeting place in Komaba?—this potential form 来られます (koraremasu), can come, is, as it is, converted into the form of the passive voice. That is, as far as the irregular verb 来る (kuru) is concerned, there is no difference in form between the potential and passive voice, as in the case of vowel stem verbs in these forms.

e.g. 明朝殺人犯が大阪から東京の警視庁に連れてこられます。(Myōchō satsujin han ga Ōsaka kara Tōkyō no Keishichō ni tsurete *koraremasu*)—Tomorrow morning a murderer will be brought in from Osaka to the Metropolitan Police Board in Tokyo—こられます (koraremasu) in this sentence is in the passive voice; a passive form such as こられます (koraremasu), to be come, is generally applied in a compound verb, as 連れて (tsurete), taking someone by the hand＋こられます (koraremasu). And thus, 連れてこられます (tsurete koraremasu) means "to be brought in".

Drill

1. この政治家は国の将来への正しい道を見い出すことができます (or: 正しい道が見い出せます)。

   This politician can discover the right path for the future of the country.

2. 言論弾圧の弊害を自覚することができます (or: 弊害が自覚できます)。

   One can become conscious of the evils brought about by the suppression of speech.

3. 彼は彼女との友情を取りもどすことができした (or: 友情が取りもどせました)。

   He could restore his former friendship with her.

4. 彼は彼女に対し責任をのがれることができませんでした (or: 責任がのがれられませんでした)。

   He could not escape his responsibility towards her.

5. 彼は知人に手紙を託すことができました (or: 手紙が託せました)。

   He could entrust a letter to his acquaintance.

6. この英語会話クラブはパンフレット型の雑誌を刊行することができました (or: 雑誌が刊行できました)。

   This English Speaking Club could produce a pamphlet-sized magazine.

7. この会社は従前通り業務を**運営**することができました（or: 業務が**運営**できました）。

This company could carry out its business as usual.

8. この検事はあの事件を**糾弾する**ことができました（or: 事件が**糾弾**できました）。

This public prosecutor could find fault with the incident.

9. 彼は餓死を**覚悟する**ことができました。（or: 餓死が**覚悟**できました）。

He could make up his mind to face death through starvation.

10. この国は天然ゴムの不足を**補う**ことができません（or: 不足が**補えません**）。

This country cannot make up for the lack of natural rubber.

11. 私は京都でのびやかな一日を**過**ごすことができました（or: 一日が**過ごせました**）。

I could spend one day of relaxation at Kyoto.

12. 私は広い庭を**見る**ことができます（or: 広い庭が**見られます** or: 広い庭が**見えます**）。

I can see a large garden.

13. 私たちはこの冬休みにスキーに**行く**ことができます（or: **行けます**）。

We will be able to be off for skiing this coming winter vacation.

14. この商人は相当の産を**作る**ことができました（or: 相当の産が**作れました**）。

This merchant could amass a considerable fortune.

15. 彼女はこの数年間続いていた自分の危機を**解決する**ことができました（or: 危機が**解決**できました）。

She could solve the crisis that had gripped her these several years.

Exercise

Rewrite the Gothic words ことができます into the expressions られます, ます, or できます, taking into consideration the verb, given below each sentence, in the plain present/future form from which the potential form can be induced:

1. 人は座禅で心を**鍛える**ことがで

One can train his own heart in

きます。
鍛える (kitae-ru), to train

religious meditation.

2. 彼はこの外人に何ほどかの信頼
をおくことができます。
信頼をおく (shinrai o ok-u), to trust

He can place some measure of trust in this foreigner.

3. 彼は身動きもならない惨澹たる
立場から友を救い出すことができ
ました。
救い出す (sukuidas-u), to save

He could save his friend from a helpless position in which he could not stir an inch.

4. 彼は恋愛という感情を経験する
ことができました。
経験する (keiken suru), to experience; 経験 (keiken), an experience, is a noun

He could experience the feeling of love.

5. 彼女は悲劇を吹き飛ばすことが
できました。
吹き飛ばす (fukitobas-u), to throw off

She could throw off disappointments.

6. 彼は冷静さを取りもどすことが
できません。
取りもどす (torimodos-u), to regain

He cannot regain his composure.

7. 彼はよくよく女の復讐の恐ろし
さを認識することができました。
認識する (ninshiki suru), to know; 認識 (ninshiki), recognition, is a noun

He could know completely the dreadfulness of a woman's revenge.

8. 彼は人間本来の生き方を探究す
ることができました。
探究する (tankyū suru), to pursue; 探究 (tankyū), pursuance, is a noun

He could pursue a human being's instinctive way of life.

9. 僧は欲念を除去することができ
ます。
除去する (jokyo suru), to get rid of; 除去 (jokyo), removal, is a noun

A priest can get rid of a diversity of passion.

10. 高僧は是非善悪を超越した人間
本来の姿を描くことができます。

描く (egak-u), to draw

A high priest can draw the true picture of a man, transcending right or wrong and good and evil.

11. 私は勝利を叫ぶ自分の朗らかな
姿を予想することができます。
予想する (yosō suru), to anticipate; 予想 (yosō), anticipation, is a noun

I can anticipate my own cheerful rejoicing of victory.

12. 彼は自信を回復することができ   He could regain his confidence.
ました。
　　回復する (kaifuku suru), to regain; 回復 (kaifuku), recovery, is a noun
13. 私は電車の中で若い女子事務員   I could listen in the tramcar
の会話を聞くことができました。   to the conversation of some young
office girls.

　　聞く (kik-u), to hear
14. 私は彼女のあけすけな述懐を聞   I could listen to her straight-
くことができました。   forward reminiscences.
　　聞く (kik-u), to hear
15. 離婚後彼女は再び心を取りもど   She could regain her heart again
すことができました。   after separation from her husband.
　　取りもどす (torimodos-u), to regain

Answers:
1. 心が鍛えられます　2. 信頼がおけます　3. 友が救い出せました
4. 感情が経験できました or 感情の経験ができました　5. 悲劇が吹き飛
ばせました　6. 冷静さが取りもどせません　7. 恐ろしさが認識できまし
た or 恐ろしさの認識ができました　8. 生き方が探究できました or 生き
方の探究ができました　9. 欲念が除去できます or 欲念の除去ができます
10. 姿が描けます　11. 姿が予想できます or 姿の予想ができます　12.
自信が回復できました or 自信の回復ができました　13. 会話が聞けました
14. 述懐が聞けました　15. 心が取りもどせました

第 四十五 課　Lesson 45

The Voice

Rule

The passive voice is classified by three categories—the direct passive voice (the objective case with the particle を [o] in the active voice being changed into the nominative case in this passive voice), the indirect passive voice (the objective case preceding either of the particles に [ni] or と [to] in the active voice being expressed as the subject in this passive voice), and the third person passive voice (the subject of the sentence in the active voice being expressed as the objective case with the particle に [ni] and the receiver of a troublesome action taking the role of the nominative case in this passive voice).

In the case of vowel stem verbs ending with either *e*-ru or *i*-ru, the passive voice can be obtained by dropping the last syllable *ru* and adding られる (rareru), plain form, or られます (raremasu), polite form, to the stem.

e.g. 先生はこの学生をほめます。(Sensei wa kono gakusei *o home-masu*)—The teacher praises this student—ほめます (home-masu) from ほめる (home-ru), to praise, can be converted into the passive voice ほめられます (home-raremasu). The direct passive voice of this active voice sentence is as follows: この学生は先生に (or 先生から) ほめられます。(Kono gakusei wa sensei *ni* [or: sensei *kara*] *home raremasu*)—This student is praised by the teacher—に (ni) or から (kara) in 先生に (sensei ni) or 先生から (sensei kara) indicates the agent of passive action.

Note: In the case of an inanimate object as the perpetrator of an action in the passive voice, から (kara) is never used; the particle に (ni) always replaces the particle から (kara).

e.g. 私は富士山の美しさに魂を奪われます。(Watakushi wa Fuji-san no utsukushii sa *ni* tamashii o ubawaremasu)—I am fascinated by the beauty of Mt. Fuji—美しさ (utsukushi sa), beauty, is an inanimate object as the perpetrator of the action in this passive voice.

e.g. 彼女は彼を信じます。(Kanojo wa kare *o shinjimasu*)—She puts confidence in him—信じます (shinji-masu) from 信じる (shinji-ru), to believe, can be converted into the passive voice 信じられます

(shinji-raremasu). The direct passive voice of this active voice sentence is as follows: 彼は彼女に (or 彼女から) 信じられます。 (Kare wa kanojo *ni* [or: kanojo *kara*] *shinji raremasu*)—He is held in confidence by her.

e.g. 先生は学生に英語を 教えます。(Sensei wa gakusei *ni* Eigo *o oshiemasu*)—The teacher teaches a student English—教えます (oshie-masu) from 教える (oshie-ru), to teach, can be converted into the passive voice 教えられます (oshie-raremasu). The indirect passive voice sentence is as follows: 学生は先生に (or 先生から) 英語を 教えられます。(Gakusei wa sensei *ni* [or: sensei *kara*] Eigo *o oshie raremasu*)—A student is taught English by the teacher. Otherwise, we may say and write as follows: 先生は学生に英語を 教えてやります。(Sensei wa gakusei *ni* Eigo *o oshiete yarimasu*)— The teacher teaches a student English—教えてやります (oshiete yarimasu) consists of the two verbs 教えて (oshie-te) from 教えた (oshie-ta), taught and やります (yar-imasu) from やる (yar-u), to give. This passive voice is as follows: 学生は先生に (or 先生から) 英語を教えてもらいます。(Gakusei wa sensei *ni* [or: sensei *kara*] Eigo *o oshiete moraimasu*)—A student is taught English by the teacher—教えてもらいます (oshiete moraimasu) consists of the two verbs 教えて (oshie-te) from 教えた (oshie-ta), taught and もらいます (mora-imasu) from もらう (mora[w]-u), to receive.

e.g. 警官が手を 押えました。(Keikan ga te *o osaemashita*)—The policeman seized a criminal by the hand—押えました (osae-mashita) comes from 押える (osae-ru), to seize; the owner of the objective term 手 (te), one's hand, is not explicitly evidenced in the sentence; that is, the omission of the owner who is affected by some interests is standard in the third person active voice. This owner, however, can be expressed at the beginning of the sentence in this passive voice, enabling it to take the role of the nominative case. The third person passive voice of this active voice sentence is as follows: 犯人が警官に手を 押えられました。(Han-nin ga keikan *ni* te *o osaeraremashita*)—A criminal was caught hold of by the hand by the policeman—押えられました (osae-raremashita) comes from 押えられる (osae-rareru), to be caught.

Note: The form of the passive voice of vowel stem verbs and that of the potential of these verbs are quite the same; that is, such forms as the passive voice and the potential can be similarly induced from any vowel stem verb in the present/future form.

e.g. 私は彼からこの仕事を任せられます。(Watakushi wa kare kara

kono shigoto *o* makase *raremasu*)—I am left to this work by him—
任せられます (makase-raremasu) from 任せる (makase-ru), to leave
A to B, is the passive voice; and を (o) in the phrase この仕事を
(kono shigoto *o*), this work, is used as an objective particle in the
passive form.

e.g. 私は彼にこの仕事が任せられます。(Watakushi wa kare ni kono
shigoto *ga* makase *raremasu*)—I can leave this work to him—任
せられます (makase-raremasu) from 任せる (makase-ru), to leave
A to B, is the potential; and が (ga) in the phrase この仕事が
(kono shigoto *ga*), this work, is treated as an objective particle
in the potential form.

In the case of consonant stem verbs ending with *u*, a consonant
+*u*, the passive voice can be obtained by dropping the last syllable
u and adding れる (areru), plain form, or れます (aremasu), polite
form, to the stem.

e.g. 教授はこの学生の卒論を読みます。(Kyōju wa kono gakusei no
sotsuron *o yomimasu*)—The professor reads this student's graduation thesis—読みます (yom-imasu) from 読む (yom-u), to read, can
be converted into the passive voice 読まれます (yom-aremasu).
The direct passive voice of this active voice sentence is as follows:
この学生の卒論は教授に 読まれます。(Kono gakusei no sotsuron wa
kyōju *ni yom-aremasu*)—This student's graduation thesis is read
by the professor.

e.g. 彼は彼女にダンスを 申し込みました。(Kare wa kanojo *ni* dansu
o mōshikomimashita)—He offered to dance with her—申し込みま
した (mōshikom-imashita) from 申し込む (mōshikom-u), to offer,
can be converted into the passive voice 申し込まれました (mōshi-
kom-aremashita). The indirect passive voice of this active voice
sentence is as follows: 彼女は彼に (or 彼から) ダンスを 申し込まれ
ました。(Kanojo wa kare *ni* [or: kare *kara*] dansu *o mōshikoma-
remashita*)—She was offered a dance by him.

e.g. スリがさいふをすりました。(Suri ga saifu *o surimashita*)—A
pickpocket relieved someone of his purse—すりました (sur-imashita)
comes from する (sur-u), to steal; the owner of the objective term
さいふ (saifu), a purse, is not explicitly evidenced in the sentence;
that is, in third person active voice sentences, the person whose
interests are being affected is commonly left unmentioned. In the
passive voice, however, this person may take the nominative role
at the beginning of the sentence. The third person passive voice
of this active voice sentence is as follows: 田中さんがスリにさい

ふをすられました。(Tanaka-san ga suri *ni* saifu *o suraremashita*)
—Mr. Tanaka had his purse stolen by a pickpocket—すられまし
た (sur-aremashita) comes from すられる (sur-areru), to have something stolen.

In the case of such irregular verbs as する (suru), to do, plain form,
or します (shimasu), polite form; and 来る (kuru), to come, plain
form, or 来ます (kimasu), polite form, the passive voice will be され
る (sareru) or されます (saremasu) and こられる (korareru) or こられ
ます (koraremasu).

e.g. 彼はみんなに馬鹿にされます。(Kare wa min-na *ni* baka ni *sare-
    masu*)—He is made fun of by everybody—馬鹿にされます (baka
    ni saremasu) from 馬鹿にする (baka ni suru), to make fun of, is
    in the passive voice; and such a verbal form as 馬鹿にする (baka
    ni suru) assumes the grammatical change of the irregular verb
    group.

e.g. 彼女は彼に絶交されました。(Kanojo wa kare *ni* zekkō *sarema-
    shita*)—She was alienated by him—絶交されました (zekkō sarema-
    shita) from 絶交する (zekkō suru), to break off with, is in the
    indirect passive voice; and such a verbal form as 絶交する (zekkō
    suru) assumes the grammatical change of the irregular verb group.
    This active voice sentence is as follows: 彼は彼女と絶交しました。
    (Kare wa kanojo *to* zekkō *shimashita*)—He broke off with her.

e.g. 急病患者は通常救急車で病院に連れてこられます。(Kyūbyō kanja
    wa tsūjō kyūkyūsha de byōin ni tsurete *koraremasu*)—An emer-
    gency patient is generally brought in to the hospital by an ambu-
    lance—こられます (koraremasu) in 連れてこられます (tsurete kora-
    remasu), to be brought in (a compound verb), comes from the
    irregular verb 来る (kuru), to come.

Note: In addition, the form of the passive voice of both vowel and consonant stem verbs can be used as the auxiliary of respect and that of
spontaneousness.

e.g. 私の会社の社長は，急用できょう夜行で京都の支店へ出かけられま
    す。(Watakushi no kaisha no shachō wa, kyūyō de kyō yakō de
    Kyōto no shiten e *dekakeraremasu*)—Because of some urgent busi-
    ness, the president of my company is going to a branch office in
    Kyoto today by night train—られます (raremasu) in 出かけられま
    す (dekake-raremasu) from 出かける (dekake-ru), to go out, in the
    passive voice shows an auxiliary of respect.

e.g. 私は彼の厚意がしみじみ感じられます。(Watakushi wa kare no
    kōi ga shimi jimi *kanjiraremasu*)—I'm heartily touched by his

kindness—られます (raremasu) in 感じられます (kanji-raremasu) from 感じる (kanji-ru), to feel, in the passive voice shows an auxiliary of spontaneousness.

e.g. 私たちはなき旧師のお顔がしのばれます。(Watakushi-tachi wa naki kyūshi no okao ga *shinobaremasu*)—We remember the face of our dead former teacher—しのばれます (shinob-aremasu) from しのぶ (shinob-u), to remember, in the passive voice shows an auxiliary of respect.

e.g. この写真を見るたびに, 私は両親や兄弟の事が思い出されます。(Kono shashin o miru tabi ni, watakushi wa ryōshin ya kyōdai no koto ga *omoidasaremasu*)—I never look at this photograph without remembering my parents and brothers—思い出されます (omoidas-aremasu) from 思い出す (omoidas-u), to recall, in the passive voice shows an auxiliary of spontaneousness.

The passive and potential forms of irregular verbs such as 来る (kuru), plain form and 来ます (kimasu), polite form, meaning "to come" are quite the same; that is, each of these forms is こられます (korare-masu). The expression こられる (korareru) or こられます (koraremasu) in the passive voice can also be used as an auxiliary of respect.

e.g. 先生がこられると, みなよろこびました。(Sensei ga *korareru* to, mina yorokobimashita)—Everybody was glad when the teacher came—こられる (korareru), to come, in the passive voice, shows an auxiliary of respect.

Auxiliary verbs such as "may", "can", "must", "will (shall)", etc. can be used with the passive voice main verb as follows:

e.g. 彼はこのげてものを食べるかもしれません。(Kare wa kono gete-mono *o taberu kamoshiremasen*)—He may eat this epicurean food —食べる (tabe-ru), to eat, in the plain present form＋かもしれません (kamoshiremasen), may. This passive voice is: このげてものは彼に食べられるかもしれません。(Kono getemono wa kare *ni taberareru kamoshiremasen*)—This epicurean food may be eaten by him—食べられる (tabe-rareru), to be eaten; can be eaten, in both the plain present passive and potential form＋かもしれません (kamoshiremasen), may. But, in fact, such an inanimate subject as げてもの (getemono), epicurean food, in the passive voice would not be evident in Japanese sentences. Thus, the formation of the passive voice such as this can be wholly ignored.

e.g. 彼は誕生日に彼女を招くかもしれません。(Kare wa tanjōbi ni kanojo *o maneku kamoshiremasen*)—He may invite her on his birthday—招く (manek-u), to invite, is in the plain present form.

This passive voice is 彼女は誕生日に彼に 招かれる かもしれません。 (Kanojo wa tanjōbi ni kare *ni manekareru kamoshiremasen*)—She may be invited by him on his birthday—招かれる (manek-areru), to be invited, is in the plain present passive form.

e.g. 彼はあなたを 憎むでしょう。 (Kare wa anata *o nikumu deshō*)— He will hate you—憎む (nikum-u), to hate, is in the plain present form and でしょう (deshō) from だろう (darō) signifies conjecture; that is, the speaker conjectures about someone and his situation. This passive voice sentence is あなたは彼に 憎まれる でしょう。 (Anata wa kare *ni nikumareru deshō*)—You will be hated by him —憎まれる (nikum-areru), to be hated, is in the plain present passive voice.

When an animate object is in subjectivity and an inanimate object in objectivity and then a transitive verb is used, the person worthy of subjectivity is, as it were, left behind; and instead a thing itself will be underlined in its own spontaneous action, phenomenon, and quality—such a tendency as this is quite Japanese. In particular, the subject denoting an inanimate object is often applied with verbs of perception such as *see* and *hear*. And thus, the expressions 見えます (miemasu), to be visible, an intransitive verb and 聞こえます (kikoe-masu), an intransitive verb or 聞こえてきます (kikoete kimasu), to be audible, are in use much more commonly than the expressions 聞け ます (kikemasu), can hear or 聞かれます (kikaremasu), to be heard and 見られます (miraremasu), can see; to be seen.

e.g. 私の家のうしろは音楽学校なので，いつも軽音楽の演奏や歌声が聞 こえます (or 聞こえてきます)。 (Watakushi no ie no ushiro wa ongaku gakkō na no de, itsumo keiongaku no ensō ya uta goe ga *kikoe-masu* [or: *kikoete kimasu*])—Behind my house there is a college of music, so the performance of light music and singing voices can often be heard—both 軽音楽の演奏 (keiongaku no ensō), the performance of light music, and 歌声 (uta goe), singing voices, are the subjects denoting inanimate objects; and the expression 聞こえてきます (kikoete kimasu), to be audible, is made up of two verbs, 聞こえて (kikoe-te) from 聞こえた (kikoe-ta), was audible, from 聞こえる (kikoe-ru), to be audible + きます (kimasu), to come; that is, a compound verb. This form enables the readers to successively catch up with portions of the movement of the object; therefore, in this type of sentence the expression 聞こえてきます (kikoete kimasu) is more common than the expression 聞こえます (kikoe-masu).

-e.g. 国会議事堂の 前に立つと，天皇・皇后両陛下のおられる皇居が**見え
ます**。(Kokkai gijidō no mae ni tatsu to, Ten-nō Kōgō ryō heika
no orareru kōkyo ga *miemasu*)—When we stand in front of the
National Diet, the Imperial Palace where the Emperor and the
Empress live can be seen—皇居 (kōkyo), the Imperial Palace, is
the subject denoting an inanimate object.

When the subject of the sentence is given some help by somebody
else, the expression もらいます (mora-imasu) from もらう (mora[w]-u),
to obtain, here loosely "kindly", can be used as the form of the
indirect passive voice—it is put after the て (te) or で (de)-form of
any verb.

e.g. 叔父さんが弟に本を**買います**。(Oji-san ga otōto *ni* hon *o kaimasu*)—Uncle will buy a book for my younger brother—otherwise,
we may say and write as follows: 叔父さんが弟に本を**買ってやり
ます**。(Oji-san ga otōto *ni* hon *o katte yarimasu*)—Uncle will buy
a book for my younger brother. The passive voice sentence is
弟が叔父さんに (or 叔父さんから) 本を**買ってもらいます**。(Otōto ga
oji-san *ni* [or: oji-san *kara*] hon *o katte moraimasu*)—My younger
brother will have Uncle buy a book—買って (kat-te) comes from
買った (kat-ta), bought.

e.g. 山田さんは田中さんに写真を**見せました**。(Yamada-san wa Tanaka-san *ni* shashin *o misemashita*)—Mr. Yamada showed a photograph to Mr. Tanaka—otherwise, we may say and write as follows:
山田さんは田中さんに写真を **見せてやりました**。(Yamada-san wa
Tanaka-san *ni* shashin *o misete yarimashita*)—Mr. Yamada showed
a photograph to Mr. Tanaka—this passive voice sentence is 田
中さんは山田さんに (or 山田さんから) 写真を見せてもらいました。
(Tanaka-san wa Yamada-san *ni* [or: Yamada-san *kara*] shashin *o
misete moraimashita*)—Mr. Tanaka was shown a photograph by
Mr. Yamada—見せて (mise-te) comes from the plain past 見せた
(mise-ta), showed.

Note: The difference of the use between the subsidiary verb ～てもらい
ます (. . .te moraimasu) and the subsidiary verb ～てくれます (. . .te
kuremasu) is as follows:

e.g. 私が弟に万年筆を**買ってやります**。(Watakushi *ga* otōto *ni* man-
nen hitsu *o katte yarimasu*)—I will buy a fountain pen for my
younger brother—this sentence is transformed into 弟が私に (or
私から) 万年筆を**買ってもらいます**。(Otōto *ga* watakushi *ni* [or:
watakushi *kara*] man-nen hitsu *o katte moraimasu*)—My younger
brother will have me buy a fountain pen. In the case of this

subsidiary verb, a rearrangement of the subject and object occurs, as seen in 弟が私に (Otōto *ga* watakushi *ni*) from the original 私が弟に (Watakushi *ga* otōto *ni*).

e.g. 母が私に花を買います。(Haha *ga* watakushi *ni* hana *o kaimasu*) —Mother will buy some flowers for me—this sentence is transformed into 母が私に花を買ってくれます。(Haha *ga* watakushi *ni* hana *o katte kuremasu*)—Mother will buy some flowers for me. In the case of this subsidiary verb, there occurs no change of position between the nominative and objective cases, as seen in 母が私に花を (Haha *ga* watakushi *ni* hana *o*) of both sentences.

Drill

1. 彼は川風に吹かれていました。

   He was buffeted by the river breeze.

2. 彼は彼女の目にうながされました。

   He was caught by her accusing eyes.

3. 彼は廊下に連れ出されました。

   He was taken out to the corridor.

4. きのう彼は友だちに冷やかされました。

   Yesterday he was teased by his friends.

5. きのう彼は先生に冗談を言われました。

   Yesterday he was the subject of a joke by his teacher.

6. 彼女は彼に近くの氷屋へ誘われました。

   She was invited by him to a refreshment shop nearby.

7. 彼女との仲が両親に感づかれているらしいです。

   The affair between her and I might have been noticed by my parents.

8. 彼女は彼に待ちぼうけをくわされました。

   She was kept waiting for no purpose by him.

9. 生まれたらすぐ彼はこの家へ連れてこられました。

   As soon as he was born, he was brought to this house.

10. 大塚のある乾物問屋の長女が内々彼の嫁に選ばれました。

    The eldest daughter of a certain wholesale grocer's in Otsuka was informally chosen for him as a wife.

11. 店の主人はそんな素性の子は置 The master of the shop said he
けないと . . . 彼は店を追い出され would have nothing to do with
ました。 such a lowborn person—he was
thrown out of his shop.

12. このお手伝いさんは，五時より This maid has neither mornings
おそく起きた朝はなく，十一時よ when she gets up later than the
り早く寝た夜はなく，日がな一日 hour of five nor nights when she
こきつかわれています。 goes to bed earlier than eleven;
all day long she is driven hard
and tired out.

Exercise

Change the following sentences into the Passive Voice:

1. 彼女は田中というでっちを愛 She loved an apprentice named
していました。 Tanaka.

2. 高利貸しは彼を だましました。 A money lender deceived him.

3. だれかが私の足を 踏みつけま Somebody stepped on my foot
した。 in the crush.

4. 父は長女をできそこないと呼ん The father calls his eldest daugh-
でいます。 ter a failure.

5. 犯人を 連れてきました。 We brought in a criminal.

Answers:
  1. 田中というでっちは 彼女に 愛されていました。 2. 彼は高利貸しに
だまされました。 3. 私はだれかに足を踏みつけられました。 4. 長女は
父にできそこないと呼ばれています。 5. 犯人が連れてこられました。

Change the following sentences into the Active Voice:

1. 彼女の危機の解決が今日まで延 The solution of her crisis has
ばされてきました。 been left untouched until now.

2. 自分の悲劇は自分で解決されな Her own tragedies have to be
くてはなりません。 solved by herself.

3. 彼はアパートを追い出されまし He was evicted from an apart-
た。 ment house.

4. 彼は釈放されました。 He was set free.

5. 彼の犬は犬小屋へ連れていかれ His dog was taken to its dog

ました。	house.
6. 彼はみんなに**軽蔑**されています。	He is despised by everybody.
7. 彼女は社長に高く**評価**されています。	She is highly esteemed by the director.
8. 彼女は老婆に子供をあずかってもらいました。	She arranged for an old woman who would take care of her child.

Answers:

1. 彼女は危機の 解決を今日まで**延ば**してきました。 2. 自分の悲劇を自分で**解決**しなくてはなりません。 3. 彼をアパートから**追い出**しました。 4. 彼を**釈放**しました。 5. 彼は犬を犬小屋へ**連れ**ていきました。 6. みんなは彼を**軽蔑**しています。 7. 社長は彼女を高く**評価**しています。 8. 老婆は彼女の子供をあずかりました。

Change the following sentences into the third person passive voice, using the word, given below each sentence, as the nominative case:

1. むすこが死にました。 — The son died.
   * 父は (chichi wa), the father
2. 子供が泣きます。 — The child cries.
   * 母は (haha wa), the mother
3. 雨が降りました。 — It rained.
   * 彼は (kare wa), he
4. 病人が隣にすわりました。 — A patient sat down beside her.
   * 彼女は (kanojo wa), she

Answers:

1. 父はむすこに死なれました。(The father had his son die).
2. 母は子供に泣かれます。(The mother has her child cry).
3. 彼は雨に降られました。(He was caught in the rain).
4. 彼女は病人に隣にすわられました。(She had a patient sit down beside her).

Change the following sentences into the indirect passive voice, using ～てやります and ～てもらいます:

1. 兄が弟の顔をふきます。 — The elder brother wipes his younger brother's face.
2. 姉が郵便局に行きます。 — The elder sister will go to the post office.
3. 私がこの子供におもちゃを**買い**ます。 — I'll buy some toys for this child.

Answers:

1. 兄が弟の顔をふいてやります。 (The elder brother wipes his younger brother's face).

　弟が兄に顔をふいてもらいます。 (The younger brother has his elder brother wipe his face).

2. 姉が郵便局に行ってやります。 (The elder sister will go to the post office).

　妹が姉に郵便局に行ってもらいます。 (The younger sister will have her elder sister go to the post office).

3. 私がこの子供におもちゃを買ってやります。 (I'll buy some toys for this child).

　この子供が私におもちゃを買ってもらいます。 (This child will have me buy some toys).

Rewrite the following sentences with the subsidiary verb ～てくれます:

1. 先生が私の絵をほめます。 The teacher praises my picture.
2. 彼が私の家まで送りました。He saw me off up to my house.
3. 父が税務署に行きます。 The father will go to the taxation office.

Answers:

1. 先生が私の絵をほめてくれます。(The teacher kindly praises my picture). 2. 彼が私の家まで送ってくれました。(He kindly saw me off up to my house). 3. 父が税務署に行ってくれます。(The father will kindly go to the taxation office).

The Causative Form

Rule

In the case of vowel stem verbs ending with *e*-ru or *i*-ru, the causative form can be obtained by dropping the last syllable *ru* and adding させる (saseru), plain form, or させます (sasemasu), polite form, to the stem.

e.g. 娘が花をいけます。(Musume *ga* hana o *ikemasu*)—The daughter arranges flowers. The causative form of this basic sentence is as follows: 母は娘に花をいけさせます。(Haha wa musume *ni* hana o *ikesasemasu*)—The mother gets her daughter to arrange flowers —いけさせます (ike-sasemasu), to get one to arrange, comes from いける (ike-ru), to arrange. The agent of causative action is indicated by the particle に (ni) in 娘に (musume ni), daughter.

Note: The nominative case in the basic sentence can be expressed by the particle に (ni) or を (o) in the case of the causative form. Only the particle に (ni) is used in transitive verbs; but either the particle に (ni) or を (o) can be used in intransitive verbs.

The causative passive of the causative expression させます (sasemasu) is させられます (saseraremasu). So, 母は娘に花をいけさせます。(Haha *wa* musume *ni* hana o *ikesasemasu*)—The mother gets her daughter to arrange flowers—can be converted into the causative passive sentence 娘は母に花をいけさせられます。(Musume *wa* haha *ni* hana o *ikesaseraremasu*)—The daughter is made to arrange flowers by the mother—いけ (ike) in いけさせられます (ike-saseraremasu) comes from いける (ike-ru), to arrange and させられます (saseraremasu) comes from させられる (saserareru), the plain present causative passive expression.

e.g. 今度の土曜日に、弟が上野国立西洋美術館の展覧会を見ます。(Kondo no doyōbi ni, otōto *ga* Ueno kokuritsu seiyō bijutsu kan no tenrankai o *mimasu*)—Next Saturday my younger brother is going to go and see the exhibition at the Ueno National Western Art Gallery. The causative form of this basic sentence is as follows: 今度の土曜日に，私は弟に上野国立西洋美術館の展覧会を見させます。(Kondo no doyōbi ni, watakushi wa otōto *ni* Ueno kokuritsu seiyō bijutsu kan no tenrankai o *misasemasu*)—Next Saturday I'll get my younger brother to go and see the exhibition at the Ueno National Western Art Gallery—見 (mi) in 見させます (mi-sasemasu), to get one to see, comes from 見る (mi-ru), to see. The causative passive of the causative 見させます (mi-sasemasu) is 見させられます (mi-saseraremasu), to be made to see.

In the case of consonant stem verbs ending with *u*, a consonant +*u*, the causative form can be obtained by dropping the last syllable *u* and adding せる (aseru), plain form, or せます (asemasu), polite form, to the stem.

    e.g. むすこが郵便局へ行きます。(Musuko *ga* yūbinkyoku e *ikimasu*) —The son will go to the post office. The causative form of this basic sentence is as follows: 父はむすこに (or むすこを) 郵便局へ行かせます。(Chichi wa musuko *ni* [or: musuko *o*] yūbinkyoku e *ikasemasu*)—The father will get his son to go to the post office—行かせます (ik-asemasu), to get one to go, comes from 行く (ik-u), to go. In this case, the nominative case in the basic sentence can be expressed by either the particle に (ni) or を (o) in the causative form because the intransitive verb 行きます (ikimasu) is used in it. The causative passive of the causative 行かせます (ik-asemasu) is 行かせられます (ik-aseraremasu), to be made to go.

    e.g. 次男が三男をなぐります。(Jinan *ga* san-nan o *nagurimasu*)—The second son strikes the third son. The causative form of this basic sentence is as follows: 長男は次男に三男をなぐらせます。(Chōnan wa jinan *ni* san-nan o *nagurasemasu*)—The eldest son gets the second one to strike the third one—なぐらせます (nagur-asemasu), to get one to strike, comes from なぐる (nagur-u), to strike. The causative passive of the causative なぐらせます (nagur-asemasu) is なぐらせられます (nagur-aseraremasu), to be made to strike.

In the case of such irregular verbs as する (suru), to do and 来る (kuru), to come, the causative form will be させる (saseru), plain form, or させます (sasemasu), polite form, and こさせる (kosaseru), plain form, or こさせます (kosasemasu), polite form.

    e.g. 妹がこの仕事をします。(Imōto *ga* kono shigoto o *shimasu*)—The younger sister does this work—the causative form of this basic sentence is as follows: 姉は妹にこの仕事をさせます。(Ane wa imōto *ni* kono shigoto o *sasemasu*)—The elder sister gets her younger sister to do this work. The causative passive of the causative させます (sasemasu) is させられます (saseraremasu), to be made to do.

    e.g. 弟が正月休みに実家に来ます。(Otōto *ga* shōgatsu yasumi ni jikka ni *kimasu*)—My younger brother will come to our parents' house during the New Year holidays—the causative form of this basic sentence is as follows: 両親は弟に正月休みに実家にこさせます。 (Ryōshin wa otōto *ni* shōgatsu yasumi ni jikka ni *kosasemasu*)— Our parents will get my younger brother to come to their house during the New Year holidays. The causative passive of the causative こさせます (kosasemasu) is こさせられます (kosaseraremasu), to be made to come.

Besides, some sentences in the causative form occasionally denote permission or noninterference.

e.g. 庭で近所の子供を (or 子供に) 遊ばせます。(Niwa de kinjo no kodomo *o* [or: kodomo *ni*] *asobasemasu*)—We let the neighboring children play in the garden—遊ばせます (asob-asemasu), to let one play, comes from 遊ぶ (asob-u), to play.

Also, some sentences in the causative form have such a nuance that one can't do anything in his own capacity.

e.g. 私はむすこを戦争で死なせました。(Watakushi wa musuko *o* sensō de *shinasemashita*)—I had my son die in the war—死なせました (shin-asemashita), had one die, comes from 死ぬ (shin-u), to die.

Drill

1. 先生は用務員にいって，教材を買わせます。

The teacher will tell the janitor to buy some teaching materials.

2. 日本語の先生は昨日教えた箇所を留学生に読ませます。

A teacher of Japanese has the foreign students read what he taught the day before.

3. 先生は学生に詩を作らせます。

The teacher makes the students compose poems.

4. 先生は留学生に漢字を書かせたり，質問に答えさせたり，短い文を作らせたりします。

The teacher gets the foreign students to write *Kanji*, answer questions, compose short sentences, and so on.

5. 新しい言葉を使って，日本語の先生は私たち研修生に聞かせます。

By using new words, a teacher of Japanese makes us trainees listen.

6. 日本語の先生は，研究留学生に同じことを幾度も幾度も聞かせま

A teacher of Japanese makes the foreign research students listen

す。

7. 日本語の主任教授は新しい言葉を使って，私たちインドの学生に文を**作らせます**。

The chief professor of Japanese makes us Indian students compose sentences, using new words.

8. この女教師は生徒に一人ずつ読本を**読ませます**。

This female teacher makes each of the pupils read a reader.

9. 母は娘に新家庭の**準備をさせま**した。

The mother got her daughter to make preparations for a new home.

10. 両親は私に彼女に対しての愛情を極力**押えさせました**。

My parents made me do my best to stifle affection toward her.

11. 彼は私に彼女との同宿を**避けさ**せました。

He made me avoid staying in the same house with her.

12. 彼は私に**手数をかけさせ**ました。

He made me cause trouble.

13. 彼は彼女に当時の心境を**語らせ**ました。

He made her relate her mental state at that time.

14. このお坊さんは彼女を素直な良い女に**生まれ変わらせ**ました。

This priest let her be reborn into an obedient and good woman.

15. 先生はこの学生に体刑の処分を**受けさせ**ました。

The teacher made this student receive the penalty of corporal punishment.

Exercise

Fill in the following blanks with させます or せます, taking into consideration the verb, given below each sentence, in the plain present/future form from which the causative form can be induced:

1. 兄は私にきらっていた仕事を（   ）。

My elder brother made me do the work I had previously refused to do.

する (suru), to do, is an irregular verb

2. 彼はあなたを改悛（   ）。

He made you repent.

改悛する (kaishun suru), to repent—the noun 改悛 (repentance)＋する—assumes the grammatical change of the irregular verb group

3. 彼が彼女を堕落（　　）。
   堕落する (daraku suru), to degenerate

   He caused her to degenerate.

4. この国の首相は善良な国民を危
   険に（　　）。

   The prime minister of this country let his decent people be exposed to danger.

   危険にさらす (kiken ni saras-u), to expose one to danger

5. 彼は運転手に新宿駅まで車を
   （　　）。
   飛ばす (tobas-u), to hasten to...

   He made the driver speed the car directly to Shinjuku Station.

6. 帰宅途中で買ってきた酒を彼は
   妻に（　　）。

   He had his wife warm the *sake* which he had bought on his way home.

   暖める (atatame-ru), to warm

7. 主人の出張は妻の心に空虚を
   （　　）。

   The husband's business tour made the wife feel a vacuum in her heart.

   感じる (kanji-ru), to feel

8. 彼女はこの職人に座ぶとんを
   （　　）。
   作る (tsukur-u), to make

   She had this craftsman make a cushion.

9. 彼女はお手伝いさんに何回も火
   ばちに火を（　　）。
   つぎ足す (tsugitas-u), to add

   She made the maid kindle the fire in the brazier many times.

10. 妻は夫に友だちの就職口を（
    ）。
    さがす (sagas-u), to seek

    The wife got her husband to find her friend a position.

11. 社長は秘書に夜十時ごろまでも
    会社に（　　）。

    The director made his secretary stay at the company as late as about ten in the evening.

    残す (nokos-u), to leave behind; to remain at

12. 社長は事務員に仕事を（　　）。
    整理する (seiri suru), to put in order

    The director made the clerk put his work in order.

13. 帰りみちに，私は友だちの家に
    寄って，夕飯を（　　）。

    On my way home, I dropped in at my friend's house and got him to treat me to supper.

ご馳走する (gochisō suru), to treat a person to something

14. 先生はこの女生徒にヒステリックな態度を（　　）。
The teacher helped this schoolgirl get rid of her hysterical attitude.

改める (aratame-ru), to get rid of; to remedy

15. 主人はお手伝いさんに引っ越しそばを（　　）。
The master had the maid order buckwheat noodles to celebrate moving into his new home.

注文する (chūmon suru), to order

16. 貧乏な彼は妻に酒場づとめを（　　）。
He, in destitution, made his wife work at a bar.

酒場づとめをする (sakaba zutome o suru), to work at a bar

Answers:
1. 仕事をさせました　2. 改悛させました　3. 堕落させました　4. 危険にさらさせました　5. 飛ばさせました　6. 暖めさせました　7. 感じさせました　8. 作らせました　9. つぎ足させました　10. さがさせました　11. 残させました　12. 整理させました　13. ご馳走させました　14. 改めさせました　15. 注文させました　16. 酒場づとめをさせました

第 四十七 課　Lesson 47

The Use of "After . . ."

Rule

"After . . ." in English is expressed by から (kara) or あとで (atode). The expressions から (kara) and あとで (atode) are never influenced by the tense of the principal clause in a sentence. When using the expression から (kara), it is placed after the て (te) or で (de)-form of any verb, this form being obtained by replacing the final vowel *a* of the plain past form by *e*. Otherwise, the expression あとで (atode) is put after any verb in the plain past form; that is, the た (ta) or だ (da)-form of any verb in the plain past form+あとで (atode).

e.g.　私はしばらく庭を散歩してから（or 散歩したあとで）, 部屋にもどり，朝食まで新聞を読みました。(Watakushi wa shibaraku niwa o sanpo shite *kara* [or: sanpo shita *atode*], heya ni modori, chōshoku made shinbun o yomimashita)—After strolling in the garden for a while, I went back to my room and read the newspaper until breakfast—散歩して (sanpo shite) comes from 散歩した (sanpo shita), strolled.

e.g.　ゆっくりからだを洗ってから（or 洗ったあとで）, 私はお風呂を出ました。(Yukkuri karada o aratte *kara* [or: aratta *atode*], watakushi wa ofuro o demashita)—After washing myself slowly, I got out of the bath—洗って (arat-te) comes from 洗った (arat-ta), washed.

e.g.　私は洋画を見てから（or 見たあとで）, 帰宅します。(Watakushi wa yōga o mite *kara* [or: mita *atode*], kitaku shimasu)—I'll go home after seeing a foreign film—見て (mi-te) comes from 見た (mi-ta), saw.

In the case of nouns (time), あとで (atode) or 後 (go) is put after them.

e.g.　四年あとで（or 四年後）, 私は日本へ留学します。(Yo nen *atode* [or: Yo nen *go*], watakushi wa Nihon e ryūgaku shimasu)—I will go to Japan to study after four years—四年 (yo nen), four years, is a noun.

Drill

1. 夜がふけてから，夫は帰宅しました。　　The husband returned home after dark.

2. お酒を一本つけてから，彼は話　　After heating a bottle of *sake*,

を切り出しました。

he broached the topic.

3. 男は中年を過ぎてから放蕩の味を覚えたら，手がつけられません。

If a man should learn the dissipated life after middle age, **he** would be unmanageable.

4. 彼女と縁切りしてから，彼は気の弱い男になってしまいました。

He turned out to be a faint-hearted man after severing relations with her.

5. 時機をみてから，新規なことに手を出す方がよいです。

You had better try your hand at any new undertakings after the right occasion arises.

6. この店の主人は四十五歳を過ぎてから，株に手を出しました。

The master of this shop played the stockmaker after he was past forty-five.

7. 彼はすわり直してから，せきを切ったようにしゃべり出しました。

He began to speak like the floodgates had been opened after sitting up straight.

8. 彼女はさびしく首を振ってから，下を向きました。

After shaking her head sadly, she hung her head.

9. 彼はしみじみと一人ごとのようにつぶやいてから，彼女にほほえみかけました。

He beamed at her after murmuring to himself reflectively.

10. 近所の火事の焼け跡を見てから，彼は帰宅しました。

He returned home after visiting the ruins of the fire in the neighborhood.

11. 何の仕事も持たずにうかうか日を過ごしてから，彼は旧師の所へ相談に行きました。

He went to see his old teacher to confer with him after spending his days idly without work.

12. やせた背中を震わせてから，彼女はまくらの上へ涙を落としました。

She wept upon the pillow after her slender back trembled.

13. 彼女は転々と淪落の道をたどってから，郷里へ舞いもどって来ま

She came back to her home town finally after treading the

した。

14. 路地を幾曲がりして**から**，彼は西大久保の区役所に着きました。

After making many turns on the alley, he was at the ward office in Nishiokubo.

15. 旅行かばんをあみだなの上にのせて**から**，彼を見送りに来た彼女の手をしっかりつかんで離しませんでした。

After putting his travelling bag on the rack, he kept clasping firmly the hand of her who had come to see him off.

16. いいなずけがゆくえ不明になったといううわさを聞いて**から**，彼女は修道尼になることを決心しました。

She made up her mind to go into a convent after hearing the rumor of the disappearance of her betrothed.

Exercise

Fill in each bracket with a verbal form suitable for the expression から, taking into consideration the verb given below each sentence:

1. 夕食が（　）から，娘が帰ってきました。

The daughter came home just after dinner was ready.

始まった (hajimat-ta), was ready; began＜始まる (hajimar-u), to begin

2. 通産省の役人生活を（　）から，彼は父の会社にはいりました。

He joined his father's company after resigning his official life at the Ministry of International Trade and Industry.

やめた (yame-ta), resigned＜やめる (yame-ru), to resign

3. 左官屋さんは茶を（　）から，又仕事に取りかかりました。

The mason went back to work again after sipping tea.

すすった (susut-ta), sipped＜すする (susur-u), to sip

4. 玄関で先生に向かって（　）から，この学生は静かな足どりで帰っていきました。

After bowing toward the teacher at the front door, this student went home with quiet steps.

一礼した (ichirei shita), bowed＜一礼する (ichirei suru), to bow

5. 大学の経済学部を（　）からすぐに，彼は経済研究所にはいりました。

Immediately after graduating from the faculty of economics of a university, he joined the Economic Research Institute.

出た (de-ta), graduated from＜出る (de-ru), to graduate from

6. 官服を（　　）から，この警官
は駒込のダンスホールへ出かける
つもりでした。

After taking off his official uniform, this policeman intended to go to a dance hall in Komagome.

脱いだ (nui-da), took off＜脱ぐ (nug-u), to take off

7. もう一本煙草を（　　）から，
彼は机のわきの石油ストーブに両
手をかざしました。

After putting another cigarette in his mouth, he stretched both hands out over the oil stove by the desk.

くわえた (kuwae-ta), put something in one's mouth＜くわえる (kuwae-ru), to put something in one's mouth

8. たんすから衣類を（　　）から，
彼女は質屋へ出かけていきまし
た。

After taking some clothes out from the chest of drawers, she went out to a pawn shop.

出した (dashi-ta), took out＜出す (das-u), to take out

9. ひと通り閲覧室を（　　）から，
彼はストーブのすぐそばの机にこ
しかけました。

After glancing about the reading room, he sat down at the desk next to the stove.

見まわした (mimawashi-ta), glanced about＜見まわす (mimawas-u), to glance about

10. 友人と二人で新橋で（　　）か
ら，また銀座へ出ました。

After drinking with a friend at Shinbashi, we went drinking again on the Ginza.

飲んだ (non-da), drank＜飲む (nom-u), to drink

11. 彼女は熱い飲み物を（　　）か
ら，口を切りました。

She ordered a hot drink and began to speak.

取った (tot-ta), ordered＜取る (tor-u), to order

12. しばらく間を（　　）から，彼
女は静かな調子で言いました。

After a pause, she spoke in a quiet tone.

間をおいた (ma o oi-ta), made a pause＜間をおく (ma o ok-u), to make a pause

13. 前もって寮へ電話を（　　）か
ら，彼は彼女をたずねてみました。

After telephoning to the dormitory beforehand, he called on her.

電話をかけた (denwa o kake-ta), telephoned＜電話をかける (denwa o kake-ru), to telephone

14. 客に煙草を勧め，自分も一本
（　　）から，ゆっくりと彼は話し
始めました。

After offering the visitor a cigarette and taking one himself, he slowly began to speak.

くわえた (kuwae-ta), took something in one's mouth＜くわえる (kuwae-ru), to take something in one's mouth

15. すぱすぱと煙草を（　　）から，
彼はわけもなく火をうめたりかき
たてたりしていました。

After puffing on a cigarette, he aimlessly stirred and poked at the fire.

すった (sut-ta), puffed＜すう (su[w]-u), to puff

16. から紙をぴしぴしと（　　）か
ら，彼女は泣き始めました。

After slamming shut the sliding paper-door, she began to weep.

しめた (shime-ta), shut＜しめる (shime-ru), to shut

17. 昨夜彼は会社で夕食を（　　）
から，帰ってきました。

He went home after finishing supper at the company last night.

すませた (sumase-ta), finished＜すませる (sumase-ru), to finish

18. 彼女は母に子供を（　　）から，
昔の友だちをたずねてみました。

After leaving her child in the care of the mother, she called on her old friend.

預けた (azuke-ta), left someone in the care of＜預ける (azuke-ru), to leave someone in the care of

Answers:
1. 始まって 2. やめて 3. すすって 4. 一礼して 5. 出て 6. 脱いで 7. くわえて 8. 出して 9. 見まわして 10. 飲んで 11. 取って 12. 間をおいて 13. 電話をかけて 14. くわえて 15. すって 16. しめて 17. すませて 18. 預けて

第 四十八 課　Lesson 48

The Use of "When . . ."

Rule

"When. . ." in English is expressed by と (to), 時 (toki), 時は (toki wa), 時に (toki ni), or 時には (toki niwa). The expression と (to), never influenced by the tense of the principal clause in a sentence, is always put after the plain present/future form of any verb. The expression 時 (toki), 時は (toki wa), 時に (toki ni), or 時には (toki niwa) is put after either the plain present/future form or the plain past form of any verb. The expressions 時は (toki wa), 時に (toki ni) and 時には (toki niwa) are more emphatic than 時 (toki).

e.g. 風呂から上がると，彼は晩酌を始めました。(Furo kara agaru *to*, kare wa banshaku o hajimemashita)—When he got out of the bath, he began to enjoy his evening drink—this と (to) serves as a connective particle which means "and at once"; so, this sentence can be written as "He got out of the bath, *and at once* began to enjoy his evening drink". The verb 上がる (agar-u), to get out of, in 上がると (agaru to) is in the plain present/future form.

e.g. 家へ帰ると，だれもいませんでした。(Ie e kaeru *to*, dare mo imasen deshita)—When I returned home, no one was there—this と (to) shows a case in which something happened or in which one unexpectedly becomes aware of something that happened. In other words, this と (to) serves as a conjunction which means "and then"; so, this sentence can be rewritten as "I returned home; *and* I found no one was there". 帰る (kaer-u), to return, in 帰ると (kaeru to) is a verb in the plain present/future form.

e.g. 春になると，きれいな花がたくさん咲きます。(Haru ni naru *to*, kirei na hana ga takusan sakimasu)—When spring comes round, many pretty flowers bloom—this と (to) is used in a conditional clause that is necessarily linked with the subsequent items or actions. That is, this と (to) is a connective particle which takes the same role as ば (ba), the suffix indicating a hypothetical subjunctive condition; and thus, the clause 春になると (haru ni naru *to*) can be rewritten as 春になれば (haru ni nare *ba*). なる (nar-u), to become, in 春になると (haru ni naru to) is a verb in the plain present/future form.

e.g. 雨が降ると, テニスを中止します。(Ame ga furu *to*, tenisu o chūshi shimasu)—If it rains, we will stop playing tennis—this と (to) shows a slight connection, the preceding word or sentence acting upon the following as a mere subjunctive condition. That is, this と (to) has such shading as ば (ba), the suffix imposing a subjunctive meaning もし~ば (moshi...ba); and thus, the clause 雨が降ると (ame ga furu *to*) can be rewritten as (もし) 雨が降れば ([moshi] ame ga fure *ba*). 降る (fur-u), to fall, in 雨が降ると (ame ga furu to) is a verb in the plain present/future form.

e.g. 彼は重労働をしていました。夕方帰って来る時には, 疲れ切って, 食卓にすわってもしばらくはしを取らずにじっとしていました。(Kare wa jūrōdō o shite imashita. Yūgata kaette kuru *toki niwa*, tsukare kitte, shokutaku ni suwatte mo shibaraku hashi o torazu ni jitto shite imashita)—He was engaged in some heavy work. On returning home in the evenings, he was so tired out that he would remain motionless for a while at the table without taking up his chopsticks—the principal clause in this sentence is in the past form, but the clause 夕方帰って来る時には (yūgata kaette *kuru* toki niwa) is in the present/future form. If the clause preceding the principal clause suggests a habitual or customary shading like "in such a case when..." or "whenever...", the tense in such an adverbial clause can be indicated by the plain present/future form. And thus, the clause 夕方帰ってくる時には (yūgata kaette kuru *toki niwa*) can necessarily be replaced by 夕方帰ってくると (yūgata kaette kuru *to*).

e.g. 私が父にそのことを相談した時, 父は反対しませんでした。(Watakushi ga chichi ni sono koto o sōdan shita *toki*, chichi wa hantai shimasen deshita)—When I talked this matter over with my father, he would not object to my request—the tense of this adverbial clause will be influenced by the tense of the principal clause because the expression 時 (toki) in this sentence can be understood as "just at that time" or "and just then"; therefore, the clause 相談した時 (sōdan shita toki) can not be replaced by the syntax with と (to). 相談した (sōdan shita), consulted, in 相談した時 (sōdan shita toki) is a verb in the plain past form.

In the case of nouns, such expressions as の時 (no toki), の時に (no toki ni), の時は (no toki wa), and の時には (no toki niwa) can be used; these expressions are similarly put after the noun.

e.g. 私が子供の時, 彼はいつも手を引っぱって, 学校へ連れて行ってくれました。(Watakushi ga kodomo *no toki*, kare wa itsumo te o hippatte, gakkō e tsurete itte kuremashita)—When I was a little boy, he always took me by the hand to the school—子供 (kodomo), a child, is a noun.

"Even when..." in English is expressed by 時にも (toki nimo).

e.g. むすこを失った時にも、この父親は涙一つこぼしませんでした。 (Musuko o ushinatta *toki nimo*, kono chichioya wa namida hitotsu koboshimasen deshita)—Even when this father lost his son, he did not shed one tear.

Drill

1. 子供の時に，彼は実母を失いました。

In his boyhood, he lost his real mother.

2. お暇の時には，おたずねください。

I hope you will visit me at your leisure.

3. 笑うと，彼女は少女のようにあどけなく見えました。

When she smiled, her expression became as naive as that of a child.

4. 立とうとすると，彼女はうるんだ目を大きく開きました。

As she rose to her feet, she opened wide her tear-filled eyes.

5. 看護婦がはいって来た時，この患者は真剣な表情で，ベットの上から彼女を迎えました。

When the nurse came in, this patient, looking serious, welcomed her from the bed.

6. 駅のホームに立っていると，彼女は眼鏡をかけた青年に不意に肩をたたかれました。

Standing on the platform at the station, she was suddenly tapped on the shoulder by a young man with eyeglasses.

7. 門の前で車を降りる時，社長は「ひとつ君，よく考えてくれたまえ」と言いました。

Just as the director was getting out of the car in front of the gate, he said, "Well,—I want you to think over what I have said".

8. 風邪を引いて寝ている時，郷里から電報が来ました。

When I was in bed with a cold, a telegram came from my home town.

9. 娘が死んだ時にも，父はいつも穏やかな微笑を失いませんでし

Even when the daughter died, the father did not lose his usual

た。

quiet smile.

10. 帰ってみると，父と母が二人だけで食卓にすわっていました。

On my return, my father and mother—just the two of them—were sitting at the table.

11. アメリカから帰って来た時，横浜で叔父が迎えてくれました。

When I came from America, I was met at Yokohama by my uncle.

12. いい気持ちで東京へ帰って来ると，彼のレコードが発売禁止になっていました。

On his return to Tokyo in pleasant spirits, he found the sale of his record had been prohibited.

13. 冷やかされたり，冗談を言われたりすると，彼はすぐむっとなる性質です。

His nature is to take offence when he is teased or is the subject of a joke.

14. 彼女の話を聞くと，彼は思わず目がぬれました。

As he listened to her story, tears came to his eyes in spite of himself.

15. 今から思ったら，私が渡りかけた時は，もう橋が燃えてたようです。

I remember that the bridge was already on fire when I was about to cross it.

16. はなやかに舞台で踊っている踊り子たちを見ていると，敗戦のことも忘れてしまいます。

Looking at the bright-colored dancers performing on the stage, I forget even the gloomy time of the surrender after the war.

17. 彼の研究の話を聞いてみると，その研究は大変なものでした。

When I listened to his explanation of this research, I found it very wonderful.

18. 彼の話を聞いていると，彼女は夢物語ではないかという気がしました。

While listening to his story, she felt that it was dreamlike.

19. 雨の中を家にやって来る恋人のレイン・コートを見ると，彼女はなにかがっかりしました。何かそ

Looking at her lover's raincoat when he came to her house in the rain, she was somehow disap-

のレイン・コートが軽薄なような
気がしました。

pointed. She felt that his rain-coat was a sort of mark of fickleness.

Exercise

Fill in the following blanks with と，時，時は，時に，時には，or の時：

1. やさしい兄を失った（　），妹は泣き悲しみました。

When she lost her gentle elder brother, the younger sister wept and grieved.

2. 彼は十七歳（　），父に連れられて歌舞伎を見ました。

When he was seventeen, he was taken by his father to see a "kabuki" play.

3. 新宿の兄の家へ着いた（　），もう夜もふけていました。

It was already late at night when I got to my elder brother's house in Shinjuku.

4. 彼女が笑う（　），妙に素直な表情です。

There is a strange air of obedience when she laughs.

5. 税務署からの書類を読み終わる（　），彼は思わずため息をつきました。

When he read through the documents from the tax office, he unwittingly drew a long breath.

6. 母が部屋をのぞいて見る（　），娘は着物のすそで足を包んで寒そうに畳にすわっていました。

Peering into the daughter's room, the mother found her sitting on the mat, shivering, with her legs wrapped in the skirt of her kimono.

7. 彼が社長室を去ろうとする（　），秘書が急に振り向きました。

When he was about to leave the director's room, the secretary suddenly looked back.

8. 車が家に着く（　），彼はお手伝いさんを呼んで，客を応接間に案内させました。

When the car got to his house, he called the maid and had her take the visitor to the reception room.

9. 彼がはいろうとする（　・）, 離れの玄関口にこじきの女が子供を抱いて立っていました。

When he was about to step inside, he found a beggar woman standing with a child in her arms in the detached vestibule.

10. 会社で夕食を済ませて帰ってみる（　）, 妻は六畳の間借りにいませんでした。

When he went home after finishing supper at the company, he found that his wife was not in his six-mat rented room.

11. 避暑地で彼女が書いた彼あての手紙は, 彼が出かせぎから自宅へ帰った（　）, 彼の手にとどきました。

The letter addressed to him, which she had written at a summer resort, reached him when he returned home from being at work in another place.

12. 彼のような犯罪者を社会に放置する（　）, 善良な国民は常に危険にさらされます。

If such a criminal as he is set free, uncontrolled in society, decent people will always be exposed to danger.

13. 私はあの花売りと交渉のあった（　）, 彼女を愛しておりました。

When I was associating with that flower girl, I was in love with her.

14. 四・五年前, 観光バスで品川を通った（　）, この町は繁華をきわめていました。

Several years ago, when we passed by Shinagawa in a sightseeing bus, this street had reached the height of its prosperity.

15. 困った問題が起きた（　）, 彼はいつも夫人に処置をまかせました。

When faced with some difficult problem, he always left its disposal to his wife.

16. 自動車の修理作業をしていた（　）, 何かのはずみで車輪がはずれ, 彼の頭部にあたり大怪我をしました。

While he was engaged in repairing cars, by some mistake a wheel was released, and it struck his head, seriously injuring him.

17. 彼は十六歳（　）, この継母に

When he was sixteen, he was

養われました。

brought up by his stepmother.

18. 紙に向かってみる（　　）、彼女は何をどう書いていいか見当がつきませんでした。

When she faced the paper, she had no idea as to how and what she was going to write.

19. 友だちは彼が恋文を書いたと聞いた（　　）、だれも何とも言いませんでした。

When his friends heard that he had written a love letter, nobody made any comment.

Answers:

1. 時 2. の時 3. 時は 4. と 5. と 6. と 7. と 8. と 9. と 10. と 11. 時 12. ときは 13. 時に 14. 時 15. とき には 16. 時 17. の時 18. と 19. 時

Noun Phrases and Clauses

Rule

の (no) is the possessive adjective ("of" or "'s" in English) used in sentences employing modifying nouns. Besides this use, の (no) also functions to form nouns, noun phrases and clauses as there are no relative pronouns or relative adverbs in Japanese. の (no) here can nearly be rendered as "to-infinitive or that clause" in English. Therefore, this use of の (no) in noun forms can necessarily be replaced by such expressions as こと (koto), the fact and もの (mono), that which; things which.

In the case of verbs, this form is as follows—the plain present/future, plain past, plain present progressive, or plain past progressive form of any verb＋の (no), or こと (koto), or 人 (hito), a person, or もの (mono), or a noun.

e.g. 三カ月足らずで，日本語の文法を習得するの (or 習得すること) はきわめて困難です。(San ka getsu tarazu de, Nihongo no bunpō o shūtoku suru *no* [or: shūtoku suru *koto*] wa kiwamete kon-nan desu)—It is quite difficult to master Japanese grammar in three months or so—習得する (shūtoku suru), to master, is a verb in the plain present/future form. The noun phrase 日本語の文法を習得するの (or こと) (Nihongo no bunpō o shūtoku suru *no* [or: *koto*]), to master Japanese grammar, comes from the regular noun 日本語の文法の 習得 (Nihongo no bunpō *no shūtoku*), the mastered Japanese grammar.

e.g. はしかは子供のうちにかかっておくものです。(Hashika wa kodomo no uchi ni kakatte oku *mono* desu)—Measles is evidently best caught in childhood—かかっておく (kakatte ok-u), to suffer from an illness beforehand, is a verb in the plain present/future form. The noun clause かかっておくもの (kakatte oku *mono*), with a verb in the present form, shows a natural tendency in the light of reason or habit. So, this sentence can be written as はしかは子供のうちにかかっておくのは当然です。(Hashika wa kodomo no uchi ni kakatte oku *no wa tōzen desu*)—It is natural that one should catch measles in his childhood.

e.g. 若いころ私はよくこのいなか道を散歩したものです。(Wakai koro

watakushi wa yoku kono inaka michi o sanpo shita *mono* desu)
—When young, I used to take walks along this country road—
散歩した (sanpo shita), took a walk, is a verb in the plain past
form. The noun clause 散歩したもの (sanpo shita *mono*), with a
verb in the past form, denotes past experience or habit.

e.g. 先生はこの学生の行動について疑い過ぎたの (or 疑い過ぎたこと)
に気が付きました。(Sensei wa kono gakusei no kōdō nitsuite utagai sugita *no* [or: utagai sugita *koto*] ni kigatsukimashita)—The
teacher realized that he was much too suspicious of this student's
actions—疑い過ぎた (utagai sugita), was much too suspicious, is
a verb in the plain past form. The noun clause 疑い過ぎたの (or
こと) (utagai sugita *no* [or: *koto*]) comes from the regular noun
余りの疑惑 (amari no giwaku), one's excessive suspicion.

e.g. 洋風の応接室にかけてある軸を見ているの (or 見ている人) は私の
父です。(Yōfū no ōsetsushitsu ni kakete aru jiku o mite iru *no*
[or: mite iru *hito*] wa watakushi no chichi desu)—The person who
is looking at a scroll hung in the foreign-style drawing room is
my father—見ている (mite iru), to be looking at, is a verb in the
plain present progressive form. The noun clause 軸を見ているの
(or 人) (jiku *o* mite iru *no* [or: *hito*]) comes from the regular noun
軸の鑑賞者 (jiku no kanshōsha), a person appreciative of a scroll.

e.g. 彼の吹いていたハモニカの曲はうらぶれたものがなしい「枯れすす
き」のメロディーです。(Kare no fuite ita hamonika no *kyoku* wa
urabureta monoganashii "Kare Susuki" no merodii desu)—The
music he was playing on a harmonica is the doleful and sad
melody "Kare Susuki" (Withered Zebra Grass)—吹いていた (fuite
ita), was playing on, is a verb in the plain past progressive form,
and ハモニカの曲 (hamonika no kyoku), the music on a harmonica,
is a noun. The noun clause 彼の吹いていたハモニカの曲 (kare no
fuite ita hamonika no kyoku) comes from the regular noun ハモ
ニカの吹奏曲 (hamonika no suisōkyoku), the music played on a
harmonica.

In the case of nouns, the form is as follows—nouns＋だという (da
to iu), plain present, or だった (datta), plain past＋の (no), こと (koto),
人 (hito), or a noun.

e.g. 彼がタイ国からの研究留学生だというの (or 研究留学生だというこ
と) を知っていますか。(Kare ga Taikoku kara no kenkyū ryūga-
kusei da to iu *no* [or: ～kenkyū ryūgakusei da to iu *koto*] o shitte
imasu ka)—Do you know that he is a foreign research student
from Thailand?—研究留学生 (kenkyū ryūgakusei), a foreign re-

search student, is a noun.

e.g. 彼がこの殺人事件の犯人だったの (or 犯人だったこと) が判明しま
した。(Kare ga kono satsujin jiken no han-nin datta *no* [or: han-nin datta *koto*] ga hanmei shimashita)—It was proved that he was the criminal in this murder case—犯人 (han-nin), a criminal, is a noun.

In the case of な (na)-adjectives and い (i)-adjectives, both of them, as they are, relate to の (no), こと (koto), 人 (hito), もの (mono) and nouns.

e.g. あなたが妹に親切なの (or 親切なこと) をお聞きして，私は大へん
うれしいです。(Anata ga imōto ni shinsetsu na *no* [or: shinsetsu na *koto*] o okiki shite, watakushi wa taihen ureshii desu)—I am very happy to hear that you are so kind to my younger sister—親切な (shinsetsu na), kind, is a な (na)-adjective. The noun phrase 親切なの (or こと) (shinsetsu na *no* [or: *koto*]) comes from the noun form 親切さ (shinsetsu *sa*); kindness.

e.g. あなたがまだ結婚前の娘さんかと思われるほど若々しいのは大へん
結構ですね。(Anata ga mada kekkon mae no musume san ka to omowareru hodo wakawakashii *no* wa taihen kekkō desu ne)—It is very nice that you still look as youthful as an unmarried girl—若々しい (wakawakashii), very young, is an い (i)-adjective. The noun phrase 若々しいの (wakawakashii *no*) comes from the noun form 若々しさ (wakawakashi *sa*), youthfulness.

In the past form of な (na)-adjectives in this noun form, the final な (na) is dropped, this termination enabling them to add だった (datta). This だった (datta) relates to の (no), こと (koto), 人 (hito), もの (mono) and nouns.

e.g. 彼の四・五年前の生活はでたらめだったの (or でたらめだったこと)
を知っているでしょう。(Kare no shi go nen mae no seikatsu wa detarame datta *no* [or: detarame datta *koto*] o shitte iru deshō)—You probably know that he led a purposeless life several years ago—でたらめだった (detarame datta) from でたらめな (detarame na), purposeless, is a な (na)-adjective in the plain past form. The noun clause 四・五年前の生活はでたらめだったの (or こと) (shi go nen mae no seikatsu wa detarame datta *no* [or: *koto*]) comes from the regular noun 四・五年前の生活のでたらめさ (shi go nen mae no seikatsu no detarame *sa*), one's purposeless life several years ago.

In the past form of い (i)-adjectives in this noun form, the final い (i) is dropped, this termination enabling them to add かった (katta).

This かった (katta) relates to の (no), こと (koto), 人 (hito), もの (mono) and nouns.

e.g. 十五年前自動車で渋谷を通った時，この町はいかにもわびしかったの (or わびしかったこと) を覚えています。(Jū go nen mae jidōsha de Shibuya o tōtta toki, kono machi wa ikani mo wabishikatta *no* [or: wabishikatta *koto*] o oboete imasu)—I remember that fifteen years ago I passed by Shibuya in a car and the streets were vividly lonely—わびしかった (wabishi katta) from わびしい (wabishii), lonely, is an い (i)-adjective in the plain past form. The noun clause いかにもわびしかったの (or こと) (ikani mo wabishi katta *no* [or: *koto*]) comes from the regular noun 大へんなわびしさ (taihen na wabishi *sa*), extreme loneliness.

Drill

1. 困ったことができました。 — I had some trouble.
2. 困ったことになったと思いました。 — He realized he had a problem.
3. あなたは私のことなんか忘れてしまうでしょう。 — You'll surely forget a person like me.
4. きちんと生活を立てて行くことを彼は息苦しく感じました。 — He felt suffocated by having to go on making an orderly living.
5. 玄関でくつをはいているのは私の下宿の主人です。 — The man putting on his shoes at the door is the landlord of my lodging house.
6. ホステスのような女を愛することはできません。 — It is impossible for me to love a woman such as a barmaid.
7. 今までのところ，私は良心に恥じることはありません。 — I have nothing so far to trouble my conscience.
8. 彼が彼女を新劇に招待したのは，もちろん理由がありました。 — His inviting her to a modern drama was, of course, intentional.
9. しょんぼり明日のご飯のことを思案している人は私の母です。 — The person who is wondering how she, greatly dejected, will find something to eat tomorrow is my mother.
10. この青年を罪におとしいれた責 — I have come to think that I am

任が私自身にあったことを思いいたりました。

11. きょうこの教会において, 私は彼女と結婚することを誓います。

12. いつまでも先輩のことを根に持っているのは, あなたが彼に負けたことになります。

13. 勤めの帰りみちに, たびたびおねえさんの家に寄るのが彼女の楽しみの一つです。

14. 困ったことになったと, 社長は机にひじをついて考えこみました。

15. 公務の忙しいあいだに友だちの就職口の世話をやくのは容易ではありません。

16. 勤めから帰ってきた姉はひとりでだまって火ばちの前にすわりました。

17. 昨日彼女が買ってきた酒を, 彼は暖めて飲みました。

18. 彼は彼女の家をさがすことはやめようとしました。

19. 彼はあの女に親切過ぎたことを少し引け目に感じています。

20. 部屋の窓から白い煙が流れ出て

responsible for having driven this young man into crime.

Today, in this church, I vow that I will marry her.

The fact that you're still bearing a grudge against your senior shows that you have been defeated by him.

It is one of her pleasures to frequently drop in at her elder sister's house on her way home from the office.

The director, worried about being in an awkward position, rested his elbows on the desk, lost in thought.

It is not so easy for me to find my friend a position while I am busily engaged in my official duties.

My elder sister, coming home from the office, sat down alone and silent before the brazier.

He warmed the *sake* which she had bought for him the previous day.

He decided not to seek her house out.

He is feeling a bit embarrassed because of his excessive kindness to that woman.

A stream of white smoke flow-

いる**の**は，中で煙草をすっている
証拠です。

ing out of the window in a room
shows that someone is smoking
inside.

21. まともにこんな人に腹を立てて
いる**の**は，よほど自分の方が間抜
けに見えました。

He felt that getting seriously
angry with such a fellow as this
was rather foolish on his part.

22. なまじっかに教養のある**の**が，
かえってこの女にとって抜きがた
い困難の原因をなしています。

Because she has picked up some
culture halfheartedly, it is difficult
for her to root out the cause of
her difficulties.

23. この子をこのまま継母へ渡すこ
とは妥当でもないし，得策でもな
いように思います。

One could see no point and no
significance in sending this child
to a stepmother in his present
state of mind.

24. 事柄がうまくいかなかったから
といって，一方にだけ罪をなすり
つけることはよくありません。

It's no good for you to say that
things didn't go well and pin the
blame only on the other party.

25. そんな無責任な男を好きになっ
たのは，あなたが軽率であったか
らではありませんか。

Weren't you a bit rash in falling
for such an irresponsible man?

26. 友人のおくさんがまだ若くて美
しい**の**が，私には意外でした。

I was surprised to find that my
friend's wife was still young and
beautiful.

27. 橋の上に鉛のようにじっと動か
ず，たたずんで川風に吹かれなが
ら，流れる水をのぞきこんでいた
男の人は私のいとこです。

The man who stood on the
bridge, quite motionless in the
river breeze, looking down at the
water flowing by, is my cousin.

Exercise
Fill in the following blanks with の, こと, 人, or もの:

1. 彼はまた悪い（　　）をしまし
た。

He again committed a crime.

2. 私は何か良い（　　）をしたい
です。

I want to do something good.

3. 「前に職業についた（　　）はありますか。」

"Did you ever work before?"

4. 詩を書く（　　）はおもしろいです。

To compose poems is interesting.

5. あなたが立腹している（　　）も当然かもしれません。

I suppose it's also quite natural that you're angry.

6. 彼は喫茶店にいる（　　）も忘れたように「ベニスの商人」に読みふけっていました。

He was absorbed in reading the book "Merchant of Venice", as if he had forgotten he was in a coffee-shop.

7. この人が詩を書くという（　　）は意外でありました。

It was strange that this person should write poetry.

8. 彼女がなぜこうも彼を信用する（　　）か不思議です。

One is puzzled why she places such confidence in him.

9. どこかへ勤めに出て働く（　　）を約束しなさい。

I want you to promise that you'll go out and work somewhere.

10. 働いて子供を立派に養育する（　　）を心がけたらどうですか。

Why don't you make up your mind to work and bring up your child in a good way?

11. 私は前借で身をしばられる（　　）になりました。

I became tied down by a loan in advance.

12. 彼女の私生活を知っている（　　）が興ざめる気持ちです。

I feel that my interest in this woman would be sapped by the fact that I know what her private life has been.

13. なるべくならこのままで，彼女の（　　）は忘れてしまおうと彼は思っています。

He is thinking that he would, if possible, try to forget her in this situation.

14. むすこから何のたよりもないからには，無事に勤めている（　　）だと，両親は思っていました。

With no letter from their son, the parents concluded that he was working without any trouble.

15. 彼女との関係が深くなってしまっては抜きさしならない事態にな

He felt uneasy over difficult situation that might result from

る（　　）を彼は懸念しました。

16. 眠っている子供のまくらもとに
すわっている（　　）はこの子の
母親です。

17. 父はむすこがまじめに勤めてい
る（　　）とばかり思っていまし
た。

18. 子供は姉夫婦に養ってもらう
（　　）にしました。

19. あなたはいつか職員室で私がこ
んこんと話して聞かせた（　　）
を覚えていますか。

20. 生きている（　　）はつまらな
いと思うようになりました。

21. この留学生の帰国手続がとられ
ていない（　　）は遺憾です。

22. このような政治犯を重く処罰す
る（　　）は，社会に対してなん
の利益をももたらしません。

23. 私は日産自動車会社に勤務し，
常務取締役の職にある（　　）で
す。

24. 私はかわいそうな女だという
（　　）を考慮にいれてください。

25. この少年にとって必要な（　　）
は，彼を愛する人があって，彼を
しあわせにしてやる（　　）です。

deepening his relations with her.

The person sitting down beside the bed of the sleeping child is the mother.

The father just thought that his son was a hard worker.

I have asked my elder sister and her husband to bring up my child.

Do you remember the fact that I once seriously admonished you in the faculty room?

I came to think there was no use in living.

It is regrettable that no procedure to enable this foreign student to go home has been prepared.

Severely punishing a political offense such as this would never benefit society.

I'm now serving in the Nissan Automobile Company in the position of an ordinary managing director.

Please take into consideration that I am a pitiable woman.

What this boy needs is a person to love him and help make him happy.

Answers:
1. こと 2. こと 3. こと 4. こと 5. の 6. こと 7. の 8. の 9. こと 10. こと 11. こと 12. こと 13. こと 14. もの 15. こと 16. 人 17. もの 18. こと 19. こと 20. こと 21. の 22. こと 23. もの 24. こと 25. こと, こと

Connective Particle Referring to Cause or Reason

Rule

"Because; so; as; since" in English is expressed by から (kara) or のて (node). When using the expression から (kara) or のて (node) which refers to cause or reason, it is placed after any verb in either the plain present/future or past form. And, in this adverbial clause there is that rule of concord which relates to the tense in the principal clause; that is, if the tense in the principal clause is the present/ future form, the tense in the subordinate clause preceding it will also be the present/future form; and accordingly, if the tense in the main clause is the past form, the same tense will naturally be induced in the subordinate clause. In the normal polite style, the ending of a sentence employs the polite form whereas all other verbs, adjectives, and copulas within the sentence are in the plain form. The use of the polite style in this manner is, as a rule, quite fashionable and the common spoken Japanese. But, these plain forms within the sentence will occasionally be transformed into the polite style; it must be acknowledged that this is mainly due to the speaker's subjective feelings. Besides, if the subordinate clause preceding the principal clause suggests a habitual or customary shading, or a universal truth, the tense in this clause can be indicated by the plain present/future form, never influenced by the tense of the principal clause in the sentence.

e.g.　この留学生は日本語が非常によくわかるから (or のて)，日本語劇の主役に選ばれました。(Kono ryūgakusei wa Nihongo ga hijō ni yoku wakaru *kara* [or: *node*], Nihongo geki no shuyaku ni erabaremashita)—This foreign student understands Japanese quite well, so he was chosen for the leading part in the Japanese language drama —the verb 選ばれました (erabaremashita), was chosen, in the principal clause is in the past form, but the clause 非常によくわかる (hijō ni yoku wakar-u), to understand quite well, is in the plain present/future form; this is because the clause preceding the principal clause suggests an established fact.

e.g.　私には日本人の友だちがいないから (or のて)，寂しいです。(Watakushi niwa Nihonjin no tomodachi ga inai *kara* [or: *node*], sabi-

shii desu)—I feel lonely because I haven't any Japanese friends—
いない (inai), to not have; there is not, in this connective particle
is in the plain present/future negative form.

e.g. 彼は生活に困ったから (or ので), 窃盗事件を起こしました。(Kare
wa seikatsu ni komatta *kara* [or: *node*], settō jiken o okoshima-
shita)—He committed a theft because he was hard pressed in life
—困った (komatta), suffered, in this connective particle is in the
plain past form.

e.g. きょうは私の行きつけの床屋にお客さんが一人もいなかったから
(or ので), 少しも待たされませんでした。(Kyō wa watakushi no yuki
tsuke no tokoya ni okyaku-san ga hitori mo inakatta *kara* [or:
node], sukoshi mo matasaremasen deshita)—Today there were no
customers at the barber shop where I go, so I did not have to
wait at all—いなかった (inakatta), there was not, in this connective particle is in the plain past negative form.

In the case of nouns, such expressions as だから (da kara) and な
ので (na node) can be used; these expressions are similarly put after
the noun.

e.g. きょうは土曜日だから (or なので), 私は友だちと映画を見に行きま
す。(Kyō wa doyōbi *da kara* [or: *na node*], watakushi wa tomodachi to eiga o mi ni ikimasu)—Today is Saturday, so I'll go to
see a film with a friend of mine—土曜日 (doyōbi), Saturday, is a
noun.

e.g. きのうは日曜日だったから (or だったので), 新宿には人が大勢出て
いました。(Kinō wa nichiyōbi *datta kara* [or: *datta node*], Shinjuku
niwa hito ga ōzei dete imashita)—It was Sunday yesterday, so a
great number of people were out around Shinjuku—日曜日 (nichiyōbi), Sunday, is a noun and だった (datta), was, a copula in the
plain past form.

The negative form of this expression is the noun＋で(は)ないから
(de [wa] nai kara), and で(は)ないので (de [wa] nai node). The expressions ではないから (de wa nai kara) and ではないので (de wa nai
node) are more emphatic than でないから (de nai kara) and でないの
で (de nai node).

e.g. この汽車は急行でないから (or でないので), どの駅にも止まりま
す。(Kono kisha wa kyūkō *de nai kara* [or: *de nai node*], dono
eki ni mo tomarimasu)—This train is not an express, so it stops
at every station—急行 (kyūkō), an express, is a noun.

e.g. きのう見た映画は現代のものではなかったから (or ではなかったの
で), 私は筋がわかりませんでした。(Kinō mita eiga wa gendai no

mono *de wa nakatta kara* [or: *de wa nakatta node*], watakushi
wa suji ga wakarimasen deshita)—Since the film I saw yesterday
was not a modern one, I did not understand the plot—ではなかっ
た (de wa nakatta), was not, is a copula in the plain past negative
form.

In the case of な (na)-adjectives, the final な (na) may be dropped,
this omission enabling them to be used as the noun forms. Such a
noun as this relates to だから (da kara), なので (na node), だったから
(datta kara), だったので (datta node), で(は)ないから (de [wa] nai kara),
で(は)ないので (de [wa] nai node), で(は)なかったから (de [wa] nakatta
kara), and で(は)なかったので (de [wa] nakatta node), as in the case
of a noun.

e.g. 漢字の筆順はめんどうだから (or なので), どの留学生も漢字の勉
強には相当の時間をさかなければならないはずです。(*Kanji* no hitsu
jun wa mendō *da kara* [or: *na node*], dono ryūgakusei mo *Kanji*
no benkyō niwa sōtō no jikan o sakanakereba naranai hazu desu)
—The stroke order of *Kanji* is troublesome, so all foreign students
will have to spare much time in its study—めんどう (mendō),
troublesomeness, comes from the な (na)-adjective めんどうな (mendō na), troublesome.

e.g. 政府の奨学金が不十分だったから (or だったので), 日本滞在中こ
の留学生は国の両親から送金してもらっていました。(Seifu no shōga-
kukin ga fujūbun *datta kara* [or: *datta node*], Nihon taizai chū
kono ryūgakusei wa kuni no ryōshin kara sōkin shite moratte
imashita)—The scholarship from the government being insufficient,
this foreign student, during his stay in Japan, was getting some
remittance from his parents at home—不十分 (fujūbun), insuf-
ficiency, comes from the な (na)-adjective 不十分な (fujūbun na),
insufficient.

e.g. この工員の意見は不当ではないから (or ではないので), 工場長は
聞き入れざるを得ません。(Kono kōin no iken wa futō *de wa nai
kara* [or: *de wa nai node*], kōjōchō wa kiki-ire zaru o emasen)—
Since this factory hand's views are not unreasonable, the factory
superintendent is obliged to comply with them—不当 (futō), un-
reasonableness, comes from the な (na)-adjective 不当な (futō na),
unreasonable.

e.g. この建物の土台は堅牢ではなかったから (or ではなかったので), 昨
年の地震でひどくいたみました。(Kono tatemono no dodai wa kenrō
de wa nakatta kara [or: *de wa nakatta node*], sakunen no jishin
de hidoku itamimashita)—As the foundation of this building was

not solid, it was greatly damaged by the earthquake in the previous year—堅牢 (kenrō), solidness, comes from the な (na)-adjective 堅牢な (kenrō na), solid.

Each い (i)-adjective ending with either the short vowel い (i) or the long vowel *ii*, as it is, may be put before the expression から (kara) or ので (node).

e.g. 私は頭が痛いから (or ので), 今晩は早く寝ようと思います。(Watakushi wa atama ga itai *kara* [or *node*], konban wa hayaku ne yō to omoimasu)—Since I have a headache, I think I will go to bed early tonight—痛い (itai), painful, is an い (i)-adjective.

e.g. 着物は洋服より働きやすくないから (or ので), このごろは日本の女性は皆洋服を着ています。(Kimono wa yōfuku yori hataraki yasuku nai *kara* [or: *node*], kono goro wa Nihon no josei wa mina yōfuku o kite imasu)—It's not easier to work in kimono than in foreign clothes, so nowadays almost every Japanese woman wears Western-style clothes—やすくない (yasuku nai) from やすい (yasui), easy, is the predicative use of an い (i)-adjective in the plain present/future negative form.

e.g. ゆうべ少し寒かったから (or ので), 私はかぜを引きました。(Yūbe sukoshi samukatta *kara* [or: *node*], watakushi wa kaze o hikimashita)—It was a little cool last evening, so I caught a cold—寒かった (samukatta) from 寒い (samui), cold, is the predicative use of an い (i)-adjective in the plain past form.

Note: から (kara) and ので (node) show cause or reason; they are commonly used in the same way. The difference in nuance between them is that から (kara) is used in a sentence which denotes the speaker's volitional attitude through an order, intention, or temptation; that is, as to two affairs, the speaker, with から (kara) in use, narrates one affair as the reason or cause for another, joining the former to the latter. On the other hand, ので (node) is generally used in the sentence which denotes an objective affair; that is, two separate affairs can be applied with ので (node) as a series of affairs connected through causality and unaffected by the speaker's volition.

e.g. 遅れてもよいから, こんどのクラス会には出席しなさい。(Okurete mo yoi *kara*, kondo no kurasu kai niwa shusseki shinasai)—Please attend the class reunion this time, even if you are late. As is illustrated with this sentence, the connective particle ので (node) cannot be used with an imperative expression.

The adverbial phrase "because of . . ." in English is expressed by で (de) or のために (no tame ni).

e.g. きのう病気で (or のために)，私は学校を休みました。(Kinō byōki *de* [or: *no tame ni*], watakushi wa gakkō o yasumimashita)—I was away from school yesterday because of illness—病気 (byōki), illness, is a noun.

e.g. 邦画の鑑賞は日本語の知識の不足で (or のために)，私には大へん めんどうなことと思います。(Hōga no kanshō wa Nihongo no chishiki no fusoku *de* [or: *no tame ni*], watakushi niwa taihen mendō na koto to omoimasu)—It seems to me that the appreciation of Japanese films is a very difficult task because of my deficiency in the Japanese language—不足 (fusoku), deficiency, is a noun form of the な (na)-adjective 不足な (fusoku na), deficient.

"Now that . . ." in English is expressed by からには (kara niwa).

e.g. 弟に一応の生活が立つようにしてやったからには，私としても気の 済むものがありました。(Otōto ni ichiō no seikatsu ga tatsu yō ni shite yatta *kara niwa*, watakushi to shite mo ki no sumu mono ga arimashita)—Now that I had enabled my younger brother to make a decent living, I felt relieved.

Drill

1. 気候や風土で，好みの料理は国 によって大へん違います。

Because of the climate and natural environment, favorite dishes greatly differ according to the country.

2. 私は農科の出だから，開墾のこ とは自信があります。

Since I graduated from the agricultural course, I'm confident I can handle farming of any sort.

3. 自分の店で作っているお菓子の 名前の半分も知らないから，私は 商人になっても仕方がありませ ん。

Since I do not know even half the names of the cookies that we are making at our own shop, there is no point in my being a merchant.

4. 彼女の姿が見当たらないので， 「葉子さんは……?」と彼はたずね てみました。

He did not see her about, so he asked where Miss Yoko might be.

5. 彼女は貧しい家に育ったので， 義務教育も受けませんでした。

She was brought up in a poor family, so she did not receive even the compulsory education.

6. 寒くなった**ので**，彼は立って洋服を着にかかりました。

He began to feel chilly, so he stood up to get dressed.

7. 乳が出ない**から**，この母親は牛乳を買ってきました。

This mother went out and bought milk for the baby because she is not able to feed it at the breast.

8. 試験の箇所を前もってよく調べてある**ので**，彼はゆうゆうとしていました。

Having taken care of every detail of the examination beforehand, he felt composed.

9. 私は少し急ぎます**ので**，これで失礼いたします。

I'm in a little hurry, so I'll have to leave now.

10. この子供はかわいそうです**から**，できれば，私がお世話したいです。

I feel sorry for this child, so if circumstances allow, I would like to take care of him.

11. 彼がいつも学校を遅刻するのは，病気の母の**ため**でした。

He often comes late for school because of his mother's illness.

12. 両親に迷惑をかけたくない**から**，私の病気のことは知らせません。

I'll not inform my parents of my illness because I don't want to make a nuisance of myself to them.

13. もう少し調べることがある**から**，あなたを帰せません。

Since I have to question you a little more, I can't let you go yet.

14. 友だちのことを口にしたくない**ので**，私は彼のことは何も家内に話しませんでした。

I told my wife nothing about him because I did not want to bring up the topic of my friend.

15. あなたは何でもわかる人**だから**，私は真面目に言って聞かせているのです。

Since you're a person who seems to understand things, I'm trying to talk to you seriously.

16. 今夜は同じクラスの者で忘年会をやる予定になっていた**ので**，彼は会社の帰りに池袋の会場へ出かけるつもりでした。

Tonight his classmates were planning a "year-end party", so, he intended to go to the meeting place in Ikebukuro on his way home from the company.

17. 野菜の煮付けがご飯の量を食べ

Since boiled vegetables were

過ぎないように，わざとまずい味を付けてあるので，この店の奉公人は年中腹がすきました。

purposely cooked with an unsavoury flavour in order not to stimulate the appetite for overeating boiled rice, the apprentices in this shop were always hungry.

Exercise

Fill in the following blanks with から, ので, or からには：

1. 彼女は男に捨てられた（　　），自分で死にたいと思っていました。

She was deserted by a man, so she hoped to die by herself.

2. 長い間貧乏でした（　　），私はいろんな物が買えませんでした。

As I had been poor for a long time, I couldn't afford to buy many things.

3. 姉の夫は大工で，子供がなかった（　　），よろこんで私の子供を預かってくれました。

My elder sister's husband was a carpenter with no children, so he was glad to take care of my child.

4. 「なぜ死のうと思いましたか」「生きていてもつまらなくなった（　　）です。」

"Why did you think you were going to die?" "Because I came to think there was no use in living."

5. 彼はだいぶ貧乏している（　　），困るらしいです。

He seems to be embarrassed because he is very poor.

6. 夫から無情な仕打ちを受けた（　　），妻は離婚しました。

The wife divorced her husband because she was cruelly treated by him.

7. 彼女の方から求愛してきた（　　），彼は彼女にいや気がさしてきました。

Since she did court him, he felt disgusted with her.

8. 長男からも次男からも何のたよりもない（　　），無事に働いているものだと両親は思っていました。

Now that no letter came either from the eldest son or from the second son, the parents concluded that they were working without

9. 彼は彼女の私生活をよく知って
   いる（　　）, 彼女を本当に愛せま
   せんでした。

He was unable to become truly attached to her because he knew what her private life had been.

10. 隣室のラジオの流行歌が大きな
    声でわめいていた（　　）, この大
    学生は昨夜よく勉強ができません
    でした。

This university student could not study well last night because popular songs were blaring on a radio in the next room.

11. このホステスは顔もいいし, 気
    性もさっぱりしている（　　）, 客
    に大変好かれています。

All the customers have a crush on this barmaid because her face is well proportioned and she is open-hearted.

12. この少年はひどく母親にしから
    れた（　　）, こたつにもぐり込み,
    ふとんに顔を伏せました。

Since this boy was scolded by his mother so snappishly, he sat down, putting his legs into the foot-warmer, and dropped his face on the bedding which covered the warmer.

13. 授業中生徒が鼻唄を歌っていた
    （　　）, 先生は彼を廊下へ引きず
    り出しました。

The teacher dragged a pupil out into the corridor because he was humming a song during the lesson.

14. 東京には友人も親戚も何もない
    （　　）, 彼女はいろいろの面で本
    当に困っているようです。

She seems to be quite distressed in many ways because in Tokyo she doesn't have any friends, relatives, or anything.

15. あてのない女子供をこの極寒の
    夜ふけに, 追いかえすわけにもい
    かなかった（　　）, 彼は自分の家
    に泊めさせました。

Since he found it impossible to send this helpless woman and her child away this late at night in the depth of cold, he put them up at his house.

16. 夜もすがら本を読みふけった
    （　　）, この学生は不眠に疲れ果
    てて, 机にうつ伏したままで, う

Since this student had been absorbed in reading books the whole night, he was so fatigued

たた寝をしてしまいました。

from lack of sleep that he put his face down on his desk and took a nap.

17. 夫が十二時を過ぎて，もう一時 になろうとしていたのに，帰らな かった（　　），妻は夫の身に何か 不慮の災難でも起こったのではな いかと心配しました。

Although twelve o'clock had passed and it was already almost one o'clock, the husband made no appearance; so, finally the wife began to fear that an unexpected accident or something might have happened to him.

Answers:

1. ので 2. から 3. から 4. から 5. ので 6. から 7. ので 8. からには 9. ので 10. ので 11. ので 12. ので 13. ので 14. ので 15. ので 16. ので 17. ので

Conjunctions

Rule

Conjunctions, freed from their own transformation, are, as they are, placed at the beginning of the sentence. The so-called conjunctions play the role of absolute terms, which identify the various relationships between the host sentence and the previous sentence. The use and classification of conjunctions is as follows:

(1) These conjunctions refer to the fact that the sentence containing them is out of, ill-proportioned to and against the contents of the previous sentence. Such conjunctions are だが (daga), が (ga), しかし (shikashi), けれど (keredo), けれども (keredomo), だけど (dakedo), でも (demo), それでも (sore demo), and ところが (tokoroga); these expressions can be rendered as "but; and yet; though" in English.

(2) The sentence with the conjunction shows result and conclusion induced from the cause and reason in the previous sentence. Such conjunctions are だから (dakara), それで (sorede), それゆえ (sore-yue), ゆえに (yueni), したがって (shitagatte), そこで (sokode), and すると (suruto); these expressions can be rendered as "therefore; accordingly" in English.

(3) The sentence with the conjunction serves to make an additional statement to the previous sentence. Such conjunctions are そして (soshite), それから (sorekara), また (mata), かつ (katsu), および (oyobi), それに (soreni), あわせて (awasete), さらに (sarani), and なお (nao); these expressions are rendered as "and then; moreover; besides" in English.

(4) The sentence with the conjunction serves to make up for explanations and details not in the previous sentence. Such conjunctions are つまり (tsumari), すなわち (sunawachi), たとえば (tatoeba), なぜなら (naze nara), ただし (tadashi), and もっとも (mottomo); these expressions are rendered as "that is; because" in English.

(5) The sentence with the conjunction presents a choice connected with affairs in the previous sentence. Such conjunctions are または (mata wa), あるいは (arui wa), もしくは (moshiku wa), and

それとも (sore tomo); these expressions are rendered as "or; either…or" in English.

(6) The sentence with the conjunction serves to change the topic of conversation. Such conjunctions are さて (sate), ところで (tokoro de), ときに (toki ni), つぎに (tsugi ni), and では (dewa); these expressions are rendered as "by the way; well" in English.

Also, among conjunctions like these, aside from the relationship between sentence and sentence some are used in a parallel between term and term—they denote the nature of the arrangement—such conjunctions are A または B (A mata wa B), A or B, A あるいは B (A arui wa B), either A or B, A そして B (A soshite B), A and B, A および B (A oyobi B), both A and B, and A ならびに B (A narabi ni B), B in addition to A.

e.g. 娘が寝がえりを打って、ふとんの中へ顔を埋めました。しかし，眠れないらしく重いため息が時々母の耳に聞こえてきました。(Musume ga negaeri o utte, futon no naka e kao o umemashita. *Shikashi*, nemurenai rashiku omoi tameiki ga toki doki haha no mimi ni kikoete kimashita)—The daughter turned over in her bedding, burying her face in the quilt. But occasionally her mother could hear her restlessness and heavy sighs—しかし (shikashi) means "but". This conjunction refers to the fact that it stands in contrast to the previous statement.

e.g. 彼女に縁談がもちあがっていました。が (or けれども)，彼女は田中という警官を愛していました。(Kanojo ni endan ga mochiagatte imashita. *Ga* [or: *keredomo*], kanojo wa Tanaka to iu keikan o aishite imashita)—She was made a proposal of marriage. But she loved a policeman named Tanaka—が (ga) and けれども (keredomo) means "but". が (ga) and けれども (keredomo) are generally used in the same way—two matters are coexistence and continuation in time. There are many cases where the two matters are substantially different from expectation in general; but this is not so often adaptable.

Note: その日は雨は降ったが (or 降ったけれど)，風は吹きませんでした。(Sono hi wa ame *wa* futta *ga* [or: futta *keredo*], kaze *wa* fukimasen deshita)—That day it rained, but it was not windy.

その日は雨も降ったが (or 降ったけれど)，風も吹きました。(Sono hi wa ame *mo* futta *ga* [or: futta *keredo*], kaze *mo* fukimashita)—That day it rained and the wind blew, too.

e.g. あなたは何でもわかる人です。だから私はまじめに言って聞かせているのです。(Anata wa nan demo wakaru hito desu. *Dakara*

watakushi wa majime ni itte kikasete iru no desu)—You are a
person who seems to understand things. Therefore, I'm trying
to talk to you seriously—だから (dakara) means "therefore". This
conjunction shows conclusion induced from reason in the previous
sentence.

e.g. 私は商売のことは何も知らないし，父の会社の常務になっても仕方
がありません。それに，私がただ社長のむすこだというそれだけの理由
で常務になるのは，およそ民主主義ではありません。(Watakushi wa
shōbai no koto wa nani mo shiranai shi, chichi no kaisha no jōmu
ni natte mo shikata ga arimasen. *Sore ni*, watakushi ga tada
shachō no musuko da to iu soredake no riyū de jōmu ni naru
nowa, oyoso minshushugi dewa arimasen)—Since I'm not interested
in trade, there's no point in my being an ordinary director of my
father's company. Moreover, I can fill that position only because
I am the son of the director, an idea far from democratic—それ
に (sore ni) means "moreover". This conjunction serves to make
an additional statement to the previous sentence.

e.g. 自分の生活をもっと大切に扱うことを考えるべきではありません
か。つまり一度しか経験できない人生です。(Jibun no seikatsu o
motto taisetsu ni atsukau koto o kangaeru beki dewa arimasen
ka. *Tsumari* ichido shika keiken dekinai jinsei desu)—You ought
to handle your own life more carefully. Don't you think so?
After all, life is something you can experience only once—つまり
(tsumari) means "after all". This conjunction serves to introduce
explanations concerning the previous sentence.

e.g. 家庭の危機の解決が今日まで延ばされてきたのは，両親の怠慢によ
るのではないでしょうか。または自分の怠慢によるものであるにちがい
ありません。(Katei no kiki no kaiketsu ga kon-nichi made noba-
sarete kita nowa, ryōshin no taiman ni yoru no dewa nai deshō
ka. *Mata wa* jibun no taiman ni yoru mono de aru ni chigai
arimasen)—The solution of the family crisis had been left until
now—one wonders whether or not that could be due to carelessness on my parents' part. Or, it might have been due to my own
carelessness—または (mata wa) means "or". This conjunction
presents a choice connected with affairs in the previous sentence.

e.g. 「どうです横浜は，お変わりありませんか」と彼は煙草を取りあげま
した。「ところで，相談があるのですが」("Dō desu Yokohama wa,
okawari arimasen ka" to kare wa tabako o toriage mashita.
"*Tokoro de*, sōdan ga aru no desu ga")—"How is Yokohama?
How's the family there getting along?" he asked, picking up a

cigarette. "By the way, I've got something I want to talk with
you about."—ところで (tokoro de) means "by the way". This
conjunction serves to change the topic of conversation.

e.g. 彼女は畳に両手をつき「大へんごやっかいになって申し訳ありませ
んでした。きょうのうちにアパートまたは下宿をさがして，引っ越しま
すから...」と言いました。(Kanojo wa tatami ni ryōte o tsuki
"Taihen goyakkai ni natte mōshiwake arimasen deshita. Kyō no
uchi ni apāto *mata wa* geshuku o sagashite, hikkoshimasu
kara..." to iimashita)—She put both hands upon the mat, bowed,
and said, "I'm sorry to have been so much trouble to you. I'll
find an apartment or a lodging house today and move there,
so..."—または (mata wa) means "A or B". This conjunction
shows a difference by way of paralleling.

e.g. 弟あるいは私が郵便局へ手紙を投函しに行かなければなりません。
(Otōto *arui wa* watakushi ga yūbinkyoku e tegami o tōkan shi
ni ikanakereba narimasen)—Either my younger brother or I have
to go to the post office to post some letters—あるいは (arui wa)
means "either A or B".

e.g. 野菜そして卵が彼のおもな食事です。(Yasai *soshite* tamago ga
kare no omo na shokuji desu)—Vegetables and eggs have been
his main foods—そして (soshite) means "A and B".

e.g. 彼およびあなたが男性の共同の責任において，彼女の生活の窮地を
救う必要があります。(Kare *oyobi* anata ga dansei no kyōdō no
sekinin ni oite, kanojo no seikatsu no kyūchi o suku-u hitsuyō
ga arimasu)—Both he and you, because of your common responsibility as men, have to help her from her tight corner of life—
および (oyobi) means "both A and B".

e.g. 重要書類ならびに貴重品は，かぎつきの机の引き出しにしまってお
いてください。(Jūyō shorui *narabi ni* kichō hin wa, kagi tsuki no
tsukue no hikidashi ni shimatte oite kudasai)—Valuable things,
in addition to important documents, are requested to be kept in
the locked drawer of the desk—ならびに (narabi ni) means "B
in addition to A".

Drill

1. 彼女は間もなく再婚しました。
   そして主人との間に女の子が生ま
   れました。

   Soon she remarried. And by
   the husband she had a female
   baby.

2. 彼女は大きな商店のおじょうさ

   She was reared "a young lady"

んとして育ちました。**が，**彼女は本当は芸者の子でした。

in a big shop. But, she was, in fact, the child of a geisha.

3.「あなたのおとうさんが，あなたと同じ考えでいてくれるでしょうか。」「**だから，**父は私が説き伏せると言っているではありませんか。」

"I'm afraid that your father would not have the same idea as you." "That being so, I think I'll be able to persuade my father."

4. 思わず涙がこみ上げてきました。**しかし，**なぜ涙が出たか，彼女はその理由を母にも親友にも言えませんでした。

She was overcome with tears; but the reason for her tears she could not disclose to either her mother or her close friend.

5. 彼はふとその時の事を思い出して，遠いおもいに胸を熱くしていたが「．．．**ところで，**葉子さんは．．．?」その葉子の姿が見あたらないので，やはり彼はそうたずねてみました。

Unintentionally recalling that time, he was moved deeply by the distant memory; "Well, where is Miss Yoko?" He did not see Miss Yoko about, so, at length, he asked where she might be.

Exercise

Fill in each bracket with the conjunction だから，つまり，しかし，が，or さらに:

1. 秋だ（　　）、まだむし暑いです。

It is autumn, but still the weather is sultry.

2. お手伝いさんが昼の食事を知らせに来た（　　）、彼女は食べたくなかったのです。（　　）、食欲がないのは暑さのせいばかりではありませんでした。

The maid came in to inform her that lunch was ready, but she did not want to eat. It was not merely because of the heat.

3. むすこが放蕩しては手がつけられません。（　　）、今のうちに父は宗教につかせるのがいいかも知れないと思いました。

If his son led a dissipated life, the father would find him unmanageable. So, before long, he thought that it might be desirable to direct him toward religion.

4. この大学生は私の不在中に転居

This university student changed

していきました。（　　），私には
新しい住所も知らせてよこしませ
んでした。

5. 横堀の瀬戸物町では軒なみに並
んだ瀬戸物問屋がまん幕を張り，
ちょうちんをつるし，いっせいに
商売を休む年に一度の陶器祭があ
ります。（　　），大阪一の夏祭り
です。

his residence during my absence.
Moreover, he did not inform me
of his new address.

In the quarter of Yokobori, the
chinaware district, there is held
a pottery festival once a year when
the rows of wholesale chinaware
shops hang bunting, string paper
lanterns at the shop front, and
rest from business altogether. In
other words, we might say, this
is the summer festival, the
grandest one in Osaka.

Answers:

1. が 2. が, しかし 3. だから 4. さらに 5. つまり

第 五十二 課　Lesson 52

The Use of Important Particles, Conjunctions, etc.

In Japanese the discrimination of cases is not strictly pursued—this causes foreigners, especially foreign students of the Japanese language, to find its further study tiresome and cost them a good command of the usage of cases. In most foreign languages, the difference of such cases as the nominative, possessive, objective, dative, genitive, and accusative is very distinct, permitting the mutual relations between word and word to be explicitly distinguished. In Japanese, however, there is no difference in a word itself but the so-called particles (the post words) such as て (te), に (ni), を (o) or は (wa), take over this function. This lesson will be sufficiently clear to secure an understanding of them as a whole, giving the reader the most enjoyment and profit out of his being familiar with their uses.

* A term can be used by itself as one sentence or an absolute term within the sentence, enabling it to indicate accosting or presentation.

　e.g.　先生，おはようございます。　　Good morning, teacher.
　　　The term 先生 (sensei), teacher, denotes accosting.

　e.g.　四月二十二日，この日がこ　　The 22nd day of April—this day
　　　の大学の創立記念日です。　　is the anniversary of the foundation
　　　　　　　　　　　　　　　　　of this university.
　　　The term 四月二十二日 (shigatsu ni jū ni nichi), April 22nd, shows presentation.

* In the case of a noun denoting time, it is applied as a circumstantial term.

　e.g.　きのう東京外国語大学で語　　Yesterday the festival of language
　　　劇祭が行なわれました。　　dramas was held at the Tokyo
　　　　　　　　　　　　　　　　University of Foreign Studies.

　e.g.　きのうの朝都心に近い盛り　　There was a fire in a busy section
　　　場に火事がありました。　　near the center of Tokyo yesterday
　　　　　　　　　　　　　　　　morning.

* In the case of a noun denoting quantity, it is applied as a continuous regular term.

e.g. この教室にビルマの国費留 学生が**十人**います。

There are ten foreign students from Burma on government support in this classroom.

e.g. この少年はおやつにお菓子 を**四つ**食べます。

This boy eats four cookies for a snack.

* Such a personal pronoun as あなた (anata), you or 私 (watakushi), I, becomes the nominative case in conversational terms.

e.g. **きみ**, こんどのソビエトの ボリショイ氷上サーカスを見 たか。

Did you see the Bolshoi ice circus from the Soviet Union this time?

The personal pronoun きみ (kimi), you, is commonly used among schoolboys or intimate friends.

e.g. **私**, そのようなことは知り ませんよ。

I don't know such things.

* The Gothic terms are used in a conversational style—they serve as the objective case を (o) which indicates the receiver of an action.

e.g. **コーヒー**飲みましたか。

Did you drink coffee?

e.g. 机の上の**学用品**どこに置き ましたか。

Where did you put my school things that were on the desk?

* The following Gothic terms become the predicate in the sense of だ (da) or です (desu), is; am; are. They are chiefly used as conversational terms.

e.g. あれが**富士山**, あの白く立 ちのぼっている湯気が**熱海の 温泉**。

That is Mt. Fuji, and that white vapor rising into the air is the Atami hot spring resort.

* Such particles as は (wa), も (mo), and さえ (sae) serve as the subject or the objective case, an indication of the receiver of an action.

e.g. **私は**駐米日本大使です。

I am the Japanese Ambassador to America.

私は (watakushi wa), I, shows the subject.

e.g. **あなたも**私費留学生です。

You also are a privately supported foreign student.

あなたも (anata mo), you also, shows the subject.

e.g. 私は**果物は**食べました。

I ate some fruit.

果物は (kudamono wa), fruit, is an objective term which shows the receiver of an action. The expression 果物は (kudamono *wa*) is more emphatic and descriptive than the expression 果物を (kudamono *o*).

e.g. 私はおでんは食べませんで I did not eat *Oden*.
した。

おでんは (Oden wa), *Oden*, is an objective term which shows the receiver of an action. The expression おでんは (Oden *wa*) is more emphatic and descriptive than the expression おでんを (Oden *o*).

e.g. 彼は魚さえ食べません。 He doesn't eat even fish.
魚さえ (sakana sae) shows the objective case.

* Nouns, with particles of coexistence such as と (to) and や (ya), are concurrent.

e.g. 本と帳面と鉛筆は学用品 Books, notebooks and pencils are
です。 school things.

と (to) is used between each of a series of nouns when all of the series of articles are being enumerated.

e.g. 石けんやちり紙やハンカチ Soap, toilet paper and handker-
は日用必需品です。 chief are daily necessities.

や (ya) is used when only part of the series of articles is being stated.

* The use of は (wa) and が (ga) is as follows:

e.g. 私は芸術家です。 I am an artist.

は (wa) in this sentence includes the idea of "The profession of artist is one of my attributes".

e.g. 私はこの飲み物を飲みま I will have this beverage.
す。

は (wa) in this sentence places emphasis on self-speciality; that is, this は (wa) implies that consciousness which emphasizes the difference between self and others.

e.g. 雪は昨日から降り続いてい It is still snowing since the previ-
ます。 ous day.

は (wa) in this sentence places emphasis on 雪 (yuki), snow; that is, this は (wa) implies that consciousness which emphasizes the difference between snow and other natural phenomena like wind and rain.

e.g. 後楽園は都市対抗野球をや An intercity baseball game is
っています。 being held at Korakuen, a baseball
field.

This は (wa) refers to continuous occurrences.

e.g. 彼は軍国主義者ではありま He is not a militarist.

せん。

When the negative form is used, the subject as a rule is followed by は (wa).

e.g. 大根は練馬に限ります。   If it's a radish, there is nothing so good as those in Nerima.

This (は) can be rendered as なら (nara), If it is... or と言えば (to ie ba), Speaking of..., so, If it is a radish or Speaking of radishes, ...

e.g. 夏は烈日が草を焼き，大地   In summer the strong sun burns を熱します。冬は富士おろし   the grasses and scorches the earth. の寒風が広野を吹き荒らしま   In winter the cold wind off Mt. す。   Fuji blows hard over the wide plain.

The は (wa) following 夏 (natsu), summer and 冬 (fuyu), winter, is used because this sentence is a contrast of two ideas and thus the subject of each idea takes special emphasis. Namely, は (wa) is used to restrict a topic especially in a fixed sphere.

e.g. 社長のテーブルの上の電話   The telephone on the director's が鳴りました。   table rang.

The meaning of this が (ga) can be read as: The telephone on the director's table *now* rang; that is, が (ga) indicates a temporary or accidental relationship.

e.g. 私の家の近所に保健所があ   There is a health center in the ります。   neighborhood of my house.

Nouns (inanimate objects) preceding あります (arimasu), there is..., are followed by the particle が (ga).

e.g. この辺に浮浪者がいます。   There are some tramps around here.

Nouns (animate objects) preceding います (imasu), there is..., are followed by the particle が (ga).

e.g. 彼の家に三毛ねこがいま   There is a tortoiseshell cat at す。   his house.

Nouns (animate objects) preceding います (imasu), there is..., are followed by the particle が (ga).

e.g. 日が当たって，風が吹いて   It is sunny and the wind is blow-います。   ing.

This expression is found to be merely that in which two subjective cases in a state of action are described in enumeration.

e.g. 日本でどこが一番好きです   Where do you like best in Japan? か。

いつ (itsu), When, どこ (doko), Where, だれ (dare), Who, なに (nani), What, and どれ (dore), Which, in the subjective tense always use が (ga).

e.g. 「犬が来た！」「あの犬は私   "A dog came." "That dog seems
の知人の田中さんの犬らし   to be Mr. Tanaka's, my acquaint-
い。」   ance."

が (ga) fixes the framework of a story and then は (wa) is used as a receiver within its framework; that is, 犬が (inu ga), a dog—this が (ga) corresponds to the English "a" or "an", an indefinite article and あの犬は (ano inu wa), that dog, to the English "the", a definite article.

e.g. 私が書いた絵が展覧会に出   The picture I drew has been
品されています。   shown at the exhibition.

私が (watakushi ga), I, in the phrase of 私が書いた (watakushi *ga* kaita), I drew, is related to 絵 (e), a picture; therefore the phrase 私が (watakushi ga) can also be written and spoken with the use of の (no), as 私の書いた絵 (watakushi *no* kaita e), the picture I drew.

e.g. この子供は漢字が読めま   This child can read Chinese
す。   characters.

e.g. 彼女は花が好きです。   She likes flowers.

が (ga) in these sentences takes the role of the secondary theme under は (wa) presenting the major topic.

* The use of the particle へ (e) is as follows:

(A) へ (e) shows a spatial point of arrival or direction.

e.g. 彼の乗った超特急「ひか   The "Hikari", super express, on
り」は大阪へ五時に着きま   which he got, will arrive at Osaka
す。   at five.

e.g. この道を左へ行きなさい。   Take this road to the left.

(B) へ (e) shows an abstract point of arrival or direction.

e.g. 日本の映画はもうすぐ世   Japanese films will soon get near
界的水準へ近づきます。   the international level.

(C) へ (e) shows an indefinite spatial point of arrival or direction.

e.g. 高校へ進学する日も遠く   The day when I will go to a
ありません。   high school is coming soon.

(D) へ (e) shows the other party.

e.g. ゆうべ私は恋人へ手紙を   Last night I wrote a letter to my
書きました。   sweetheart.

e.g. このお祝い物を先生へと   Please send this congratulatory

どけてください。　present to the teacher.

* The use of the particle に (ni) is as follows:

(A)　に (ni) shows spatial whereabouts.

    e.g.　机の上に日本語の本や英　There are Japanese and English
語の本や辞書などがありま　books, dictionaries, and so forth on
す。　the desk.

    e.g.　担任の先生は海岸に別荘　The teacher in charge has his
をもっています。　villa at the seaside.

(B)　に (ni) shows abstract whereabouts.

    e.g.　私はゴルフに自信があり　I have self-confidence in playing
ます。　golf.

    e.g.　彼は今名誉教授の地位に　He is now in the position of an
あります。　emeritus professor.

(C)　に (ni) shows a spatial point of arrival or direction.

    e.g.　季節労務者として，私は　I, as a seasonal worker, am going
働きに東京に行きます。　to Tokyo to work.

    e.g.　彼はポケットに雑誌を押　He shoved a magazine into his
しこみました。　pocket.

(D)　に (ni) shows an indefinite spatial point of arrival.

    e.g.　姉の病気は快方に向かっ　My elder sister, in bad health, is
ています。　progressing favorably.

    e.g.　娘は都会の女子大学に入　My daughter is going to enter
学します。　a women's college in the city.

(E)　に (ni) shows an indefinite spatial whereabouts.

    e.g.　この工業都市は海岸に近　This industrial city is near the
いです。　seashore.

(F)　に (ni) shows the other party or the object.

    e.g.　兄は弟にドイツ語を教え　The elder brother is teaching his
ています。　younger brother German.

    e.g.　このたびの人事異動をき　He became aware of his own
っかけに，彼は自分の欠点　defects with the personnel changes
に気付きました。　this time.

(G)　に (ni) shows standard.

e.g. 日本の映画の質は外国の　　Japanese films are inferior in
映画に劣ります。　　　　quality to foreign ones.

e.g. 大学生にふさわしい服装　Please wear clothes becoming to
をしなさい。　　　　　　a university student.

(H) に (ni) shows result.

e.g. 彼女は立派な歌手になり　She became a fine singer.
ました。

e.g. あたりが静かになりまし　It became quiet about.
た。

(I) に (ni) shows an abstract whereabouts as well as the content
of one's thought.

e.g. 彼女の服装がはでに見え　The way she wears her dress
ます。　　　　　　　　looks showy.

e.g. 初対面の印象では，彼女　She seemed to be a rather com-
は平凡な人妻に見えました。　mon married woman by my first
impression in meeting her.

(J) に (ni) shows a spatial point of an action.

e.g. 私は窓ごしに彼の書斎を　I peered into his study through
のぞいてみました。　　　the window.

(K) に (ni) shows purpose.

e.g. きのう快晴だったので，　It being fine yesterday, all of my
家じゅうでハイキングに出　family went on a hike.
かけました。

e.g. 来週洋舞を見に行きま　I'm going to go and see European
す。　　　　　　　　　dances next week.

(L) に (ni) shows cause or reason.

e.g. あまり彼女のずうずうし　He was quite disappointed at her
い態度に，彼はいささか失望　overly impudent attitude.
しました。

e.g. 大売り出しの赤い幕が風　The red hangings for the bargain
にひらひらしています。　sale are flitting in the wind.

(M) に (ni) shows time or a case.

e.g. 父はいつも五時に起床し　My father always gets up at five.

ます。

e.g.　運動会には，仮装行列を
　　　やります。

We are holding a fancy-dress parade at the athletic meet.

(N)　に (ni) follows subsidiary terms.

e.g.　彼も医学生にちがいあり
　　　ません。

He also must be a medical student.

e.g.　私にとって日本研究は必
　　　要です。

It's necessary for me to pursue the studies of Japan.

* The use of the particle で (de) is as follows:

(A)　で (de) shows the spatial place where an action is performed.

e.g.　私たちは公園で野球をし
　　　ます。

We play baseball in the park.

e.g.　去年私は大阪で恩師に会
　　　いました。

Last year I met my respected teacher in Osaka.

(B)　で (de) shows an abstract place or scene where an action is performed.

e.g.　彼は日本留学試験で失敗
　　　しました。

He failed in the examination to study in Japan.

e.g.　今の社会では，あなたの
　　　ような考えは通用しません。

In the present society such an idea as you harbor does not pass current.

(C)　で (de) shows an association or organization as the subject of an action.

e.g.　文部省ではつぎのような
　　　国費留学生受け入れの要項
　　　を発表しました。

The Ministry of Education made known the following essential points on taking in foreign students on government support.

e.g.　きのう東京外国語大学で
　　　は助教授三名を教授に昇任
　　　させました。

Yesterday the Tokyo University of Foreign Studies allowed three assistant professors to be promoted to professors.

(D)　で (de) shows a period.

e.g.　現在では，電燈のない農

Nowadays we seldom find any

村はあまり見あたりません。 farm village without a lighting installation.

e.g. あと三日で卒論を書きあげなければなりません。 I have to write up my graduation thesis in another three days.

(E) で (de) shows the condition in which an action or operation is conducted.

e.g. この少年はひとりで上京しました。 This boy went up to Tokyo alone.

e.g. 私はこの中古車を十万円で買いました。 I bought this slightly used car for 100,000 yen.

(F) で (de) shows a tool or means.

e.g. 留学生にとって筆で字を書くのは大へんめんどうなことです。 It is quite troublesome for foreign students to write letters with a brush.

e.g. この方法で外人に日本語を教えれば，きっと成功します。 Teach foreigners Japanese in this way and you will surely be successful.

(G) で (de) shows cause or reason.

e.g. 私はかぜで熱を出しました。 I became feverish because of a cold.

e.g. 彼はこの作品で有名になりました。 He became famous for this work.

* The use of the objective particle を (o) is as follows:

(A) を (o) shows the object (the receiver) which alters from being worked upon.

e.g. 母は洗濯物を物干しざおに干しています。 The mother is drying the wash on a clothes pole.

e.g. むすこはかぜをこじらせました。 My son's cold got worse.

(B) を (o) shows the object of shift of possession or ownership.

e.g. この苦学生は東京へ出て勉強するためにお金をためています。 This self-supporting student is saving money to go up to Tokyo and study.

e.g. この地主は北海道にもか
なりの土地をもっています。

This landowner possesses a lot
of land even in Hokkaido.

(C) を (o) shows the object in which one's mental activities take
part.

e.g. 彼女は故郷を恋しがりま
す。

She feels a longing for her home
town.

e.g. 私はこの夏休みの旅行を
計画しています。

I'm planning a tour in this summer vacation.

(D) を (o) shows a place of shift, a place of passage and a starting
point.

e.g. 「つばめ」は東海道線を
走っています。

The "Tsubame" runs on the
Tokaido Line.

e.g. 門柱を通って，私は商店
街に出ました。

Passing through the portal, I went
out into some rows of shops.

e.g. 彼女は先月家を出ました。

She left home last month.

(E) を (o) shows quantity in time and space.

e.g. この老人は一日平均十キ
ロメートルを歩きます。

This aged man walks ten kilometers on the average per day.

e.g. この学生は東大受験に失
敗し，この四・五日をぼん
やり過ごしています。

This student failed in the entrance examination to Tokyo University and has spent his time
listlessly these several days.

* The use of the particle と (to) is as follows:

(A) と (to) shows the other party of an action which needs a
companion.

e.g. 私は時々兄とけんかしま
す。

I sometimes quarrel with my
elder brother.

e.g. 盲人は電柱とぶつかりま
した。

A blind man walked into a tele-
graph pole.

(B) と (to) shows the other party with whom one behaves.

e.g. きのう私は友だちと教会
に行きました。

Yesterday I went to church with
a friend.

e.g. 昨夜おそくまで恋人と話

Last night I talked with my

し合いました。	sweetheart far into the night.

(C)　と (to) shows the standard of comparison.

e.g.　いなかと比べて，都会は森や林にめぐまれていません。	Compared with the country, towns are not blessed by woods and forests.
e.g.　この見本と同じきれを見せてください。	Please show me the same cloth as this sample.

(D)　と (to) shows the result of change.

e.g.　横須賀から平塚一帯もやがて工業地帯となるでしょう。	The whole area extending from Yokosuka to Hiratsuka will soon be turned into an industrial zone.
e.g.　これをもっと売れる週刊誌とするにはどうしたらよいか教えてください。	Please tell me how to enable this to be a more salable weekly magazine.

(E)　と (to) shows the content of one's thoughts and terms, or it receives the sentence in a quotation.

e.g.　父は次女をできそこないと呼んでいます。	Father calls his second daughter a failure.
e.g.　正直は最高の道徳と信じています。	We believe that honesty is the highest morality.
e.g.　「先生，おはようございます」と生徒はあいさつしました。	The pupils greeted, "Good morning, teacher."

(F)　と (to) shows condition.

e.g.　私は北海道・青森県と一まわりしてきました。	I returned home after making my rounds in Hokkaido and Aomori Prefecture.
e.g.　この入り江から向こうの一本松まで五百キロメートルとはありません。	It's a distance of less than five hundred kilometers to one pine-tree on the opposite side of this inlet.

* The use of the particle から (kara) is as follows:

(A)　から (kara) shows a spatial starting point, via point or direction.

e.g. 来月の下旬おじさんはビ My uncle will return home from
ルマ**から**帰国します。 Burma at the end of next month.

e.g. 風は東**から**吹いています。 The wind is blowing from the
east.

(B) から (kara) shows an abstract starting point, via point or direction.

e.g. 日本政府は軍国主義の思 The Japanese Government could
想**から**やっとぬけだせまし finally get rid of the thought of
た。 militarism.

e.g. いろんな面**から**この問題 Let's consider this problem from
を考えてみましょう。 various aspects.

(C) から (kara) shows the other party from whom one receives some action.

e.g. この留学生は下宿で日本 This foreign student is learning
人の家庭教師**から**日本語を Japanese from a Japanese tutor at
習っています。 his lodging house.

e.g. 私は路上で見知らぬ人か I was accosted by a stranger in
ら声をかけられました。 the street.

(D) から (kara) shows material.

e.g. パンは小麦粉**から**つくら Bread is made from wheat flour.
れます。

e.g. この洋書は三つの部分か This foreign book consists of
らなっています。 three parts.

(E) から (kara) and ので (node) show cause or reason; they are
commonly used in the same way. But the difference in nuance
between から (kara) and ので (node) is as follows: から (kara) is
used in a sentence which denotes the speaker's volitional attitude
through an order, intention, or temptation; that is, as to two affairs,
the speaker, with から (kara) in use, narrates one affair as the
reason or cause for another, joining the former to the latter. On
the other hand, ので (node) is generally used in the sentence
which denotes an objective affair; that is, two separate affairs can
be applied with ので (node) as a series of affairs connected through
causality and unaffected by the speaker's volition.

e.g. 彼の不注意**から**大火事を He set off a big fire by his care-

引き起こしました。

e.g. 空には黒い雲が出ている**から**，午後は雨が降りだすかもしれません。

Black clouds have appeared in the sky, so it will probably be rainy in the afternoon.

e.g. 雨が降った**ので**，運動会は中止になりました。

It rained, so the athletic meet was called off.

e.g. 時間がおそい**ので**，彼をたずねることをやめました。

It being so late, I gave up calling on him.

Note: この事業に失敗してもよい**から**，最後までがんばりなさい。

Please do your best up to the last moment, giving no mind to possible failure in this enterprise.

As can be understood from this sentence, ので (node) cannot be used with an imperative expression.

(F) から (kara) shows a starting point in time.

e.g. 四月**から**新学期が始まります。

The new term commences from April.

e.g. 朝**から**降りつづいた雨は，夜になってやみました。

The rain which had kept falling from morning stopped towards evening.

(G) から (kara) shows order.

e.g. まず勉強部屋の掃除**から**始めよう。

First, I'll set about cleaning my study.

e.g. あなた**から**お先に試食してください。

Please taste some of this ahead of me.

* The use of the particle まで (made) is as follows:

(A) まで (made) shows limit.

e.g. この本の二十五課**まで**進んだら新しいテキストを使用します。

We'll use a new textbook when we have proceeded to Lesson twenty-five of this book.

e.g. 私は骨のずい**まで**も冷えきっています。

I am chilled to the marrow of my bones.

(B) まで (made) shows the other party.

e.g. ご用の方は係**まで**お申し出ください。

Those who have some business are requested to come up to the man in charge.

e.g. 身分証明書を紛失した学生は教務課まで申し出てください。

Those students who have lost their identification cards are requested to come and report it at the Registrar's Office.

(C) まで (made) shows limit in time.

e.g. 明後日までこの文学書を貸しましょう。

I'll lend this literary book to you until the day after tomorrow.

(D) まで (made) takes up an extreme case and emphasizes it.

e.g. 戦時中，食糧不足で私は雑草まで食べたことがあります。

During the wartime, I once ate even weeds because of the food shortage.

e.g. 今ではこんないなかまで映画館があります。

Nowadays there are movie theatres even in such rural areas as this.

* The use of the particle より (yori) is as follows:

(A) より (yori) shows the standard of comparison.

e.g. 私はそばよりうどんが食べたいです。

I would rather eat plain noodles than buckwheat noodles.

e.g. 一般に女子留学生は男子留学生よりよく勉強します。

Generally female foreign students study harder than male ones.

(B) より (yori) shows the denial of other things.

e.g. 彼との妥協よりしかたがありませんでしょう。

There would be no other way than making a compromise with him.

e.g. この父にとっては，長男を勘当するより道はありません。

For this father, there is no other way than to disinherit his eldest son.

(C) より (yori), as a written expression, can be used in the same way as から (kara), from.

e.g. 諸外国よりオリンピック選手団が東京に到着しました。

The Olympic champion teams from various countries arrived in Tokyo.

e.g. 「春の踊り」は午後六時　　"A Dance of Spring"—the curtain
　　　より開演の予定です。　　　is to rise at 6 p.m.

* The use of も (mo) is as follows:

(A)　も (mo) shows similarity.

e.g. あなたも映画に行きませ　　Won't you go to see a movie,
　　　んか。　　　　　　　　　too?

e.g. 彼は酒も煙草も飲みませ　　He neither drinks nor smokes.
　　　ん。

(B)　も (mo) shows emphasis.

e.g. この辺は人っ子ひとりも　　It's a solitary place where not
　　　通らないさびしい所です。　a soul passes by around here.

e.g. この外人は日本に二十年　　This foreigner has stayed in
　　　間も滞在しています。　　　Japan for as long as twenty years.

(C)　も (mo) shows entire or maximum quantity.

e.g. あと百円もあれば，あの　　To my regret, I could buy that
　　　地球儀が買えるのですが。　globe if I had only one hundred yen
　　　　　　　　　　　　　　　more with me.

e.g. この都電の停留場から外　　It will not take more than ten
　　　大まで十分もかかりません。minutes from this streetcar stop to
　　　　　　　　　　　　　　　the Tokyo University of Foreign
　　　　　　　　　　　　　　　Studies.

(D)　も (mo) shows a thing on the whole in the circumstance of
doubt.

e.g. だれも彼女の再婚を信じ　　Everybody believes in her remar-
　　　ています。　　　　　　　riage.

e.g. あなたの写真機には何も　　I suppose there may be nothing
　　　欠陥はありません。　　　the matter with your camera.

* The use of こそ (koso) is as follows:

こそ (koso) shows emphasis.

e.g. 彼こそ真の道徳家です。　　He is the real moralist.

e.g. 今年こそ早稲田に勝って　　This year we'll surely beat Wa-
　　　みせます。　　　　　　　seda.

* The use of さえ (sae) is as follows:

(A) さえ (sae) takes up an extreme case and emphasizes it.

   e.g. この医者は患者にさえほ　　This doctor doesn't smile at even
     ほえみかけません。　　　　his patients.

   e.g. この歌手のショーのとき　　At this singer's show, there were
     には，あまりの混雑に死傷　even some cases in which people
     者が出たという例さえあり　were killed or injured because of
     ます。　　　　　　　　　　overcrowding.

(B) さえ (sae) serves as the objective case, an indication of the
receiver of an action.

   e.g. 彼は肉さえ食べません。　　He doesn't eat even meat.

(C) さえ (sae) shows such shading as それで十分です (sore de jūbun
desu), that's enough, together with the conditional expression ～
ば (...ba) or ～たら (...tara).

   e.g. あと歴史さえ予習すれば，　My preparations for tomorrow's
     あしたの授業の準備は完了　lessons are finished only when I
     です。　　　　　　　　　　have prepared history.

   e.g. 父にさえ賛成してもらえ　　I'm going to visit America to
     たら，私は社会学の勉強に　study sociology if I can only get
     渡米します。　　　　　　　approval from my father.

* The use of しか (shika) is as follows:
しか (shika) denies other matters.

   e.g. 適当な日本語の参考書と　　There is no more proper reference
     しては，これしかありませ　book than this on the Japanese
     ん。　　　　　　　　　　　language.

   e.g. 富士山は七合目までしか　　I once climbed merely to the
     登ったことがありません。　seventh stage of Mt. Fuji.

* The use of すら (sura) is as follows:
すら (sura) takes up an extreme case and emphasizes it.

   e.g. へんとうせんがひどくて，　My tonsils being very bad, I
     水すらのどを通りませんで　could not drink even water.
     した。

   e.g. この事は子供にすらわか　　This matter can be understood
     ります。　　　　　　　　　even by a child.

* The use of でも (demo) is as follows:

  (A) でも (demo) takes up a partial example and regards it as equal to the case in point.

     e.g. そんな仕事は女子供でも　　Such a job as this can be done
        できます。　　　　　　　　even by women and children.

     e.g. 私でもそんなミスはしま　　Even I do not make such a mis-
        せん。　　　　　　　　　　take.

  (B) でも (demo) shows the whole matter together with the expression of a doubt.

     e.g. 今のようなあなたの生き　　Under your present way of living,
        方では，家族の者はだれで　all of your family would be annoyed.
        も困るでしょう。

     e.g. いつでもそのような服装　　The way you always wear such
        をしていると，人に笑われ　clothes will be laughed at by peo-
        ます。　　　　　　　　　　ple.

  (C) でも (demo) shows a light illustration.

     e.g. 一つ野球でもしましょう　　How about playing a little base-
        か。　　　　　　　　　　　ball?

     e.g. 大阪へでもご出張なさっ　　Please drop in at my house when
        た折りは，私のうちにお立　you are on a business trip or some-
        ち寄りください。　　　　　thing to Osaka.

* The use of ぐらい (gurai) or くらい (kurai) is as follows:

  (A) ぐらい (gurai) shows a rough quantity.

     e.g. 私のさいふにはあと千円　　Only about one thousand yen
        ぐらい残っています。　　　remains in my purse.

     e.g. あなたの仕立て物は四日　　Your tailoring will be ready in
        ぐらいでできあがるでしょう。about four days.

  (B) くらい (kurai) shows the standard of quantity.

     e.g. 彼は野うさぎくらいもあ　　He saw a water rat as big as a
        る大きなどぶねずみを見ま　hare.
        した。

     e.g. あの中国人くらい漢字が　　I wish I could write *Kanji* as
        よく書ければいいのですが。well as that Chinese.

(C) くらい (kurai) shows a minimal standard of comparison.

e.g. ピンポンくらいだれだっ　　Everybody can play pingpong at
てできますよ。　　　　　　least.

e.g. たまには日光浴するくら　　It's not good for the health un-
いしなくてはからだによく　less you occasionally bathe in the
ありません。　　　　　　　sun at least.

* The use of だけ (dake) is as follows:

(A) だけ (dake) restricts extent.

e.g. あしたの遠足には弁当だ　　Please carry only a lunch with
けもってきなさい。　　　　you for the excursion tomorrow.

e.g. ここだけは大都会であり　　In this metropolis, here only is
ながら，静かで，周囲の空気　quiet, and also the air around is
もすがすがしいです。　　　refreshing.

(B) ～だけあって (...dake atte) or ～だけに (...dake ni) expresses
reason.

e.g. 彼の苦心の作だけあって，　This picture, worthy of his im-
この絵は実にみごとなもの　mense amount of labor, is quite
です。　　　　　　　　　　wonderful.

e.g. 私にとっては初めての経　　I have to operate this machine
験だけに，この機械の操作　cautiously chiefly because it is my
を慎重にしなければなりま　first experience.
せん。

* The use of ばかり (bakari) is as follows:

(A) ばかり (bakari) expresses a rough quantity.

e.g. 十羽ばかりのはとが神社　　About ten pigeons are pecking
の境内でえさをついばんで　at food in the precincts of a shrine.
います。

e.g. もう三日ばかり借金の返　　Please wait another three days
済を待ってください。　　　for my debts to be payed back.

(B) ばかり (bakari) restricts extent.

e.g. 家の中にばかりいるのは　　It is not good for the health only
健康によくありません。　　to stay indoors.

e.g. 私ばかりが厚遇を受けて　　I must apologize for my receiv-

は申し訳ありません。　　　　ing all the hospitality.

* The use of のみ (nomi) is as follows:

のみ (nomi) restricts extent.

e.g. 合格は受験生のみが知る　　Passing an examination is a joy
よろこびです。　　　　　　which only examinees know.

e.g. この件については，本人　　As to this matter, decision on
の決断のみが残されていま　　the side of the person in question
す。　　　　　　　　　　　is all that remains.

* The use of など (nado) or なんか (nanka) is as follows:

など (nado) or なんか (nanka) shows an example.

e.g. あなたになどこの本が読　　Is this book read by people like
めますか。　　　　　　　you?

e.g. 外人への贈り物には，日　　As a present for a foreigner, a
本人形なんかがいいのでは　　Japanese doll or something is good,
ないですか。　　　　　　isn't it?

* The use of し (shi) is as follows:

し (shi) shows the coexistence of more than two things or the reason
for the coexistence of more than two things.

e.g. その日は雨も降ったし，　　That day it rained, and the wind
風も吹きました。　　　　blew, too.

e.g. その日は雨も降ったし，　　I was really disturbed that it
風も吹いたし，まったく困っ　　was rainy and also it was windy
てしまいました。　　　　that day.

* The use of のに (noni) is as follows:

のに (noni) shows that something happened contrary to one's expectation.

e.g. 病気なのに，彼は会に出　　In spite of illness, he attended
席しました。　　　　　　the meeting.

e.g. あれだけ練習したのに，　　They did not win the match
彼らは試合に負けてしまい　　although they trained so much.
ました。

* The use of かどうか (ka dō ka) is as follows:

The expression かどうか (ka dō ka) is used when the speaker

relates in conjecture the state or condition of an object which is not realized.

e.g. 彼女が来る**かどうかわか** I don't know whether or not she
りません。 will come.

e.g. このなしがおいしい**かど** Just taste and see whether this
うか食べてみてください。 pear is delicious or not.

第 五十三 課　Lesson 53

Common Adverbs

* Adverbs denoting the state of affairs.

e.g.　母親は子供の手を取って
ゆっくり歩いて行きました。

The mother walked on *slowly*, taking the child by her hand.

e.g.　国会議事堂が青空にどっ
しりと立っています。

The National Diet stands *imposingly* high in the blue sky.

e.g.　この町の中をいくつかの
小川が**さらさら** 流れていま
す。

Several streams flow *murmuring* through this town.

* Adverbs denoting quantity or extent.

e.g.　私にもお菓子を**すこしく**
ださい。

Please give *a few* cookies to me, also.

e.g.　バナナもりんごも**たくさ
ん**冷蔵庫の中にあります。

There are *a lot of* bananas and apples kept in the refrigerator.

e.g.　妹の手料理のこのえびは
かなりうまいです。

This lobster my younger sister cooked is *rather* delicious.

e.g.　タイ国の留学生の日本語
の試験の成績は**きわめて**よ
かったです。

The result of the Japanese examination of a foreign student from Thailand was *quite* fine.

e.g.　もずが**しきりに**鳴いてい
ます。

A butcherbird is chirping *incessantly*.

* Adverbs denoting time.

e.g.　寒い冬が過ぎると，**やが
て**暖かい春がやってきます。

When the cold winter is over, the warm spring will *soon* come.

e.g.　**もう**日が暮れます。

It will be dark *before long*.

e.g.　あしたは旅行に行く日な
のに，彼は**まだ**準備が終わ
っていません。

Although tomorrow is the day for the trip, he has *not yet* completed the arrangements.

* Demonstrative adverbs indicating the appearance of an action or condition.

e.g. こうやれば，もっとうま　　　You should be able to carry out
く仕事を進めていけるはず　　your business more smoothly if you
です。　　　　　　　　　　　do it *in this way.*

e.g. 主人をなくして，どう生　　　Now that I have lost my hus-
きていくべきでしょうか。　　band, I wonder *how* I should lead
　　　　　　　　　　　　　　my life.

* Demonstrative adverbs indicating an action, a condition, quantity, quality, or extent.

e.g. 日本語の会話の勉強はそ　　　The study of Japanese conversa-
うむずかしくありません。　　tion is not *so* difficult.

e.g. こう熱いお風呂には，は　　　I can't get into so hot a bath *as*
いられません。　　　　　　*this.*

* Adverbs of declaration denoting the speaker's feeling or attitude in response to the predicate are as follows:

e.g. そのような事は**決してし**　　You should *never* do such a thing.
てはいけません。
This adverb shows denial.

e.g. 彼女が来るとは**すこしも**　　I did *not in the least* expect that
期待していませんでした。　　she would come.
This adverb shows denial.

e.g. **とうてい**始発には間に合　　I can *not possibly* be in time for
いません。　　　　　　　　the first train.
This adverb shows denial.

e.g. 彼は**たぶん**学校を休むで　　*Perhaps* he will stay away from
しょう。　　　　　　　　　school.
This adverb shows conjecture.

e.g. **おそらく**彼は返事をよこ　　*I'm afraid* he will not answer.
さないと思います。
This adverb shows conjecture.

e.g. **さぞ**北海道旅行でお疲れ　　*I am sure* you must be very tired
でしょう。　　　　　　　　from your trip in Hokkaido.
This adverb shows conjecture.

e.g. 彼は**きっと**当選します。　　He *is sure to* be elected.

This adverb shows conjecture.

e.g. まさかこの雨空はもう続   *Surely* this wet weather can *not*
くまい。   last much more.

This adverb shows a negative conjecture.

e.g. よもや彼は自衛隊には，   It is *not probable* that he is going
はいらないだろうね。   to join the Self Defense Force.

This adverb shows a negative conjecture.

e.g. ぜひクラス会に参加して   Please take part in the class
ください。   reunion *without fail.*

This adverb shows anticipation.

e.g. どうか私には離婚の理由   *Do* tell me the reason for your
を話してください。   divorce, *please!*

This adverb shows anticipation.

e.g. 父は朝食前に**かならず**一   Father *never fails to* take an
時間散歩します。   hour's walk before breakfast.

This adverb shows the affirmation of one's strong will.

e.g. もし彼が約束の時間に来   *If* he should not come at the
なければ，私はひとりで出   appointed time, I'll go off by my-
かけます。   self.

This adverb shows hypothesis.

e.g. 万一雨が降れば，修学旅   *If* it should rain, the school ex-
行は延期になります。   cursion is to be postponed.

This adverb shows hypothesis.

e.g. たとえどんなことがあっ   *Whatever* may happen, I'll carry
ても，最後までこの仕事を   out this work to the last moment.
やりとげます。

This adverb shows hypothesis.

e.g. やっぱりそれは本当でし   It turned out to be true *after all.*
た。

This adverb shows the confirmation of one's expectation.

e.g. あなたは**また**同じ間違い   You made the same mistake over
をくりかえしましたね。   and over *again.*

This adverb shows the confirmation of repetition.

第 五十四 課　Lesson 54

The Use of Particles at the End of Sentences

* The use of か (ka) is as follows:

Notes: The expression in each bracket is in the polite form.

(A) Question.

e.g. あなたも昨夜の火事を見に行ったか (行きましたか)。　Did you also go and see the fire on the previous night?

e.g. 習字の練習はおもしろいか (おもしろいですか)。　Do you find the practice of penmanship interesting?

(B) Irony: か (ka) in this case indicates denial of a matter in the form of a question.

e.g. 娘の離婚についてこの父はどれだけの理解をもってくれるか (もってくれますか)。　How much could this father bring himself to understand his daughter's divorce?

e.g. 二十五や六で未亡人で暮らせるやつがあるか (暮らせる方がありますか)。　Is there anybody at twenty-five or six who can go on living as a widow?

(C) Rhetorical question: か (ka) in this case requires no answer of the other party, different from an ordinary question.

e.g. 実際, あなたは運が悪かったかなぁ。　You know, you were quite unfortunate.

e.g. その時になってから, だれが責任をもってくれるだろうか (もってくれるでしょうか)。　When the time comes, I wonder who would be willing to take the responsibility.

(D) Impression.

e.g. 主人が生きて帰って来るのを彼女はどんなに待っていたか (待っていましたか)!　How she must have waited impatiently for her husband to be back alive!

e.g. 彼もとうとう戦死してし　He also must have been finally

まったか（戦死してしまいま   killed in action.
したか）!

(E) Agreement.

e.g. 「お暇なら，一緒に奈良   "If you're free, I think we should
の名所旧跡をたずねたいと   go together to visit noted and
思っています。」「ああ，そう   historic places in Nara." "Oh, is
ですか。わかりました。」   that so? Yes, I see."

(F) Wish: か (ka) in this case can be used with a negative form.

e.g. はやく端午の節句がこな   I wish the Boy's Festival would
いかなぁ。   come soon.

(G) Invitation: か (ka) in this case can be used with a negative
form.

e.g. あなたも私の誕生日に来   Won't you also come and join us
ませんか。   on my birthday?

(H) Calling one's attention: か (ka) in this case can be used in
the form of ではないか (dewa nai ka).

e.g. 野球をしに行こうではな   Aren't you going to go and play
いか（行こうではありません   baseball?
か）!

e.g. これはにせものではない   This is an imitation, isn't it?
か（にせものではありません
か）!

* The expression かい (kai) shows a question—the use of かい (kai)
applies to familiar persons, as compared with the expression か
(ka).

e.g. 本当かい。   Really?

e.g. そんなにこの小説はおも   Do you find this novel so inter-
しろいかい。   esting?

* The use of かしら (kashira) is as follows: かしら (kashira), women's
usage, is a slightly more polite term than か (ka).

(A) Question.

e.g. あなたもあの時同窓会へ   Did you also attend the alumni
いらっしゃったかしら。   reunion at that time?

(B) Doubt.

    e.g. はてな, むすこはどこへ   Let me see; I wonder where my
        行ったかしら。   son has gone.

(C) Wish: かしら (kashira) in this case can be used with a negative form.

    e.g. 早く夕飯ができないかし   I wish supper were ready soon.
        ら。

* The use of さ (sa) is as follows:

(A) Relating as a prescribed fact: さ (sa) in this case is men's
usage.

    e.g. 「早慶戦はおもしろいで   "Is the Waseda-Keio match in-
        すか。」「そりゃ, おもしろい   teresting?" "It's very interesting."
        さ。」

    e.g. 英語ができるのはあたり   Of course he is good at English;
        まえさ。彼は二世だから。   he is a Japanese-American.

(B) Cross-question: さ (sa) in this case can be used with a term
expressing doubt.

    e.g. その答えはどこがいけな   What is wrong with that answer?
        いのさ。

* The expression ぜ (ze), men's usage, makes assurance in an intimate
way.

    e.g. じゃあ当直をたのんだ   Well then, I'm depending on you
        ぜ。   for the night duty.

    e.g. 日本語の勉強をしっかり   Let's study Japanese hard!
        やろうぜ。

* The use of ぞ (zo) is as follows: ぞ (zo) is men's usage and generally
connected to a common syntax.

(A) Persuading a person of one's own judgement.

    e.g. おかしいぞ。庭に足あと   Strange! There are some foot-
        がある。   marks in the garden.

    e.g. このサーカスはおもしろ   I feel sure this circus is going
        そうだぞ。   to be interesting.

(B) Calling attention and insistence: ぞ (zo) in this case has such
a nuance as to threaten or warn the other party.

e.g. こんな落書きをしたら承　　I won't forgive you any more if
　　知しないぞ。　　　　　　you make scribblings like this.

* The use of っけ (kke) is as follows:

(A) Relating the recollection of past things.

e.g. 大阪城を見に行ったのは　　I wonder when I went to see the
いつのことだったっけ。　　Osaka Castle.

(B) Making a question again about something once familiar with,
in either case—the present time or the future; っけ (kke) in this
case is attended with such a term as to express condition, quality,
or kind.

e.g. 卒業式は来月だっけ。　　The graduation ceremony is next
　　　　　　　　　　　　　　　month?

e.g. あなたは今神田に住んで　　You are now living in Kanda?
いたっけ。

* The expression とも (tomo) denotes certainty or an attitude leaving
no room for objection:

e.g. 「あなたの国はフットボ　　"Football is popular in your
ールが強いですね。」「そう　　country, isn't it?" "That's right."
だとも！」

* The use of な (na) is as follows:

(A) A mood of inspiration and admiration.

e.g. にじはきれいだな。　　How beautiful the rainbow is!

(B) A gentle insistence.

e.g. 家をふしんしたばかりで,　　I have just built a house, so I
今のところ金銭的余裕があ　　have no money to spare for the
りませんので, お貸しできか　　present; I can't accommodate you
ねます。まあそうゆうわけ　　with money. Well, that's the
ですな。　　　　　　　　　reason.

(C) A mood of a gentle request with the use of such expressions
of favor as ください (kudasai), なさい (nasai), and ちょうだい (chō-
dai).

e.g. かきを三つくださいな。　　Please give me three persimmons.

* The use of なあ (nā) is as follows:

(A) A mood of inspiration and admiration.

e.g. 長い鉄橋だなあ。   How long the steel bridge is!

(B) A mood of asking the other party's agreement.

e.g. うそじゃないね。そうだ   It's not a lie, is it? Are you sure?
なあ。

* The use of ね (ne) or ねえ (nē) is as follows:

(A) A gentle insistence.

e.g. 私なんかもそう思います   I myself think so.
ね。

e.g. さあ，彼のことはよく知   Well, I don't know him well.
りませんね。

(B) Asking the other party's agreement.

e.g. わかりましたね。   Did you understand?

e.g. 一緒に行きましょうね。   Let's go there together.

(C) A question or cross-question with the form of doubt.

e.g. なんですね! 子供のくせ   What! And you but a child!
に。

* The use of や (ya) is as follows:

(A) Sounding out the other party with the volitional form.

e.g. もう帰ろうや。   Let's go home now.

(B) A mood of stating positively in a gentle way.

e.g. まだ仕上げていません。   I've not yet got it finished.
まあいいや。   There's no need to be so serious.

(C) Calling a person with a tone of insistence.

e.g. 太郎や。ここへおいで。   Taro, come here.

* The use of よ (yo) is as follows:

(A) A mood of insistence.

e.g. この本は私のだよ。   This book is itself mine.

e.g. 私の郷里はとてもしずか   My home town is very quiet.
よ。

(B) A mood of urging the other party's action with the volitional
form expressing imperative or inviting.

e.g. はやくこいよ。   Come here quickly.

e.g. 一緒に行こうよ。   Let's go together.

(C) Calling a person: よ (yo) in this case is the written form.

　e.g. 少年よ，大志をいだけ。　　Boys, be ambitious!

* The expression わ (wa) shows a mood of a light insistence. This
expression is women's usage.

　e.g. わたし知らないわ。　　I don't know.

* The expressions ね (ne), ねえ (nē), and さ (sa), placed after terms
within the sentence, assure the other party of something:

　e.g. きのうね。おもしろいこ　　Yesterday—something interest-
　　　とがあったんだ。　　　　ing happened.

　e.g. うちへ帰ってさ，辞書を　　On returning home, I consulted
　　　引いてみたらすぐその意味　　the dictionary and found the mean-
　　　がわかった。　　　　　　ing at once.